The Rise and Fall of Civic Education

The Rise and Fall of Civic Education

The Battle for Social Studies in a Shifting Historical Landscape

Michael Learn

ROWMAN & LITTLEFIELD
Lanham • Boulder • New York • London

Published by Rowman & Littlefield
An imprint of The Rowman & Littlefield Publishing Group, Inc.
4501 Forbes Boulevard, Suite 200, Lanham, Maryland 20706
www.rowman.com

86-90 Paul Street, London EC2A 4NE, United Kingdom

Copyright © 2025 by Michael Learn

All rights reserved. No part of this book may be reproduced in any form or by any electronic or mechanical means, including information storage and retrieval systems, without written permission from the publisher, except by a reviewer who may quote passages in a review.

British Library Cataloguing in Publication Information Available

Library of Congress Cataloging-in-Publication Data

Names: Learn, Michael, 1971– author.
Title: The rise and fall of civic education : the battle for social studies in a shifting historical landscape / Michael Learn.
Description: Lanham, Maryland : Rowman & Littlefield, 2024. | Includes bibliographical references and index. | Summary: "This book investigates the changing definitions and purposes ascribed to social studies in the United States through time"—Provided by publisher.
Identifiers: LCCN 2024025774 (print) | LCCN 2024025775 (ebook) | ISBN 9781475858853 (cloth) | ISBN 9781475858860 (paperback) | ISBN 9781475858877 (epub)
Subjects: LCSH: Civics—Study and teaching—United States. | Citizenship—Study and teaching—United States. | Social sciences—Study and teaching—United States.
Classification: LCC LC1091 .L32 2024 (print) | LCC LC1091 (ebook) | DDC 370.11/5—dc23/eng/20240702
LC record available at https://lccn.loc.gov/2024025774
LC ebook record available at https://lccn.loc.gov/2024025775

For my wife, Tracy, who made this journey possible
For my boys, Gus & Eli, who make me a better person

Contents

Acknowledgments		ix
Introduction: Social Studies Is/Are . . .		xi
1	Making History Part of the Curriculum	1
2	Defining Civic Education	13
3	Combining History and Civic Education	27
4	A Social Studies Curriculum	43
5	What Happened to History Education?	57
6	Cold War Comes to Social Sciences	69
7	A New Set of Controversies	87
8	Creating a National Crisis	101
9	Standards to Address the National Crisis	113
10	The Realm of Accountability	129
11	The Nation's Report Card	147
Appendix A: Chart of Major Social Studies Committees		167
Appendix B: Timeline of Social Studies Standards		177
Appendix C: NAEP Schedule		181

Notes	185
Bibliography	225
Index	259
About the Author	275

Acknowledgments

The origins of this book date from a simple question that Professor David Silkenat posed. Is social studies a singular or plural word? After great reflection and thought, this book is a testament to that simple question. The examination of social studies is a long, winding path that never seems to have an end point. David started me on the path, Claudette Peterson dried my tears and encouraged me, and Brent Hill allowed me to finish the first draft of this book as an appendix to my dissertation. I am thankful for their wisdom and guidance.

At Rowman & Littlefield, Tom Koerner and Carlie Wall first accepted my vision. April Snider gave me the deadline that provided all the incentive I needed. Finally, assistant acquisitions editor Jasmine Holman held my hand through this process. I wish to thank each of them for their time and encouragement.

The librarians at the North Dakota State University and North Dakota State College of Science were amazing at getting me copies of hard-to-find books and articles. Amy Carson at the NDSCS Library located some outrageous articles. She was always able to find things so quickly. I owe her a debt of gratitude.

To those colleagues and friends who formed my social studies sounding board throughout this process, I offer my sincere thanks. Without the ongoing dialogue with Dr. Angela Smith, Professor Nate Wood, Professor Jeff Hart, Chesney Thompkins, Dr. Chris Whitsel, Veronique Walters, Dr. Sheri Okland, and Stephen Disrud, the final product would not have been what I wanted it to be. I also owe a special thanks to all my students who challenged me to become a better teacher. I hope they learned as much from me as I learned from them.

Over time, mentors became friends and friends became mentors. I must acknowledge three individuals who fit into both categories. Dr. Claudette Peterson guided me to conceive a theoretical framework based on my understanding of social studies. The depiction of social studies in the introduction was created through her dogged insistence that I explain what I believe. Linda Quigley volunteered to give a fresh set of eyes to my book. She found numerous inconsistencies, offered suggestions, and provided encouragement. That friendship has been invaluable over the years. To Dr. Angela Smith, the long discussions about teaching history did not fall on deaf ears. Thank you for sharing your insight and your time.

I offer special thanks to my parents, Susan and Howard Learn, who gave me the tools and opportunities to find my own path, even if they did not always understand it. My late grandmother, Kitty Learn, made me realize that social studies is more than simply memorization. She encouraged me to look at my family and society as more than names and dates. To my second family, I thank Dr. Roby Barrett, who made me become a better articulator and showed me how to speak up if I want to be heard. To Cheryl Barrett, my second mom and friend, I have tortured you with reading this manuscript almost as many times as me, and you have greatly improved the quality.

To my family, the three most important people in my life, I owe a debt of gratitude that can never be repaid. At times you kept me sane, at times you drove me to a necessary insanity, but through it all you loved me, cared for me, and believed in me. Dr. Tracy Barrett, Gus Barrett-Learn, and Eli Barrett-Learn, this book is a testament to your patience and dedication. Thank you.

As always, any mistakes are my own doing. Please enjoy this journey.

Introduction

Social Studies Is/Are . . .

Social studies is a field in crisis. Whether students just do not like it or elementary teachers focus too much on tested subjects, social studies departments are being eliminated across the United States. To understand why the field is in crisis, it is imperative to examine its past and its fluctuating purpose through the curricular narrative that has characterized its tenure in the American educational system. More significantly, perhaps, this book investigates the changing definitions and purposes ascribed to social studies in the United States through time.

DEFINING SOCIAL STUDIES

To start, is "social studies" a singular or plural noun? The answer at first seems simple, yet it is not. Many social studies teachers do not think about either grammatical choice. I know that when I started teaching, I never considered it. Is social studies a grouped single subject like mathematics, language arts, and science? Or is it a diffuse amalgamation of different disciplines that are simply jammed together? Or as one critic called it, "social stew."

For the purposes of this work, social studies is a singular noun because it is a single field that, similar to the other core subjects, incorporates different disciplines beneath one label. It is not a group of many distinct disciplines that happen to be taught under a larger umbrella. Like mathematics, language arts, and science, social studies uses interconnected disciplines to form its field.

Many educators view social studies as simply a history course with mention of other disciplines. In many American high schools, world and American history comprise two years of the required curriculum. Geography often occupies a third year and civics is a single to half a year course. In middle schools, two history courses generally form the curriculum for those three grades. Yet, just like science, history is not the only discipline taught in social studies. In fact, history is not at the heart of social studies; it is merely an important part of the field.

The different disciplines that comprise social studies are interconnected (see figure I.1), but the heart of social studies is an understanding of culture. This can be seen through history, civics, geography, economics, anthropology, psychology, archeology, and sociology. These disciplines do cross each other, which often blurs the lines between them just as the lines between biology and chemistry blur in science. Making connections among the disciplines is one of the purposes of social studies.

PURPOSE OF SOCIAL STUDIES

The purpose of social studies is confusing and conflicting at times. In its early incarnation, historians viewed social studies as a means of educating people about social institutions. Another common belief is that social studies enables students to think critically about evidence. As social studies developed, the

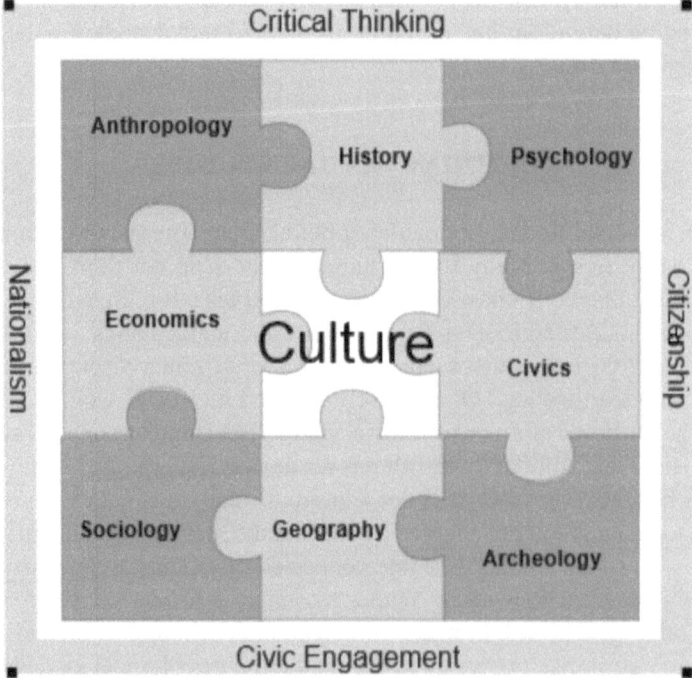

Figure I.1   Conceptualization of Social Studies

leading intent revolved around citizenship. Other potential rationales for social studies are suggested, but ultimately advocates insist that the rationale for social studies is for the citizenry.

If educators define the purpose of social studies as citizenship, then teaching social studies is about making students good citizens. What is a good citizen? What are the roles, responsibilities, behaviors, and characteristics that comprise good citizenship? The underlying debates over social studies center on the differences of opinion about how to attain good citizens. Which disciplines lead to good citizenship: history, social sciences, social studies, or something else? No single answer is correct. Additionally, historians, politicians, educators, social scientists, and parents all have competing ideas about citizenship.

Robert D. Barr, James L. Barth, and S. Samuel Shermis identify three traditions to communicate citizenship in social studies: citizenship transmission, citizenship through social science, and reflective inquiry. Teachers using social studies for citizenship transmission can be conservative or liberal depending on the local or state politics. Nationally, the political slant is often a pendulum swinging between two contrary sides that clash in culture wars. Teachers adhering to the second tradition use the discipline to train citizens to view society through the discipline. Teachers using reflective inquiry want students to think about problems driven by the interests of the students. This tradition is often thought of as encouraging critical thinking.

THE LAYOUT

The narrative of this book takes the reader from the evolution of social studies as a field through its current crisis of marginalization, devaluation, and content debates. In the first three chapters, this book looks at the establishment of the field. The first section looks at the establishment of history education and social studies within the curriculum. Chapter 1 addresses how history established itself in the American curriculum. The establishment of the American curriculum started with determining what courses college-bound students needed to succeed.

As America moved into the twentieth century, issues regarding questions of citizenship arose. What makes a good citizen and how does the government control the making of citizens? Chapter 2 addresses the foundation of civic education. By 1910, the number of children attending schools was increasing rapidly. The government latched upon the idea of using schools to foster civic education for all students, not only those who were college-bound. Chapter 3, the final chapter in this section, examines how the government transformed history and its kindred subjects into the field of social studies.

With social studies as part of the educational curriculum, the second section focuses on developing pedagogy addressed by the various disciplines within the field. Chapter 4 examines how educators aimed to create social studies materials for the schools. History advocates attempted to guide the social studies curriculum with an unexpected outcome. The foundation of progressive theories in social studies material is examined. Chapter 5 explores the first "culture war" over the new progressive-infused social studies material. This chapter introduces another player into the educational policy debate: the federal government. With the passage of the National Defense Education Act in the late 1950s, chapter 6 explores the origins of the "New" social studies movement. The "New" social studies movement is when the other social sciences pushed back against a history-centric social studies curriculum. The movement developed in two distinct stages. The first one was very ideological with little course material; the second was more pedagogical with an abundance of material.

The third section explores the origins of a new disunity arising within the field. Chapter 7 examines the cultural controversy that brought an end to the "New" social studies, namely a temporary disruption of federal intervention in education and the rise of a new educational crisis. Chapter 8 considers how the federal government's concern about an educational crisis influenced the field and laid the foundation for the development of national standards. A rebirth of the conflict between history and social studies education arose during this time. In chapter 9, history education achieves an apparent victory with the development of the National Standards for History. Then, the chapter scrutinizes the third cultural "war" and the failure of the National Standards for History and its implications.

The final section explores how social studies education has progressed since the crashing of the National Standards for History. Chapter 10 investigates federal accountability efforts, including the No Child Left Behind era and the state-inspired Common Core. Both efforts left social studies educators feeling marginalized. The chapter also addresses how local controversies impacted social studies, including a discussion of critical race theory, which has set off another culture war. Chapter 11 utilizes the Nation's Report Card, the National Assessment for Educational Progress, as a foil for investigating the recent problems for social studies. This chapter looks at the evolution and devolution of the field of social studies. These concluding chapters consider potential futures for social studies. Is the field in a state of crisis or is this simply the new norm for social studies? If it is a field in crisis, there is little consensus when it comes to choosing its new direction.

Chapter 1

Making History Part of the Curriculum

Contrary to many traditional views, the social sciences[1] were part of our schools even before the formal establishment of the curriculum framework. Formalizing the American curriculum arose as college and university leaders codified which subjects they deemed essential for preparing students for college. This first codification affected less than 1 percent of the total population, yet it eventually impacted all students. In American curriculum studies, the codification started with the Committee of Ten's work during the 1890s. For the social sciences, the Committee of Ten established history and its "kindred subjects" as part of their essential curriculum. Yet within five years, historians revised the requirements and recommendations. This revision also included a curricular path for non-college-bound students who were starting to enter public schools at an increasing rate. In other words, two potential frameworks for social sciences existed by the turn of the century.

RISE OF THE SOCIAL SCIENCES

Education was essential to create informed participants in the community. After the American Revolution, education included teaching students how to be informed on civic matters. Many state constitutions viewed education as an essential duty. "Citizens must be properly instructed so that they could, in turn, instruct their government in an orderly way" was a common rationale for any public education.[2] To be *good* citizens, students needed instruction starting in the lower elementary grades. Even in early America, most children had at least a fleeting exposure to these earliest years of instruction.

The discipline of history became an identifiable subject in American schools sometime between 1830 and 1860. Yet history during this period is not the same history that is taught today. Its purpose was to expose students to the sacrificial costs of their American forefathers.[3] Its pedagogy relied on rote memorization of essential US documents, for example, the Gettysburg Address, the Preamble to the Constitution, and the Declaration of Independence. During the nineteenth century, history books often synthesized other works; some were accurate and some were not so accurate.

For history writers, the narrative was more important than the facts. Popular biographies of the nineteenth century included Parson Weems's *The Life of Washington* and Washington Irving's *The Life and Voyages of Christopher Columbus*. These biographies often included facts, hearsay, historical myths, and moral lessons. Weems's work, for example, is the first to record the story of George Washington chopping down the cherry tree, which many later books incorporated into their descriptions of our first president as a trustworthy leader. Irving claimed that Columbus was attempting to prove the world was not flat.[4] Both of these "facts" have been proven to be fabrications. Yet, for the better part of the next one hundred years, these stories were accepted facts for students to know.

History was not the only social science discipline developing during the nineteenth century. In 1865, the American Social Science Association (ASSA) formed as an interdisciplinary professional organization.[5] This organization examined social problems as they related to politics and economics. The ASSA allowed individuals who had an interest in reforming society to meet in an academic setting. Some scholars suggest that the term *social* was almost automatically attached to any reform efforts later in the Progressive Era.[6]

Similar to ASSA, study clubs were first organized in Chicago during the late nineteenth century with the goal of investigating "social conditions and institutions and to study social questions."[7] Social science soon became "the social sciences" with a new focus on examining social problems scientifically through connected disciplines. Scientific study was conceived as a method for solving many of the societal problems of the late nineteenth century. One of the common terms used was "social study" as a way to parallel science's "nature study."

Despite ASSA's relatively early arrival on the reforming scene, it did not take the lead in public education for the social sciences. Members of the ASSA agitated for the inclusion of the social sciences into public education in the 1880s. As an emerging interest, the social sciences were not a well-established field within higher education, but other discipline organizations in the new field were more established at the higher education level.

The two earliest professional organizations promoted economics and history. The American Economic Association (AEA) held its first meeting in 1884. The study of economics was a recent specialty with two distinct factions arguing over the political uses of economics.[8] The Association was heavily preoccupied with its own infighting for the next ten years. By the time economists arrived at a cordial détente, other social scientists were better positioned to influence the curriculum. Andrew D. White, cofounder of Cornell University, and Herbert Baxter Adams (HB Adams), professor at Johns Hopkins University, also organized professional and amateur historians into the American Historical Association (AHA) in 1884. The AHA was a forum to discuss ways to promote professional history.[9] Even though there was a large crossover between AHA and ASSA membership, the leaders of educational reform were more active in AHA. History was a more established discipline in higher education, so its adherents took a leadership role.

This professionalization of history and economics eventually expanded through the social sciences, further diluting the influence of the ASSA. The other social sciences created their own professional organizations: the American Psychological Association (1892); the American Political Science Association (1903); the Association of American Geographers (1904); and American Sociological Society (1905).[10] By the turn of the century, the venerable ASSA was in full decline and, by the 1920s, it ceased to exist.[11] The professionalization of the social sciences had resulted in the establishment of a group of disparate professional organizations for its various disciplines.

THE REFORM EFFORTS

Progressivism as an American political ideology dominated the late nineteenth and early twentieth century and frequently spilled into other areas of reforms. As already mentioned, the birth of the social sciences was taking place, yet education also saw an intense period of transformation. In terms of curricular reform, Kliebard identifies four curricular factions that dominated the first seventy years of mass public education. They include the mental disciplinarian/humanistic (traditional) faction, the developmental/experiential (child-centered) faction, the social efficiency (scientific) faction, and the social reformers (social meliorists).[12] As they intersect social studies, this book will address each faction.

The *humanist* or *traditional* faction dominated education through much of the nineteenth century. It advocated the notion that students learned best through a teacher-centered model. For them, what students learned through repetition and exact content was less important than the practice of learning. Both HB Adams and White advocated the idea that history provided both a method for learning and improved mental discipline because they believed it gave "a comprehensive or holistic view of the world."[13] The professionalization of history was new and HB Adams and White recognized the need for change, yet they could not comprehend its manner of change.[14]

Several issues quickly arose with the traditional method for teaching history. One was the problem of books as already mentioned. The written word in the form of textbooks was believed to be more reliable than the spoken words of the teacher.[15] In fact, Europeans believed American education relied too heavily on the use of textbooks and began calling this style of education the "American system."[16] More importantly, historians needed to shift away from celebrated stories and their reliance on other people's synthesis of facts or events.

Albert Bushnell Hart became a vocal advocate within the AHA for a more scientific approach to history.[17] He taught historians to examine primary sources utilizing scientific research methods.[18] The "scientification" of history was a major shift for the discipline and became the main methodology of historians. Despite this, Hart did not want history to become a science. Unlike scientific inquiry, he believed that the role of a historian was to evaluate the accumulation of facts.[19] This methodology was thought to create a mechanism so that "citizens . . . participate fully and intelligently in a democratic society" by creating more than a simple collection of facts.[20] Historians wanted to create a "habit of comparison" within textbooks that would help students develop a critical manner of thinking.[21] To Hart and many historians, history provided a way to understand basic aspects of human existence (historicism) and was not simply a recitation of facts. This approach laid a solid foundation within the field for Kliebard's *social meliorists* or *social reformers* faction, who believed education could help correct societal problems.

The early AHA membership did not focus on the boundaries between history and other social sciences.[22] As late as 1911, at least a third of its members held positions in another social science or held dual positions with another social science (i.e., professors of history and geography). Consequently, discussions about history's relationship with the other social sciences did not seem important.[23] Early AHA members considered history and the burgeoning social sciences as complementary to rather than in competition with each other. Hart himself was a professor of history and government at Harvard University, so when Hart and his Harvard colleagues sought some basic entry standards for students, they did not think only in terms of history but freely incorporated aspects of other disciplines as well.

THE MADISON CONFERENCE: A SET OF STANDARDS

In 1892, Harvard's president, Charles W. Eliot, and other university presidents petitioned the National Education Association (NEA)[24] to create basic college-entry standards as per a request from his faculty. The NEA formed the famous Committee of Ten, chaired by Eliot, to create the first educational standards in the United States. These standards were designed to determine which subjects should be included in the general college-ready curriculum. The membership provided recommendations concerning curricular content, the preparation of teachers, the organization of the curriculum, and pedagogical methods for teachers.[25] These were guidelines for secondary schools that laid the foundation for America's future curriculum.

In the late nineteenth century, many students attended elementary schools but only about 10 to 15 percent attended secondary schools. Only 2 percent of the college-aged population attended college in 1900.[26] The curricular decisions made by this Committee were designed to impact a relatively small population. The rise of mass education did not happen until the twentieth century, which made the decisions of the Committee less complicated. To accomplish its task, the Committee of Ten established discipline-specific committees "to consider the proper limits of the subject area, methods of instruction, methods of testing for pupil accomplishment, the most desirable time allotment for each subject, and college admission requirements."[27] Each subcommittee forwarded their recommendations back to the Committee of Ten. One unifying task given to all subcommittees under the Committee of Ten was to transform American public curriculum into a curriculum for all students, regardless of whether the students planned to attend college. There was some acknowledgment that the percentage of students in public education was increasing, but committee members gave little consideration to what the purpose of public education should be.

The subcommittee assigned to social sciences was headed by the president of the University of Wisconsin, Charles Kendall Adams, and became known as the Madison Conference. The composition of the Madison Conference included four history professors, three government/political economics professors, and three school administrators (see appendix A). Hart served as the principal secretary for the Madison Conference. Over the course of two years, the Conference drafted new "curricula for the subjects of history, civil government, and political economy."[28] Most of the professors were members of the AHA and had strong ties to history education. Other noteworthy members included James Harvey Robinson, history professor and cofounder of the "New" history movement, and Woodrow Wilson, political historian and future president.

In their analysis of the social sciences in schools, the Madison Conference determined that about a third of high school students were already taking some form of history in 1890.[29] History was the third most common subject taught in education after Algebra and Latin. Even though the curriculum was dominated by history, its content was blurred by the other social sciences, or "allied subjects."[30] The Conference spent most of its time addressing two areas: the course of study and the benefits of history to education. They proposed two curricula for schools to choose from in order to establish history, civics, and economics as "legitimate disciplines."[31] The Madison Conference asserted that the purpose of the social sciences was to prepare students for life, not simply for college.[32]

The Madison Conference proposed a preferred foundational social sciences curriculum, which was an eight-year sequence of history and "kindred subjects" (see table 1.1).[33] No longer were the social sciences simply allied subjects; they were deemed essential like history and given a footing within education. They also proposed a shorter six-year program, which eliminated French history and combined the second year of American history with civic education.

The Madison Conference employed two themes for education: promoting the idea of mental discipline and promoting civic good.[34] The conference adopted an approach dominated by *humanistic* attitudes; classics and rational thinking were its key ideological paradigms. But to help students be a part of society, Conference members also wanted them to understand the origins of America and its democratic values. To this end, they recommended a more aggressive focus on cause and effect, arguing that this focus would assist students' capacity to reason through problems. This created a balance between historians' historicism and educators' civic mindedness.[35] Additionally, they called for the revision of poorly written textbooks, improvements in teacher preparation, and the inclusion of more innovative teaching practices such as debates, student presentations, and use of primary sources.[36]

From the moment that the recommendations were made public, criticism abounded. The College Board, which oversaw college entrance exams, countered that rote memorization of facts, a preferred evaluative tool by Harvard's history department, was not a good measure for college readiness.[37] Several members of the AEA argued for a separate course of

Table 1.1 Sequence of Study Based on Madison Conference

Grades	Content
5th and 6th grades	Myths and famous individuals
7th grade	American history
8th grade	Greek and Roman history
9th grade	British history
10th grade	French history
11th grade	American history
12th grade	Civic education

Based on the Madison Conference, 1894.

economics outside of the realm of the other social sciences. Social scientists viewed this criticism with disdain because they felt that students could not comprehend the concepts of economics.[38] Debates over the organization and content of the social sciences began with the very first attempt to draft standards.

REVISITING HISTORY EDUCATION STANDARDS: THE COMMITTEE OF SEVEN

Many historians accepted the proposals of the Madison Conference because history received a preferred status over the social sciences, but not everyone was pleased. Some historians and educators wanted to alter the focus of the curriculum. The AHA convened its own committee to examine and refine the history curriculum with a greater emphasis upon historicism. The foundational issues included best practices for history, history's relationship with social sciences, and history teacher preparation.[39] Three years later, the AHA appointed seven members to make recommendations for these best practices. This group was simply called the Committee of Seven (Seven). The Seven was chaired by University of Michigan professor Andrew C. McLaughlin, but AHA cofounder HB Adams and Madison Conference secretary Hart dominated the Committee. In addition to these three professors, three more members were history professors and the last was a headmaster at a private secondary school (see appendix A).

The Committee of Seven sent a survey to American secondary schools regarding history education. About 250 schools responded to the survey as did a number of state education agencies.[40] Eventually, they extended their study to evaluate history education internationally: in Germany, France, England, and Canada. Ironically, their recommendations were more in line with other social science methodology than a more traditional history methodology. After completing the survey, the Seven reorganized the Madison history program. They then shortened the length of study into a chronological progression of Western civilization: ancient history, medieval and modern history, British history, and American history. Even though they detailed a course progression, they did not explicitly state the grades these courses aligned with in secondary schools. Further, the Committee's members demonstrated a bias toward European history over American history.

In the Madison Conference, the members considered a more holistic view of the social sciences with history as the main discipline. HB Adams regarded this interpretation as favoring the other social sciences above history. He wanted to turn the curriculum more towards a *traditionalist* viewpoint with a lens of historicism. History was "to be studied for its own sake and not merely for disciplinary purposes."[41] History education was "to provide students with an understanding of their environment," which differed from the Madison Conference's purpose of teaching a holistic worldview.[42]

The Seven believed that history could synthesize civic endeavors but should not teach civics.[43] History should be apolitical. In his 1902 AHA presidential address, Charles Francis Adams spoke of the *unwritten rules* of history being outside of politics.[44] Likewise, Professor Lucy M. Salmon, a member of the Committee of Seven, expanded on the relationship between history and its *kindred* subjects. She expressed the belief that history was separate and no longer connected to its *kindred* subjects.[45] Hart thought history permitted students to discover universal truths about civics through its narrative. History deserved precedence over all other social science disciplines, thus creating what some recent scholars view as a *golden age* for history education.[46]

With regard to the other social sciences, Seven suggested that schools themselves determine if they needed to include other social sciences.[47] For example, the discipline of economics could not be part of the history curriculum, but economic conditions could be included in the study of historical processes.[48] A separate course for economics was not deemed appropriate for high school students and the Committee argued that economics as a class should be taught only at the college level. In its final recommendations, the Seven did not address the issue of other social sciences.[49]

In the five years between Madison and Seven, the number of students in public education had continued to expand. The Committee of Seven recognized how few of these students were advancing to college; thus, they limited history coursework for non-college-bound students.[50] Instead of the four-year progression of history courses, Seven recommended a two-year progression of modern European and US history. Finally, Seven provided critiques on teaching practices. Both Madison and Seven criticized the preponderance of rote memorization and recitation in common teaching practices. The Seven reiterated the need for a move away from memorization of facts. They wanted students trained "to gather evidence, generalize upon data, estimate character, apply the lessons of history to current events, and lucidly state conclusions."[51]

Unfortunately, the pedagogical recommendations were lost in their translation to the classroom. American teachers continued to rely on textbooks, but textbooks relied on the historical narrative structure, not pedagogical techniques. Textbook publishers eventually followed either the recommendations of the Madison Conference or the Seven for content, which meant that the curriculum focused heavily upon history.[52] Madison and Seven had influenced the curriculum using textbooks, but they achieved little change when it came to pedagogy.

The AHA hoped that the Seven had addressed some of the needs of teachers and school administrators. Many among the AHA leadership saw the importance of maintaining a connection with K-12 educators; however, the majority of the work the AHA accomplished concerned postsecondary issues.[53] The one major area of overlap, teacher preparation, saw little direction from the association. The AHA recognized the importance of teacher participation in the association; however, the AHA did very little to entice teachers or teacher educators to join.

Problems and critiques soon arose from the recommendations of the Committee of Seven. The first problem was the general disconnection between university professors and classroom teachers. The Committee did not foster an understanding between historical research at universities and the teaching profession. This lack of communication only increased the disunity between the two groups of professionals.[54] History professors possessed only a cursory understanding of how primary and secondary schools were changing. This became an enduring problem as the AHA attempted to reform a system to which they did not belong.[55]

In terms of pedagogical issues, Seven issued a very general curricular plan for the major topics covered but provided little guidance in terms of best practices. Even though the Committee criticized rote memorization, some members favored the recitation method. While some others preferred a seminar style, the seminar was not a practical method within the ideology of teaching at the time.[56] In terms of the situation within the schools, the Committee felt that too many teachers were forced into teaching additional subjects or that their real focus was coaching, not teaching.[57] Yet they did not offer any solutions.

In terms of critiques, several AHA members and state boards of education demanded an increase in the amount of American history in schools.[58] Administrators were afforded doubts about how critical history courses were to the curriculum due to the two conflicting curricular guides provided by the Committee. These doubts furthered the tendency of administrators to use history as a stopgap for additional courses for teachers or to permit sports coaches to teach history classes. Further, by not addressing history and social science, school boards had to determine whether history or the social sciences was important without any clear guidance on why they needed to be part of the school curriculum in the first place.

In the end, regional teacher associations were left to fill in the gaps left by Seven's recommendations. The two largest teacher associations for history were the New England History Teachers' Association and the Middle States and Maryland Association of History Teachers. The New England association produced syllabi for the new courses for educators. The Middle States association filled in some professional development gaps.[59] Even with higher participation in these associations, participation in any professional organization was the exception rather than the rule.

IMPLICATIONS

Even though the differences between the Madison Conference and the Committee of Seven seem relatively minor, the Committee of Seven was generally considered an improvement over the Madison Conference.[60] Many administrators adopted the new Seven mandates because they had fewer requirements. The recommendations of the Seven became the standard for public education. In recent years, scholars have argued that the Seven's report should be the foundation for public education. History remains the dominant discipline: most schools even now follow a form of their four-block system with an expanded role of citizenship within history education.[61]

During the first decade of the twentieth century in the years following the Seven, historians conducted numerous discussions about how to evaluate history education. In 1905, an AHA committee (Eight) looked at elementary education and made recommendations to align elementary education with Seven curriculum.[62] Other AHA committees reexamined the secondary curriculum. Nevertheless, the views of the Committee of Seven remained largely in place for most public schools. Through the 1930s, AHA held to the belief that the Committee of Seven provided the final statement for all history education from 1898 into the future.

For historians such as HB Adams, Robinson, and Hart, citizenship was an often-unspoken motivator for the purpose of history. Their recommendations contained a civics component within the curriculum. Hart wanted to blend historical inquiry with civics, while citizenship education played a secondary role.[63] Students of history were supposed to understand the origins of their roles as citizens within the Progressive Era of American culture. The Committee of Seven, as well as other AHA committees, recognized the civic aspect but did not perceive it as critical to the essential curriculum.

Some scholars indicate that Seven established the *golden age* of history education where educators agreed upon the organization, content, and methods of teaching the curriculum.[64] Hertzberg states that the Committee of Seven report "cemented a connection between the historical profession and the schools," which lasted until the 1930s.[65] On the contrary, Saxe believes that the Seven undermined the work of the Madison Conference by allowing criticism of *traditional* history, thereby providing an opening for the other social sciences.[66] One side sees history as the hero, while the other wants to see history as the villain; reality often lies in the middle.

The first attempts to incorporate social sciences in public education were highly influenced by the AHA. The early supremacy of the AHA was less dramatic than it might seem. Many of the members of the American Political Science Association and American Sociological Society were also members of the AHA, so the AHA often met in conjunction with those organizations.[67] In addition, the differences between the various social sciences were not as distinct as they are today. For example, sociologists worked as economists and economists worked as historians, and so on.

Both the Madison Conference and Committee of Seven tolerated the other social sciences if they anchored history at the center of their paradigms. The other professional organizations wanted to imprint their own interests upon the public education curriculum; however, the AHA controlled nearly all access to public dissemination of information on "social science" curricula.[68] The social sciences were going through a process of professionalization where the cohesiveness of the field was fragmenting into discrete disciplines. The disciplines were adopting their own methodologies and pedagogies, and even history was in the midst of its own development of methodologies at the time.[69] The modern belief that *traditional* history was under attack in the first decades of the twentieth century is true, but not by social studies advocates—by other historians.

Robinson, a member of the Madison Conference, became a critic of the Committee of Seven's recommendations. While the majority of the AHA membership perceived history as a separate discipline and superior to the other social sciences, Robinson imagined an adjustment to history's value, its purpose, and its relationship with other social sciences.[70] Robinson and cofounder professor Charles A. Beard articulated a revolutionary paradigm shift that became known as the "New" history. "New" history sought to shift the discipline away from the study of famous people, politics, and military history and toward more social history, the history of all people. They were shifting the paradigm away from old stories toward a more inclusive history. Historians came to see history's value in making historical social and economic issues relate to current problems.[71] The "New" history movement likewise sought to examine historical events through the lenses of other social sciences. "New" historians were interested in the development and evolution of societal thoughts and beliefs. This type of history made it more relevant to the problems and issues of the present day—in other words, the *social meliorism* interest group.[72]

Madison and Seven were not perfect curricula and they needed revisions, but they did provide a start to a social science curriculum. Both committees raised necessary issues, but their decisions did not solve all of social studies' problems. For example, the state of Illinois held a conference to determine its high school curriculum in 1908. They needed to address the diversity of various districts. They also needed to formulate "what is now practicable rather than a programme based solely on philosophical considerations, and therefore ideal."[73] In the plan, they followed some of the recommendations but also considered the needs of non-college-bound students. Moreover, they wanted twelfth grade to be a combined American history, civics, and basic economics course. Events in American history influenced the debate, but that would come as a surprise to certain members of the AHA.

Chapter 2

Defining Civic Education

The rising tide of democracy was paralleled by the rise of public education. Nations saw public education as an important vehicle for developing their citizenry. Within schools, history and the other social sciences provide the most direct link between education and civic education. At first, civic duty was the notion of citizenship, but as democracy became more complex, notions of citizenship became more complex as well.[1] Prior to the codification of curriculum, patriotic education was evident in education in often performative ways: the recitation of pledges; singing of the "Star-Spangled Banner," which was not yet the national anthem; and memorization of the Constitution. New Hampshire required all eighth-graders to read out loud both the state and US Constitution; students who did not participate could be prosecuted under the law.[2] The theory was that these activities would help students gain insight and understanding into the American system, but, as most educators today would attest, these methods often did not translate into understanding.

NOTIONS OF CITIZENSHIP

In the late nineteenth century, education was often tasked with the promotion of citizenship that supported the nation-state. An example from the French Third Republic is the French primary school reader, *Le tour de France par deux enfants* (*The Tour of France by Two Children*). This reader relates a tale about two boys (André and Julien) from the former French province of Lorraine. They honor their father's dying request to become the most loyal French citizens possible by wandering through France. As they did so, they related cultural, historic, and physical aspects of the state to the various French *departments*.³ *Le Tour de France* teaches about the diversity of French society while laying the groundwork for a unified French vision.

Fouillée⁴ published this elementary reader six years after the defeat of the French in the Franco-Prussian War (1877), and it dominated French education for the next fifty years.⁵ Language arts and social sciences were blended at the primary levels to educate students on their roles as *responsible* French citizens. Fouillée's use of two boys from Lorraine was a deliberate choice representing a form of French nationalism. Through the inclusion of maps, André and Julien became "geographically informed citizens."⁶ In their wandering, they learned the history of France. The two orphans are exposed to their place in Belle Époque French society. By World War I, nearly two generations of French children had learned to read through André and Julien's eyes.⁷ Interestingly, Fouillée's story was also infused with anti-Germanic viewpoints that contributed to French attitudes leading up to World War I. These attitudes became part of the French identity in terms of how it defined what constituted a *good* citizen.

American education had a plethora of textbooks, but few achieved the renown of *Le tour de France*. As a result, American identity determined how the United States wanted to shape civic education. In the early formation of American identity, two types of citizenship coexisted: civic republicanism and political liberalism.⁸ Civic republicanism was a popular view of an indoctrinated citizen, as seen in *Le tour*. This aligned with the *traditional* faction of curriculum. The other view, political liberalism, advocated that students learn civics so that they could perform their civic obligations as informed citizens.⁹ This aligned more readily with the *social meliorism* faction.

Whether schools promoted English as a common language or as a method for educating minorities to understand *their* place within American society, education became an important vehicle by which to instill civic identity in students.¹⁰ The justification for civic education has traditionally been the need to prepare students for the continued future of America. The conflict in civic education has been and continues to be about the methods and final outcomes that define a *good* citizen.

Looking back at the Madison and Seven Committees, the nuances of understanding their society and their place in world society is evident. An alliance needed to be developed between educators and historians to infuse civic education into the curriculum. Historians embraced citizenship as the primary objective of history in the schools, and educators accepted the thesis that historical mindedness was an essential characteristic of the *good* citizen.¹¹ But this alliance was an uneasy union. Today, citizenship is the most common explanation given for the inclusion of social sciences in the curriculum. Civic education is a highly politicized subject within schools because the definition of citizen keeps changing. Below are some illustrations of how the United States used education with citizenship.

EDUCATING EXISTING GROUPS

In nineteenth-century America, efforts were made to "educate" two ethnic groups while having no intention of making "equal" citizens of either group. The two ethnic groups were Native Americans and African Americans. Early efforts were mostly informal endeavors by missionaries, volunteers, free schools, and self-education. Eventually, more institutionalized approaches to "educate" took place. This is the focus of this section. The importance of these efforts would be that educators would utilize some of these practices to "educate" other groups.[12]

American identity is a factor in the way that policy developed regarding the other groups. For educational purposes, American identity begins during the colonial period.[13] The cultural identity of America was White Anglo-Saxon Protestant (WASP) as exemplified by New Englanders. Americans adopted the narrative of the pilgrims over the settlers in Jamestown. Thus, even the Protestant ethic was not English, but uniquely American. This debate over American identity was also linked to the arguments for America to adopt cultural pluralism or multiculturalism within the curriculum. Cultural pluralism is the recognition of many cultures but the existence of a single dominant culture (WASP). Multiculturalism is the belief that there is not a single dominant culture and America is composed of all its ethnic cultures.

New England settlers recounted how, if Native Americans had acted more like them, harmony could have existed between the two groups.[14] Numerous examples of American missionaries and educators narrated their attempts to Christianize and *civilize* Native Americans.[15] Evidence clearly points to the fact that some Native Americans did indeed adopt European and American systems, yet even they did not find success. For example, the Cherokee, a *civilized* tribe, codified their native language, adopted a constitution based on the US Constitution, and embraced Christianity, and yet President Andrew Jackson forced them off their land during the 1830s. Settling in the Indian Territory, the Cherokee continued using schools to impart their culture; however, the Bureau of Indian Affairs constantly sought another model of education.[16]

In 1879, the Carlisle Indian Industrial School was set up in Carlisle, Pennsylvania, as a boarding school for Native Americans. Richard Henry Pratt, founder of the Carlisle School, developed another path for *civilizing* Native Americans.[17] He espoused the idea of "Kill the Indian inside, Save the Man." Total assimilation became the common practice among most Indian boarding schools. Native American children were forcefully removed from their homes and transplanted in these military-style schools, often thousands of miles away from their people.[18] Curriculum included the exclusive use of English, forced conversion to Christianity, and training in vocational or domestic labor.[19] The cultural impact of the boarding schools was devastating upon Native cultures: it wiped out many tribal customs.

In another example, former Union general Samuel C. Armstrong founded Hampton Normal and Agricultural Institute,[20] commonly called the Hampton Institute, in Virginia. Armstrong established Hampton to educate free African Americans in 1867 and "to train them to go back into their communities and educate their people, to give them the tools necessary to earn a living, and teach them respect for labor."[21] Students ranged in age from the late teens through the mid-twenties. Institute leaders admitted Native Americans in 1878 after their release from military prisons in Florida.[22] The Hampton Institute became another model of Americanization for both African Americans and Native Americans.

The fundamental idea behind the Hampton curriculum was to teach both Native Americans and African Americans to understand how society worked and the roles they should play in that society.[23] To accomplish this goal, "classes in American history, English, sociology, and economics were attended jointly."[24] Additionally, the administrators created an *outing* program where students learned trades. This was not the total assimilation of the Native American boarding schools; rather this was placement indoctrination.

Even within the Hampton Institute, a form of segregation existed between Native Americans and African Americans. Administrators held differing goals for each group. Native Americans took courses aimed at *civilizing* them so they could become *real* members of society.[25] The administrators sought total assimilation, but most Native Americans came out with trade skills and little formal education. African Americans, on the other hand, obtained both trade skills and an advanced education. Booker T. Washington was a graduate of the Hampton Institute and established the Tuskegee Institute, which was modelled on the Hampton Institute.

This process at Hampton was colloquially called Americanization. Americanization was increasingly seen as a means of controlling minorities, specifically African Americans and Native Americans. Francis Kennedy, a Native American, reflecting upon his experience with the Hampton Institute, provides insight:

> We want good mechanics, blacksmiths, carpenters, bricklayers, and above all, good farmers. We must make our own plowshares and the farmer till the dormant lands, and then we shall be independent and rise as our white brothers—the Anglo-Saxon have risen. Our race shall then be loyal to our God and

country as long as the stars and stripes wave over this broad land of ours—the United States of America.[26]

The institute was training its Native American students, like Francis Kennedy, to be *good* American citizens. For them, this meant placement indoctrination.

Thomas Jesse Jones and the other instructors utilized the Madison Conference as an impetus to "educate" these minorities at the Hampton Institute using courses labelled social studies.[27] In his sociology course, he strove to "persuade Blacks to accept the leadership and goals of Whites."[28] In other words, Jones and the Hampton Institute used social studies to get minorities to understand their roles within society. To further this program, Jones created a course called the *Problems of American Democracy*. He had students examine America through the lenses of economics, sociology, and civics instead of focusing on history.[29] By using these techniques, students would understand not only the history, but the economics, sociology, and civics of their place in society.[30] His hope was for them to better comprehend their roles as citizens in American society.

Both the Carlisle School and the Hampton Institute were important transitions in terms of the notion of citizenship in education. Both embodied America's *civilizing* mission and its responsibility to minorities. They also embodied the WASP identity of American culture during the late nineteenth century. Most importantly, these two schools provided a laboratory for implementing an educational process of Americanization that aimed to teach minority groups how to be *good* citizens within American society.

AMERICANIZING IMMIGRANTS

As the United States transformed into an industrial power that needed new sources of labor, the question of how to incorporate this new labor into American society became an issue. The labor force increasingly consisted of immigrants from new ethnic groups. Even though America required new labor, ethnic nationalists[31] sought governmental restrictions on certain ethnic groups. These included the Chinese Exclusion Act of 1882 and the Alien Contract Labor Acts of 1885 and 1887. Ethnic nationalists (e.g., the American Party, aka Know Nothings—1850s, American Protective Association—1880s and 1890s, and the Ku Klux Klan—1880s–1920s) were not new to the American political landscape. These ethnic nationalists felt that the best way to create *good* citizens was to keep undesired immigrants from entering America.[32] However, there were certain groups they could not keep out, especially when the flood of immigrants from Europe began and American industry sought the cheap labor force.

Civic nationalists favored an Americanization process like those examples used with African Americans and Native Americans. Civic nationalists had some success at assimilating German immigrants during the middle to latter half of the nineteenth century with the adoption of the German kindergarten model.[33] Buoyed by the perceived success of places like the Carlisle School and Hampton Institute, they wanted to apply similar techniques to the rising numbers of immigrants from around the world.[34] The education movement that swept the country was the Americanization movement with assistance from civic and business leaders.

Detroit's Americanization program exemplified a blended model of governmental, business, and community groups. The foreign-born population of Detroit doubled between 1910 and 1920 due to the car industry.[35] Detroit city officials structured student learning in public schools with that reality in mind. Using Kliebard's *social efficiency* or *scientific* faction, city officials used data to streamline the student curriculum to promote Americanization. They implemented a historicism agenda that was designed to forge a common historical narrative into a common civic mindedness.

While city officials focused on students, the community and city businesses focused on the adult working population. The YMCA offered English language lessons to adults to help them find employment. The largest business, the Ford Motor Company, joined forces with the YMCA to provide additional classes. These classes focused primarily on teaching English language, but they also devoted several classes to educating adults about American history.[36] The nighttime instructors at Ford were mostly full-time public-school teachers who used their school curriculum with both jobs.[37] Henry Ford's intention was the "complete social, cultural, and ideological transformation of the immigrant."[38] Detroit combined the city's various Americanization efforts into a total assimilation of numerous and varied immigrant groups. This form of the Americanization movement lasted only for a few decades in the early twentieth century. But even with this example, civic nationalists implemented two approaches to the Americanization movement: a*ssimilationists* sought to assimilate immigrants into the existing American narrative; *amalgamationists* endeavored to advocate the superiority of Anglo-Saxonism until a new American race emerged.[39]

At the 1904 AHA convention, historian John Bach McMaster provided the Americanization justification for the need for history in public schools.[40] McMaster acknowledged that foreigners might not understand American history, but he suggested that they needed to take history courses as "medicine" to appreciate America. One of the biggest problems with an assimilationist perspective is that it tends towards indoctrination rather than understanding. Assimilation and indoctrination were two sides of the same coin with this form of Americanization. It generally required very little thinking from those who were subjected to it.

A third approach also developed during this period: *cultural pluralism*. This approach strove to embrace the impact that specific immigrant cultures had upon America. Foreign-language newspapers printed in the United States included lessons on American history as a form of Americanization; however, their lessons did not always play to the *traditionalist* version of history. They often revealed their own ethnic slant to American history, looking for ethnic heroes. For example, the popularization of Christopher Columbus as a national Italian American hero dates from this period. Columbus Day was a direct outgrowth of Italians seeking an American hero. This was neither assimilation nor amalgamation.

Cultural pluralism found an advocate in social work doyenne Jane Addams. Addams warned the NEA about the effects of assimilating students into American culture and its impact on the students' relationships with their immigrant parents.[41] The year before, she delivered a speech to the North Central History Teachers' Association Convention suggesting that history courses embrace cultural differences.[42] Even though Addams and McMaster differed on the reasons for the use of history in public schools, both agreed that history could be used as a tool to influence civics.[43] During the Americanization movement, assimilationists and amalgamationists dominated governmental positions. Places such as Detroit and other urban districts tended to favor the assimilationist approach. Competing theories and motives spilled over in the curriculum wars that developed during this period, specifically around issues of civic education. Civic education became a progressive reason for education.[44]

THE EXISTING CURRICULUM VERSUS AMERICANIZATION

> The firm alliance between leading educators and historians was due in large measure to the willingness of the historians to embrace citizenship as the primary objective of history in the schools and the educators' acceptance of the thesis that historical mindedness was an essential characteristic of the good citizen. . . . As long as citizenship was defined in vague terms, it offered no serious threat to the professional integrity of the historians; they simply assumed the good citizen was one who thought historically.[45]

Eventually, civic nationalists, assisted by progressive educators, focused on the education of children in an effort to Americanize ethnic groups. When this process expanded beyond already existing minorities into immigrant communities, the role and purpose of education became more relevant. The question was whether education could play a major role in Americanizing these groups or whether ethnic background was too large a hurdle for the education system to overcome. The very nature of citizenship and education was changing.

The Committee of Ten's recommendations were designed with higher education in mind. Assimilationists tended to agree with the Madison Conference and the Committee of Seven in terms of history education and more *traditionalist* historians. The traditional form of Americanization imparted upon students included learning English, teaching American history through events and individuals, and infusing democratic principles and attitudes.[46]

Chicago elementary schools were directed by the school administration to teach immigrant children American history through the glory of American heroes.[47] Several examples of the elementary curriculum exposed students to US history via biographies of Columbus, Magellan, De Soto, Washington, Lincoln, and Penn. Additionally, students were exposed to such semi-historical literature as the stories of Homer's *The Odyssey*, Howard Pyle's *Robin Hood*, Washington Irving's *Rip van Winkle*, and Henry Wadsworth Longfellow's "Paul Revere's Ride."

Education transformed from a basic general education with a small percentage heading to secondary education and on to college into a mass movement. Progressivism sought to educate all children through mass education. Education became a factory system for children.[48] Thus, the rise of a *social efficiency* faction occurred during this period. Education no longer stopped when children turned ten years old. The high school student population rose sharply, but college education was not the goal.

Those core subjects from the Committee of Ten needed some reevaluation, including history education. Educators did not introduce the AHA historical narrative until seventh grade.[49] Often history textbooks focused upon traditional political and military history with a single objective of exemplifying Anglo-Saxon culture as the model American culture.[50] History education needed to educate "students to be better citizens of the community, nation, or world."[51] School administrators requested that the AHA update the Seven's curriculum plan. They sought changes to pedagogical methods, especially the reliance on rote memorization, wanted to limit the study of ancient history, and hoped to address concerns about civic education. They also reiterated their desire for more American history. The AHA's response was to create a committee to examine these requests.

The Committee of Five is often overlooked in the evolution of standards for a rational reason: this Committee examined these requests with a focus on college entrance exams. They suggested that the College Board focus on a wide breadth of historical knowledge instead of a literal interpretation of the Seven.[52] Both Madison and Seven advocated for a more balanced view of history. *Social efficiency* advocates wanted a test that could best streamline the curriculum. For *traditionalists*, providing a list of specific content knowledge became the main means to measure student achievement. They favored history that focused upon military, politics, famous persons, and dates and thus the textbooks favored these perspectives.[53]

The Committee of Five noted that textbooks still aligned with a reliance on rote memorization because this was the teaching method needed to get students into college.[54] The textbook publishers did update the books to align with Seven's four-block plan. And they researched a model for what was considered a good textbook. This model included "abundant maps . . . instructive illustrations . . . [and] genealogical tables, chronological summaries, topical outlines, questions for further study."[55] The research was based on what school districts bought.

The Committee of Five did not point out the issues with the textbooks nor provide for alternative ways to measure student abilities; they simply blamed the College Board for encouraging rote memorization as a pedagogical practice.[56] The Committee of Five could be viewed as the high point for *traditional* history, but, in actuality, its sheer ineffectiveness and failure to understand the complexity of the new reality epitomized the traditional history arguments.

In a study of textbooks published in 1916, William C. Bagley and Harold O. Rugg analyzed textbooks for their distribution of topics. When military topics and democratic traditions were covered thoroughly, they became the heart of most history textbooks, implying that the purpose of most textbooks was nationalism or patriotism.[57] This reflected the notion of historicism as the foundation of historians' attitudes towards Americanization.

After two years of deliberations, the Committee of Five decided to maintain four years of curriculum, including ancient history (see table 2.1). This was a major complaint of the "New" history wing of the AHA as they wanted more relevance in the history curriculum. The Committee altered the structure somewhat but mostly followed the recommendations of Seven. "The thing that [the Committee] deplore[s] is that young men and women should leave the schools and encounter the work and pleasure of mature years without a knowledge of history."[58] They were also willing to modify the curriculum for the general population and for trade schools. Non-college-bound students

Table 2.1   Sequence of Study (1911)

Grade	Content
9th	Ancient history to 800 BCE
10th	English history (through 1760)
11th	Modern European history (since 1760)
12th	US history (3/5) and US government (2/5)

Based on the Recommendations of Committee of Five

required three years of history. Trade school students required two years of history (modern and United States). This is the first Committee to address the College Board's reliance on exams for college entrance. Additionally, they recommended the creation of another committee to look at history teacher preparation.

The Committee on the Preparation of Teachers of History in Schools[59] developed out of this request, as well as from similar requests made by professors at normal colleges.[60] Charles E. Chadsey, superintendent of Detroit schools (1912–1920), and Kendric C. Babcock,[61] who started working at the Bureau of Education in 1910, became the first non-social scientists to participate in these discussions. In professional organizations like the AHA and in the teacher organizations like New England History Teachers' Association, questions abounded regarding the preparation of history teachers.

The US Bureau of Education, the precursor to the Department of Education, explored the teacher preparation process for all subjects, not only history. After an examination of history teacher requirements in various locations, they determined that a wide variance existed. The Bureau of Education recommended that history teachers have at least fifteen hours of postsecondary credit in history. But neither the bureau nor the Committee were able to create standards for certification without the support of the AHA Council.[62]

Also worth noting, a philosophical shift in education was happening through the influence of John Dewey. Dewey, the most influential educational theorist during this period, suggested that education should provide intellectual development as well as infuse the need for social change.[63] He was the leader of the *developmental* or *child-centered* faction. Students would learn by doing work in content that interested them. Dewey believed that these purposes would promote the ideals of democracy. The Frontier Group, disciples and colleagues of Dewey, sought to use education to provoke social change following a liberal-socialist model. Their main tool was infusing progressive values into the educational system.

In the 1910s, educators reduced the dominant role of "professional" history and promoted other disciplines as well as education to foster their own views of a *good* citizen. "As long as citizenship was defined in vague terms, it offered no serious threat to the professional integrity of the historians; they simply assumed the *good* citizen was one who thought historically."[64] The division between *traditionalists* and "New" history adherents further distracted the AHA from what was happening in public schools. In 1909, both the New England Teachers Association and Albert McKinley's *The History Teacher's Magazine* voiced the need for a civics course separate from American history.[65] The fragile unity between historians and educators regarding history as the basis for civic education was cracking.[66]

IMPLICATIONS

When scholars look back upon notions of citizenship from this era, they call these reforms "cultural imperialism."[67] The citizenship training forced upon Native Americans, African Americans, and immigrants was about assimilation into a WASP political identity. With the outbreak of World War I, the Americanization movement took on a more nationalistic and idealist view of America. For example, former President Theodore Roosevelt, on Columbus Day 1915, said "there is no such thing as a hyphenated American who is a good American. The only man who is a good American is the man who is an American and nothing else."[68] The dominant WASP majority in America felt threatened by the rising number of immigrants in the late nineteenth century. This fear became acute during World War I and the Red Scare that immediately followed the war as the wealthy majority felt that a potential fifth column might now reside in America.[69] Frances A. Kellor, director of the National American Committee, began a national campaign prior to the US entry into World War I to Americanize immigrants with the intention of bringing the issue to the forefront of the public consciousness.[70]

The American Legion proposed to mandate the requirement for schools to teach civic education to Americanize America. They promised their fellowship that within the next generation they "will see this country rid of the undesirable element not present in its citizenship, . . . the spirit of true Americanism prevailing throughout the length and breadth of our country, and our ideals of government secure."[71] The fears of World War I and the questions over immigrant loyalty laid the groundwork for a renewed patriotic education movement that changed public education (see table 2.2). The inclusion of US history was mandatory in 30 out of 45 states in 1903. This inclusion rate increased to 43 out of 48 states by 1923.

In this milieu, reformers sought to impose a civic agenda upon education. Regardless of whether it was for nationalism, assimilation, or other more nefarious reasons, the groundwork laid in the 1890s did not fully address this civic agenda. Bohan, Doppen, Feinberg, and O'Mahony suggest that both

Table 2.2 Number of States Prescribing Patriotic Instruction

	1903 (45 states)		1913 (48 states)		1923 (48 states)	
	N	%	N	%	N	%
US history	30	67	32	67	43	90
Constitution	9	20	9	19	21	44
State history	13	29	20	42	29	60
Citizenship	1	2	1	2	39	81

Adapted from David B. Tyack, Thomas James, & Aaron Benavot, *Law and the Shaping of Public Education, 1785–1954* (Madison, WI: University of Wisconsin Press, 1987), 171.

the Madison Conference and the Committee of Seven were progressive in nature. Furthermore, both committees wanted to extend history education to non-enfranchised individuals so that they "receive the same benefit of social education as the males destined to exercise legal rights."[72] The Committee of Seven even considered a separate twelfth-grade course dedicated to civics.[73] But they amalgamated it with the American history course.

Progressive educators argued that the purpose of general education was to create *good* citizens. Educators wanted students to think critically about their world, not be subjugated by traditional ways.[74] At this time, some educators adopted an assimilationist policy that forced students to adopt all American values and customs while discarding their own native cultures.[75] As calls for civic education became increasingly common, many felt that civic education was in actuality strong patriotic education.[76] Nevertheless, some immigrant groups approved of governmental policies (both ethnic and civic nationalists), while others felt that Americanization was "a bitter process of cultural oppression and loss."[77]

The Americanization movement started to decline by 1930, but these conflicting approaches continued for decades to come. Not until the middle part of the twentieth century did America begin to embrace the nation of immigrants, or melting pot, mentality of cultural pluralism.[78] However, assimilationist attitudes still abounded in the curriculum, especially among groups that believed the 1890s curriculum was usurped from its patriotic historical legacy. Bohan, Doppen, Feinberg, and O'Mahony argue that the concept of citizenship altered in the 1890s. Citizenship underwent a change from a strict legal construct to a cultural concept. For example, "what it means to be a citizen" expanded the idea of citizenry to include women, African Americans, and children.[79] Citizenship was typically about understanding one's position within society, and it was beginning to evolve into protecting political rights.

The AHA opened the door to altering the structure of history courses as long as history was the subject binding the social sciences together. The Committee of Five's concession to allow the fusion of US history with government would create unintended consequences. The Committee felt that they could only "present our views of the relations of government to history and make proposals for adjustment of time and proportional emphasis."[80] This concession was a watershed movement for the social science wing of the AHA, aka "New" history. This victory over the traditionalist influenced curricular debates and the future role of the AHA in K-12 education. For several members of the social science wing of the AHA, they realized that the AHA was not going to be able to adjust to the new reality.[81] In hindsight, during the subsequent seventy years, historians gave up their dominant voice in curricular discussions.

Wallace Foster gathered material to create a patriotic primer for the "little citizen." Published in 1898, the author details how "little citizens," children from ages three to fifteen, can become *good* citizens. Foster starts with a list of rhetorical questions and their answers. He describes what a good little citizen is by stating "every little boy or girl born in this country . . . is a LITTLE AMERICAN CITIZEN, who is learning every day how to be a big citizen."[82] And the reason every little citizen is in school is for "self-protection against the evil of ignorance, [states have] undertaken to see that its people are duly prepared for AMERICAN CITIZENSHIP. To that end, therefore, there has been established by law in each State a system of public schools—THE SCHOOLS OF THE PEOPLE."[83]

Chapter 3

Combining History and Civic Education

In the twenty years following the formation of the Committee of Ten, public education underwent various radical changes. The massive influx of immigrants coincided with the need to guarantee employment for them. This parallelled politically progressive reformers' desire for changes in child labor laws. With children being removed from the workforce, public education became more significant politically. Schools now represented an avenue for keeping children out of the workforce. Progressives once again viewed education as a pathway to creating an American civic identity. The uneasy relationship between historians and educators was deteriorating as they saw different ways to attain *good* citizens. Fear over immigration allowed progressive educators to blend the "promise of a socially engineered future with reassuring traditional values of hard work, self-help, honesty, and efficiency . . . [as well as] if the rising generation were properly educated, the problems besetting the society might be solved without drastic disruption."[1] In order to accomplish this promise, they discarded the preparatory-school model in favor of the public-school model.

THE HISTORIANS AND EDUCATORS

University historians forged a spot for history and its *kindred* subjects as an essential subject for college-bound students. They favored using a broad history of the world in public education as the most effective way to instill a civic identity.[2] However, amid changing demographics and notions of citizenship, history education failed to keep up with the changes. Amid this failure on the part of history educators, those kindred subjects that aligned better with the "New" history movement provided another path to prepare *good* citizens.

The American Historical Association (AHA) dominated the conversations over curriculum, but changes in the organization contributed to a diminishing return on their control. In 1908, Waldo Gifford Leland became secretary of the AHA and his interests were in archival and higher education, causes to which he devoted most of his attention during his eleven-year tenure. The AHA had always struggled to attract history teachers, but Leland's focus on establishing the National Archives meant that other interests fell completely away.[3] The "New" history movement under James Harvey Robinson and Charles A. Beard further exacerbated the disunity within the organization.

The AHA interest in history education fell to their publication, *The History Teacher's Magazine*. The editor, Albert McKinley, became the AHA's voice for teachers. Even though McKinley received funding from the AHA, he controlled the publication, which meant that the AHA's connection to teachers was not directed by Leland's faction.[4] Nearly two-thirds of paid subscribers were not members of the AHA, but rather teachers looking for advice.[5] By 1913, the magazine advocated that "the civics course should be what the subject inherently warrants—the most fascinating, inspiring, and profitable in the whole school curriculum."[6]

A second historical association formed in 1907, the Mississippi Valley Historical Association (MVHA).[7] The MVHA advocated for more regional and local history and an emphasis on American history. These attitudes aligned more with the "New" history movement's desire for relevancy. The MVHA felt the AHA should direct state curriculum, but they wanted to direct local interaction with educators into encouraging the use of local historical sites and museums.[8] Unfortunately, neither national association successfully recruited an appreciable number of teachers.

The MVHA and the regional historical teacher associations repeatedly requested guidance from the AHA on history education. The MVHA requested that the AHA take the lead in enacting state history curriculum. They also sought more opportunities for teachers to participate in MVHA-AHA conferences.[9] The AHA response was to create a committee. The Committee of Five was already finishing its defense of the early recommendations, so the new Committee on Teacher Certification was organized. This Committee showed a marked tendency to defer to state authority.

Dissatisfied with the AHA's response, the MVHA and regional teacher associations acted on their own and formed the Committee on the Certification of High School Teachers of History. The report, called the Paxson Report, declared that the real problem for teachers was lack of content knowledge during their preparation.[10] They wanted college courses that would focus on what teachers would have to teach. The Committee focused on the adequate preparation of history teachers within university content courses but it neglected pedagogical issues. The Paxson Report advocated that a teacher candidate should take ten history courses while only recommending a single education course.

The MVHA committed a mistake that had plagued the AHA for decades: their Committee was comprised almost entirely of university historians (see appendix A). The Association of History Teachers of the Middle States and Maryland offered a more realistic approach by trying to balance both education and history courses, but the national associations consistently ignored the calls of the teachers.[11] The MVHA Committee existed at the same time as the AHA's Committee on Teacher Certification. Awareness of problems with teacher certification was apparent, but no viable solution was found.

Having produced their recommendations, the MVHA Committee disbanded. The MVHA reformed the Committee on the Certification of High School Teachers of History in 1913 with only three members from the original Committee. This Committee reconfirmed the prior findings and suggested a pedagogical course. The new chairman, Wayland Chase,[12] provided suggestions for a course on methods of teaching history.[13] But very little heed was paid to these suggestions as other events were overtaking these issues.

EDUCATORS TAKE ON CURRICULUM

By 1910, educators revisited the recommendations of the 1890s Committee of Ten to make it align better with the changing demographics of public schools. The National Education Association (NEA) formed the Committee of Articulation.[14] This Committee morphed into the Committee of Nine on the Articulation of High School and College with the intent to examine the "curriculum confusion in secondary schools . . . [due to] the conflicting demands of collegiate and of noncollegiate constituencies."[15] To head this Committee, the NEA appointed Clarence D. Kingsley, a math teacher in the Manual Training High School of New York. The other eight members were either public school administrators or education professors. Neither university presidents nor university content experts were on this NEA Committee.

The Committee resolved "to return to society intelligent, able-bodied, and progressive citizens."[16] They felt that public education was about more than sending students to college; it should be an avenue for correcting social problems in society. Their report provided the foundation for the Commission on the Reorganization of Secondary Education School Subjects. This latter Committee became as critical to American curriculum as the Committee of Ten had been years earlier. The NEA again appointed Kingsley, soon to be a high school inspector in Massachusetts, to oversee the Commission. The

NEA stated that they wanted the Commission to examine all educational subjects because of the demographic, ideological, and pedagogical shifts that had occurred since 1892. The Commission's first action was to rename itself the Commission on the Reorganization of Secondary Education (CRSE).

The CRSE focused on the public aspect of curriculum with six concentrations: English, social science, natural science, physical training, mathematics, and foreign language. Because the focus was on all students, they narrowed the curriculum to what they felt students needed to learn. Each concentration had to justify its inclusion in the reorganization and explain how it was useful to both students and society for its final reports.[17] Another major shift was the composition of the committees: membership consisted primarily of government officials, public school administrators, professors of education, and teachers.

COMMITTEE ON SOCIAL SCIENCE (AKA COMMITTEE ON SOCIAL STUDIES)

Kingsley replaced history with a concentration in social science, a reflection of demands by educators. Additionally, educational theorists John Dewey and David Snedden highly influenced him.[18] Dewey was the leader of the *child-centered* faction of curriculum. Snedden was a leading advocate for the *social efficiency* faction. Neither of these two theorists directly participated in the CRSE, but their influence can be clearly seen.[19]

Focusing on the social sciences, both Dewey and Snedden conceived of history as two distinct disciplines, one academic and another for the general public. Academic history should be left for the postsecondary levels. Public history should focus on having a social purpose such as assimilation, indoctrination, citizenship education, or social meliorism. Dewey worked within the AHA history framework, but he favored a more *student-centered* approach that made history more relevant to all students. This appealed to "New" history followers and cultural pluralists. He opposed the notion that teaching should be confined by a strict structure. He proposed that teachers be free to conform to changes in society. Although he did not participate, several quotes were lifted directly from Dewey's writing on education and included in the Commission's final report, the *Cardinal Principles*.[20] His presence is felt within the ideology, recommendations, and implementation of CRSE's curriculum.

Snedden, Commissioner of Education for Massachusetts and *social efficiency* advocate, hired Kingsley in 1912 to oversee secondary education for Massachusetts. As Kingsley's supervisor, Snedden mentored Kingsley through the critical stages of writing the *Cardinal Principles*. Snedden pushed for a radical break from traditional history.[21] He favored scrapping all vestiges of the previous history curriculum and replacing it with courses based on the social sciences. These courses would focus on citizenship education. Snedden's education program consisted of indoctrination in the lower grades through use of American stories, fables, and biographies. In the upper grades, students would be introduced to techniques, ideals, and attitudes about interacting with other social groups, as well as to considering the problems of society.[22] Snedden's pedagogy, based on the beliefs of Herbert Spencer, fostered knowledge intended to help students understand and change the current situation (*social meliorism*).

While Snedden and Kingsley shared many educational beliefs, they differed on some key aspects of the curriculum.[23] Kingsley wanted to incorporate diversity among the student population to meld a new social order—in many ways a blending of *social meliorism* with *social efficiency*. These influences played an important role in Kingsley's choice of the chair of the Committee on Social Science, because Kingsley felt that this Committee was at the crux of progressive education and thus all public education.[24]

Kingsley settled on Thomas Jesse Jones as the chair of the Committee on Social Science. The Hampton Institute professor had recently started working at the US Bureau of Education. Arthur William Dunn, another employee of the US Bureau of Education, was appointed the Committee's secretary. The rest of the Committee was composed of mostly secondary school educators from regional history teachers' organizations (particularly on the East Coast), professors of education, or administrators. Only William H. Mace and Robinson, the cofounder of "New" history, could be labelled academic historians.

Jones's opening statement to the Committee "attack[ed] and dismiss[ed] traditional history instruction and to introduce a secondary curriculum that specialized in attending to the present growth needs and interests of the learner."[25] Then, the Committee's first action was to rename itself the "Committee on Social Studies."[26] Jones applied a term he had used back at the Hampton Institute for teaching about society, the first official use of the term "social studies" in the curriculum. From one viewpoint, historians could claim that the Committee on Social Studies was eliminating traditional history from the curriculum. They would be correct.

The powerful influence of Kingsley, Jones, and Dunn led the Committee to adopt a sociological perspective towards the social studies curriculum that eliminated the chronological emphasis of traditional history.[27] Jones acknowledged that history education could develop *good* citizens; however, he believed that history should not be taught just because it was taught in the past. He wanted history to "answer the test of good citizenship" as with all the social sciences.[28] Over the next four years, the guiding principle of the Committee on Social Studies and its model, the Hampton Institute, was doing what was best for the students in order to make the students viable employees.[29] To make students viable employees, the Committee on Social Studies determined that the focus should be on reforming the secondary curriculum while permitting decisions made by the AHA about the elementary curriculum to remain.[30]

These new curricular developments moved away from Seven's recommendations. The Committee eliminated the study of ancient history as a separate course. They kept the two-cycle program but recommended that student courses repeat themselves. Accordingly, the six-year course of study was divided into two similar cycles of study. The lower cycle consisted of geography, European history, and American history/civics. The upper cycle repeated European history, American history, and a *Problems of Democracy* course. The Committee believed that student learning would be less reliant on content, thereby turning education into a more effective tool for socialization.[31]

> Too frequently, however, does mere information, conventional in value and remote in its bearing, make up the content of the social studies. History should so treat the growth of institutions that their present value may be appreciated. Geography should show the interdependence of men while it shows their common dependence on nature. Civics should concern itself less with constitutional questions and remote governmental functions, and should direct attention to social agencies close at hand and to the informal activities of daily life that regard and seek the common good.[32]

According to this interpretation, the three core disciplines of social studies should be history, geography, and civics. But the recommendation was not to teach them in the manner that they had been taught, because that approach did not foster the training of socialized and thoughtful citizens.

The *Problems of Democracy* course exemplified the personality of the Committee and its differences with previous reforms. Using previous teaching methods, teachers explained US government through the history of the Constitution, the powers of the presidency, and the actions of Congress. The course was visualized as a capstone for social studies courses. Civics was to be infused into all levels of the curriculum.[33] The *Problems* course integrated civics with history, economics, and social issues with the hope that students would be able to address social problems.

The Committee agreed on the course, but they did not fully agree on the direction of the course. Jones and Dunn disagreed about the direction of civic education. Jones believed the social studies curriculum should use Americanization policy to maintain the current status of ethnic minorities but should also encourage assimilation for the new European immigrants. Thus, rather than representing an attempt to induce equal democracy, social studies "sought to legitimate social, economic, and political inequality" among immigrants and minorities.[34] In other words, Jones wanted the *Problems of*

Democracy course to reflect the same values he had created in his work at the Hampton Institute.

On the other hand, Dunn advocated for a civic engagement model. He was the primary author of the Committee's first publication, *The Teaching of Community Civics*. This publication was considered a vital part of the Committee's Final Report (submitted to CRSE). Students would solve problems in a pseudorealistic community in order to make civics relevant to them. These problems were not only to be used in the capstone course, but should also be incorporated throughout the social studies curriculum.

The Committee report, composed mostly by Dunn, ended up describing a course like the one Dunn promoted. Civic education required a more active role than that urged in the previous pedagogical model. Students could not simply memorize the role of the president during one year; civics was part of the yearly curriculum. Dunn stated that schools "should have for their conscious and constant purpose the cultivation of good citizenship."[35] Furthermore, the Committee had a problem with history because "the past becomes educational to [children] only as it is related to the present."[36] History was not relevant to students; solving social problems would engage students. This was Dewey's influence. Dunn even had his own working mock-up of his vision—Indianapolis schools were his test case.[37]

In January 1913, *History Teacher's Magazine* published the preliminary report of the Committee on Social Studies. In 1916, the Committee issued their Final Report and referred to *Community Civics* as an "integral part of the Report of the Committee on Social Studies."[38] The Final Report laid out the structure of the social studies curriculum, including why social studies should replace traditional history courses. The argument was civic education.

In 1918, Kingsley's CRSE issued the *Cardinal Principles of Secondary Education* to address the optimal organization, administration, and focus of American secondary schools. Kingsley's view of civic education was to socialize students into a cohesive blend (amalgamationists) along the ideas of the melting pot theory of America.[39] The *Cardinal Principles* did not reprint the reports of each of the committees; rather it attempted to synthesize them into a progressive ideal for education. In their conclusion, the Committee wrote,

> While seeking to evoke the distinctive excellencies of individuals and groups of individuals, the secondary school must be equally zealous to develop those common ideas, common ideals, and common modes of thought, feeling, and action, whereby America, through a rich, unified, common life, may render her truest service to a world seeking for democracy among men and nations.[40]

Thus, civic education became one of the key elements of this new progressive education model that American schools would emulate.

HISTORY EDUCATION VERSUS SOCIAL STUDIES EDUCATION

Throughout the 1910s, the AHA formed numerous committees examining history education in public schools, but few made significant changes to the curriculum.[41] Prior to the publication of the *Cardinal Principles* report, the NEA asked the AHA to examine the Final Report. The AHA wanted to limit the influence of social studies while expanding the role of history.[42] When the members of the AHA examined the Final Report, most felt it had "very little immediate impact" on them because this social studies curriculum was not history.[43] Another reason historians did not fret over the Final Report was because of American participation in World War I. The National Board for Historical Service recommended Americanization as a war measure.[44] Historians, educators, and civic leaders closed ranks and assessed history textbooks for their attitudes towards the British and the Germans. Citizen committees burned some existing textbooks and made formal calls for new textbooks.[45]

As in the past, the unity among historians and educators was fleeting. World War I changed the dialogue within the curriculum. The curriculum included indoctrination via Americanization, which meant an increase in citizenship education. The AHA decided to address the changes in curriculum. In 1918, a committee was formed called the Committee on History and Education for Citizenship (CHEC). The AHA appointed Professor James Schafer as head of the Committee, but the principal author of CHEC's report was Henry Johnson, a former Minnesota history teacher and a pedagogical professor at Columbia University's Teachers College. He was one of the few K-12 educators who preferred the Seven's recommendations.[46] The AHA viewed him as their education *expert*. The AHA also changed tactics by relying on non-academic historians as a part of the Committee (see appendix A). In addition to Johnson, the Committee secretary, Daniel C. Knowlton, was a high school teacher.[47]

The Committee was charged with "prepar[ing] *as soon as possible* a report on the changes and readjustments which should be made in the study and teaching of history in all schools," yet the reality was impossible.[48] The CHEC tried to parallel the work of the Committee of Five, but the shift to Americanization by the CRSE could not be ignored. So, the CHEC conceded that most students needed only two years of history. Civics needed a larger role in the curriculum.

Johnson maintained that history education served "to illuminate current events, to impress festivals, ceremonies, and holidays, to enforce moral or civic ideas, and in general to stimulate love and reverence for existing institutions."[49] A division in the Committee can be seen here between Schafer and Johnson. Schafer wanted to use history to improve citizenship while Johnson wanted to use history to indoctrinate students, thereby transforming them into citizens. Johnson wanted to foster the abstract parts of history education by teaching government in a more traditional manner.

In their report, the Committee tried to balance the desires of historians and educators. Johnson focused on the primary grades, Knowlton on tenth grade, and Schafer on ninth, eleventh, and twelfth grades.[50] The Committee suggested a two-course minimum for graduation. The first course was to be a modern European history course in tenth grade and the second was an American history course in eleventh grade. The Committee was also willing to replace European history with a World history course, which they believed aligned more closely with the worldly focus of the social studies curriculum. In terms of primary education, the Committee took third to sixth grades and divided them into four segments of US history with half a year of government to be taught during sixth grade. Professor James Alton James, former chair of the Committee of Eight, thought the Committee should have avoided focusing on the elementary grades, a disagreement that caused more disunity. But Johnson insisted, seeking to use history to assimilate even younger students into American society.

The CHEC tried to appease all parties because they supported certain aspects of the Committee on Social Studies. In particular, the Committee on Social Studies granted teachers the authority to articulate curriculum within their classrooms, a stance favored by the CHEC. The CHEC also legitimized the *Problems of Democracy* course.[51] Schafer argued that history education "is to give positive direction to the growth of those mental and moral qualities of children which, rightly developed, constitute the basis of the highest type of citizenship."[52] For the first time, an AHA committee espoused that history was no longer about historicism; rather it was about students' futures in society.

As the first papers were coming out it became clear that the CHEC did not garner the approval of either side. The CHEC's report was disavowed by the AHA governing council. Previous committee reports had been published in the AHA's annual report, but not this time. *Traditionalists* felt betrayed by the Committee's recommendations because they felt that it had rejected all the work of the Committee of Seven. And they supported the Committee on Social Studies.[53] Many members wanted a minimum of three years of history study in high school. *The Historical Outlook,* which replaced *The History Teacher's Magazine* (1911–1918), did publish CHEC's recommendations in a series of six articles, but within those editions the pro–social studies editors included comments criticizing the Committee's recommendations. Anna Stewart, a Los Angeles teacher, wrote that history need not be discarded, rather revised. Her statement that if "social science leaders to damn history in order to boost civics" the reverse might happen to social studies.[54] She pointed out that history suffered from its dedication to rote memorization and reliance on chronology. Edmund S. Noyes suggested that teachers "should continue to teach history *as* history, to try to recreate some appreciation of the past."[55]

Sandwiched between the CHEC's recommendations and its critics were the social studies advocates. Harold O. Rugg, a teacher at Teachers College's Lincoln School, wrote an open letter to Johnson pointing out how *social efficiency* adherents were whittling down the curriculum to essential courses. History was viewed as less essential because it kept changing its purpose within the curriculum while social studies allowed for incorporation of history and had the added bonus of providing civic education.[56] Rugg's open letter sparked a public response from Schafer. Schafer retreated towards a more *traditionalist* stance. He said that his Committee had no authority over curriculum and that ultimately the opinions of the local boards made all the decisions. Rugg responded in kind by providing a list of experts that could inform school boards about social studies curriculum.

The timing of these events is important. Dunn identified "the immediate needs of the nation and of the individual pupil as the starting point of any promising attempt to reorganize the social studies."[57] The Americanization calls during World War I focused attention on the need to indoctrinate students into American culture. If history could indoctrinate students in American civics, then social studies would not be needed. But historians' focus was on "true historical-mindedness, . . . includ[ing] a realization of the continuity of events, of development, of the fact that present is intelligible only when seen by the light of the past."[58]

Cardinal Principles of Secondary Education is believed to be the beginning of the progressive education movement that dominated education for the next forty years.[59] Progressive educators justified the new curriculum as a means "to transform the children of immigrant factory workers into individuals who considered themselves Americans, by intentionally fostering a common civic consciousness."[60] The progressive administrators were attempting to establish their authority and control over their curriculum. They also had to find room for the recommendations from the *Cardinal Principles*, including social studies. The new field would replace courses because students could take only a finite number of courses. These replacements happened at the expense of history-only courses. Administrators were not the only individuals exerting influence. Modern local school boards came into existence as small non-political bodies controlling school curriculum while overseeing superintendent's decisions.[61]

Even in education, events were changing the fabric of educational theory. Progressive theorists (who supported the *social meliorism* and *developmentalist factions*) wrested control away from the more *traditionalist* faction. For example, in 1910, the NEA elected their first female president, Ella Flagg

Young, who was the recently appointed superintendent of Chicago public schools. This election was a shock to the NEA establishment.[62] She got the support of such social reformers as Addams and Dewey. The union between historians and educators was beyond cracked; it was fractured.[63]

IMPLICATIONS

Hofstadter asserted that the CRSE was a revolution in education, but it was not a good revolution because college professors and presidents were not involved.[64] He argued that schools should be utilized only for preparation for college; he rejected the CRSE premise of general education and vocational education.[65] Conservatives later critiqued the CRSE because they believed it was a political attempt to recapture the nationalist narrative for preparing citizens. The concept of relevance was irrelevant to history education. For conservatives, promotion of progressive education in the *Cardinal Principles* was the final betrayal of American education. And social studies was the culmination of progressive reform efforts under CRSE.

Several *denunciations* of the Committee on Social Studies have occurred throughout the past century. The main ones include its attitudes towards college, its prominence regarding relevancy, its adoption of untried learning techniques, and its usurpation of history courses. The denunciations have come from all forms and places. But the fundamental issue revolves around the interpretation of citizenship or civic education. Looking at these denunciations highlights some of the issues related to the field moving forward.

Hunt indicates that the Final Report created greater confusion than understanding because the College Board ignored the social studies recommendations for nearly twenty years.[66] Ironically, Hertzberg argues that social studies educators only wanted to force students to go to college.[67] This accusation neglects that both Madison and Seven were primarily focused upon college entrance requirements. In terms of the second denunciation, the *humanistic* leanings of the 1890s turned into progressive education that needed to be relevant to a person's normal life.[68] The noncausal relationship between partial dismantling of traditional history in an effort to renew focus upon modern history was a problem.[69] The relevancy of modern history undermined the notion of historical continuity that had been a key concept for traditionalists who believed students needed to study ancient, medieval, and European history. Unfortunately for *traditionalists*, the general rise of progressive education also coincided with the rise of social studies.

Social studies adopted many contemporary educational trends like *social efficiency* that required the teaching of relevant information.[70] Progressive educators and "New" history advocates de-emphasized political history and attempted to connect history to current social and economic problems. Several of the other social sciences already focused on the relevancy of their discipline to contemporaneous society. "Civics should concern itself less with constitutional questions and remote governmental functions and should direct attention to social agencies close at hand and to the informal activities of daily life that regard and seek the common good."[71] Social studies is more interested in the problems of the present.[72]

Looking at pedagogical interpretations, Dewey is often credited with laying the pedagogical foundation for social studies.[73] *Traditionalists* favored an adult-centered classroom, which is often how history classes are taught. Social studies classes remained more student-centered. The Committee on Social Studies repeated the same problem that the Madison Conference and the Committee of Seven exposed: the lack of teaching material and training on what the new curriculum should look like for students. Saxe considers this evolutionary approach to be very Deweyian.[74] Jorgensen dismisses the historiographical interpretations of Dewey's influence on social studies and these recommendations.[75] Another explanation for these events is the triumph of *social meliorism* in social studies pedagogy over Deweyian *developmentalism*. Despite Dewey's apparent ambiguity, he interacted with his colleagues at Teachers College who later implemented the social studies curriculum.

Hertzberg challenges the need for a student-centered classroom to teach history and civic education.[76] Saxe resolves that the Committee's perspective on the purpose of social studies was to address socialization and citizenship education and to infuse *social efficiency* into the curriculum.[77] At first glance, *social efficiency* is not that important to the social studies debate, but its influence during this period cannot be ignored. According to Jorgensen, Edward Krug interpreted *social efficiency* as a quest for social reform via the avenue of creating social control through education. The goal, of course, was to improve the well-being of society.[78] Jorgensen explains how later authors like Michael Lybarger and Herbert Kliebard suggested that social efficiency influenced the *Cardinal Principles* and led to progressive education. He adds that Diane Ravitch, by contrast, simply confirmed the trend toward progressive education. Regardless of when the connection between social studies and progressive education happened, the social meliorist link will dominate the progressive education ties.

Conservatives have taken the term efficiency to mean *scientific* management, which is applying a modern interpretation to the context.[79] Actually, *social efficiency* attempted to blend efficiency with science, which is part of the political ideology of progressivism. Political progressivism was a spectrum with conservatives favoring *scientific* application. Moderates were Theodore Roosevelt's New Nationalism and Woodrow Wilson's New Freedom with government oversight on the abuses of society. Leftists were social reformers like Dewey, Addams, and other democratic progressives.

All other denunciations pale in comparison to the indictment that social studies destroyed history education. *Traditionalists* believe that historians established civic education and provided a preferred way to train students. Then, social studies not only usurped history's traditional place in the curriculum, but it also fosters a civic education model that did not properly train students. Jackson and Jackson argue that history education had been in a *golden age* as a dominant subject from 1890 until 1920.[80] The Committee on Social Studies ended that *golden age* by incorporating social studies into the curriculum and forever downgrading history education.

Hertzberg supports this claim because the Committee on Social Studies criticized the idea of four years of history as a long-standing tradition.[81] The elimination of ancient history seemed to matter to the AHA because many of its members studied those periods. Rising American nationalism was a potential rationale for eliminating the study of English history. From this point of view, it appears that the Committee on Social Studies was attempting to eliminate traditional history from the curriculum; however, this oversimplification is only the latest made by political factions who tried to control the education of citizens by discrediting social studies.

By the 1980s, paleoconservatives[82] would put a different spin on the formation of social studies. Lerner, Nagai, and Rothman argue that the foundation of history education was not controversial and that it laid the foundation for natural civic education.[83] In this view, the efforts of the Committee on Social Studies destroyed the unified work of historians by creating a new mishmash of subjects and skills.[84] Saxe claims that social studies "insurgents" had a four-step process: undermine traditional history's purpose, eliminate traditional history from the curriculum, introduce social studies proposals, and replace traditional history with social studies.[85] Saxe does not truly believe that these insurgents had thought through what they were doing to history. To him, the other denunciations seem to lead to the replacement of history education. Saxe stipulates that change happened between the Committee of Five report (1911) and the organization of the Committee on Social Studies.[86] Educators viewed history as both intellectual and individual, yet by 1913 educators felt that education had a social purpose for change: *social meliorism*. Kingsley and other "insurgents" formed the social studies Committee to circumvent national history organizations and apply social reforms to history education.[87]

The preordained design by social studies educators did not actually undermine the role of history education. Social studies is a history-dominated field. The courses were reliant on traditional historical teaching methods of rote memorization, political history, and narrow focus on WASP identity. Many reformers felt that history did not always address the changing needs of training citizens. Historians, educators, and administrators had created two distinct curricula for a diverging population. Bohan, Doppen, Feinberg, and O'Mahony indicate that all the committees recognized the need for differences between high school plans, one for college-bound and one for non-college-bound students.[88] However, this fact is often glossed over by contemporary commentators because they want to find a person to blame for the reduction of history education within the current curriculum.

The Final Report was part of the process for developing a curriculum for the social sciences and civic education. By framing social studies as destroying a *golden age* of history education, commentators raise questions about the overall value of social studies to the current curriculum. As an unintended consequence, they also raise questions about the value of history in the curriculum. The Final Report had "very little immediate impact on historians" and caused confusion about what really constituted a social studies curriculum.[89]

In the end, the argument cannot be about history or social studies education because all sides are focused on civic education. This disagreement over civics became the crux of a conflict between history education and social studies education that has not been resolved.[90] Most of the controversies stem from the questions surrounding civic education. The end problem is that different groups have different theories about how to be a *good* citizen and these conflicting civic theories are at the heart of the history-versus–social studies debate.

The Committee on Social Studies erroneously defined the purpose of traditional history as creating nationalism or a national American identity, a lack of understanding of the changing concept of citizenship. The Madison Conference and Committee of Seven did not view history as nationalism building. Further, the ideology of citizenship radically altered between 1899 and 1913.[91] The *Cardinal Principles* states that the purpose of education was "the comprehension of the ideals of American democracy and loyalty to them should be a prominent aim of civic education."[92] Social studies insurgents believed that all Americans would see the benefit of social studies as a model for developing citizens. When political debates about citizenship arose, they were shocked that people would question the social studies curriculum. The Final Report was more a continuation of the other reports, and its importance became apparent only in later decades.[93]

In many ways, advocates for social studies conceived of the subject as a way for oppressed Americans to understand "their place" within society; however, to the dismay of *humanists/traditionalists*, social studies adopted an aggressive form of *social meliorism* as progressive education became more popular. Eventually, courses such as the *Problems of Democracy* helped social studies identify some of the continual problems with society instead of simply maintaining a status quo. From this point forward, *social meliorists* influenced social studies curriculum and undermined notions that social studies should maintain the traditional attitudes of America. Critical comments about the Final Report's emphasis on permitting students to have serious discussions about contemporaneous social problems are valid; however, Saxe states that the report called for these curricula, but the lack of material following the report did not permit the opportunity to engage students with contemporaneous social ills.[94]

The publication of the *Cardinal Principles* was on the eve of the first Red Scare in American history. Anything that might question traditional American society became problematic. Fifty years after the Final Report was published, the public held common discussions on the concept of social studies because it was "a kind of heterogeneous mixture" or some nefarious concept based on the word social (i.e., socialism).[95]

State government attitudes stressed the importance of civic education. Illinois passed a law that required middle school educators to teach an hour of civics education, with attention to the Declaration of Independence, the Illinois state constitution, and the US Constitution.[96] Michigan required all graduating students to successfully complete a semester of civics.[97] Administrators and educators were implementing their own educational Americanization programs and they sought innovative ways to teach civics.

During the 1914 Pennsylvania Education Association meeting, a high school principal attempted to differentiate between traditional history as espoused by the AHA and social studies, explaining that "the gods and goddesses of Ancient Greece [traditional history] are engaged in mighty conflict with the ashman and garbage collector of to-day [social studies]" over the direction of the relevance of the curriculum.[98] Both sides simply allowed state legislatures, boards of education, education professionals, and practitioners to decide.[99] And thus, the real conundrum of civic education arises as gods and goddess stop dictating *good* citizenry.

Chapter 4

A Social Studies Curriculum

The first thirty years of the development of history/social studies standards constitutes one of the most chaotic periods in the evolution of social studies education. Three major committees established a place for the social sciences, but each committee offered different perspectives. By 1920, history and/or the social sciences were included in nearly every school's curriculum. The use of the social studies moniker did not necessitate that the stakeholders adopt the social studies philosophy. Many school districts adopted this label to describe the social science department. Regardless of the influence, civic education became the justification for these courses.

High school administrators were already under pressure to maximize courses while minimizing staff expenditures due to the rising numbers of students. Hiring three different individuals to be a history teacher, a civics teacher, and an economics teacher was neither possible nor cost effective. Social studies provided them with an appealing alternative: a single all-encompassing teacher. Many administrators found it easier to utilize a single organizational umbrella and continue with a traditional history curriculum. For the most part, the social studies curriculum ties itself to these three committees in terms of general purpose and structure. Moving forward has been primarily about what content and pedagogy are best for implementing civic education.

BUILDING A SOCIAL STUDIES COMMUNITY

At first, broad consensus was built among some of the professional organizations, including the AHA, NEA, and American Sociological Society.

The AHA, the biggest supporter, provided funds, permitted the use of its official journal (edited by McKinley), and encouraged social studies teachers to join. But, then the AHA claimed all *good* and *efficient* teachers were history teachers, not social studies teachers.[1]

The other social sciences saw a chance to exert their place in the curriculum for the first time since their professional organizations formed. In 1914, the Organization of the National Council of Geography Teachers was formed. The American Political Science Association (APSA) published its guidelines for teaching social studies, which recommended a year of social science and at least a semester dedicated to the study of American government.[2] By 1922, APSA advocated expanding the American government semester to a full year of government study, a curricular change intended to replace the *Problems of Democracy* course.

The American Economic Association likewise advocated for a broader social studies approach to the curriculum. Economists wanted to infuse principles of economics into the entire high school social studies curriculum. Sociologists, under the Finney Committee, issued reports permitting the NEA/AHA vision of the social studies curriculum. Sociologists and economists advocated for a more general social science program of study to replace *Problems of Democracy*.

A major ideological division happened between the discipline advocates and social studies promoters when it came to the pedagogical direction of the curriculum. During the Rugg-Schafer exchanges, Earle Rugg, Harold Rugg's brother, called for a reconvening of the Committee on Social Studies to detail plans for a social studies curriculum beyond the structural recommendations. The Committee on Social Studies met again in conjunction with the 1921 AHA meeting to form the nucleus of the National Council for the Social Studies (NCSS). Albert McKinley, J. Montgomery Gambrill, Daniel C. Knowlton, Harold Rugg, Earle Rugg, Roy Hatch, Rolla Tyron, and Edgar Dawson laid the council's foundation. The curriculum was not focusing upon one disciplinary approach; it took a more integrated tactic.

The Rugg brothers, Earle and Harold, argued that the new organization be dedicated to recruit social science educators and teachers.[3] So NCSS labelled those AHA *good* teachers as too close-minded about social studies; they needed to adopt more diverse approaches. The founders of the NCSS used McKinley's editorship over *The Historical Outlook* (originally *The History Teacher's Magazine* until 1918) to find "those who wish to make the social studies useful."[4] However, McKinley did not provide enough space for non-historical pedagogy.[5]

Historical Outlook was heavily subscribed to by teachers.[6] McKinley published several sample syllabi recommendations for grades one through six, modern European history, and American history that included lessons with other social sciences.[7] McKinley's syllabi recommendations soon became the established standards for the field. *Historical Outlook* started to examine more pedagogical issues related to social studies content and strictly historical issues. Eventually, *Historical Outlook* became *The Social Studies* (1934) under the auspices of the NCSS.

The NCSS formally adopted the stance that social studies was "history and the social sciences in schools."[8] Dawson, a NCSS founder, was concerned about the absence of historians in the curriculum debate and personally felt that history and social studies were interchangeable, but he meant "New" history.[9] By the middle of the 1920s, the AHA concern became apparent as it lost its preeminent position as the leader of the social science curriculum. Likewise, the other professional organizations never connected themselves with the NCSS.

As the influence of professional associations waned, university educators increasingly directed the shape of the field. The NCSS was gaining in strength and popularity among teachers. They formed their own department in the NEA to oversee social studies disciplines within schools, including economics, civics, sociology, and history.[10]

ORGANIZING THE SOCIAL STUDIES CURRICULUM

C. E. Martz, an AHA member and advocate for more traditional history education, argued for the preeminence of history over the other social sciences because "history, taught well, encompasses every value claimed for social studies."[11] But despite the increasingly complicated landscape of history and social studies, history did dominate social studies curriculum because historians were still the primary authors of the textbooks.[12]

Dawson, first secretary-treasurer of NCSS, conducted a survey of the state of history and social studies education in schools. More than 2,400 schools responded. He concluded that social studies was expanding throughout the curriculum; new teachers were more likely to be social studies minded, and history content was shrinking. In fact, school leadership wanted "to increase space in the curriculum for civics and economics and had a general preference for recent history [American history] over the more distant past."[13] This report is the basis for subsequent views that history shrank while social studies expanded.

Additionally, college admission boards decreased the requirement for history in favor of social science, but the decrease by the College Board corresponded with the rise of mandatory American history courses for high school graduation by states.[14] American history was the most popular course taught under social studies (table 4.1). As American history courses increased, European and Ancient history courses were being offered less and less often by public schools. In the classroom, only about 12 percent of history teachers were able to teach history courses alone. An additional one third of history teachers taught as social studies instructors, meaning that they were also responsible for teaching subjects like civics, economics, and geography. More than half of the history teachers—the remaining majority—became general teachers, responsible for teaching English, mathematics, and foreign language courses in addition to history classes.[15]

History was demoted to an important role within the social studies curriculum, but it was no longer the single voice in the curriculum. University historians broke ties with the social studies movement as national organizations focused on the collegiate level. Education schools were taking the lead in the curriculum debates for social studies and other education fields. Within social studies, history-minded educators held the dominant role in the leadership of the NCSS. Thus, the organization was not truly articulating the needs of the other social sciences.

A problem with social studies was finding places for other social sciences within the curriculum. Administrators focused on courses containing history, civics, and geography content. As theoreticians created the formula for social studies, they relied upon history and civics as the main foundations, even ignoring geography.[16] As social studies further developed, geography was transferred to the physical sciences and economics was elevated in importance.

By the end of the 1920s, the divisions between the various social scientists and social studies educators centered on the capstone social studies course, *Problems of Democracy*.[17] The broad social studies model had become the standard curriculum model. Educators such as the Ruggs marginalized traditional history teaching methods and won allies in the AHA. Some AHA members recognized that teaching methods in social studies were more effective than the unreliable pedagogy of rote memorization. Even though the Final Report called for *Problems of Democracy* to be taught as the senior capstone, several schools taught simple American history, while other schools taught government, economics, sociology, or social problems. The National Association of Secondary School Principals followed many of the suggestions of *Cardinal Principles*, including advising the *Problems of Democracy* course (at first a single semester course that was eventually expanded to a full

Table 4.1 Percentage of High School Students Taking Social Studies Courses

Social Studies Courses	1928	1934
American history	17.9	17.4
European history	6.7	6.2
World history	6.1	11.9

Adapted from R. B. Townsend, *History's Babel: Scholarship, Professionalization, and the Historical Enterprise in the United States, 1880-1940* (Chicago, IL: University of Chicago Press, 2013), 176.

year), an economics course during twelfth grade, and the cessation of history courses at tenth grade.[18]

As schools started adopting social studies curriculum, the *Problems of Democracy* course became very popular. As a capstone course, the Hampton Institute's *Problems of Democracy* for the social studies curriculum differentiated history and social studies education. Students chose the topics they wanted to cover. This aligned with Dewey's *experiential* beliefs where students had input in their learning.[19] This course also was an experiment in *social meliorism*.[20] But teachers complained about a lack of materials that prevented further adoption. Additionally, social scientists disliked the capstone course because they wanted space for other disciplines. Principals and social studies educators were the only groups advocating for the inclusion of *Problems of Democracy* into the curriculum to incorporate the various social sciences. They agreed that the primary purpose of social studies was citizenship education; however, they disagreed on the best method of obtaining civic education.[21]

More teachers adopted the *Problems of Democracy* model once materials started to appear on the market. Educators, not university professors, were the major contributors to the new course material. Dawson commented that the social sciences disagreement over the *Problems* course was a missed opportunity. Dissension among the social sciences festered instead of coalescing around a single vision for the field.[22] Some trends emerged in social studies education: a broadly based social science approach to social studies with an active *social meliorist* leaning and a social studies curriculum firmly rooted upon a historical center but actively supported by the other social sciences. The tendencies varied yet citizenship education seemed to be at the heart of each method of teaching: "Good citizenship in an efficient democracy was set up as a primary objective of public education."[23]

Educators began to see civics as a method to value a democratic society and defend democratic institutions.[24] This notion of valuing democratic institutions conformed to the progressive ideal of protecting the general welfare of the citizen and their democratic rights. This continued the trend towards more pluralistic attitudes in civic education.

CREATING TEXTBOOK MATERIALS

With the arguments of Charles Beard and Robinson taking center place, "New" history philosophies began appearing in American history textbooks. Thus the elimination of patriotic-laden narratives as well as hero-worship biographies began. *Traditionalists* favored keeping the patriotic content over social science skills. Immigrant groups wanted a return to patriotic content but only if it included the roles of important immigrants. Cultural pluralists were fighting an anti-discrimination trend by preferring a more multicultural approach to history.[25] Even though textbooks in all subjects have had episodes of politicization, social studies has continually been politicized by all political and social groups.

Elementary education in urban Midwest schools still relied upon biographies and holidays as the primary form of social studies curriculum. However, sixth-graders were now being introduced to traditional American history as part of the curriculum. These schools tried to blend traditional history with social studies skills and civic education. Nevertheless, "few educators at the time considered including people other than white Anglo-Saxon Protestants [WASP] in the teaching of American history or in explicating lessons related to American citizenship."[26]

In a different approach to textbooks, older immigrant groups (e.g., Irish and German) were the most vocal critics of the dominant WASP narrative to American history. They advocated for the inclusion of their heroes into the narrative of American history as individuals who helped to build the country.[27] After World War I, shifts in attitudes regarding the dominant WASP narrative happened because immigrants comprised nearly a fifth of the fighting army and immigrants began to assert themselves against anti-immigrant feelings.[28]

In 1922, William Randolph Hearst, the famous New York City newspaper publisher, started questioning the integrity of school textbooks. He printed in his newspapers that school textbooks were biased towards British values and attitudes. The following year, New York City's mayoral office scrutinized the bias in the district's history textbooks; the investigation confirmed Hearst's claims and the mayor's office banned several history textbooks.[29] In Chicago, a mayoral candidate criticized school textbooks for their British bias in order to win favor from immigrant groups.[30]

Harold Rugg, an education professor at Teachers College, started publishing a series of social studies textbook pamphlets during the 1920s. As a colleague of Dewey, Rugg supported *experimental* interests; but he favored *social meliorism* over *experimental*. Both Harold and Earle Rugg determined that "utility and practicality as the criteria for the selection of content" were essential when developing social studies curriculum.[31] Rugg sought to control the textbook because he could not control the teachers or their educational background. Rugg's social studies curriculum started in 1922 as a pamphlet series, *Man and his Changing Society*. Over the next fifteen years, Rugg sold more than five million textbooks; it was quite successful.[32] He avoided the historian's point of view; his pamphlets were the first full integration of the social sciences into curricular material. Additionally, his *Problems* pamphlet cemented the course in the curriculum for the next twenty years.

Social studies had suffered from "curriculum fragmentation and unnecessary compartmentalization" that could be reversed only by a fully integrated social studies curriculum.[33] In terms of pedagogy, Rugg introduced a problem-solving approach to social studies that melded the various social sciences. He argued that "the entire social studies curriculum should be organized around problems of contemporary life" as opposed to focusing upon historical issues.[34]

These pamphlets laid the groundwork for his textbook series, which schools started adopting along with the social studies curriculum model. In Terre Haute, Indiana, the local school board adopted the Rugg series to introduce a "fused" course of social studies. One of the teachers conducted a study comparing two local schools and found that the school that used the Rugg textbook "will rate higher in solving present day problems;" whereas the school using the traditional textbook scored higher on factual knowledge.[35] The biggest divide between social studies advocates and history education advocates remained the same: what does citizenship education mean?

In the mid-1930s, Paul R. Hanna and James Mendenhall started generating another textbook series called *Building America*. Hanna and Mendenhall produced their first issue in February 1935 on "Housing," an examination of different aspects of American houses from the colonial era to more recent times.[36] They created a new pamphlet every year. These pamphlets were small, roughly twenty-four to thirty-two pages, and they focused only on a specific part of American society and included illustrations. They published a total of thirteen pamphlets.

THE COMMISSION ON THE SOCIAL STUDIES

In 1925, the AHA, at the behest of the NEA, set up another committee to examine the curriculum at the elementary level. The Final Report dealt only with courses at the upper level of secondary schools. The Association hoped to regain the upper hand in the curricular struggle. The AHA considered two candidates to lead: Max Farrand, a history professor at Yale, and August C. Krey, a professor at the University of Minnesota and former teacher.[37]

Each choice had differing views. Farrand insisted that the AHA be open to dialogues between history and the other social sciences. Several colleagues seemed willing to explore this possibility. However, senior historians were entrenched in the notion of traditional history and the inability to compromise on any curriculum other than that of the Committee of Seven.[38] On the other side, the members were concerned about Krey's connection to the NCSS. Dawson thought Krey was a good choice because he was not stuck in outdated notions of history education.[39] The AHA ended up choosing Krey to head the committee.

Investigation on History and Other Social Studies in the Schools were tasked with investigating with little direction or support from the governing council.[40] This Committee proposed a unified social studies curriculum be developed with the assistance of social scientists and education specialists from various university.[41] The work of the Committee was intent on making history education a core subject without social studies. But after three years of general inactivity, this Committee ceased operation when fortune suddenly shined upon it.

Working from within the AHA *Committee on Teaching,* Krey received a huge boost from the Carnegie Corporation. Carnegie offered to fund work that sought ways to improve the curriculum starting with objectives, better organization, grade leveling, teaching methods, and teacher preparation.[42] The financial support provided by Carnegie was immense for the period; the $250,000 grant to the Committee was eight times the annual budget of the American Historical Association.[43] The Committee had to meet certain conditions for the grant. Composition of the Committee altered with fewer academics: university professors were replaced by individuals with an interest in measuring student learning.[44]

The committee was renamed the *Commission on the Social Studies* and became one of the biggest endeavors the AHA would ever undertake in secondary education. Some similarities exist between the *Committee on the Social Studies* and the *Commission on the Social Studies*. Both groups were composed of members with diverse social science backgrounds, not simply history (see appendix A). Both groups advocated for Robinson's "New" history as an important pedagogical foundation. Charles A. Beard, Robinson's "New" history cofounder, was named to the Commission. Other individuals of note were Johnson, former member of the CHEC, and education professor George Counts. Several members of the Commission had strong ties to Teachers College and thus were influenced by Dewey.

The differences were apparent as well. The *Committee on Social Studies* had been summoned by the NEA whereas the AHA *Commission* did not have direct connection to the NEA but was willing to associate with other national organizations (American Association of School Administrators and NCSS). The *Commission on the Social Studies* relied on academics and administrators, rather than teachers.[45] Again, it was one of the perennial problems among the AHA committees.

The *Commission on the Social Studies* marked an important departure from previous AHA committees: they endorsed the term "social studies."[46] Building on the Final Report, the Commission also advocated for a more foundational approach toward education over indoctrination of students to the narrative.[47] They detailed the purported knowledge, skills, attitudes, and values that social studies was to include. They advocated for the inclusion of the social sciences within the curriculum, although they believed history should still be at the forefront of social studies.[48] The Commission also favored expanding the *Problems of Democracy* course within the curriculum.

The one area that the members of the Commission could not agree on was how to present their recommendations. Krey favored a series of consensual reports for the curriculum, whereas Beard and Counts wanted to provide more general instructions.[49] Ultimately, the Commission started to generate random reports that reflected the different perspectives among its members. A plethora of publications (at least eighteen volumes) came out of the Commission's work over the next six years. The majority of publications were written by Beard and Counts, the Commission's research director.

Beard attempted to bridge the gaps between history and the other disciplines, merging them into a progressive educator worldview.[50] He created a *seamless web* where "the perspective of the present and the needs of the future shaped the teaching" of history and other social sciences.[51] Counts adopted Beard's vision of history as "a continuing revision of the past based on the historian's values and tempered by this particular time, circumstances, and personality," which for Counts meant that history was a reflection of his own time that could be used to solve current problems.[52]

Counts wanted to bring civic education to the forefront of social studies.[53] Likewise, he laid out an ideal for educating democratic citizens that aligned with Rugg's textbook series as well as with the *Problems of Democracy* course. Counts' vision did not include an accompanying social studies curriculum. His vision was at the heart of public schools, which meant all courses needed to incorporate democratic education. He continued moving away from traditional theories of education. American society needed to work for the general good will of all over the needs of individuals.[54]

The influence of Counts over the Commission had lasting implications. His desire to transform American society into a form of collectivism with striking similarities to the Soviet model was highly suspicious within American society. His design was intended to critique American society and create "democratic collectivism."[55] The need to address the problems in American society was more apparent because of the Great Depression. For the future of American society, American schools needed to be integrated into all aspects of society and function as an agency of change for social institutions.[56] The Commission's final publication, *Conclusions and Recommendations* (1934), called for new social studies materials, yet "the commission's majority membership seemed to agree on a few things."[57] Presenting the information to the AHA community, some Commission members voiced their dissent openly.[58] Isaiah Bowman signed with reservations; Frank Ballou, Edmund E. Day, Ernest Horn, and Charles E. Merriam declined to sign due to opposition over terms such as *collectivism* and the perception of indoctrination.[59]

The Commission's recommendations required schools to implement a curricular upgrade when most districts struggled even to fund schools during the Great Depression. Further, the Commission's efforts were not always practical and relevant for teachers.[60] Counts' suggestions were abstract, which might be a plausible pedagogical method, but districts wanted measurable learning. The Commission did not try to change or reform the general framework. Instead, Counts and the others focused on developing curricular material.[61] The one lasting recommendation the Commission did have was that decisions about curriculum should be left to the local level, thus the rationale for not making a uniform national curriculum.[62] As a result, most of the recommendations and work of the Commission never filtered down to the teachers, administrators, specialists, and organizations.

The legacy of the *Commission on the Social Studies* is often glossed over as simply allowing the AHA to legitimize the creation of social studies as a field for public schools. Advocating for the Rugg textbook series and its leftist leanings had a lasting negative impact. Nevertheless, the *Commission on the Social Studies* did several important things: AHA accepted the term of social studies over history; they acknowledged the changes within society with regards to student-teacher relationship; and they embraced the importance of citizenship education within social studies.[63] This was the last major attempt by the AHA to influence primary and secondary education.

TRANSITIONS

The perceived close relationship between AHA and NCSS altered after the Commission. In 1934, the AHA ended its association with the NCSS. The AHA focus became postsecondary education and the role of the historian in professional settings. The AHA would not get involved in secondary education again until the 1990s. NCSS took control over *The Historical Outlook* and renamed it *The Social Studies* with funds from the Carnegie grant. Two years later, the NCSS became totally independent. Upon editor McKinley's death, NCSS rebranded its journal to *Social Education*. *Social Education* received recognition from APSA, AHA, and American Sociological Society but no financial support from them. This journal's focus was on assisting teachers with social studies curriculum, but history instruction dominated the journal.[64]

Counts' vision of social studies laid the foundation for the Progressive Education Association (PEA). The PEA, centered at Columbia University, was connected to the ongoing debates in social studies. After the Commission finished its work, Counts continued to advance democratic education using social studies as the exemplar. He feared that local school districts were incapable of handling the changes to society, thus the PEA needed to direct changes.⁶⁵ He called for social reconstruction of society through education, or dynamic education. Dynamic education would allow citizens to adjust to problems and issues that might arise in the American democracy.⁶⁶

The *social meliorist* attitudes that many *traditionalists* despised within progressive education served to link the work of Counts and the PEA. The PEA condemned the continual reliance on textbooks and rote memorization as a teaching pedagogy. The PEA negatively criticized the goals and accomplishments of the Committees of Ten and Seven.⁶⁷ It praised the revolutionary nature of the Final Report; however, the PEA suggested that the Final Report was hampered by practices ingrained by previous recommendations. It even criticized the *Commission on the Social Studies* for not providing instructional direction even though it developed more curricular material than all three previous efforts had.

The *Committee on the Function of the Social Studies* was a subcommittee within the PEA. Its aim was to foster a curriculum for comprehending social interactions with others.⁶⁸ This Committee defined the purpose of social studies as providing students with the means to interact with others within a democratic society. The Committee desired students to learn to understand and appreciate all parts of society, not only the part from which they came. Tolerance was a main value to be instilled through students' learning.

By the end of the 1930s, two visions for social studies emerged due to the efforts of the Commission.⁶⁹ The NCSS advocated for "the education of citizens for a democratic society in concrete curricular scope-and-sequence recommendations" alongside a more traditional *social efficiency* model.⁷⁰ The other vision also incorporated citizen education but infused a social awareness among the students. This awareness, or *social meliorism*, was organic in that it would develop from the students, in other words, Dewey's *developmentalist* approach. This latter vision valued student examination of contemporary societal problems above *traditional* historical content.

IMPLICATIONS

One of the biggest issues in the social studies curriculum is the belief that during this period, social studies edged history from the curriculum. This belief continually arises through the development of social studies.⁷¹ Yet the Final Report "should be recognized for protecting history during [1920s and 1930s], not eroding it" as many historians like to believe. Despite the criticisms, history remained the centerpiece of social studies curriculum over the other disciplines.⁷² According to Hertzberg, the 1930s really saw the various social science disciplines being fused with one another into the field of social studies.[73] But she neglects to address the changes within the discipline of history.

The AHA was transforming away from traditional political and military history, even if it moved slowly. "New" history was becoming more popular among its members, and it was more inclusive with the other social sciences. Likewise, the role of the other professional organizations tends to be silent on whether or not they favored the social studies curriculum. In fact, sociologists and economists viewed government as a larger threat to the curriculum than history.[74] So the Final Report expanded the reach of the social sciences, but it did not create the network of social sciences working together to create a cohesive curriculum.

Nearly every committee or critique of social studies curriculum involved the lack of materials. One educator said that "social studies will be successful only when they supply an abundance of descriptive material. Furthermore, this descriptive material must be given through a long period of school life in order that it may slowly permeate the whole experience of the pupil."[75] The Madison Conference urged teachers to move away from lectures and utilize a "wise" textbook, include class activities such as debates and discussion, and concentrate on written expression. The Committee of Seven suggested, in conjunction with a textbook, the use of primary sources. After the *Cardinal Principles*, the pedagogy was more on student-centered problem-solving with textbooks fostering discussions. The Rugg textbook series finally seemed to address this issue. Social studies curriculum developed more thematic units rather than specific discipline approaches. The Rugg textbook series was extremely popular due to its thematic approach.

In the 1990s, Nash, Crabtree, and Dunn assert that the AHA tried to regain its dominance over the NCSS and failed due to the work of the Commission.[76] The Commission focused less on structure and more on pedagogy and materials. The fusion of the social studies field muted many of the discussions over what should be taught. By the end of the 1930s, Deweyan and the philosophy of progressivism dominated the educational agenda, which also meant that citizenship education became a hidden assumption for all education, not just social studies.[77] King believed that only the Committee of Seven and Committee on the Social Studies were positively received by secondary schools.[78]

There are some potential explanations why the Commission failed: firstly, it started during a prosperous period and finished during the Great Depression (funds were scarce); secondly, diverse publications with three differing opinions confounded administrators; and finally, decentralized school districts evolved that could choose which programs to implement.[79] Previous efforts generally received near-unanimous support from the committee members largely because the committees worked to make consensus. Consensus is something that was lacking in the Commission.

The intransigence of Counts would influence his work in the PEA. The PEA focus was to use all subjects to address the problems with American democracy, not only one course. Ideological shifts meant that progressive educators like Counts wanted to stress democratic traditions throughout the curriculum, not just social studies. The notion of cultural pluralism as civic education was being infused into the new progressive conception of education and social studies. Changes that immigrant leaders urged upon curricula also sought to infuse civic nationalism into education.[80] The impact of Counts and his PEA linked social studies with a leftist philosophy that influenced the first major cultural controversy.

A Slovenian immigrant and editor, Louis Adamic, toured the urban centers of the Northeast and Midwest during the early 1930s. He noted a rising trend among second-generation immigrants who were no longer part of European society: they did not feel they were part of American society either, harkening back to Addams' comments in 1910.[81] Adamic called for a more inclusive history as part of the American history narrative in order to make immigrants feel pride in their new country's history as well as to combat nativist sentiments.[82] New York City politicians embraced Adamic's call for a change, and they began changing the traditional narrative to create a more pluralistic vision of America.[83]

Chapter 5

What Happened to History Education?

By the end of the 1930s, American history was an essential part of the "core" public curriculum.[1] Non-American history (e.g., British, ancient, medieval) declined and transformed into a single yearlong "world history" course. Administrators adopted the *Problems of Democracy* course that fused civil government, sociology, and economics. This course provided the first real change to traditional teaching methods within the curriculum. The arguments were no longer about whether social studies was part of the curriculum, rather they revolved around methodology and content.

General Omar Bradley, commenting on his own soldiers during World War II, felt that Americans did not participate in the political life of the United States because they lacked interest in its philosophical foundation. The purpose of education is to maintain a status quo by keeping a connection with the elder and younger generations as close as possible.[2] Older Americans picked up on Bradley's concern, which developed into a struggle over the direction of social studies that created a major educational cultural war. Traditional historians sought to maintain a continuum of the status quo while progressive educators, such as Dewey and Counts, sought to examine problems in the contemporary world and seek changes.[3]

FIRST CULTURAL BATTLES

Rugg's attempt to correct the ills of society through education received a boost with the onset of the Great Depression in 1930s. The problems associated with the Great Depression turned the contemporary problems, social ills, and problems with American democracy into the bread and butter of social studies classes. Counts wanted education to deal with the reality that America was no longer a united solidarity of WASP culture.[4] Social studies provided the vehicle to discuss the current situation and move forward.

Even though there had been previous attempts to examine textbooks, these events tended to be small and local. The 1930s catapulted these textbook controversies into national debates.[5] The Mississippi State Textbook Purchasing Board banned Rugg's textbook series because of its *progressive* ideas.[6] William Randolph Hearst banned any mention of Counts in his newspapers.[7] As a consequence of this ban on Counts, any individual associated with him was tarnished with the same paintbrush, including Dewey and Rugg.

The Americanization policies of the early twentieth century were directed more at total assimilation to the WASP narrative. The Americanization policies of the 1930s and 1940s attempted to extol the virtues of various cultures that helped to build the American experience.[8] A shift from assimilation to amalgamation was happening and many groups did not favor this change. Racial restrictionists proclaimed that this Americanization created a weakness within the American system.[9] Conservatives and isolationists saw national history and civics as acceptable courses but questioned social studies courses.

Throughout the 1920s, the American Legion led a campaign against Rugg's textbook series and other "progressive" social studies textbooks. They wanted a straight traditional history that would indoctrinate students.[10] Yet they did not make much headway into disrupting textbooks until the late 1930s. In a 1934 NEA report, Harold Rugg was tagged with supporting Soviet collectivism, which led many to conclude he was a communist. In the late 1930s, businesses complained about urban education budgets due to their "failure" to successfully Americanize immigrants. The National Association of Manufacturers (NAM) commissioned a study to examine the view of private enterprise within various social studies textbooks.[11] Not surprisingly, NAM concluded the Rugg's textbook series was socialist. Bertie Forbes, founder of *Forbes* magazine, joined the attack, claiming the series was anti-capitalist and "un-American." Forbes garnered the support of the American Legion, Hearst, and other like-minded groups, which lobbied school boards to stop adopting Rugg's textbooks.[12] In 1938, sales of Rugg's textbooks dropped to less than 300,000 copies a year.[13]

Building on the critique against Rugg, Professor Allen Nevins, an American historian at Columbia University, penned an article for the *New York Times* that was the opening shot for the first cultural war.[14] Nevins beseeched the readers for a return to more *traditional* pedagogy over the leftist ideology of his *progressive* colleagues at Teachers College. He contended that history education was an essential part of being an American.[15] He verbalized the unhappiness over the "mistreatment" of history at all levels.[16] Even though Nevins tried to include history in college's general education requirements,

Columbia's faculty decided against his recommendation and did not mandate history in their revised general education requirements.

Erling Hunt, editor of *Social Education*, responded with the social studies position. He argued that students learned more history under the new mantle of social studies than they had under the old history education model. The diversity of "New" history combined with the social studies curriculum allowed students to learn more than political history.[17] Further, he argued that students did not have to learn history by memorizing facts and then repeating them. Hunt and Nevins voiced their differing opinions over the course of several months. Nevins had the benefit and support of the *New York Times* owners to assist in the persuasion of the public.

Nearly a year later, the *New York Times* released the results from a survey on college freshmen's knowledge of US history. The results demonstrated that the high school graduates did not know much US history. Nevins, who assisted in the survey construction, portrayed this lack of historical knowledge as un-American and un-patriotic in the middle of World War II.[18] To Nevins, the identifying factors for poor student performance were obvious: school curriculum, shrinking of history courses, ill-prepared teachers, immature students, and a lack of parental involvement in education. Initially, the public accepted the results of the survey.

Historical organizations like the Mississippi Valley Historical Association (MVHA) praised the survey for pointing out the lack of historical knowledge. The president of the AHA, Guy Stanton Ford, publicly remained silent while privately supporting the NCSS leadership.[19] After supporting, MVHA allowed for some critiques to be published in their journal, *Mississippi Valley Historical Review*. Edgar Wesley, former NCSS president and education professor at Minnesota, explained that this knowledge problem stemmed from historians' unwillingness to participate in designing curriculum, refusing to assist in school issues, holding low opinions of public teachers, neglecting the preparation of teachers, offering poorly constructed history textbooks, and finally resisting the development of a set of common standards within social studies.[20] Hunt also noted that the survey sample was skewed to avoid students at elite colleges. Likewise, many students did not take the survey seriously. He questioned the validity of the survey. Yet, he also identified the poor preparation of teachers and the poorly constructed textbooks, primarily written by historians, as potential reasons for the results.[21]

The *New York Times* and the Committee on American History, a group dedicated to the improvement of history education in schools, constructed a second survey to validate their results.[22] The *Times* was not interested in a rigorous analysis of the survey. Most questions relied on factual recall or rote memorization. For example, participants needed to name all thirteen colonies, not a particularly arduous task. But participants received credit only if they identified *all* thirteen colonies correctly. High school students performed better on questions connecting people with their achievements, especially on more contemporary individuals.

The supporters of the survey had achieved their dedicated goal: American schools were failing, and social studies was the culprit. Supporters of the *Times* survey argued that the reason for the decline lay in promotion of social studies educators who ignored history like the NCSS and the Teachers College.[23] Nevins and the *New York Times* focused on the belief that history was not taught if it was not required by the state. Additionally social studies was more focused on current events and problem solving than on understanding traditional US history.[24]

To combat these accusations, another history survey was conducted. The Committee on American History in Schools and Colleges, including members from the AHA, MVHA, and NCSS, tasked themselves with examining the scope of American history in schools, administering a "fairer" test to students as well as to the general citizenry, providing recommendations for teacher preparation in history, and creating a national standard for American history.[25]

This assessment's results showed that social studies teachers scored the highest (69 percent), followed by "important" Americans (68 percent) as listed in *Who's Who*. The general population scored 29 percent, while high school students scored the lowest with 22 percent.[26] The Committee had anticipated better scores on their test; however, the dismal scores were blamed on the poor design of their multiple-choice test. The test did show that students generally had a better grasp of general social studies concepts than specific content knowledge. They also often recognized more contemporary individuals (such as current government officials) than the average citizen.[27] The committee provided constructive recommendations for history instruction starting in the middle grades through college.

This public debate resulted in factual knowledge being deemed more important to education than skills or thinking.[28] That this reconceptualization occurred in the middle of World War II is not coincidental. Historical understanding was a critical component of patriotism and both were required in order to construct *good* citizens who were willing to fight in the war. The *humanistic* interest group aligned themselves with social efficiency interests for practical reasons. *Social efficiency* methods made measuring student learning easier than it was for the *developmentalist* and *social meliorist* interest groups.

Ultimately, World War II and the rise of American patriotism undermined the Rugg textbook series due to its "un-American" perspective.[29] Many of the criticisms concerning Rugg's textbook were more about how his classes were structured than about contentious content. Content knowledge would also have been a valid criticism, but Rugg's methodology was at the heart of Forbes's critique. The textbook continued to be adopted for several more years by some school districts, but after 1943 sales declined dramatically. Social studies remained the named subject over straight history, educators continued to examine the pedagogical foundations of social studies and align disciplinary skills, and the lines between the factions within the social studies debate continued into the next decade. The AHA further distanced itself from public school education, while MVHA attempted to incorporate an education piece into their publications and conferences but with little success.[30]

IN OTHER NEWS RELATED TO SOCIAL STUDIES

In 1940, the US Supreme Court heard a case, *Gobitis v. Minerville*, that required students to salute the American flag. A pair of Jehovah's Witness students were expelled for violating Pennsylvania state law. A patriotism education movement had passed into law several years earlier, but the students claimed it violated their First Amendment rights.[31] The Court ruled in favor of the school district, citing its desire to remain out of educational policy. The victory was fleeting; it lasted for only three years. In 1943, the Supreme Court overturned a similar law in *West Virginia v. Barnette*. The courts were starting to get involved in educational matters.

For the most part, the other disciplines remained quiet during the 1940s. The American Political Science Association (APSA) set up a committee to look at social studies in 1939. The committee published in the NCSS bulletin, *Teaching of the Civil Liberties* (1941). Otherwise APSA did very little to promote civics education in secondary schools.[32] Sociologists also created a committee but garnered little support from professional sociologists for public schools. The American Economic Association focused on higher education during this period. Any publications regarding economics for educators came from NCSS.

At the postsecondary level, Columbia University introduced a new comprehensive course called Western Civilization. Their premise was to expose the roots of American society through the study of Western European culture. By the 1980s, Western Civilization was the most common non-American course taught at universities and served to underscore the Eurocentric model of America's development. European, or a very Eurocentric world history, became the standard course taught in secondary school with some attention spread among Africa, Asia, Latin America, and the Middle East. Considering internationalism was part of the relevancy focus of social studies, this Eurocentric focus was problematic for progressives.

Defending social studies fell upon the NCSS; educators were disconnected from the disciplines for teacher preparation. The NCSS promoted citizenship education throughout the 1940s as the field's main purpose. Textbooks also started including more multicultural perspectives.[33] Critics claimed that social studies' cultural pluralism attempted to indoctrinate minorities into a system that was undemocratic.[34] The focus shifted away from national citizenship towards international citizenship.[35] This shift likely began to take root due to events in Europe prior to World War II.

In 1946, the Sons of the American Revolution based in California attacked the *Building America* series because it undermined the American government. The series also supported civil rights. The opponents expanded to other groups; these groups attempted to link the series to communist organizations.[36] The pressure at the California Board of Education finally forced Paul R. Hanna and James Mendenhall to end the series in 1948.

UNDERTAKINGS IN SOCIAL STUDIES

During the height of World War II, racial riots erupted in Detroit over living and working conditions. Following the war, various groups within Detroit set up the Detroit Citizenship Education Project (DCEP) to identify ways to prevent more race riots. The project, using eight diverse Detroit schools, examined the fundamental principles of American democracy taught within schools. Their findings harken back to General Bradley's comments that students did not relate those principles to their own lives.

Whether this view is correct or not, many Americans agreed with it, including Stanley Diamond. Diamond oversaw the social studies department for Detroit public schools during the DCEP.[37] The initial study determined that students were not able to discover "alternative solutions to social problems, evaluating evidence, critical thinking, and studying contemporary affairs" within the framework of citizen education.[38] Not surprisingly, the project found the biggest problems were happening in lower socio-economic schools.

Diamond sought to shift the social studies curriculum. He wanted to move away from content-driven citizens toward citizens who dealt with real-world problems.[39] This aligned with Counts, progressive educators, and *social meliorist* advocates. In elementary settings, the DCEP noted that students wanted a purpose to their history learning.[40] At the secondary level, though, marginalizing content was inconclusive for impact on citizenship education.[41] The DCEP validated many progressive education pedagogy theories including student-centered active learning techniques. They were found to be effective and relevant for student learning. Likewise, disciplined-centered education was inconclusive for fostering good education.[42]

In another example, the city of Denver, Colorado, conducted an eight-year study of its curriculum for college-bound students within its schools.[43] This action research was an important departure from university-prescribed guidelines. Study leaders asked teachers to assist in the development of curriculum. Denver schools blended social studies within English classes. The *social efficiency* members of the study believed this would trim "the deadwood off the traditional academic curriculum."[44] They also anticipated eliminating algebra, foreign languages, and history from the curriculum because average citizens did not need them. Denver's experimental schools produced students with slightly higher tests results. *Social efficiency* took the results and advocated applying this to the general curriculum. This provided another theory of how to utilize social studies in the curriculum, blending it with language arts.

Denver's theory of fusing social studies and language arts developed out of an education reform movement in the 1920s that wanted to fuse several subjects. Ultimately, all disciplines would be totally integrated and there would be no distinction. Many schools attempted this fusion model with social studies and language arts. They implemented a block plan where social studies and English became a two-period integrated class. The effect of this fusion model is not known, but eventually most schools returned to separate language arts and social studies courses.

Teachers College initiated a Citizenship Education Project to combat the lack of instruction of American citizens. Funding for this project came from Carnegie Corporation, which had on its board Gen. George C. Marshall. The dean of the Teachers College, William R. Russell, also enlisted the help of Columbia's new president, Dwight D. Eisenhower. Russell initiated a fifteen-year plan to revise the nation's schools so that "students became active, responsible citizens through actual, practical citizenship participation."[45]

Even though Dewey had retired, this project reflected a very *developmentalist* approach to education. Students were actively determining what in their community needed civic participation and then would go out and participate. The project's major weakness was the lack of tools to assist teachers in the implementation of their lab practices.[46] Overall, local efforts to reform social studies produced some interesting test cases but no lasting change to the overall curriculum or curricular material.

NATIONAL PARADIGM SHIFTS

The return of *social efficiency* coincided with America's rise as a world power. Before World War II, most high school graduates went out and found jobs. After World War II, the US government introduced several pieces of legislation to handle its massive returning forces. The most famous of these legislative initiatives was the G.I. Bill for education. Unlike American soldiers returning in 1919, returning soldiers in 1945 could locate employment or the government would provide aid for college. Providing two options diluted the need for full employment. The G.I. Bill opened college to groups that never considered it an option. Colleges were more than willing to expand their enrollment with the infusion of federal money.

As the 1950s began, social studies educators started to focus on how to teach rather than why to teach. Historiographical discussions about the origins of social studies as a field disappeared from teacher preparation and textbooks as social studies became the new accepted paradigm.[47] The reasons for this shift are not entirely clear: social scientists were not involved in making the curriculum; educators were more focused on teaching; and a rise in specialization all might be contributing factors.

The rising political tension with the Soviet Union following World War II made criticism of America even more taboo. Progressive education and its call for constructive education came under attack as part of a communist plot to undermine America's global superiority. The rise of McCarthyism was not limited to high-profile individuals; school districts also implemented their own hunt for communists. A round of loyalty oaths was initiated for teachers; state-mandated loyalty oaths still exist as part of teacher contracts today. Discussions over the purpose and philosophy of schools were relegated to educational theorists. Schools of education began turning towards curriculum development and teacher preparation.

Social studies educators, such as Counts and Rugg, were seen as a haven for red-leaning communist sympathizers. Their imprint on the curriculum needed to be removed.[48] Many social studies teachers were placed under a microscope and questioned about their loyalty to America. Politics again played into the social studies debate and ultimately proved the downfall for the *Problems of Democracy* course. McCarthyism also accelerated the attacks on textbooks like Rugg's *Man and his Changing Society* and calls were made to ban any textbook deemed un-American.[49] A high percentage of textbooks deemed un-American came from social studies.

The impact of the early Cold War on classroom curriculum was also quite remarkable. Curriculum reverted from highly integrated courses back to stand-alone subject courses with content focus. *Traditionalists* called for a return to the 1894 vision of history education. *Social efficiency* advocates favored social studies as a method for teaching the social sciences. The question of how to reorganize social studies, make it a core subject, and define its purpose became the central issue again for the field.

These post-WWII influences forced a redefinition of social studies in the 1950s. Attempts to abandon social studies altogether were passed over in favor of returning to a social sciences model. For example, the citizenship education model, which often utilized the problem-solving model to produce *good* citizens, became increasingly popular. Ironically, this citizenship model mimicked the original conception of social studies. Social studies educators wanted to focus on the present and its needs.[50]

Some groups still pressed for history to replace social studies, but most of their calls were not as public as in the 1940s. Even within the history camp, conflicts about what kind of history should be taught became contentious: some advocated a more science-modeled history (inventions), others advocated a larger civilizational approach, and still others liked the more *meliorist* approach to history.[51] Many historians were utilizing the "New" history lens over the more traditional political/event lens.

The one exception was Arthur Bestor, who studied at Teachers College experimental school. He claimed that social studies was not a sound theory of practice. As a professor in the social studies department at Teachers College, he wanted teachers to rely on content knowledge over methods of instructions. He unsuccessfully strove for the AHA to rethink its boycott of teacher preparation and public education affairs.[52] He promoted five disciplines: mathematics, English, science, history, and foreign language. The rationale for history over the use of social studies was that it allowed for the education of citizens who would be able to grasp perspectives of change within an ever-changing society.[53] Bestor enticed historians to recapture the *golden age* of history education, which social studies educators corrupted with social activism and life adjustment theories. The unintended consequence of Bestor's attacks on social studies was that historians began to have a negative view of all social studies educators.[54]

Educators looked at ways to make social studies more equitable among the other disciplines. They approached the other social sciences for curricular materials. They felt that this material could help students deal with current problems. The concept of dealing with real social problems was reconceived as a need for relevancy within the field. This attitude aligned with an innovative theory for teaching social studies. This new teaching method looked at issues. Classes converted to issues-centered courses. This theory dealt more with contemporary social issues and represented a quasi-return to the *Problems of Democracy* course model. Issues-centered courses utilized the problem-solving skill method and incorporated a single large-scale research project for learning. New problems arose as the theory of social studies and the practice of social studies diverged; teachers found the theories of social studies difficult to implement due to the *humanistic* attitudes still held by the policymakers.

The launch of Sputnik in 1957 triggered a turbulent transformation in American education. Stories spread that "American schoolchildren were learning how to get along with their peers or how to bake a cherry pie . . .

Soviet children were being steeped in the hard sciences and mathematics." These stories lent credence for an adjustment within American curricula.[55] Sputnik spurred the federal government to invest money in public education for the first time. A huge influx of capital was poured into education, and an unintended side effect was the return to prominence of *humanistic* interests and the concurrent focus upon content in curriculum. The monetary national objectives were on mathematics, sciences, and foreign languages; English and social studies were relegated to secondary status. The focus on mathematics and science impacted the social studies debates.

The social sciences were going through a paradigm shift of their own unrelated to Sputnik. This shift dramatically impacted secondary education. By 1960, the impacts of the G.I. Bill were bearing fruit in the halls of colleges and universities. A changing demographics in faculty started to filter down to teacher preparation courses. Social scientists wanted to explain how America fit into a new global world.[56] Universities began using global history courses over Western Civilization courses.

As for public education having "absorbed significant elements of both social efficiency and social reconstruction [*meliorism*]," social studies continued to develop with little governmental oversight.[57] The NCSS rebranded the mission of social studies to be "the most inclusive . . . part of general education in the United States [so] to help young people learn to carry on the free society they have inherited, to make whatever changes modern conditions demand or creative imagination suggests that are consistent with its basic principles and values, and to hand it on to their offspring better than they received it."[58]

IMPLICATIONS

In *Educational Wastelands*, Bestor called social studies the "social stew" of education.[59] He believed that social studies did not have a purpose in the curriculum. Many scholars utilize Bestor's comments to prove that liberalism was too infused in social studies, along with its great champions Rugg and Counts.[60] Into the 1950s, the American Legion was still victimizing Rugg as a model for "subversive activity—teaching the youth of America to find fault with its government."[61] Society worried that social studies was radical—"at least *pink*"—in its political leanings, which led to questions on citizenship education.

The *New York Times* survey was not the first survey to be conducted on historical knowledge. The public mostly ignored a 1935 survey conducted by the AHA. Other surveys examined the number of public schools teaching history or whether history was required for admission into college. These were also ignored. The previous debates concerning history and social studies were isolated to universities and educational professionals. Now the *New York Times* brought the issue into the public eye.[62] The *Times'* survey developed into the enduring myth put forth by *traditionalists* suggesting that students at some point in the past knew their country's history and that ignorance about the past is the provenance of the current generation.[63]

Halvorsen believes that this very public attack, as well as subsequent attacks, were a strictly political effort to sensationalize the plight of American schools.[64] The struggle between educators and the public over social studies became a recurring event. NCSS and educators argued for thinking (skills); supporters of the *Times* survey argued for content knowledge (facts). In the larger public arena, politicians tended to agree with *traditionalist* attitudes towards history while Progressive and left-leaning individuals tended to support social studies. Part of the issue might have been that most politicians had learned social studies using traditional methods like rote memorization and considered those methods to be effective.

In *Teaching the Social Studies*, Wesley relates the first academic history of the evolution of social studies education. He is portrayed as a critic of history education who sought to eliminate all history courses from the curriculum.[65] But, he, like so many others before him, argued that history provided no purpose for students other than memorization of facts. He advised teachers to move away from the pedagogy of rote memorization. *Traditionalists* could see these curriculum decisions as a violation of the notion that history could remain objective and apolitical, whereas social studies was enmeshed in examining societal problems. Historians, believing that social studies could remain out of these political fights, forgot that history can be corrupted for political reasons just as easily as social studies can be used for political activism.[66] The AHA responded by setting up a committee to examine the teaching of history in schools.[67] The first cultural war did not resolve any curriculum matters nor any content matters; it simply laid the groundwork for future conflicts.

Some of efforts of the period identified existing problems that continue in today's society. Tyack, James, and Benovat argue that the Supreme Court's shift from upholding the majority to listening to the minority laid the foundation for the *Brown v. Topeka* decision.[68] In the Detroit public school study, the members identified a problem regarding elementary education, with students not understanding why they study history. Still, students today often do not understand why they study history.[69]

Nash, Crabtree, and Dunn assert the new Western Civilization course hampered the development of history education.[70] In hindsight, scholars believed global history would have been introduced in lieu of the more Eurocentric focus. The traditional attitudes of maintaining a Western perspective ran counter to the progressive attitudes of many social studies educators. Hunt foreshadowed the doom of the *Problems of Democracy* course as a victim to the ideological battles of the Cold War.[71] As America started to "slip" behind the Soviet Union, students needed to be indoctrinated with the superiority of democracy so they would become *good* citizens.

James A. Michener wrote a story titled "Who is Virgil T. Fry?" According to Michener, Fry was a high school social studies teacher in Indiana. Michener replaced him. Michener tells how he discovered why the school board fired Fry. Fry was fired because he was trouble. When talking with Dr. Kelley, a school board member and father of a pupil, Michener inquires about Fry as a teacher. Kelley says "Virgil T. Fry was a truly great teacher. . . . [because] Fry seems to have been the only teacher who ever really got under [the students'] skins and taught them anything."[72]

Michener wonders why the school board would fire a great teacher. Kelley tells Michener that he would rather have his daughter "study under Fry than under [him]. In the long run she'd learn more."[73] But Michener's traditional approach might teach her what she ought to know. This story appreciates the conflict between social studies and history. The story's editor poses the following question: "What kind of teacher do we want in the high schools of the next ten years—a staid conformist to the traditional pattern, a brilliant, erratic not-conformist, or one of well-balanced qualities?"[74] What kind of curriculum does America want social studies/history to be?

Chapter 6

Cold War Comes to Social Sciences

After a relatively stable period for social studies during the early 1950s, the Cold War came to education. In 1957, the Soviet Union launched Sputnik into space. The federal government responded with the passage of the National Defense Education Act. They flung millions of dollars into both higher and secondary education to compete with the Soviets. In the mid-1960s, the Civil Rights movement came to education in President Lyndon B. Johnson's Elementary and Secondary Education Act (ESEA). This brought another influx of funds from the federal government. These funds were not to address Civil Rights but the achievement gap among minorities. Although social studies was not a primary recipient, all education shared in the wealth of the period.

By 1960, many social studies educators felt that reform within the field needed to take place.[1] One contemporary scholar identified citizen education as the source of the *doldrums* within the field of social studies.[2] Progressivism had laid the foundation that citizenship education should occur throughout the school curricula, not be limited to social studies alone. If this were the case, revised approaches to citizenship would free up some time within the social studies curriculum to devote to other efforts.

EDUCATION IN THE FIFTIES

As the 1950s progressed, most schools had a set course of study that looked similar (see table 6.1). The courses focused on three areas: history, geography, and civics. In one study examining the composition of textbooks, history textbooks were "massive complications of information."[3] Few history textbooks integrated other social science material. Few districts vertically aligned

Table 6.1 Frequent Course of Study for Twenty-Four Cities during the 1950s

Grade	Subjects
7th	World history and geography; Geography and history
8th	US and state history with geography; US history and government; US history, 1865 to present; US history to 1865
9th	Community civics; Occupations
10th	World history and geography; World history
11th	US history, 1500 to present; Modern US History
12th	*Problems of Democracy*; American, state, and local government; Personal problems

Adapted from A. N. Cruikshanks, The Social Studies Curriculum in the Secondary School: 1893–1955 [Unpublished doctoral dissertation]. Stanford University, Stanford, CA, 1957, 185.

the courses to build upon each other. Teachers taught history as a "series of unrelated facts" that relied heavily on readings from the textbooks.[4]

The *Problems of Democracy* course was still being taught, but far less effectively than it had been during the 1930s.[5] Amid Cold War turmoil, teachers tended to avoid controversial topics and also tended limited liberal-slanted material.[6] In Howard Elmer Brown's civic textbook, *Your Life in a Democracy*, about a third of the book was devoted to "Your Job as a Citizen (government, vocations, consuming)."[7] Additionally, many districts were transitioning to a semester government course that relied on "formal and descriptive" textbooks about government.[8]

In the early 1950s, intellectuals such as Arthur Bestor and James Bryant Conant believed the new focus on vocational and practical knowledge was problematic. They sought to reintroduce the disciplines into the high school curriculum through the use of postsecondary academics with the hope of creating "insightful, liberated minds" for America.[9] This gave rise to another historical movement: *consensus history*.[10]

Consensus history sought a homogenous interpretation of American history with a downplay of strife.[11] It harkened back to Frederick Jackson Turner's idea of American exceptionalism. Historians, as described by HB Adams, must act as an observer rather than an activist.[12] In the *consensus* vision, American democracy solves America's problems. *Consensus history* fit nicely into the politics of the 1950s and the Norman Rockwell–style vision of small-town America; unfortunately, it did not fit well into the changing realities of American society. *Consensus* historians created a narrative within American history that focused on American exceptionalism without discussing such topics as race, gender, and ethnicity.

Another reform effort within history was to move away from dates, wars, and politics towards a full embrace of the methods and thinking of "New" history. Historians started looking at bigger pictures. Additionally, new voices and perspectives were being added to the narrative of history. A focus on different social perspectives led to a re-evaluation of traditional theories and conceptualizations of the discipline. Historians abandoned the idea that there was only one "correct" historical narrative.[13] Then came a renewed call for teachers to utilize primary sources, especially those showcasing diverse voices. A multicultural approach to the narrative of history included the voices of hitherto such neglected constituencies as African Americans, women, and other ethnic groups. The belief that "one cannot study any nation's history as the whole without understanding the parts in all their variety" became the backbone of the social history movement.[14]

THE PROJECT MODEL

Typically, education research or projects had been funded either through professional organizations (e.g., AHA, APSA), private foundations (e.g., Carnegie, Ford Foundations), or local districts (e.g., Denver schools). The advent of Sputnik changed the research funding model. The federal government would provide mostly universities with funds to create educational centers across the United States. The federal government swerved into the realm of educational reform. However, it provided little direction or oversight, simply the money.

The trickle of federal money after Sputnik does not compare to the flood of federal money that flowed after 1965. President Lyndon B. Johnson's War on Poverty had education as its cornerstone piece legislation. The Elementary and Secondary Education Act (ESEA) was enacted to address the educational achievement gap between white and black students. Other minorities were not a focus. ESEA expanded the federal education section within the government to oversee massive new programs to assist students, especially in low socioeconomic schools. To many, ESEA was an open faucet of federal money for any struggling school need with little accountability attached. Future federal education legislation has mostly been the renaming of ESEA with a particular spin by that administration, such as accountability.

In 1956, MIT professor Jerrold R. Zacharias suggested to the MIT president that they produce a series of twenty-minute films on physics content featuring his department colleagues to be distributed to high schools.[15] To facilitate this project, Zacharias sought a grant from the six-year-old National Science Foundation (NSF). By the end of 1956, NSF funded six different curriculum projects. Each project was responsible for content and distribution.[16] The project model appeared to be a successful way for university faculty to connect with secondary teachers. In response to Sputnik, the federal government handed out grants for mathematics, science, and foreign languages along the lines of the project model. Estimates suggest that more than $100 million was given out to various projects; on average each project received about $3.6 million with each social studies project getting closer to $2.6 million.[17]

Harvard University psychologist Jerome Bruner gathered influential university professors at the Woods Hole Conference in September 1959. The professors assembled with an understanding that they were to reform mathematics and science curricula.[18] Bruner articulated the following four principles: learning content knowledge and facts are not essential to learning; getting the basic structure, students can master any subject; mastering any subject is possible by any student at any level if taught effectively; and learning occurs if the material is interesting.[19] He became the spokesperson and intellectual architect of the project models going forward. Even though the focus was mathematics and science, this Conference laid the groundwork for the project model that would characterize the "New" social studies movement.

Bruner's book *The Process of Education* became the second most influential education book during the 1960s and 1970s.[20] Bruner claimed that the Deweyan model of child-centered learning did not allow for knowledge to develop, and children could gain knowledge only through studying material with which they were unfamiliar.[21] Educational specialists quickly picked up on Bruner's principles, especially social studies educators. They followed this principle of focusing upon skills over content. Students would be transformed into miniature historians if only they were given the proper tools. For the other social sciences, social studies provided the avenue to develop junior social scientists.[22] Economists saw the possibility of training little economists at the elementary levels.[23]

Pedagogy for the "New" social studies (NSS) movement should revolve around decision-making or problem solving that integrated the social sciences.[24] The biggest difference between the disciplines of the social sciences and field of social studies is that social studies' main goal is to prepare citizens, whereas social science investigates social issues.[25] Progressive educators from the 1930s wanted students to explore the social issues of the day and try to solve these problems. During the first phase of the project model, social scientists wanted to train students only to explore the problems.

THE DISCIPLINES REFLECT ON SOCIAL STUDIES

The NCSS spent the 1950s attempting to infuse social sciences into the social studies curriculum. As seen above, the traditional system was resistant to any infusion practices. They published *Social Education* for educators around theme-based curriculum. In 1958, the council included a section called the *New Viewpoints in the Social Sciences*, which examined the more scientific side of the social sciences.[26] The aim was more than simply history, civics, and geography; the contributors came from all social science disciplines.

Three years after the first article, the journal theme returned to American history. The focus was on various interpretations in American history. Historians reiterated the use of primary sources as a tool in teaching, but they did not provide the training to the teachers so teachers could not diverge from the indoctrinated curriculum of how the American Revolution was taught. This disconnection between teachers and the discipline experts increasingly became a problem.

Many social scientists from this era attended public school during the 1920s and 1930s and were exposed to those early ideas of social studies. The demographics of public schools were not the only things that had changed since the Final Report. The academy was also changing. An increasing number of individuals obtained social sciences degrees in the aftermath of World War II. Several groups who would not have been able to attend college also gained access to university education. These new social science graduates often did not want to uphold *consensus* history, nor to maintain the national status quo. Many of these scholars examined immigrant groups, ethnic minorities, and gender to redefine these groups' role in American society.[27]

With the societal changes bubbling under the surface, the first cracks in the traditional system came in 1958 when NCSS called for another Commission on Social Studies. NCSS enlisted the support of the American Council of Learned Societies (ACLS) and various social science organizations. Three years later at a joint conference, the ACLS and NCSS shared their findings. Then they published a combined volume of articles that examined the relationship between the social sciences and social studies called *The Social Studies and the Social Sciences*.[28] Upon the publication of the ACLS/NCSS volume, the *New York Times* praised the effort as a step in the right direction that could prevent social sciences from deteriorating like mathematics and science had before they started their projects. They wrote "teaching in social studies is to be attuned to the world of today rather than the provincialism of yesterday."[29]

The joint volume dealt with the idea of creating a core discipline within social studies. The introduction addressed the issue of the different perspectives that populated the field, suggesting that social studies either could foster citizenship education or introduce students to various social sciences. The results were predictable. Historians and political scientists suggested history. Anthropologists wanted anthropological concepts in the core. Geographers could not see how history permitted an understanding of global issues. Economists wanted to use economics to teach citizenship. Sociologists demanded a method of tying together different sociological themes. Finally, the psychologists looked at the situation from a psychological viewpoint. Social studies was at a crossroads.

In the buzz following the publication of *The Social Studies and the Social Sciences*, the Endicott House Conference was convened. This Conference gathered forty-seven social scientists and educators to discuss the development of a social studies program modeled after the mathematics and science projects. Robert Feldmesser, a sociologist, argued that the problem with social studies rested in the dominance of history within the field.[30] Historians at the Conference immediately came to the defense of their discipline, except for historian Edwin Fenton of Carnegie Mellon University, who built on Feldmesser's critique but focused on how *traditional* history was bad teaching. He was inspired by Bruner's vision to eliminate the focus on content, which relied on rote memorization.[31] Most of the attendees wanted students to learn social studies through present-day social issues and problems.

Social studies took an unexpected turn at this crossroads. The "New" social studies (NSS) movement was launched with the support of the social scientists.[32] This movement reinvigorated social studies from its doldrums of content with little financial help. For the first significant time, social scientists imprinted their ideology on the social studies curriculum. They would use their disciplines' theoretical framework to develop curricular materials for elementary and secondary students. Additionally, the social studies projects in the early stage adopted Bruner's inductive teaching method as a common pedagogy.[33]

Even though advocates of the NSS clung to traditional discipline-based divisions, they acknowledged the need for an interdisciplinary social science approach to social studies.[34] In the beginning, many educators advocated for interdisciplinary efforts, but once discipline specialists started to participate, interdisciplinary practices often ended.[35] The rising notion of specialization within disciplines had been part of their professionalization; disciplines had compartmentalized away from interdisciplinary views (table 6.2).

Table 6.2 Social Studies Courses Enrollment, High School

Course	1961	1973	% Change
Civics	733,000	449,000	-39%
Problems of Democracy	380,000	298,000	-22%
World history	1,471,000	1,541,000	+5%
World geography	595,000	736,000	+24%
US government	780,000	1,306,000	+67%
US history	1,994,000	3,464,000	+74%
Economics	293,000	592,000	+102%
Sociology	289,000	796,000	+175%
Psychology	140,000	590,000	+323%

Adapted from Richard E. Gross, The Status of the Social Studies in the Public Schools of the United States: Facts and Impressions of a National Survey (Paper presented at annual meeting of the National Council for Social Studies, Washington, DC, November 4–7, 1976), 18

For the field of social studies, a blending of many different disciplines had been common since the days of the Madison Conference. Scholars at Madison understood the need for some interdisciplinary to formulate a cohesive field. Even if history was the center of the field, they acknowledged the importance of the other disciplines as *kindred* subjects. Seventy years later, the various social sciences did not steer themselves with a cohesive field in mind.

THE "NEW" SOCIAL STUDIES

During the 1950s, Lawrence Senesh, an economist from Purdue University, and historian Edwin Fenton piloted their own social studies projects. They both favored an inquiry approach to learning through their disciplines.[36] Charles R. Keller, head of the new John Hays Fellows Program for Outstanding Teaching, published an article, "Needed: Revolution in Social Studies," in 1961. He claimed that social studies was not a subject but was instead a collection of diverse disciplines that did not always fit together in a recognizable pattern.[37] Keller believed the revisions laid out in the Final Report curriculum did not conform to the changes in the various disciplines. Consequently, when President John F. Kennedy expanded the federal support beyond mathematics, science, and foreign languages, Project Social Studies was initiated. The Project's aims were to disseminate research, prepare teachers more successfully, and work towards overall improvements of the field. Keller sought to focus upon teaching students what historians and social scientists do rather than attempting to foster attitudes about citizenship. This was a foundational principle among many of the new project centers set up at universities.

One of the purposes of the projects was to bypass the teacher by providing materials that were *guaranteed* to improve student learning.[38] As with the Commission on the Social Studies, reformers did not want to reorganize the curriculum; rather, they wanted to make it meaningful to students, to effectively blend together the social sciences, and to also make it accessible to teachers using a problem-centered pedagogy.[39] Moreover, if teachers and educators were providing questionable service, it was only logical that professionals in the field should be better able to relate the content. Therefore, innovative materials were going to be produced by content experts for public school children. Social studies came late to the party; reform was already in full swing in mathematics and science. It took Keller's call for a new revolution for reformers to react.[40]

The curriculum was to be determined by professional academics who could broaden the minds of students, teachers, and other policymakers.[41] Policymakers had the feeling that discipline-specific education might return under these various projects. Educators argued that they wanted to integrate social studies to create a cultural history that included anthropology and literary theory: in other words, to create "a grand synthesis of the human experience."[42] With more than forty curriculum centers throughout the United States, Project Social Studies promised to revolutionize the field; however, these centers were not coordinated and were slow to produce materials. Although a definitive number for these curriculum centers is difficult to determine, some scholars have suggested that there were one hundred of them in the initial iteration.[43]

After three years of work and with more centers opening, few curricular materials were available for use by teachers. Looking back, scholars identify two stages to this surge: the initial "New" social studies (1950s to 1968) and later "Newer" social studies (1968 to 1974). The initial stage consisted of two phases: the grassroots phase and the first round of federal funding. By 1967, initial funding for the projects was ending. Centers started producing material that examined contemporary issues. The materials produced were "among the most innovative and influential commodities ever produced for use in social studies classrooms"; however, most of the material produced in these centers never made it into classrooms (table 6.3).[44] Several attempts were made to disseminate information from the projects, but most did not make it to teachers until the early 1970s.

The "Newer" social studies movement is characterized by the term *relevance*, as it was driven more by the motivations of students to participate in civic activities, civil rights, political rallies, anti-war protests, and the like. Students became social activists instead of little social scientists.[45] Ideological fights over the direction of projects were frequent during this phase. This

Table 6.3 Frequency of "New" Social Studies Projects (1975)

Projects	States (N=36)	Districts (N=100)
High School Geography Project	8	21
Carnegie-Melon History Project	6	13
Sociological Resources for Secondary Schools	5	12
American Political Behavior	7	10
Harvard Paperbacks	4	8
MACOS	3	8
TABA Social Studies Program	3	8
Our Working World	3	4
People and Technology	1	4
Minnesota Family of Man	1	3
Anthropology Curriculum Project	4	0
Legal Programs	6	5

Based on R. E. Gross, The Status of the Social Studies in the Public Schools of the United States: Facts and Impressions of a National Survey (Paper presented at annual meeting of the National Council for Social Studies, Washington, DC, November 1976), 24.

stage can be divided into two phases as well. The first is the dissemination and activism phase and the second is the evaluative phase.

If social problems (in other words, Civil Rights, the Vietnam War, and so on) were to be integrated into the NSS model, proponents had "failed to pay much attention to the social problems or to delineate a general approach to how the social sciences could be combined or integrated for purposes of instruction."[46] The real problems of the world could not be handled under the new vision of social studies.

SUCCESSFUL PROJECTS IN "NEW" SOCIAL STUDIES?

Although many of the projects ran through the 1960s, it is hard to identify specific commonalities to the stages or phases of their development. Examining a few of the projects, though, gives us some insight into the social studies projects' character. The Amherst Project was a cooperative effort between Amherst High School and Amherst College.[47] The initial impetus was that participants wanted something "to be done to improve the teaching of American history in the secondary schools."[48] The Project's focus was on history education with an inquiry approach. Leaders typically came from non-history backgrounds. In 1969, infighting among the leadership broke out over whether the Project was successfully adapting its teaching methods to the changing student culture.[49]

The leaders used materials that were utilized in the college classroom but modified them for the inquiry model. They used primary sources and forced students to develop their own questions and arguments through primary source units. Rose Olver, a psychology professor at Amherst College, shifted the teaching model away from lectures to a discussion-based model. When the Project sent observers into classrooms, they often found "teachers did not understand the Project's philosophical, psychological and pedagogical assumptions" and thus the materials were not being used the intended way.[50] Leaders decided to change the focus of the writing units to assist teachers with using the curricular material. Teaching guides were also created. *What Happened on Lexington Green? An Inquiry into the Nature and Methods of History* was the model that Amherst Project distributed to curricular writers. This unit was significant because it hooked its students with a very contemporary event: the Watts Riots. Paralleling the eyewitness accounts of Lexington with the eyewitness accounts of the Watts Riots was an atypical but culturally relevant historical technique.

During the first few years of the Project, mostly private schools utilized the pamphlets produced. Once the Project received federal funds (1964), the leaders attempted to distribute their curriculum to public schools throughout the United States, particularly in the Midwest and West.[51] However, recruitment relied on highly motivated teachers to want to participate and attend the training program. The Project began scheduling one-week workshops teaching attendees how to utilize their material. By the end of the Project, about sixty-eight units were written.[52]

In 1961, the High School Geography Project (HSGP) was launched by a joint effort of the Association of American Geographers and the National Council for Geographic Education. Their goal was "to reinvigorate the lack of support and interest associated with classroom geography through the use of active, hands-on student involvement."[53] For the first two years, the Project got funding from private funds, then in 1964 the National Science Foundation provided support.[54] Two factions existed within the discipline over the best theme for geography: settlement or regional. This dispute spilled over into the work of the HSGP, where the settlement faction dominated.[55] As an example of the disagreements between the two factions, the settlement faction maintained that students did not need to memorize locations on a map, which was common practice under the regional faction.[56] The settlement faction aligned with Bruner's views; thus, the HSGP also utilized the inquiry approach.

Over the course of its lifespan, the Project created six self-contained units on various geographic topics. These units made a yearlong course, *Geography in an Urban Age*, for ninth- or tenth-graders with reference materials for teachers. They contracted with a commercial publisher for distribution. Teachers were provided all the materials they would need to be successful with the exception of test questions.[57] To help teachers use the curriculum, the HSGP also set up several meetings and conferences during 1967, 1968, and 1970 to familiarize teachers with the program.[58]

Arthur and Judy Getis field-tested one of the units using Judy Getis's ninth-grade class.

> [Her] students were actively, creatively, and constructively applying the ideas and methodology of the geographer to the problem of settlement in 1851 and after. By doing so, they were developing their intellectual powers to make finer judgments, more thoughtful discriminations, and wiser human decisions, which it was hoped would transcend the model of settlement expressed in Portsville [name of the unit] and relate to the problems faced in everyday urban life.[59]

The Getises had used the inquiry model to train students to think critically about questions of citizenship in geography. They wanted to create materials to engage all students. However, the leaders of the HSGP were informed by their benefactor, the NSF, that they needed to target the upper half of the student population.[60]

In another discipline project, the faculty at the University of Georgia developed and oversaw the Anthropology Curriculum Project (ACP). The ACP was a five-year project that started after receiving federal funding in 1964. Their goal was to complete a five-week unit for each year from first through seventh grades. The stated purpose was "to present the organizing concepts of anthropology in curricula suitable for use in elementary and intermediate grades."[61] Two concerns were discussed before materials were distributed: the first was whether the reading level of the curriculum was too advanced and the second was whether an untrained teacher could facilitate learning.[62] When studying reading level, they determined that the ability of fifth- and sixth-graders was not significantly different. Students in fourth grade did score lower but not because the material was too difficult.[63] In terms of untrained teachers, the study found that teachers who had been through training did not show improved student learning when compared to novice teachers.[64] The Project also allowed for the flexibility of the teaching style of the teacher when it came to inductive or deductive teaching of the material.[65]

During this first phase of the NSS movement, many projects tended to be a grassroots process, like the Amherst and HSGP. Often, these were coordinated efforts between faculty and local teaching staff. Some materials were created but very few of them were initially circulated. They mostly used the inquiry method as the main type of teaching approach. Once federal funds started to flow into the projects, more projects started, and more faculty participated. More resources could be disseminated but few projects started distributing their materials until after 1968. The popularity of the projects tended to be in suburban districts that had more money for education and served higher-achieving students.

Projects such as ACP attempted to branch out into the other social science disciplines, extending its reach beyond the one subject already being taught in the classroom. The reality of this stage of the movement was that:

> identification of the structure of the individual disciplines and/or basic social science concepts, discovery or inductive teaching and learning, use of the modes of inquiry of historians and social scientists, an attempt to build in cumulative, sequential learning, the notion that any idea can be taught successfully in some form to any child at any age, the challenge to the older subjects (history, geography and civics) by the social sciences, the proliferation of an explosive variety of new audio-visual materials, and teacher involvement, largely through field testing in experimental classes.[66]

The promise of the NSS movement was to "overhaul the entire field through projects in every area from sociology to geography, anthropology to civics, geography to history and beyond, lest students enrolled in schools throughout the United States fail to lead the post industrialized world in academics."[67]

IMPLICATIONS

The Cold War brought some impactful changes to social studies. The return of American exceptionalism in the form of consensus history reinforced some nationalistic tendencies. For America to be exceptional, it must be compared to other nations that are not better.[68] History education was thought to be indoctrination into the exceptionalism of America. After Sputnik shattered the belief in American exceptionalism, American education was thrown into a panic, desperate to catch the Soviets.

Social studies continued to be plagued by an enduring fallacy that arose during the Final Report and, frankly, continues to plague social studies in the present day. Creating *good* citizens cannot simply happen by teaching content from history or other social sciences; there needs to be a conceptualization of what constitutes a *good* citizen. How do you obtain the skills to be a *good* citizen? The most typical curriculum maps for the 1950s and early 1960s had returned to more traditionalist views (table 6.4).[69]

Reforms started in the 1950s in social studies, but the NSS movement did not really start generating materials until after 1964. The joint ACLS/NCSS volume is a perfect example of how the participants behaved in the debate regarding social studies. Hertzberg believes that educators forgot the previous conversations as evidenced by the fact that they initiated previously recommended teaching practices.[70] Further, Hertzberg points out that the *New Viewpoints'* contributors were not acquainted with the social studies curriculum. Educators did not know how to use the non-history materials to develop civic education.[71]

Cohen-Cole maintains that Bruner's work and the other initiatives in the NSS movement were attempts by academics to deal with the perceived problems created by the previous progressive movements.[72] The hands-on approach favored by many NSS educators was deemed inappropriate by a rising tide of conservativism. Those conservatives craved a return to the teacher-centered curriculum (*humanistic*) over the student-centered curriculum (*developmental*).

But reformers also understood the problem of rote memorization or reliance on the textbook. Teachers were not instructing students in history, only indoctrinating them.[73] Historians during the NSS wanted students to think like historians. They wanted them to request the evidence required to formulate their own understanding of nature of history.[74] Even though historians had these concerns, they were hesitant to participate in many of the reform efforts.

Table 6.4 Suggested Social Studies Curriculum under "New" Social Studies Movement

Grade	Subjects
1st	Life at home and at school; pets; holidays; farm life
2nd	Community helpers and workers; transportation; communication
3rd	Expanding community; food, clothing, shelter; other communities
4th	Living in other lands (type geographic regions); state history; state geography
5th	US history and geography; Latin America; Canada; Western Hemisphere
6th	Geography of Western Hemisphere; geography of Eastern Hemisphere; Old World backgrounds of the history of the United States
7th	Geography of Eastern Hemisphere; world geography; US history
8th	US history; geography; state history; civics
9th	Civics; vocations; world history; world geography
10th	World history; world geography; modern history
11th	US history; world history; *Problems of Democracy*; civics
12th	*Problems of Democracy*; government; economics; sociology; US history

Adapted from E. R. Carr, *The Social Studies* (New York, NY: The Center for Applied Research in Education, Inc., 1965), 7.

Prominent historians such as Richard Hofstadter advocated for a closer contact between the social sciences and history but along *consensus* history lines.[75] Many of the reformers believed that the bad techniques were not the fault of the academy; instead, they blamed ill-prepared teachers.

Keller claimed that social studies concepts were generally being taught well throughout most of the United States, but he argued that the lack of any context and content was a significant problem.[76] He reiterated the problem with the term social studies and suggested "history and the social sciences" replace the label to eliminate the unclear purpose.[77] Policymakers believed that the purpose of history was to return students to the notion of nationalism and patriotism; most teachers did not necessarily acknowledge this as their purpose.[78] Carr suggested that a history-centered social studies curriculum should be used to interpret the present, and the content needed to be adjusted to what *is* relevant to the present day as opposed to what *was* important in the past.[79]

Historically, efforts to revise the curriculum had been led by historians. The NSS projects, however, were the practice ground of the social sciences when it came to reform because most historians stayed away from NSS projects.[80] Few projects were developed by historians or were even participated in by history faculty. Historians continued their avoidance of public education efforts that started after the Commission on the Social Studies. The specialization and professionalization of historians also did damage to the field of social studies. Attempts to see a cohesive narrative was lost between the various paths of inquiry followed by historians. In other words, historians lost sight of the bigger picture.

In 1978, about ten years after the height of the project era, Education Professor Leonard Kenworthy reflected on the NSS movement, writing:

> a few college professors rediscovered the public schools and a few of them began to take an interest in the social studies curriculum. There were some gains from this movement, especially in developing what was called the structure of the disciplines and the pinpointing of the major concepts and generalizations of each of the social studies disciplines.[81]

Even though historians had no direct input into the curriculum, history still remained the dominant discipline within social studies, and the changes within the discipline of history eventually filtered down into public education without any direction for or understanding of the teachers.[82] Others advised that history should remain the foundation because, as a field, it establishes a set of common knowledge, concepts, and methodology. This would make it far easier for teachers to integrate the various disciplines, especially when the disciplines struggle to integrate themselves.[83] Historian H. Stuart Hughes aspired for a return to a traditional model where history included the other social sciences; this was in contrast to more interdisciplinary approaches.[84]

A concern during the NSS movement was to control the local impact on the classroom, particularly teachers. In the three projects that had some success, university faculty allowed teachers to participate in the design of the materials; however, in many of the other projects, social scientists believed that they could distribute materials that teachers could simply follow without any training. Social scientists believed the teachers needed only the map, which social scientists were now providing. The phrase that was utilized by many of the project leaders and faculty was to make the materials "teacher proof."[85]

Coincidently, the 1960s also saw the rise of schools of education in the public university and the beginning of the professionalization of the teacher position within society. Teachers were poorly prepared and lacked a clear understanding of the purpose of social studies, even though many reformers could not agree on the purpose either.[86] Teachers were not trained to handle topics the public and/or their supervisors might consider taboo (i.e., sex, religion, race, etc.). So *expert* scholars developed lessons on various topics for teachers to follow.[87] These scholars believed if teachers did not stray from the plans, they could easily replicate the lesson and keep their positions. Academic freedom at a university did not always translate to the K-12 world. Thus teachers stuck to traditional content.

Hunt and Metcalf stated that just teaching students that America is an absolute good is no better than a dictatorship (Soviet system); America needed to be viewed as one of many heritages, not a single WASP one.[88] Jackson and Jackson characterize the NSS movement as a formless curriculum that attempted to mimic science.[89] Further, "youngsters" could not be inquisitive or skilled without a through grounding in historical content knowledge.[90] The notion of relevance is critical to the growth of democratic education, and the role that teachers play in developing curriculum that is relevant to students is also very important.[91]

A criticism of some projects was their "absence of a central plan or procedure to coordinate the different activities."[92] The projects' focus was on "structure, inductive teaching, sequential learning, the discipline approach, and the integrated approach."[93] The shift toward academic disciplines and cognitive skills during the 1950s contributed to a fading tolerance for diversity. The melting pot schema was increasingly rejected in favor of cultural pluralism. Hunt and Metcalf insisted that content was the lazy method of teaching social studies, arguing that facts mean nothing without interpretation.[94] The field was invigorated by a return to the Deweyan notion of reflection over the simple rote memorization that was commonplace.[95]

Fenton claims that Carnegie Mellon collected materials from "130 experimental social studies projects."[96] Helburn believed that a quarter of California schools were using part of the HSGP, but there is no verifiable evidence to support this claim.[97] Yet the biggest impact seems to be that faculty and teachers began interacting with one another during the teacher workshops. Likewise, Rice and Bailey found that "a significant increase in achievement in anthropology" was achieved by students in first, second, fourth, and fifth grades.[98] Social studies was producing little social scientists. The sheer quantity of materials being generated by the various projects was immense. The Social Science Education Consortium under Irving Morrissett attempted to sort through some of the materials and determine which ones might actually be effective in the classroom.

More than three hundred schools requested sample materials from various projects. Many schools simply sought ways to "revise the social studies program" but not necessarily adopt an anthropological approach.[99] In the end, only about seventy school systems acquired the full materials. While the "New" social studies projects failed in eliminating textbooks as the primary instructional tool, they provided alternative avenues to materials. NSS projects helped stimulate and create a new series of commercial and teacher-made supplementary materials used in the classroom.[100]

"The High School Geography Project reflected a new confidence in teachers and in their ability to take a creative and active role in curriculum design and implementation."[101] Samec says that the most important outcome from the Amherst Project was "the model of curriculum design," which used teachers to write, as well as their use of other teachers to field-test the units.[102] No teacher acknowledged hearing about others using the Amherst Project, but a good number of teachers admitted to utilizing at least one of the Project's materials.[103]

After the funding ran out of the Amherst project, the Advanced Placement program run by Keller adopted the inquiry model utilized by Amherst. The document-based questions (DBQs) are seen as loosely modeled after the Amherst pamphlet series.[104] "The New Social Studies movement represented a technical breakthrough in pedagogy that should not be lost. Some of the innovations have been incorporated into later work."[105] These later works include several contemporary curriculum centers that model themselves after the Amherst and other NSS training programs.[106] In recent education parlance, the education reformers call the inquiry model of teaching "critical thinking."

When NSS scholars looked back on progressive education in the 1930s, they determined that progressives went to an extreme to integrate democratic education into the curriculum.[107] When recent scholars look back on the NSS, they note how "well-written textbooks" could be used in class discussions. But teachers "with a minimum of effort . . . should be able to find an acceptable combination of instructional materials to offer a stimulating course in cultural anthropology."[108] Social studies is not limited to history.

The projects were isolated to schools willing to participate in the experiment, so generalization of the concepts was not always possible. Poorer school districts were also not likely to adopt projects. Furthermore, project authors had little appreciation for the teacher's role other than as facilitators of their concepts. Project centers assumed students were passive receptacles who eagerly accepted content from their facilitator teachers.

Most schools did not adopt the materials, and by 1980 those schools that had adopted them were abandoning them.[109] Marker suggests that "misapplication" of the materials were a motivating factor in its abandonment.[110] Generally, teachers did not have a problem with material, but they also did not worry about what content their students derived from the material. Demographic and societal changes also impacted project success as material did not address those changes in the classroom.[111] Newmann contends that if each discipline developed a separate curriculum, then there was "no real value" in social studies instruction. The general social sciences form a community to create educated citizens and the essential needs of society.[112] The most daunting critiques were that social studies lacked a clear purpose and that any previous efforts were simply ill-conceived notions that undermined the field.[113]

Nelson and Drake interviewed twenty-nine social studies teachers who entered teaching in the late 1940s through the 1970s, with most entering during the mid-1950s. Most of these teachers considered themselves historians, then they became government specialists. They did not need education courses to teach history because pedagogy in-service implied that they were *"equally wretched"* teachers.[114] They did not want pedagogical material but wanted useful history material instead. Haas claims only 5 percent of social studies teacher were influenced by the NSS movement.[115] However, nearly all of these teachers were at least aware of it and utilized some aspects of those materials they liked.

In a study of social studies teachers in Oklahoma in 1968, only 11 percent of secondary teachers (n=300) were familiar with any of the NSS projects. Most of those familiar were recent graduates of teacher education programs. Even though

> suddenly a large influx of materials designed to be used with new teaching strategies appeared on the scene. These new materials appeared for the most part as self-contained teaching units with all the content materials, audiovisual aids, and teaching instructions deemed necessary. No longer did the subject of history totally dominate the social studies curriculum. Other disciplines such as geography, economics, sociology, anthropology, and political science began to receive a share of the attention . . . The materials of the new social studies projects are not radically different from the traditional social studies materials. The principal difference seems to lie in the method of instruction. The new materials are designed to accommodate and encourage the inquiry process.[116]

New materials were being created. Some of the material was cumbersome, difficult to translate to students, and financially prohibitive. Some of it was innovative, relevant, and practical. But the majority of the material never got into the classroom. Given these realities, the real question is whether the NSS movement was a success, a failure, or something else entirely.

Chapter 7

A New Set of Controversies

Coming out of the 1960s, civic education had transformed with the belief that any discipline could achieve a sense of political socialization. Hunt and Metcalf branded social studies as a way *"to help students reflectively examine issues in the problematic areas of American culture,"* which harkens back to the old *social meliorism* of Rugg and Counts.[1] The political socialization would thus create an understanding of citizenship. In order to achieve political socialization, the social sciences simply needed student- and teacher-proof materials. The pinnacle of this "New" social studies (NSS) ideology was Jerome Bruner's *Man: A Course of Study* (MACOS).

With the advent of federal money came a new problem for social studies. Before federal money was so freely available, educational oversight occurred at the local levels: even controversies over the Rugg textbook were fought at the local school board. In the 1970s, though, oversight shifted from local to state and sometimes to federal levels. The primary motivation for federal involvement came from MACOS. The aftermath of the MACOS controversy left the field adrift for the remainder of the 1970s.

THE PINNACLE PROJECT MAN: A COURSE OF STUDY

The theories developed at the Endicott House workshop in 1962 marked the official beginning of the NSS movement. Bruner, who led the workshop, tasked a group to develop an interdisciplinary upper elementary curriculum. That group, the Educational Development Center (EDC),[2] developed a textbook and curriculum over the course of the next seven years that is commonly called *Man: A Course of Study*, or MACOS.[3] The EDC was committed to the notion of interdisciplinary study for the textbook and its material.[4] Donald Oliver[5] was originally selected for project head at EDC, but he stepped aside in 1964 for family reasons. Oliver's vision was to create an entire elementary social studies curriculum centered around anthropology.[6] When Bruner personally replaced the director of the project, a drastic intellectual shift occurred. Under Oliver, the course examined the evolution of human culture, *Evolution of Man and Society*; under Bruner, the course explored what made up human nature, *Man: A Course of Study*.[7] Bruner was a visionary for this project not only in the developmental but also in the intellectual aspects. Peter Dow joined the EDC as the project director in charge of assembling and disseminating the materials.

At first glance, MACOS is like many other projects: a social science project that wanted to introduce inquiry theory to students. The project also wanted to expose students to anthropological concepts and methodology. Bruner, a cognitive psychologist, had a long history of interaction with cultural anthropology.[8] In 1960, he set up the Center for Cognitive Studies at Harvard. This center was about looking at people's social relations within psychology. At the time, he had two graduate students. One's focus was a study of Wolof children in Africa while the other studied Eskimos in Alaska.[9] Bruner joined the study in Africa and made some insights into the connection between psychology and cultural anthropology. He wanted "Eskimo and Bushman—to show what the life experience of hunting peoples is."[10] He used the basic information about the Eskimo and Bushman to formulate a question: "What is Human about Humans?" Bruner states that "the most persistent problem in social studies is to rescue the phenomena of social life from familiarity."[11] In Bruner's interpretation, teaching students about something foreign to their own knowledge would assist them in better understanding the concepts.

MACOS allowed Bruner to investigate his theory that any student could learn any content given the correct materials. Originally, he wanted to utilize the Eskimo and Bushman tribes to create a cross comparison model, but team members worried about potential backlash about perceived racism.[12] In the end, he chose the Netsilik tribe as the model for instruction. He ordered a full-length documentary of the tribe, one of the first documentaries conceived specifically for education.[13] Yet, Dow ignored other potential social issues such as the fable, *The Many Lives of Kiviok*, about a man who had many wives. He regretted keeping this fable in the material because it opened them up to criticism.[14]

Bruner was bothered by the passivity of film watching, even his documentary. He wanted an active learning environment. He utilized no narration and focused the student's attention on the sights and sounds of the Netsilik lives, posing questions for students to examine.[15] In one sequence, a young Netsilik boy captures and kills a seagull. Bruner recounts later how some Boston students initially considered the young boy a "nasty brute" but then another student pointed out that the boy's goal was to grow to be a hunter in their society.[16] Students were learning from each other.

Additionally, students were exposed to an interactive seal-hunt game and provided with Netsilik stories and folklore all designed to transport students to the frozen tundra of northern Canada.[17] As an introspective tool, MACOS field-tested the ability of students to compare Netsilik with baboons. The EDC discovered that "children were incapable of viewing the [baboon] films with any kind of objective distance;" so they adapted the project to consider how humans developed separate from animals.[18] After all, one of the main purposes of the project was for students to understand some of the universal truths of the evolution of human society.[19]

The rationale for Bruner's focus on upper elementary arose from the influence of Jean Piaget's stages of development for students.[20] Piaget implied that children could not begin to understand abstract concepts such as time until they were in the upper elementary grades, particularly fifth grade. Many educationalists adopted Piaget's theory as a sound principle, and this influenced the teaching of social studies in the lower elementary grades for several decades. Thus, MACOS attempted to transform the field by debuting social studies concepts in upper elementary grades instead of introducing social studies at the secondary level (seventh grade and beyond).

Many contemporary scholars were heartened by MACOS. They speculated that students would generally enjoy MACOS due to the "vividness of the primary sources—literary and graphic," that were infused within materials.[21] No commercial publisher would agree to publish and market the materials for several reasons, including cost and potential conflicts with their other materials.[22] But there was another problem as well. MACOS was now a single-year curriculum. Textbook companies sought aligned multiyear social studies curriculum, so using MACOS meant that schools would have to forgo the prescribed textbook curriculum and its logical sequence.[23]

The response from teachers and students was generally favorable. A Texas class wrote to Bruner explaining why they liked MACOS better than geography. In the beginning, they listed twenty-five reasons why they considered themselves to be human; by the end, they had narrowed the list to three items. The students decided that to be more human, they needed to "get along with others—here and overseas, correcting pollution of air and water, taking more time to make decisions, and try to act as humanly as possible."[24] These attitudes combined *social meliorism* and relativism for these students. A principal testified to the California Board of Education that MACOS was "the most significant, all-around educational program [he'd] ever been involved with."[25]

The idea of training little social scientists fostered the idea of infusing skills over content, as the students were trained to think like social scientists of various disciplines regardless of the content. The MACOS curriculum was introduced into general classrooms starting in 1967. Schools could buy all the MACOS materials for five classrooms at a cost of $3,000.[26] It peaked in 1972 with more than 1,700 schools utilizing the textbook, but more importantly, many teacher preparation programs utilized the textbook as a model for teaching.[27] Estimates of the number of students exposed to MACOS is somewhere between 200,000 and 328,000.[28]

Teacher training for MACOS was similar to the student experience; teachers used the discovery-based method to understand how to teach with the textbook.[29] Originally five training centers were established at universities in Florida, Oregon, Colorado, Connecticut, and New York. These centers trained more than 700 teachers in the first three years.[30] Ultimately, more than eighty-five centers were established to train teachers who wanted to utilize MACOS.[31] MACOS looked to be the success story of the Bruner's ideology and the "New" social studies.

ENTER FEDERAL OVERSIGHT

The first attempt to eliminate MACOS happened in 1970 when a Christian fundamentalist parent, Baptist minister Don Glenn, sought removal of it from his daughter's Lake City elementary school in Florida. He believed MACOS to be immoral. Glenn was critical of the film where Netsilik ritual placed the elderly or invalids on blocks of ice and sailed them out to sea.[32] The school board defended the curriculum but allowed parents to opt out. Another Baptist minister, also a teacher, supported the curriculum on the grounds of academic freedom.[33] These supporters believed MACOS provided them an avenue for "easing racial tensions" within the community.[34]

MACOS was not only attacked in Southern states, but local boards in California, Maryland, Texas, Arizona, Washington, Oregon, Georgia, New Hampshire, and Vermont all had groups demanding an end to the MACOS curriculum as well. Bruner's MACOS brought the Enlightenment to the world of social studies by allowing students to see how other cultures found happiness. Happiness was not isolated to middle-class America. The reaction to MACOS's thought-provoking method led conservatives to see the textbook as embedding "anti-American, liberal, and secular humanist" attitudes into the minds of fifth-graders.[35]

Conservative groups such as the Heritage Foundation and the John Birch Society believed MACOS was an assault on traditional American values. Conservatives claimed MACOS was influenced by Dewey's progressive education and would lead to a dismantling of the American political system.[36] Arizona parents claimed that MACOS represented secular humanism, which they deemed was a religion. Thus, they argued MACOS should be banned as a breach of the separation of church and state.[37] In Vermont, Norma Gabler, who with her husband policed school textbooks for Christian values, traveled up from Longview, Texas, to reveal the moral corruption of MACOS.[38] Another "expert," John Steinbacher, arrived from California to fight against MACOS because of its influence of "Deweyism, pragmatism, behaviorism, psychic manipulation, and above all humanism."[39] He also spoke about the apparent corruption of basic Christian values that MACOS was intended to catalyze.

In Oregon, one superintendent, Alton O. Smedstad, reported that he received a petition with more than 400 signatures demanding an end to MACOS. The town had only 12,000 registered voters. He then revealed that about 100 signatures were from individuals living outside the district. In truth, only seven families had students that would have had contact with the MACOS curricular material. Many other signatories did not have any children. Smedstad estimated that 50 people out of 12,000 were interested in the elimination of MACOS.[40] He notified all parents that if enough students signed up, MACOS would be taught. Not enough went into the district office to sign up.

In 1975, the situation worsened for MACOS. The NSF budget was unanimously approved by a subcommittee of the Committee on Science and Technology,[41] but when introduced to the Congressional Committee for full authorization, Rep. John B. Conlan (R-AZ) "threw an incendiary bomb in the full committee's deliberations with an amendment to cut off all funding" to MACOS.[42] Committee chairman Olin Teague (D-TX) was able to diffuse the initial attack, but the federal flood gates were about to open.

Conlan's legislative aide, George Archibald, led verbal and political attacks on MACOS and its ally, NCSS. Archibald's attacks "sounded the ominous tone of a renewal of the war on social studies" and against any progressive thinking educational reform.[43] He claimed that social studies had been taken over by a minority group of intellectuals with the intent of undermining American education.[44] Conlan eventually claimed that MACOS supported adultery, cannibalism, infanticide, and senilicide.[45] Conlan even suggested reviewing all NSF curriculum grants and projects on a monthly basis to maintain the safety of the children.

Another avenue of attack concerned the pedagogy of MACOS. Conlan and conservative columnist James J. Kilpatrick criticized Bruner for wanting students "to think—to think, that is, as Bruner would like them to think."[46] This was evidence that Bruner was linked to behavioral psychologist B. F. Skinner with an intention to condition students to conform to Bruner's teaching.[47] The linking of Bruner and Skinner was problematic for MACOS as Skinner was seen as indoctrinating students to a certain way of thinking by rote memorization of conditioning. Conlan decried the Bruner scientific approach where students were to observe and collect data would condition students to transform America into a Communist police state.[48]

Archibald and Conlan charged that the NSF had provided $189 million to develop and implement curricular material over a twenty-five-year period.[49] This is an exaggeration: MACOS had been around for only thirteen years and in the classroom for only five years. The *New York Times* stated that MACOS had used $7.4 million federal funds.[50] Dr. H. Guyford Stever testified to Congress that MACOS was not receiving any new funds from the NSF budget in 1975.[51] Yet, on April 9, 1975, "everybody's attention was focused on one small program involving a minuscule portion of the $755 million NSF budget."[52] Conlan feared that MACOS would lead to a "dangerous trend toward a uniform national curriculum."[53]

After the congressional fiasco, the NSF stopped all funding to MACOS, including its training centers like the one in Oregon. William Harris, director of the University of Oregon EDC center, attempted to alter and fix the problem without any funding, but with no success.[54] Then, the NSF nearly stopped funding all education projects because Congress threatened to conduct full investigations into all of its education projects. To avoid any further pressure, NSF withdrew from K-12 education for the next ten years, further reducing all federal spending on curricular material, particularly any social studies materials. Dow argued that it was "not the content of the course but the provision of federal support."[55] If federal support was provided to an immoral project, then what did that say about the government?

MACOS did not just suddenly die in 1975. Several schools continued to implement the program as long as they had strong administrative support.[56] As late as 1977, schools in California, Utah, and Chicago were adopting MACOS for the fall.[57] Defenders of MACOS were numerous compared to the very small vocal and organized group of detractors. But the defense was unorganized and random, so it was ineffective. About a year after Conlan's congressional bomb, the *New York Times* wrote that MACOS' critics were afraid that by learning about the Netsilik, students would have a "breakdown of [their] own traditional values."[58]

Some studies reviewed the impact of the MACOS, especially after the congressional inquiry. Many of the results reported *"no significant differences"* between students taking the course and the control group.[59] A few reported a slight positive effect towards MACOS students over the control group. One study in Washington State noted teachers perceived an increase in student interest for the social studies, but it was not measurable.[60] In another study, researchers determined that non-MACOS teachers tended to rely more on memory-type questions than open-ended critical thinking questions.[61] The most evidenced conclusion is that MACOS did not negatively impact student learning as Conlan so forcefully insinuated.

In another Oregon district, a mother, Vivian McElmurry, sought to eliminate all unwanted elements from the school district. She started with a Myths and Legends course (spiritualism), then the book *Carrie* (pornographic), and finally MACOS (secular humanism) in September 1976.[62] Going through several committees and discussions, the superintendent, Dealous Cox, permitted MACOS to continue, but parents who wanted to opt out would have to fill out a form. This was the reverse of the earlier controversy in Oregon.

A paleoconservative blitz was conducted on this little town. A California group, Christian Family Renewal, sent tons of pamphlets to the residents about how MACOS taught students about sex education, immorality in Oregon schools, Oregon schools being influenced by non-Oregonians, and paganism. Norma Gabler appeared on a local TV station to discuss MACOS and declared her intention to participate in the next school board hearing.

Cox could not muster many supporters to defend the project at the hearing. Despite this, the hearing appeared to go with Cox and his allies, but then the vote was postponed a week due to the lateness of the hour. A renewed effort was undertaken by opposition. At the delayed vote, a unanimous decision was reached to withdraw MACOS from the district in the following fall. Cox would go on to resign that summer, primarily over the MACOS controversy.[63]

The impact of the MACOS was felt beyond the halls of Congress. No clear rationale has been presented for Conlan's motivation. Conlan might have sought to make a name for himself. Dow and many others say parents in Phoenix rallied against MACOS. Phoenix was Congressman Conlan's home district. Conlan used the hullabaloo of the MACOS as a major platform in his reelection campaign, but he lost in the primary to another Republican.[64] His attack on the Netsilik was perceived as an ideological attack on Native American groups, like those residing in Arizona.[65] He had stated that his preference would be for Native Americans to assimilate into Western culture: the Netsilik were non-assimilationist.[66]

When President Ford appointed NSF director Stever to the post of Director for the Office of Science and Technology Policy, he came up against a brick wall. Four Republican senators criticized the president's appointment because Stever supported MACOS, and his participation precipitated a full investigation.[67] Stever was eventually confirmed and served until the end of Ford's administration. Affiliation with MACOS complicated careers in politics and education.

WHAT ABOUT THE BOOKS

There were a total of seven federal investigations into textbooks from 1850 to 1955, six of which came during the interwar period.[68] The critiques of previous reformers had been on the reliance on textbooks as the only teaching tool. The 1960s was a socially turbulent decade that upset the traditional WASP cultural identity in traditional textbooks. The postsecondary academy had already shown their desire for diversity within the curriculum. Many young scholars were calling for more socially diverse history within the textbooks.

During this period, a shift happened where content and political leanings were being examined as part of the textbook.[69] Rep. Adam Clayton Powell (D-NY), chairman of the House Labor and Education Committee, held hearings in 1966 about bias against African Americans within textbooks. When the Committee asked Commissioner of Education Harold Howe about what the national government was going to do about the bias, Howe replied that he could make recommendations, but the states held the ultimate authority over textbook selection.[70] Fenton had published a textbook that incorporated many "New" social studies concepts. His textbook was banned by the state of Georgia because it might disrupt Georgian society. Frances FitzGerald examined numerous history textbooks and bitterly criticized the influence of social studies on history education.[71] She further complained about the liberal practice of sprinkling minorities and women throughout American history. She sought a return to the idea of assimilation into American textbooks.

By the mid-1970s, the course distribution for social studies was diverse and chaotic. The most common format was as follows. In eighth grade, students were taught world history, culture, and geography. In ninth grade, students studied US history. In tenth grade, students learned about world culture and history. Students studied US history again in eleventh grade and in twelfth grade they focused on American government and another social science. Social studies curriculum was organized into a standardized form that was adopted by most schools to facilitate their students' entrance into college.

A new trend within education and particularly social studies arose, which was conflict over content within the textbooks. *Traditionalist* interest groups and political conservatives started attacking the federal funding of the textbook as in the case of MACOS. They focused their attacks on the notion that the book raised questions but did not provide answers for the students.[72] Defenders against the attacks on textbooks claimed that these groups were attacking academic freedoms of the teachers. Some of the academic freedom issues would eventually turn into textbook controversies.

The parents of Kanawha County, West Virginia, school students initiated the most famous textbook controversy in the 1970s. The school board approved more than three hundred books for use in the various classes, particularly language arts. These books had been selected in an established system with public inspection prior to adoption.[73] A minority of parents used violent intimidation, including dynamite on school property and bullet holes in school buses, as a means of forcing the county to select a school curriculum "that emphasizes basic skills and patriotic indoctrination."[74] Kanawha was not the first textbook controversy during this period, but it was the most violent. It also became a model that paleoconservatives utilized on their assault upon any curricula with which they did not agree.

IS THIS THE END OF SOCIAL STUDIES?

Despite the tensions from this time, social studies managed to endure. A new trend arose in universities that was filtering its way into the high schools: area studies courses. Several high school mini courses were developed. Most were courses offered on history or government, like examinations of contemporary America, Western America, Colonial America, the Civil War, state and local politics, the Presidency, and youth and the law.

But several courses were created on other relevant current events topics: ethnicity, race, and gender issues. The most popular courses were Black, Native American, and women's studies courses. *Social meliorism* rose again as educators strove to attain the "Great Society." In the academic year of 1976–1977 at Tamalpais High School, in California, *forty-four* social studies courses were offered.[75] The mini-course model continued into the early 1980s.[76] The diversity of courses is beyond a single school. In Kansas, 70 percent of the state schools had a course dedicated to US history. The Kansas schools included courses in state history, area studies, various forms of geography, and economics. Of the 377 public schools in Kansas, 113 offered a social studies mini courese in a non-traditional history/civics/geography discipline (see table 7.1).[77] Clearly, social studies was in the process of changing its focus. One major difference from NSS was that teachers had to create their own curricula for these mini courses. They used some NSS methods and materials, but they had to create most of their own material or rely on a textbook. The focus of these mini courses tended to be in area, ethnic, gender, and minority studies as they tried to emphasize cultural pluralism over nationalism.[78] Yet, even government would have mini courses on the Presidency, youth law, political parties, government finance, civil rights, and city government to name a few.[79]

Additionally, children's education was greatly expanding in the 1970s. During the third season of ABC's *Schoolhouse Rock*, the creators launched *America Rock*. These were short lessons on US history and civics broadcast during Saturday morning cartoons. The lessons were cartoons set to music that covered the American Revolution, Manifest Destiny, immigration, inventions, and the legislative process. The *America Rock* season impacted more children than all of the NSS projects combined. Teachers still utilize *America Rock* in their classrooms today, but the songs were written from

Table 7.1 Social Studies Courses Offered at High Schools in Kansas

| | High Schools (n = 377) | | |
Subject	Number	Percentage	Instructors
US history	260	70.0	451
US government	260	70.0	337
Introduction to psychology	241	63.9	269
Non-US history	185	49.1	200
Introduction to sociology	153	40.6	166
Current affairs	68	18.0	86
World geography	55	14.6	59
Principles of economics	50	13.3	54
International relations	37	9.8	41
Ethnic studies	15	4.0	26
Citizenship	22	5.8	24
American studies	13	3.4	23
Economics/consumer studies	19	5.0	22
Introduction to political science	11	2.9	14
Contemporary economics	13	3.4	13
Kansas history	13	3.4	13
Civics	10	2.7	13
Humanities	8	2.1	13
Economic and US history	10	2.7	11
Independent study and US history	8	2.1	11
Introduction to social studies	9	2.4	9
Introduction to geography	9	2.4	9
European history	9	2.4	9
Western civilization	9	2.4	9
Western & non-Western area studies	8	2.1	8
Anthropology	7	1.9	7
Independent study and government	7	1.9	7
Family living	5	1.3	7
Problems of US democracy	5	1.3	6
US geography	4	1.1	4
African history	3	0.8	4
Independent study and World history	3	0.8	4
Law enforcement	3	0.8	3
Introduction to philosophy	3	0.8	3
Economic geography	2	0.5	2
Latin American history	2	0.5	2
Kansas geography	1	0.3	1
Asian history	1	0.3	1

Based on J. Guenther, More Humanistic Social Studies Programs through Mini-courses [Paper presented at the Annual Meeting of the National Council for the Social Studies, Atlanta, GA, November 27–29, 1975], 6.

a *consensus* historians' point of view.[80] Diversity could not be adequately expressed within a two-minute song. For example, in "No More Kings," Native Americans are depicted for a few seconds "hiding behind a Plymouth Rock" as the Pilgrims settle.[81] Even "The Great American Melting Pot," which focuses upon immigration, is highly Eurocentric with an assimilation message for citizenship.[82] *America Rock* portrays "history as an instrument for honoring the past rather than exploring it."[83]

Social studies educators did not perceive the issue of postsecondary history problems as connected to social studies until the end of the 1970s. Failure to understand the hurdles social studies was facing significantly impacted social studies education: the field was in trouble without even knowing it.[84] Richard Gross conducted a survey comparing the number of secondary social studies classes offered in 1961 and in 1973 (see table 6.2). The results showed that history and social studies classes were being offered less frequently; however, course offerings increased in economics, sociology, and psychology courses, though these courses had low general enrollment. *The History Teacher* began publishing lesson plans for teachers in 1968, but at first the general focus was on higher education.

The Organization of American Historians (OAH, formerly Mississippi Valley Historical Association) issued an alarm for history education in 1975. The organization conducted a state of the discipline survey including most states. Among the issues cited by Richard Kirkendall, executive secretary for OAH, were too much emphasis on current events; the rising importance of the social sciences; the perception that history was not a valid school subject; too much competition with other school subjects, including multicultural education; and student views that it was irrelevant or boring.[85] Historians did not begin connecting the problems with history education at the postsecondary level to the public schools until the OAH survey.

IMPLICATIONS

Social sciences advocates succumbed to the fallacy that they could control all aspects of social studies curriculum. If students and teachers simply followed their materials, students would come out of school prepared to be *good* citizens.[86] One of the early problems with the "New" social studies as envisioned by Bruner was that postsecondary disciplines are generally out of touch with education.[87] Gallagher argues that many of the curriculum reform efforts from the 1960s lacked an important component: the language to convince the general public of the correctness in their ways of reforming education.[88] An anti-intellectual movement had been festering since the 1950s, and MACOS became a victim of it. After all, MACOS was developed by a group of intellectuals imposing a "teacher-proof" curriculum.

Wolcott comments that the NSF might have supported the development of materials, but dissemination of the materials was not a major concern. In the MACOS project, neither NSF nor Bruner were interested in training teachers. They believed that the curriculum was self-sufficient at $3,000 a set.[89] Ultimately, the "New/Newer" social studies "had a minor influence on some teachers and stimulated some change in texts and supplementary materials by major publishers."[90] But wholehearted adoption of any project was not really high; even MACOS reached only a maximum of 400,000 students out of potential pool of nearly 34,000,000 students.

The 1960s saw a slight shift where various NSS projects defined learning objectives for classrooms, but local and state politicians challenged these federally devised learning objectives by limiting or prohibiting their appearance in local classrooms.[91] State Education Agencies (SEAs) were reluctant to allow districts to adopt NSS materials due to their cost. Furthermore, adoption committees relied heavily upon publishers to market materials in sequenced approaches incorporating multiple grade levels of material.[92] Archibald's criticisms also targeted any form of academic freedom within public schools. They were successful at restricting academic freedom as teachers were increasingly limited in what they could teach. Yet student demand for different courses and content increased.

Many NSS projects required weeklong training and were single courses or parts of courses, rather than a whole curriculum. William Harris, the director of University of Oregon MACOS center, tried to get MACOS into Eugene schools but the social studies coordinator refused to utilize something she really did not understand.[93] This intellectual arrogance led to a new series of cultural controversies about curriculum centered around MACOS. "The MACOS controversy marks a re-examination of national policy relating to curriculum development and the role of the federal government in this activity."[94]

One of the lessons coming out of MACOS should have been that in any material, someone is going to find something to criticize. A reporter investigating MACOS contacted Curriculum Development Associates, publishers/distributors of MACOS, for only films that showed killing of seals and caribou. When offered other films, the reporter refused the offer.[95] Kraus points out that most of the comments are from items taken out of context.[96]

Critics of MACOS often accused Bruner of trying to brainwash students "into holding values which are counter to traditional beliefs."[97] Students were not asked to "evaluate the reasonableness of cultural practices, the texts asked the students to affirm the ongoing validity of these cultural differences within the American national context," which did not support traditional values that schools were charged with maintaining.[98] Building on Conlan's comments, a *New York Times* reporter warned his readers that "children are receiving positive teaching about killing the elderly and female infants; wife swapping and child marriage; communal living; witchcraft and the occult, and cannibalism."[99] Critics of MACOS generally favored civic education that encouraged assimilation into WASP cultural identity. Milam says that opponents to MACOS disliked the scientific approach towards social studies, fearing that students "would grow up without sufficient appreciation for their democratic freedom" because they were simply another animal like the gull or baboon.[100]

Woolfson raises the notion that MACOS supporters and anti-MACOS individuals fought over whether schools were supposed to be teaching Christian values or needed to deal with the changing society, regardless of religion. "Are schools to concentrate on the absolute truths of the Judeo-Christian heritage, or are they to prepare man for life in a constantly changing technological world?"[101] To this day, Pat Robertson's Christian Broadcasting Network still invokes MACOS as the evil of the federal government imposing humanism over Christian values.[102] In fact, this dispute helped the conservative think tank, Heritage Foundation, find its political voice.[103]

In assessing what went wrong with NSS and MACOS, Selakovich concludes that a rising mood of conservatism was washing across America. The focus when the NSS started changed dramatically in the 1970s. Accountability, assessment, performance, and basic skills became the new focus.[104] The 1970s saw a "Back to the Basics" movement in public schools. In fact, the first state assessments emerged in the 1970s and focused on basic skills. The NSS was not prepared for the impact of these changes in political trends in education.

Hegeman suggests that MACOS was a key event in the rise of Ronald Reagan and the conservatives.[105] She portrays conservatives as linking MACOS to sex education, evolution, gun control, and desegregation, thus suggesting that liberals sought to impose a communist totalitarianism regime on democratic America.[106] Just as with the Kanawha textbook controversy, other controversies were controlled by opposition who also controlled the general language of controversies. When reformers combatted the minority opposition, they were already disadvantaged by having to use language that had been tainted by the opposition.

The MACOS debate exposed a recurrent issue once again. What is the purpose of education and specifically social studies? To create citizens. What type of citizens should American classrooms create: dutiful indoctrinated citizens or free-thinking citizens? The first is more likely to be the product of a highly content-focused classroom; the other is more likely rooted in examining humanity through the lens of various social science disciplines. MACOS and many other social studies projects were more concerned with generating skills within students rather than focusing upon mastery of a certain content.[107]

Archibald advocated a return to a traditional history format of indoctrination that prevented students from drawing their own conclusions about society. The rejection of MACOS also meant the rejection of many social studies projects and the idea of the discovery method as a signature pedagogy for social studies.[108] The lessons of MACOS were forgotten as the rise of discipline education began to take shape. Parallels can be made between the defunding of the NSF because of MACOS and later attempts to defund the Common Core.[109]

> The decision as to what should be taught in American history to elementary school children . . . can best be reached with the aid of those with a high degree of vision and competence . . . Whether schoolchildren require an understanding of Frederick Jackson Turner's ideas about the role of the frontier in American history before they can sort out the facts and trends of American history—this again is a decision that requires the help of the scholar who has a deep understanding of the American past.[110]

Edwin Reynolds of Teaneck, New Jersey, was a social studies teacher starting in 1965. He started teaching American History I and American History II. Within six years, he was the social studies supervisor for the Teaneck district. Mr. Reynolds remained the social studies supervisor for the next thirteen years. In those years, he oversaw a transformation in the district's social studies curriculum. When he surveyed the students, their response was that "the stuff was dull."[111] His response was to bring the world to Teaneck. Reynolds and his social studies colleagues "junked" the curriculum in favor of semester topical courses, mini courses in all but name.[112] They offered elective courses in America's Future, the American Revolution, AP history, Psychology, Economics, and other history. They informed the students and parents that graduation required four semesters of social studies. Teachers worked in the summer to develop curriculum guides. They were encouraged to be creative and implement new ideas. By the time the program was in full production, student response was generally positive.

Reynolds displayed a creativity in his social studies department that probably would not have been possible ten years earlier. In 1975, he pioneered the first Holocaust studies program in New Jersey schools. Teaneck established a Holocaust Center within the high school. The semester courses expanded to include fifteen different electives. His innovative ideas began to filter down into the elementary grades. By the early 1980s, a change in district administration encouraged Reynolds to return to sequencing the semester courses into a more traditional approach to social studies. Soon, he returned to his classroom to serve out his years as a social studies teacher until his retirement.

Chapter 8

Creating a National Crisis

In the 1970s, the United States experienced the first cracks in its post-war prosperity and its role as *the* dominant world power. The complications of the Vietnam War, the two oil embargos, the Iranian Revolution, Watergate, and the Soviet invasion of Afghanistan highlighted some weaknesses within the American system. The 1980s found the United States in its first major economic downturn since the Great Depression. As America suffered economic hardship, other countries rose to prominence economically, particularly Japan and West Germany. As had happened in the immediate aftermath of Sputnik, leaders sought explanation for the United States' decline once again.

Within education, the MACOS fiasco left many groups wanting an end to federal government interference in education. In the 1980 presidential election, Ronald Reagan promised to eliminate the Department of Education.[1] However, by the end of the decade, federal interference in education would reach a new height with politicians from both sides attempting to direct educational reform. For the field of social studies, a new type of problem arose. A return to *consensus* history and discipline-dominated courses called into question the value of social studies.

NATIONAL COMMISSION ON EXCELLENCE IN EDUCATION

Throughout the 1970s, assorted conservative ideologies slowly spread throughout American society. These various conservative groups came to guide American political and educational movements.[2] Conservatives proclaimed their intention of moving "federal policy away from equity [as in President Lyndon B. Johnson's Great Society] to an emphasis on excellence."[3] The culmination of these conservative movements was the election of Ronald

Reagan. During his campaign, Reagan promised his constituents that he would eliminate the Department of Education. Reagan started with the appointment of Terrel H. Bell as Secretary of Education. Bell was tasked with determining how to cut or abolish his department. Bell felt he was on a mission to save education.[4] Bell assembled a blue-ribbon panel to look at education in America. This panel, the National Commission on Excellence in Education (NCEE), included teachers, business leaders, Nobel-winners, politicians, and various educational administrators. Accumulating readily available evidence from various sources, the Commission noted the "steady" decline of the College Board's Scholastic Aptitude Test (SAT), the College Board's achievement tests in English and Physics, and the National Assessment of Educational Progress (NAEP) science assessment.[5] NCEE conducted public hearings where they gathered information on graduation requirements, experts' opinions about how the United States compared to other countries' educational programs, and business leaders' desires for their potential workforces.

Bell's handpicked Commission was skewed to discover that the current economic crisis traced directly back to the lack of excellence in the schools.[6] The Commission reflected the contemporary American Cold War mentality to "see education problems as national ones, . . . [and explore the] role the Federal government could play in making improvements."[7] The NCEE laid out simple conclusions with equally simple recommendations to address the complex issues of education.[8] The report's suggestions included improving teacher salaries, training in-service teachers, and making teaching a highly desirable profession.[9] The suggestions reflected many of the concerns voiced by conservative education advocates, who pushed for a return to educational basics: a focus upon reading, writing, and mathematics.

When the Commission published its conclusions in their landmark report, *A Nation at Risk*, the public uproar was tremendous. Reagan eventually backtracked on his plans to eliminate the Department of Education. In the 1984 campaign, he demanded more reform of education through federal mandates and thus actually expanded the Department of Education.[10] For Reagan, ESEA had been a government handout to schools that was not showing any returns on America's investment, and the government needed to hold schools and districts accountable. The biggest federal mandate was the expansion of national educational research centers such as the National Center for Education Statistics (NCES) to better track the *crisis*.[11]

THE CRISIS IN EDUCATION

There are notable similarities between the impact of the Committee of Ten, discussed in chapter one, and the NCEE report. Both sent shockwaves into the realm of public education. The Committee of Ten's report influenced education for the next fifty years, and its impact is still apparent today. The NCEE's report, *A Nation at Risk: The Imperative for Educational Reform*, has required every administration to make a commitment to solve the education crisis that is now in its fiftieth year.

Secretary Bell began using the results of the National Assessment for Educational Progress (NAEP), commonly called the Nation's Report Card, for various interpretations. Using a wall chart, he displayed state results to make state comparisons. This was a new use for the NAEP because at the time, the SAT or American College Testing Program (ACT) were the only assessments used to make state-to-state comparisons and those tests only attempted to measure the potential aptitude of college-bound students. In fact, the NCES was prohibited by law from making those state-to-state comparisons using the NAEP. Nevertheless, Bell wanted to gather evidence on all students and compare states. Bell's comparison chart was a sign of things to come. Federal oversight into the general direction of education became important. The Commission suggested that the federal government needed to determine if the financial support given to states and districts was improving student achievement and reducing the achievement gap. Prior to *A Nation at Risk*, the federal government provided financial support to education in the form of initiatives like MACOS, but there was little governmental oversight to account for this money. Further, few scholars were evaluating the effectiveness of any of the programs being created. NCEE presided over a return to scientific management of education in the guise of accountability.

Conservative supporters of Reagan were in a quandary because their fiscal responsibility demanded that they cut spending, and yet most of the proposals for educational reform required increased spending on education.[12] *A Nation at Risk* also started a new round of federal attempts to reform education, which many current teachers believe has been *done to* educators not *done with* educators.[13] The impact of *A Nation at Risk* was not only felt at the federal level. State Education Agencies (SEAs) began to require more than simply a course title. Beginning in the 1970s, New York and California had expanded their statewide assessments to include more than simply basic skills.[14] Other states started to develop their own formal curricular standards for minimum competency.[15] Minimum competency was the first step to more aggressive curricular standards in the accountability cycle. One conclusion that came out of these initial findings was that southern states lagged behind many more industrialized regions of the United States.

As more states considered accountability programs, several SEAs informed the Department of Education that they needed assistance with assessing their students.[16] The leaders of the NAEP offered their assistance by comparing national results with those of the requesting state or district.[17] In 1984, the

Council of Chief State School Officers (CCSSO) and several state governors initiated a plan to start cross-state comparisons using the NAEP for the first time. In this, SEAs relinquished some their educational authority to the national government.

SOCIAL STUDIES IN THE CRISIS

With all the controversy surrounding education and the economy, social studies came out of the MACOS and textbook controversies without a clear direction for the future. The government was focused upon those disciplines they determined were of economic value for international competition: mathematics, English, technology, and foreign languages. Social studies appeared "a field adrift."[18] The old fundamental problem for social studies was that it could be defined using any number of terms, so all the struggles and clarifications dealing with social studies began to break down under new political pressure.

In true yellow journalism, the media picked up the "educational crisis" and reported on a plethora of gaps in education. History and social studies did not get mentioned specifically when talking about obtaining qualified teachers for subjects including mathematics, science, and English.[19] A *Nation at Risk* pointed out how poorly prepared teachers were when it came to training future citizens, but not in the traditional sense. When looking at the NCEE meetings in the preparation of the report, they did not hold any meetings regarding social studies or its disciplines. The closest meeting with experts that NCEE had to incorporating social studies was in their "Education for a Productive Role in a Productive Society" section. Yet even there the focus was on economics and character education.

Social studies was included in the high school curriculum but the report neglected to provide any direction for the field. The report focused upon preparing citizens for the future world economy, as well as on training citizens

Table 8.1 SPAN Recommended Scope and Sequence (1978)

Grade	Course Focus
K-6	Roles in society (citizen, worker, family, friend, group, and self)
7th	Social studies (self, family, friend, and group)
8th	US history
9th	Social studies (worker, consumer, and citizen)
10th	World cultures
11th	US history
12th	US government; social science elective

Based on Richard E. Gross & Thomas L. Dynneson, What Should We Be Teaching in the Social Studies? Fastback 199, Phi Delta Kappa (1983), 32.

to be part of an economically prepared citizenry. In five other reports from the same period, advocates put forth the notion that citizenship relied upon history. The reports called for "complex thinking skills," without the ability to address or critique any problems within the American system.[20] This form of *consensus* history dominated the K-12 textbook industry.[21] But no universal plan or agenda was adopted (see table 8.1).

SCAPEGOATING SOCIAL STUDIES

Starting in the 1970s, national historical organizations expressed their own concerns over the decline of history majors. Historians speculated about various explanations for the lack of history undergraduates. The most popular conclusion was the rise of social sciences and their K-12 stepchild, social studies. The organizations decried the twenty-year decline of history's dominant role in teacher preparation for social studies. Thus, a new onslaught was launched on social studies.[22]

For many historians, the problem was that social studies had usurped the role of history in public education.[23] Diane Ravitch penned an article in November 1985 called the "Decline and Fall of History Teaching." In her article, she stated that history as a discipline was in trouble and that the main culprit was social studies.[24] She advocated for a return to traditionalist history based on chronology and textbooks. Teachers, she felt, should ignore the questions of relevancy. The curriculum needed to rely upon history education as the foundation of citizenship. Additionally, researchers started examining the teaching of social studies and determined that bad social studies teachers further contributed to the problem.[25] In 1984, the NAEP was redesigned and social studies was replaced by a US history test with very little commentary (see chapter 11). In an analysis of this redesigned assessment, Ravitch and Finn published *What Do Our 17-Year-Olds Know? A Report on the First National Assessment of History and Literature*. Their preference for literature and history arose because students "who study [literature and history] subjects become more knowledgeable, more perceptive, and more thoughtful . . . [and thus] they [help] interpret for us the human experience."[26] For history, they concluded that high school students lacked a specific amount of content knowledge.[27]

Responses to the book were mixed. Educators tended to dismiss several of the book's conclusions. The *New York Times* criticized Ravitch and Finn's focus on students' inability to demonstrate chronology.[28] But conservatives utilized this as further evidence that the humanities and education were in a dire crisis as well.[29] For conservatives, the solution was to focus student learning on historical content knowledge. If students had the content, then chronology would follow. Gilbert Sewell, a conservative-leaning advocate working for the American Textbook Council, critiqued all social studies books as ineffective.[30] For the moment, the conservative wing of American politics favored a very nationalistic agenda for education. They found in Sewell an ally to disrupt the view that the university academy favored a multicultural perspective. This differing viewpoint between conservatives and university professors would eventually become crucial to future developments. First objective, conservatives needed to control the language of the debate.

BRADLEY COMMISSION

Conservatives led the charge to formally replace social studies with history by enlisting the aid of historians and politicians. The guiding principle of conservatives was that following World War II, liberals were determined to minimize the influence of history in the curriculum, a move led primarily by social studies educators who had a distaste for history's dominant role.[31] Ravitch herself designed an investigation into how to establish a social studies curriculum that enlisted noted historians and history teachers. With funding from the Lynde and Harry Bradley Foundation, the Bradley Commission laid out the foundations for a new curriculum in *Historical Literacy: The Case for History in American Education*. This new curriculum included social studies every year during the elementary grades (1–6) and required at least four additional years of history in the secondary grades (7–12).[32] Even though social studies was kept in the elementary grades, the Commission wanted it to revolve around historical content. But their main concern was establishing a history curriculum for the secondary levels.

The Commission stressed the importance of including teachers in the discussion about curriculum. Out of seventeen members (see appendix A), five members were teachers: two taught advanced placement (AP) high school classes (Arévalo and Bingham); another high school teacher came from a Magnet school (Byron); a single middle school teacher (Shotland) and a single elementary teacher (Hoone) were included. Three professors had affiliations with schools of education: Crabtree was exclusively in a school of education, but both Hertzberg and Ravitch taught in Columbia's history department and Teachers' College. The remaining ten members were historians. Members from other social studies disciplines were excluded and no pro–social studies teacher played a part.

The Commission also announced their intent to broaden students' understanding of the world by the study of world history.[33] The Commission's advocates wanted to teach history in the traditional manner to return to a style of indoctrination. They relied on the need to have students know specific facts, dates, and individuals. The Commission simply wanted to turn the clock back to 1892 and declare history an essential element of the curriculum at the cost of social studies.[34] They maintained that history education represented a "binding heritage" based on our democratic tradition.[35] Students needed to understand how past events established the current American citizen society. For Ravitch, knowing American history was critical for the establishment of the commonality of students.[36] The belief that "democratic citizenship and effective participation in the determination of public policy require citizens to share a collective memory" was core to the Commission's vision of citizenship.[37] Thus, the discipline of history establishes the collective memory that is essential to citizenship.

The five teachers on the Bradley Commission were very concerned about their role in the Commission, because they wanted to focus on what was being done well in schools for history.[38] Wilson and Sykes spent time talking about teacher preparation. Simply knowing dates (rote memorization) is not what makes a good history teacher, they argued; rather good teaching conveys a level of historical understanding that is often not included in general survey courses.[39] Competency required deeper level of understanding than simply knowing the chronology of events, but how events fit together. Additionally, a teacher must determine how to make the story of history relevant to the students so that they internalize the ideas, concepts, and understanding into their own personal development (*humanistic* progressivism).[40] The teachers' voices were stifled in the final recommendations.

Content was a focus of the Bradley Commission, but there was also an understanding that content should be transferred to students via a "usable pedagogy," otherwise teachers and students would simply return to rote memorization.[41] The Bradley Commission challenged the historical community to return to the classroom to assist in the preparation of teachers. Both the AHA and OAH endorsed the curriculum proposal. Supporters did not raise any concerns with the Commission's recommendations because the recommendations encouraged the direct inclusion of history in the curriculum. To help facilitate the operationalization of their findings, the Bradley Foundation promoted the development of a new national organization, the National Council for History Education (NCHE). This organization looked to promote historical thinking in schools based on the findings of the Bradley Commission.

Yet, as with any report, there were problems. The Commission did not investigate the state of history education, they simply assumed there was a problem in history education and thus created a history curriculum. As the teachers on the Commission expressed, the report did not examine the pedagogy nor how the pedagogy fit with their intended purpose: citizenship.[42]

Additionally, the recommendations relied upon a shared *consensus* history and ignored many of the recent interpretations within the discipline, including the blending of social sciences. With a focus on *consensus* history, they ignored any of the societal problems or issues within American history, thus rejecting any form of pluralism. Historians have never agreed on all historical facts. Students do not generally get the chance to see disputes within the discipline because textbooks synthesize the views of the "experts."[43] Thus, citizenship returned to an assimilationist approach with history highlighting only the positive aspects of the American story.

IMPLICATIONS

When reflecting upon *A Nation at Risk*, Schissler points out, "a crisis is defined as a short period of time when things get of control. A crisis that lasts for more than [fifty] years cannot be given this label; rather, it could perhaps be regarded as a structural feature of a major social change, accompanied by any number of crises."[44] A popular trend has been to view public education as a division of society that is still in crisis mode. As a result, the fundamental structure of education has been shaped by the educational crisis of the last fifty years.

By focusing on excellence, the federal government ignored the issues of equity that many of the programs of the 1960s and 1970s were designed to address. Instead, the government created a new education gap between suburban schools and all other schools. The NCEE wanted to improve schools in a way that would demonstrate a school's value. The NCEE vision created a one-size-fits-all model based on successful suburban schools. All schools needed to conform to this model and send their students to college. This became the goal to demonstrate the high value of the American educational system.

As shown in the MACOS clash, conservative groups wanted the federal government out of the decision-making side of educational policy. They expressed the notion that only a focus on local control of the schools would correct the problems with American education. For many conservatives, they viewed federal desegregation policies in the south "as a fight over who got to define the nature" of the schools.[45] This fight spilled over into the north with questions over urban desegregation policies, like court-mandated busing. These fights laid the foundation for paleoconservative movements to influence education. Yet SEAs encouraged federal interests because it permitted them to establish mechanisms by which to wrestle education away from local authority.[46] Thus they were able to create a uniform state curriculum.

The one-size-fits-all school model raises questions about citizenship.[47] What constituted an appropriate vision of citizenship? Some argue education is important to create individuals who value a free democratic society.[48] Others want to foster a uniform culture and use education to assimilate all students into that culture, like the Hampton Institute. Still others want students to understand how society chooses its leaders and *why* we should choose those leaders: not exactly *good* citizens, just active citizens. This disagreement over citizenship is at the heart of the culture wars that erupted in the 1990s.

Symcox points out that the publication of Benedict Anderson's *Imagined Communities* led to an increased interest in the question of national identity.[49] She implies that identity has been a question with which history and social studies have both grappled, yet she overlooks one reality. Both history and social studies have been victimized by their repeated inability to define their identities within the field of education. The multiculturalism of the 1970s was seen by conservative interests as undermining the image of "a shared national identity."[50] Moderate reformers within the conservative group "believe that social studies lacked narrative and coherence, . . . encouraged victimization, divisiveness, and negativism," which conflicted with their need to write a coherent positive history of America that minimized negative aspects and fostered national identity.[51]

Citizenship education does not predict if students will be *good* citizens or suggest that they will understand how collective memory works today. History cannot predict the future but it can help understand potential avenues of causality.[52] The teaching of history is important so that students understand the evidence as well as differing perspectives: to question what cannot be proven.[53] Ravitch does not question the teaching but supports the methodology of engraining history within the general knowledge of all students, almost to the level of reading or mathematics. Ravitch's complaint about the lack of history is more about methodology: she argues that certain facts need to be established before certain abstract concepts can be addressed (e.g., studying *Brown* v *Topeka* without discussing race relations prior to 1954).

At the beginning of the 1980s, social studies was the umbrella under which all social science and history disciplines fell. Keith Barton points out that numerically, the number of history courses required by states had not altered very much. During the forty years after the first criticism by the *New York Times*, several studies seemed to counter the argument of the critics.[54] Historians examined the decline of history at the university level during the 1970s. Historians were looking for a reason for its decline. It must be social studies.

In 1981, Hertzberg traced the origins of social studies including its transformation into a mixture of various disciplines. She promoted the notion that social studies usurped the role of history education, which created a structured curriculum. About two years later, Michael Lybarger contributed an article on the Committee of Social Studies and the origins of social studies. He depicted how social studies evolved out of the intellectual movements of the period, addressing the idea that there was a need to create multiple curricular models. Hertzberg's vision of social studies became normalized. She depicts social studies as a progressive educational mistake. Progressivists were determined to utilize anti-intellectual techniques that permitted students to control the classroom and its curriculum. In her view, the stew of disciplines known as social studies exemplifies all that is wrong with Progressive education.[55] Hertzberg accepts the idea that traditional history based upon the Madison Conference was an essential part of the curriculum, but social studies was not an essential part.[56] She overlooks the notion that history was a second-tier subject for college-bound students whereas social studies was developed for mass education. Nevertheless, she scapegoats social studies for the destruction of traditional history education.

University historians quickly embraced the idea of scapegoating because they could ignore their own negligence when it came to the preparation of teachers. For most social studies teachers, their main interaction with university academics was through large lecture classes.[57] In history classes, this required a reliance on rote memorization of dates, people, and events. In the other social science courses, prospective teachers received an introduction to general theories on a diversity of topics, but there was no formal content curriculum developed to train social studies teachers. As a result, teachers today are more grounded in educational courses than any formal blending of content and pedagogy. No one asked why students hated history.

For traditional history education to be considered a valued discipline in public schools, conservatives believed it had to be detached from the corruption of social studies. Conservative groups favored this approach because they sought to infuse morals and patriotism into the history curriculum. Historians favored this approach because it elevated their discipline and thus increased student participation in history at postsecondary levels. Properly taught, history teaches the pursuit of truth and understanding; it establishes a context for human life in a particular time and place, relating art, literature, philosophy, law, architecture, language, government, economics, and social life; it portrays the great achievements and terrible disasters of the human race; it awakens youngsters to the particularities that distinguish cultures and societies from one another; it encourages the development of intelligence, civility, and a sense of perspective.[58]

The Bradley Commission was the culmination of the longer trend of criticism over the lack of history education within the curriculum.[59] Hertzberg and Ravitch, her Teachers College colleague, were instrumental in the commission. The Commission wanted to establish the value of history within the curriculum. Educational reformers, historians, and conservative advocates identified the decline in history's value to be caused by the villain of social studies.⁶⁰ For a group that prided itself on knowing history, the Bradley Commission did not seem to be aware of the long history of struggles over citizenship and social studies. The Bradley Commission argued that civic education could be achieved only through the study of history. Further, they devalued social studies because they saw it as attempting to address civic education and too many other disciplines.

According to the Bradley Commission, history should be valued at the expense of the meaninglessness of social studies. In the 1980s John Hughes film, *Ferris Beuhler's Day Off*, the economics high school teacher epitomized the conservative vision of social studies teachers during the period.⁶¹ Ben Stein's character drones on to a classroom full of sleeping students. He describes the economics of the Great Depression very technically while his classroom remains completely unengaged. From the perspective of historians, the students are unengaged because they simply do not have the relevant historical context regarding the topic: the Great Depression. For history, Ben Stein was a metaphor for social studies.

Chapter 9

Standards to Address the National Crisis

The seismic influence of *A Nation at Risk* endured far beyond the Reagan era. Mathematics instructors looked for ways to address the slide in student test scores on national and international measures. They ended up focusing upon mathematical content, which catalyzed a push to create a national math curriculum. The national standards movement led ultimately into a national assessment movement. The federal government had begun to take a more active role in education. For social studies, the impact of the Bradley Commission on national standards had unintended consequences. Social studies had become a political football between pro-America civics and multicultural pluralism.

A NATIONAL CURRICULUM

After the publication of *A Nation at Risk*, educational issues became political hot buttons that were addressed everywhere from the national pulpit to local school boards. Evidence included the results of the re-engineered NAEP tests, which showed students not passing; a decrease in SAT scores; and a decline in American student performance when compared to international students. The truth of any given body of evidence did not matter; the perception was that American education was falling behind and the federal government and state leaders needed to act.

President George H. W. Bush requested that Sandia National Labs conduct their own study on the state of education. The Sandia Report repudiated the conclusions of *A Nation at Risk*, claiming that the analysis was simplistic and did not look at long-term trends or other influencing factors such as the increased number of students taking the SAT.[1] Furthermore, any focus on the SAT was not very reliable given that NAEP scores had remained relatively stable throughout the *crisis* years of the 1980s. President Bush, looking towards the British example, sought to implement a new national curriculum.[2]

Standards-based reform mandates that "all students should master a common core of academic material, and if they do not, then the state should hold teachers, administrators, and sometimes the students themselves accountable."[3] In the mid-1980s, national mathematics associations initiated a trend to create *standards* to be used as guidelines for the states in their responses to *A Nation at Risk*.[4] These standards-based reform measures did not require that all students be held accountable to the same standards, which might be attributable to the influence of vocational education advocates within education.[5]

In 1988, President Bush invited governors to Charlottesville, Virginia, for an education summit where he outlined his vision for education. The gathering set forth a strategy called *America 2000*. *America 2000* laid out a strategy for creating a set of national standards and assessments. President Bush's educational strategy was not per se a national curriculum, but it was intended to "inspire new ideas in education at the Federal, state, and local levels" to help America compete globally with common standards.[6] The recommended "national curriculum" included mathematics, English, science, history, and geography.

No major group came out in opposition to the notion of a national curriculum or to the possibility of a national testing program. Throughout 1991, support for the initiative continued to grow.[7] When issues arose, they concerned the national assessment and the development of a national accountability system. Things changed in 1992, which was an election year. The national assessment was killed so that President Bush would not have to veto an education bill. The national curriculum was transformed once more into guidelines for the states to adopt, yet no formal legislation was passed. George H. W. Bush ended up losing the election to President Bill Clinton.

Reforming education through standards became part of the federal program legislation in the centerpiece of President Clinton's education policy called *Goals 2000: Educate America Act and the Improving America's Schools Act* (IASA).[8] IASA was incorporated into the ESEA. The similarities between *America 2000* and IASA were very evident. Standards-based reform was mandated for any state receiving federal money; thus, to show evidence of some degree of accountability, states began the process of adopting specific state standards that were intended to accompany the national standards that were in development. The standards movement did indeed produce a set of standards for education with each state modelling them on the national standards recommendations.

SOCIAL STUDIES STANDARDS

In their discussions with reform leaders, the NCSS leadership argued that social studies could be used as an umbrella for history, geography, and the other social sciences.[9] Historians and educators ended the fifty-year silence that had characterized their relationship in order to develop standards, but only on the terms of the historians.[10] Social studies advocates were compelled to accede to the historians' point of view or be left out of the discussion.[11] The National Commission on Social Studies in the Schools (NCSSS) was formed by the AHA, the Carnegie Foundation, NCSS, and the Organization of American Historians (OAH). Its goal was to follow the example set by mathematics prior to the adoption of *America 2000*.

NCSSS was composed of members from various groups, but it favored historians because of the participation of AHA and OAH. The Commission relied on education specialists as its backbone and included two non-historians. NCSSS suggested that high school curriculum should be a three-year program of world and US history, but they also incorporated the other social sciences. Middle school was to focus more on local history, as well as local problems, topics, and issues. This Commission displayed a history-centric view of social studies: this view was quickly becoming the established trend in the field.[12] NCSSS published their recommendations, but reform events overtook its publication. Comments within NCSS were that its recommendations were simply a revision of the 1950s.[13] More importantly, the Bradley Commission published its history recommendations before the release of the NCSSS report and it was clear that public policy was already moving in that direction. History was swiftly overtaking social studies.

When California decided to adopt new social studies standards, the fractures in the field became increasingly evident.[14] California's History–Social Studies Framework was viewed as a success for discipline advocates. First, the committee relied on history academics instead of social studies teachers.[15] The key participants were professors Charlotte Crabtree and Diane Ravitch.[16] They argued for focus on history because "the social studies curriculum has been difficult to define because it is organized as a loose confederation of social science disciplines, rather than as a single discipline with a coherent intellectual framework and methodology."[17] Lynne Cheney, head of the National Endowment for the Humanities (NEH), hailed the California reform as a model for the nation.[18]

For all the praise heaped upon the new California standards, the reception was not always positive. Conservative groups were able to persuade the California SEA to permit only one textbook company, Houghton Mifflin, to provide materials.[19] In 1991, the Oakland school board rejected the social studies textbooks for being too Eurocentric.[20] Oakland laid the foundation for an alternative direction that the framework could enlist that did not conform to the conservative model. Using a different vision, New York created a new set of standards for social studies. They were also heavily focused towards history, but not a traditional historical interpretation. Rather they infused a more multicultural form of history.[21] Ravitch publicly criticized Thomas Sobol, the New York Commissioner of Education, by suggesting that New York follow the California model. Conservatives favored discipline standards aligned with California while social studies advocates favored standards like New York.

NCSS leadership viewed history as the "parent-guardian of social studies." It already held an elevated position, but opponents could not offer an alternative model (table 9.1).[22] Social studies leaders had permitted history to hold this privileged position for many reasons. They could not conceive of other ways to organize the field. Compounding the issue, most social studies advocates were classroom teachers, while discipline advocates largely came from the postsecondary arena. Further arguments arose about what constituted social studies. One interpretation was a true interdisciplinary approach to the field: social studies comprised "virtually all social knowledge—the most inclusive, overarching field that envelopes content from all other subjects."[23] Another view limited social studies to elementary grades where students were taught about the social world.[24] Social studies advocates could not form a single coherent definition and thus crippled the field.

In the face of this rising confusion, as *America 2000* became the adopted plan for educational reform, social studies was replaced by an undefined application

Table 9.1 Scope and Sequence Based on NCSS Recommendations (1989)

Grade	Focus
K	Awareness of Self in Social Setting
1st	Individual Primary Social Groups: Understanding School and Family Life
2nd	Meeting Basic Needs to Nearby Social Groups: Neighborhood
3rd	Sharing Earth Space with Others: The Community
4th	Human Life in Varied Environments: The Region
5th	People of the Americas: The United States and Its Close Neighbors
6th	People and Cultures: Representative World Regions
7th	A Changing World of Many Nations: A Global View
8th	Building a Strong and Free Nation: The United States
9th	Systems That Make a Democratic Society Work: Law, Justice, and Economics
10th	Origins of Major Cultures: A World History
11th	The Maturing of America; United States History
12th	Issues and Problems of Modern Society; Introduction to the Social Sciences; The Arts in Human Societies; International Area Studies; Social Science Elective Courses; or Supervised Experience in Community Affairs

Based on James L. Barth, *Elementary and Junior High/Middle School Social Studies Curriculum, Activities, and Materials* (Vol. 1) (Lanham, MD: University Press of America, 1991), 108–13.

of history and geography.[25] This discipline movement, promoted by the Bradley Commission, filtered down into each of the various disciplines. The federal government was set on promoting the value of history over social studies. In 1988, Crabtree received a $1.5 million federal grant to analyze history instruction and develop teaching examples for history over a three-year period.[26]

DISCIPLINE STANDARDS

As part of the *America 2000* strategy, the federal government would provide funds for the creation of standards in five key disciplines: English, mathematics, science, history, and geography. The National Endowment for the Humanities (NEH), headed by Cheney, oversaw the funding of these standards. She commissioned the UCLA-based National Center for History in the Schools (NCHS) to create history standards. This center's work became known as the National Standards for History (NSH).

With federal funds on the line, dissension erupted within groups over how the funds should be spent. In the case of science, scientists argued over how much time should be allotted to each discipline at each grade level.[27] Even though discipline specialists disagreed with each other, however, they kept the various disciplines under the broad field of science. They generally agreed to use a common methodology in the form of the scientific method. No such agreement happened in social studies.

When the other social sciences heard that history and geography received special attention, they sought their own pieces of the federal pie. Political scientists, sociologists, and economists argued that their disciplines deserved equal inclusion within the curriculum. Even geography, though included, did not want to share space with history courses. For their part, historians, including the two national historical associations, argued for a social science curriculum with history as its primary pillar. Ravitch suggested negotiating a science-style model for social studies. Cheney permitted the inclusion of multiple social science groups, but she insisted that the standards must remain history focused.[28] Eventually, a consensus model was adopted with history at its center.

Assorted national organizations established committees to generate their own K-12 discipline standards. In addition to geography, both political scientists and economists developed standards for their disciplines following the NCHS examples.[29] In 1994, federal funding (*America 2000*) finally came through with a slight modification. The government funded a total of nine standards centers. Social studies would have four dedicated standards centers including the original NSH, as well as standards centers for geography, civics, and economics. Cheney approved the work of all four social studies centers.

NATIONAL STANDARDS FOR HISTORY

Gary Nash (US history), Charlotte Crabtree (elementary education), and Ross E. Dunn (world history) oversaw the three aspects of the NSH. In addition to the university faculty, NCHS included participants from various state and national organizations[30] (see appendix A). They utilized focus groups to vet their standards: more than two hundred people were involved with this effort.[31] In the end, the NCHS employed a consensus decision model to finalize the standards. They also decided to focus on skills and thinking over content knowledge.

NCHS identifies historical thinking skills as students' ability "to evaluate evidence, develop comparative and causal analyses, interpret the historical record, and construct sound historical arguments and perspectives on which informed decisions in contemporary life can be based."[32] They wanted to build active learners over passive learners who relied on recitation of a set content. The NCHS focused on teaching historical understanding instead of historical content, which had some unintended consequences over the long term. They sought to incorporate several of history's recent approaches, among which was a desire to include the voices of diverse historical actors.[33] This not only meant including the known voices but also highlighting the voices of lesser known or voiceless individuals.

Further, "American culture has . . . the idea that history, especially the history of the nation, consists of 'the truth,' a body of fixed information, objectively known, and that the job of educators is simply to train children's memories in the facts they need to be loyal and industrious citizens."[34] This was essentially the purpose that social studies educators had been using for the previous eighty years. The center wanted to include more than the dominant political culture of America, but they also desired to create a culture that connected all of America's students.

This led to the first of several disagreements. The NSH evaluated what content should be included about the struggles, accomplishments, and civic contributions of African Americans and other minorities. Conservative members such as Chester Finn favored civic-centered Eurocentric history; educators and professors favored the inclusion of a broader base that they termed cultural pluralism. Cultural pluralism won (New York style).[35]

The next quarrel concerned whether western civilization[36] or world history courses should be taught in K-12. This disagreement fell along ideological lines again; conservatives (e.g., Finn and Ravitch) favored western civilization while academics favored global history. For the conservatives, western civilization courses were a way to teach the origins of American exceptionalism, but once again conservatives lost.[37] The dominant voice of standards-driven conservatives was silenced by the consensus of the committee.

The center divided the standards into two parts: a skills section and a general content section. The broad content items were linked back to specific skills that students were to accomplish through their course of study. Education incorporated many theories of educational psychology, which urged educators to move away from a teacher-centered classroom to an active student-centered classroom (*developmentalist*). This was not a trend unique to social studies/history but it appeared within education at large. The NCHS divided history skills into five categories: chronology; comprehension; analysis and interpretation; research; and issue analysis and decision-making.

The NCHS developed sample curricula and lesson plans to go along with their standards. They advocated for a minimum of six full years of history between fifth and twelfth grades. The standards focused upon the big picture of historical movements instead of specific content knowledge. The standards, especially the sample lessons, did indeed take a more active, student-centered tone.[38] Students were intended to develop skills and critical thinking: for example, they were to understand the daily existence of individuals living in Jamestown instead of simply reciting the year that Jamestown was founded.

The other three federally funded social studies mimicked the history model. They also focused more on skills than content knowledge when they developed their standards. Geography standards were divided into six themes that students needed to understand in order to apply geography skills.[39] These geographic themes included eighteen geographic standards across the curriculum. Each standard focused on geographic skills within each theme so that students developed skills and concepts connected to geography. Geography standards endorsed two years of study during secondary school, as well as a senior elective course.

Civics standards focused on conceptual objectives that related to citizenship and the rationale underlying civics study.[40] Five major questions formed the basis for standards that revolved around the role of citizens and how the American political system worked. Civics standards consisted of a series of questions that students should be able to answer about civics and government; the standards provided for no underlying skill development. Both the geography and civics standards were generally well received by their stakeholders.

Likewise, the Council of Economic Education focused on concept objectives for student mastery of economics.[41] The Council of Economic Education enumerated twenty standards for economics that attempted to teach the fundamental ideas and concepts of the discipline. They also sought to introduce an understanding of abstract theories like wealth distribution, the role of prices, and the morals of economic theory. Economic standards were benchmarked for students to have varying degrees of understanding of the twenty standards in fourth, eighth, and twelfth grades. In 1990, only half of the student population in America took a semester course in economics, but even though it was not represented by a specific course, the impression was that economics needed to be incorporated into lower-level curriculum.[42] The twenty standards delineated by the Council of Economic Education were content-based so that students were required to demonstrate an understanding of economic principles rather than mastery of a theoretical framework of skills.

SOCIAL STUDIES STANDARDS, AGAIN

Many educators still pleaded for a single social studies curriculum, giving attention to all social sciences. Without federal funding largesse or even federal sanction, the NCSS worked on their standards project. They hoped their own standards would become the de facto national standards for social studies. They also utilized a consensus model to generate their standards and used a new broader definition for social studies.[43] NCSS's definition maintained that social studies was "the integration of history, the social sciences, and the humanities to promote civic competence."[44] Problems arose as scholars and practitioners demanded to know what exactly was meant by the term *civic competence*. NCSS did not have a clear answer. After nearly eighty years of continual argument and struggle, social studies had produced a vague definition that left far too much freedom for stakeholders to develop their own interpretations of the value of social studies. Educators continue to argue over what *civic competence* might mean to the field.

NCSS tried to focus on skills and general content for all areas with very few specific details in any one area. Further confusing the issue, several groups attempted to create a voice for what the standards movement should look like for social studies. Parker advocated that local districts renew the curriculum of social studies skills and ignore the debates continuing at the national level.[45] Even though NCSS led the fight, several other social studies organizations attempted to formulate a future for social studies.[46] Even though there were flaws in the NCSS standards, many educators felt that these social studies standards were a reasonable alternative to the overwhelming number of other circulating standards. Others complained that the NCSS standards were a weak compromise, damaging to all the disciplines. In actuality, the standards were organized into "thematic strands that were clearly disciplinary," and thus were not really any better than the four other projects.[47] But most states did not have a chance to determine whether to use the social studies or the four discipline standards anyway, because political events temporarily brought a halt to the standards movement.

NATIONAL STANDARDS FOR HISTORICAL IDENTITY

The midterm elections in 1994 are often viewed as the beginning of the end for the standards movement. A cultural war was brewing during the summer of 1994, centering around a permanent *Enola Gay* exhibition at the Smithsonian Institute. Congress felt pressure to address the exhibit.[48] Rep. Duncan Hunter (R-CA) portrayed the Smithsonian as implementing "pseudo-history by insinuating that the United States is to blame for the unfortunate sufferings of the Japanese people rather than those really responsible; the leaders of wartime Japan, including Emperor Hirohito."[49] This national debate was over the portrayal of this event in the national memory.

Conservatives depicted the *Enola Gay* as a great victory for America. These actions made the world safe for democracy. The director of the Smithsonian and historians wanted to show that Japanese individuals were silenced. Academic historians tended to view the bomb as a mistake. The air force wanted veto power over parts of the exhibit. Historians argued that museums needed freedom from government interference when it came to displaying artifacts. The *Enola Gay* controversy politicized history, and politicians from all sides wanted their opinions heard.[50]

As the *Enola Gay* crisis raged on, the NCHS was finishing its work on their standards without realizing the controversy's implications for their work. Cheney, who stepped down from NEH after the election of President Clinton, unleashed a biting editorial criticizing the unreleased US history standards. She had received drafts and "knowingly" approved early versions of the history standards while the head of NEH. Now she led the charge against them.[51] She claimed the standards attempted to include too many groups (multiculturalism) at the expense of the "important" facts of history.

Her claims mobilized conservative radio pundits, who criticized the standards that were not yet available for public review. A counting game started: how many "historically significant" names or events appeared in the standards or lesson plans? The war of numbers between conservatives and the historians was content inclusion: should classrooms discuss George Washington or Nat Turner? Yet the central question was not about whether history or social studies should be taught, but what was the very purpose of history education.[52] This question plagued the social studies curriculum for decades.

Returning to debates between the various interpretations of citizenships, some conservatives wanted to foster patriotic subjects who were loyal to the national achievements of America.[53] Conservatives believed that the standards negatively portrayed America in certain episodes, for instance, McCarthyism and racism. Cheney and her fellow conservatives opposed the perceived *hidden agenda* in the standards. They wanted to exclude minorities in favor of assimilationist interpretations of civic nationalism.[54] Nash, Crabtree, and Dunn claim the conservatives saw that "history, like politics, is about national identity"—whoever controlled history controlled national identity.[55]

The majority of the NCHS committee was more concerned about skills over content. Yet for conservatives, the standards represented the American identity, this was the real struggle.[56] Risinger, a member of the NCHS committee, believed that the primary goal of the standards was to produce an "informed citizenry."[57] This suggests that the general feeling among the writers of the NSH was that, through the study of history, teachers can develop *good* citizens. The conservatives did not comprehend how one might craft a hagiographical narrative of how America creates a more perfect union through discussion about more than just the positive aspects of America's past.[58]

Cheney and Nash held televised public debates over the standards, and they argued for two different national identities. These factions are not new to American society, nor are they new to the social studies debate. The rhetoric used by the conservatives was that of traditionalist history, whereas Nash and others were arguing for developing historical skills akin to the "New" history or "New" social studies movements. Additionally, other parts of society were just as concerned about the lack of content as the conservatives. They viewed "extreme multiculturalism [as] . . . about turf, power, patronage, and money—it is a very lucrative business."[59] Multiculturalism became the spectator against which America was fighting.

The conservatives were not the only stakeholders eager to see the NSH fail; multiculturalists definitely had a stake in either promoting or destroying the NSH.[60] Ethnic groups saw this as a struggle between conservatives and the intelligentsia, so they felt no desire to participate in their ideological debate. Their apathy would have ramifications later. Print media was sympathetic to the standards, but few individuals or groups enthusiastically supported them.[61] Both Bill Honig, California's Superintendent of Education, and Thomas Sobol, New York Commissioner of Education, supported the NSH. They viewed the standards as a celebration of democracy and the acceptance of cultural pluralism.[62]

With the National Standards for History set to be released to the public, Senator Slade Gorton (R-WA) called for a vote to abolish all standards even before they were unveiled. The Senate vote passed 99 to 1; the Senate rejected the history standards. The opposition did not criticize the notion of making students have historical understanding; instead, they criticized the absence of their desired content. The net result of this Senate vote was not just the derailing of the US history standards; it derailed the entire national standards movement for all subjects.

AFTERMATH OF THE SENATE VOTE

The standards continued to be problematic as more people started to criticize them. Darling-Hammond insinuated that the NSH would simply consist of a list of terms that students would have to learn to pass a test.[63] She felt that standards would not allow students to learn and grow. Furthermore, she predicted that standards would "create a static and bounded conception of curriculum that is at odds with this understanding of learning."[64]

In this combative environment, the NSH became a lightning rod for educational problems and especially highlighted the perils of federal involvement in education.[65] Parents, teachers, and other stakeholders feared that standards would eventually lead to national testing, even though the national assessment aspect of standards reform had been removed prior to the convening of any standards-setting projects.[66] In 1980s, the Christian Coalition headed by Pat Robertson spearheaded another attempt to eliminate the Department of Education as a way to guarantee that funding of education would be subject to parental control. The NSH were snared in Christian conservatives' desire to question educational techniques as being too progressive or liberal.

Nash and Dunn endeavored to quell the controversy by redrafting the standards into a smaller single volume. They deleted many of the suggested lesson plans that they felt were at the heart of the controversy. Ironically, orders poured in for the NSH; many educators were simply enthralled to have a set of standards at last. By the late 1990s, twenty-eight states had adopted the revised history standards as their social studies curriculum. These revised standards included standards for civics, geography, and economics in a much more watered-down form. Three states had separate civic education standards.[67]

IMPLICATIONS

George H. W. Bush and Bill Clinton's administrations sought to use standards, assessments, and accountability to encourage a systemic reform within education.[68] This reform effort did not arise out of some personal political agenda, rather it derived from the hysteria created by the crisis found in *A Nation at Risk*. Bush's administration wanted to generate a direction by creating a set of uniform standards and assessments. By the time Clinton's term began, standards were nearly completed and national assessments were scrapped. The education reform movement was no longer systemic. The fractures were spreading.

At the time of the NSH development, America experienced a historic transitional event. The Cold War was ending and all the ideological underpinnings and rationales for American education came into question again. The idea that America needed patriotic furor in defense of the nation had dissipated with the fall of Communism.[69] Could this transition also have undermined the *consensus* notion of citizenship education? The high points of traditionalist agitation often happened at periods when America was in an apparent struggle with outside forces: 1940s, 1950s, and 1980s. History will continue to reexamine itself to determine the roles played by international politics in domestic decisions.

The brief accord between historians and social studies educators to obtain a uniform set of standards fell apart. NCSS did not defend social studies from conservative criticisms, like the Bradley Commission, to focus on discipline reforms; they believed that they would still dominate any reform. The other social sciences did not participate in the discussion and sat on the sidelines as NCSS attempted to fend off these conservative attacks to create history standards. NCSS did not understand the dilemma that the Bradley Commission had identified within social studies. The issue of a single uniform authentic pedagogy had plagued the field since its beginning. Just prior to the national standards reform, the California History–Social Science framework critiqued social studies' need for a single pedagogy among the various disciplines. By the time they finally advocated an issue-based authentic pedagogy for social studies as related to civic education in 1996, it was too late.[70] Likewise, stating a need and implementing a program to fill that need are totally different realities.

Conservatives hammered away at the need to use history as the discipline through which to teach civic education. Ravitch recycled the myth that students simply did not know history and insisted that social studies was the culprit in this travesty of ignorance. She called for civic curriculum to return to the *golden age* of history education. The other leading conservative reformers favored this increase in the importance of history, but they also tied the politics of nationalism to it. They wanted to use the NSH as "a thinly disguised attempt to inculcate students with a relatively conflict-free, consensual view of history."[71]

The rationale, according to Symcox, was that they were motivated by the notion of power "used to legitimize knowledge: to decide which knowledge or truth is the correct one," which would further legitimize their own political power in America.[72] So when the NSH were initiated, Nash, Crabtree, and Dunn echoed the recycled myth. They declared the "United States was gathering a head of steam to overcome history illiteracy" without the understanding that there had never actually been a *golden age* of students knowing history.[73] Seixas further contributed to this outlook when he looked at historical understanding in eleventh-graders and concluded that teachers did not improve the historical understanding of high school students.[74]

Having won the battle for standards, conservatives proceeded to lose the battle of control. Conservatives and progressives had originally agreed about the need for history standards, but they could not agree on the nature of American history.[75] The consensus model implemented by the NCHS committee muted conservative voices. Ironically, the conservatives fell into a similar trap as those who wrote the Committee of Seven report: they neglected the views of other groups. So instead of implementing a system of traditional values through the power of content knowledge in history, the conservatives accidently created a vehicle to bring *social meliorism* into history education.[76]

University historians dominated the standards conversation for the first time since 1910. They wanted to use academia's more inclusive vision of history to form the basis for new history standards. For many conservatives, this loss of control to university historians is often interpretated as a victory for progressive education reformers. Progressive reformers wanted to foster equity among all students as well as ensure the inclusion of their cultures into the historical narrative.[77]

Of the three standards, Symcox argues that the world history standards were the most controversial because they backed a global history over the traditional Western civilization.[78] Universities began phasing out Western civilization requirements starting in the 1980s. Stanford students led protests to eliminate its Western civilization requirement in 1987.[79] This trend was evident to the point that Nash dismisses Finn's opposition to global history as his extreme right political stance.[80] Nevertheless, the US history standards hit closer to home, and the public outcry was more politically motivated.[81]

This pattern of conflict between "political intent and educational practice in history education" has played out in similar patterns in at least a dozen countries.[82] The conservative opposition to the NSH was due to the misapprehended goals of the standards, by virtue of which university historians wanted to re-envision history education with a skills-oriented focus.[83] This idea that evidence was essential to social studies might have helped establish an authentic pedagogy for the field. Symcox places the misapprehension on "evangelical Christians [who] condemn[ed] the child-centered teaching methods by educational theorists and psychologists" because they wanted to control the factual knowledge accessible to students.[84]

Further problems arose as history education and the other content-specific standards failed to integrate other disciplines into their standards.[85] For example, the US history standards neglected the inclusion of economic reasoning, which was a major criticism from economists. Why was economic reasoning omitted? Because NCHS did not include either an economic historian or economist in the development of its standards. In fact, only the NCSS social studies standards ever gave adequate attention to the incorporation of economics.[86] In one example regarding a lesson on the Great Depression, historians created a lesson based on several traditional myths that recent economic scholars had debunked. Regardless of this fact, the political firestorm forced the NCHS to publish a revised set of standards without any of the controversial lessons including the Great Depression lesson. Consequently, teachers and social studies coordinators were left to find their own lessons without a framework or current literature to use as guidance. Textbook makers utilized some of the examples from the original NSH standards, but examples were generally left to their discretion.[87]

Costrell suggests that the most logical method for developing standards was the Massachusetts model for standards of *History and Social Science* in which the various disciplines got to supply input into the standards.[88] But Congress had changed the standards into a voluntary movement for state and local districts instead of the more national standards movement represented by *America 2000*.[89] The politicization of social studies has made it much harder to come to a consensus now that standards are being reviewed and revised by governor's mansions and state houses with politics in mind.

Symcox insinuates that conservatives won this cultural war because they used simple language to sway the public. This is in contrast to historians who understood the complexities of history but tried to argue with the public about abstractions of history teaching.[90] Nash, Crabtree, and Dunn believe that the real target of the conservatives was not the NSH. They claim the actual target was the political funding available to the National Endowment for the Humanities and the National Endowment of the Arts.[91] Whether or not history standards were the target, the standards were undermined and ultimately were not adopted by the national government. Despite the failure of standards at the federal level, SEAs still needed to find curricula for social studies and/or history education.

The standards movement resulted in reformed curricula across many social studies disciplines. Standards were created by geography, civics, and economics, and the NCSS funded their own general standards for social studies. In other words, five sets of standards were produced in the early 1990s for the field. After the derailing of the standards movement, experts reviewed the various standards.[92] Each expert considered their discipline to be as important as any other discipline, and each believed their discipline deserved equal time with every other discipline. Unfortunately, the reality was that social studies had been a second-tier subject since the 1890s. Moreover, subject experts do not have to deal with questions of relevancy to students, nor with the interconnectedness of the field of social studies. For example, the *voluntary* economic standards that were developed in the late 1990s by "non-economists, who refuse and reject professional input" did not have the same appeal to university economists.[93] Of the social studies disciplines, economists tend to be the most supportive of their discipline being incorporated into the other social studies disciplines or, more likely, into the general field *social studies*.[94]

The failure of the NSH did have some positive effects on social studies education. A new focus on historical thinking skills brought a renewed effort to conduct new research into student understanding of historical concepts. Various scholars (e.g., Barton, VanSledright, & Wineburg) started to examine student understanding of historical concepts as outlined in the NSH. Wilschut points out that "reading a source is not an historical skill, but interpreting content of a source *from some other time*" is a skill that was not a focus of social studies or history education before the 1990s.[95] Several new studies focused on elementary levels, challenging the Piagetian notion that students did not develop an ability to understand abstract concepts, especially time, until the fifth grade. Barton and Levstik conducted interviews with fifty-eight students (K-6) to determine student understanding of time. The researchers established that younger students *did* understand the concept of time; however, the researchers also discovered that student understanding and articulation of time develop over the course of the elementary school years.[96]

In a more comprehensive examination of history across various levels, Wineburg conducted several studies into the cognitive theory of student understanding of the past.[97] VanSledright and Kelly examined whether students could achieve some form of historical understanding.[98] They determined that teachers do play a role in encouraging students to use alternative sources to understand ideas but that students do not always gain an understanding of historical concepts. Barton and McCully scrutinized Northern Ireland's attempts to connect student understanding of history to identity, evaluating how student attitudes changed after exposure to the national curriculum.[99] They concluded that historical understanding is formed at an early age and that school history classes add to, but do not supersede, student identity.

The research suggests that students use various sources to mold their own national identities to conform to their beliefs. Barton followed up on the identity study that was hailed as a success.[100] But Barton also determined that national identity is formed before students are introduced to Northern Ireland's national curriculum. Civic nationalism has once again become a focus of social studies; however, the direction of the reform is in flux as scholars attempt to understand how to develop *good* citizens. The NSH should not be considered the final version that dictates all future curriculum but should instead be viewed as a good start for further development of curriculum.[101]

The controversy over the NSH "reveals how policymakers and opinion-makers, including academics, pundits, politicians, and the press, used their positions to advance particular intellectual and ideological agendas, and how their contending efforts drove curricular policy throughout the 1980s and 1990s."[102] Some sort of uneasy balance needs to be found between these groups, because unidentified generic social studies skills are just as problematic as overly content-heavy standards.[103] By the end of the national standards movement, between the four individual disciplines and social studies organizations, more than thirteen hundred pages were devoted to social studies standards.

Administrators simply could not fit the recommended amount of study into a typical school day. The various disciplinary standards, when added together, called for a minimum of eight years of study in secondary school (sixth to twelfth grades) before civics or economics were even added to the secondary curriculum. Marzano and Kendall analyzed all the standards for every social studies discipline that received federal funding. This included history, civics, economics, and geography. They determined that if a student was obliged to learn every standard, benchmark, and content identified, the student would have to be in school for *twenty-two* years![104] Provided there was no need to re-teach any standards.

Chapter 10

The Realm of Accountability

In the opening decades of the twenty-first century, state culture wars erupted, local arguments became more prevalent, and a new national debate arose around the teaching of history. These culture wars came from both conservatives and liberals who believed they should control the education narrative. As has historically been the case, social studies is particularly besieged by these culture wars.

Even though the move toward national standards went down in flames, the federal government still believed in requiring some form of accountability in order for a state or district to receive federal education dollars. Most states adopted some standards and even implemented some standardized tests for their own accountability. One of these states was Texas, where Gov. George W. Bush touted an education miracle: due to the revised Texas student accountability standards, student learning improved. Upon his election to the presidency, he translated the Texas model to the federal accountability system with a reauthorization of the Elementary and Secondary Education Act (ESEA). With bipartisan support, President Bush passed a reauthorization of ESEA, now named the No Child Left Behind (NCLB) Act of 2002.

NCLB ushered in a new era of accountability as well as a new era for social studies. As NCLB continued, state governors sought a set of common standards that were aligned with a common assessment. The development of the Common Core (CC) and its common assessment plans were widely supported by nearly all state governments until the moment of their unveiling. Again, the CC influenced educational policy toward social studies. In the end, the CC shared several of the problems that had plagued the national standards movement a generation before.

NO CHILD LEFT BEHIND ACT

As the national standards were presented and then rejected, states began to implement their own versions of these standards. Texas became a shining example of how to correct a terrible record of educating students. The Texas miracle introduced standards aligned to statewide tests that districts were required to use to show evidence of student achievement. Texas even improved its ranking in the national assessment, NAEP. Gov. Bush touted the rise in student learning and reduction in the achievement gap: thus, the Texas miracle.[1]

The federal government was set to reauthorize ESEA. The governor, by then the nation's president, sought to implement the Texas miracle across the nation and renamed ESEA the No Child Left Behind Act (NCLB). Ironically, research into the Texas miracle demonstrated only a temporary increase to student achievement. Eventually, student scores regressed to the mean.[2] Nevertheless, this became the national form of accountability. States had to adopt standards and demonstrate student achievement in math and reading or lose federal education dollars.

NCLB took many of its ideas from *Goals 2000* and *America 2000*. Yet instead of the federal government being responsible for standards and assessments, each state was now responsible for creating its own standards and assessments. The federal government wanted State Education Agencies (SEAs) to hold various stakeholders accountable for student learning. If students failed to demonstrate academic progress on state assessments, local districts or schools would be held responsible for not educating students. The SEAs would be required to take over the district or school depending on the level of repeated failed accountability.

By the time of NCLB, all states except for Nebraska and Iowa had already adopted standards for mathematics and language arts.[3] NCLB further required that states possess standards for all core subjects by 2004. Accordingly, states needed to develop standards in mathematics, language arts, science, history, and civics. In the end, the standards movement did not die; it simply shifted from federal governance to state governance, resulting in fifty-one different sets of standards and assessments. Some states developed *good* standards and others did not.

The accountability mandate continued to hold teachers, schools, and districts responsible for all student learning through data collection. Data collection translated into student learning on standardized tests. Further, all students were required to make adequate yearly progress (AYP) in their learning, including students in all subgroups. This stipulation dominated the conversation about NCLB because districts needed to demonstrate student achievement. The fastest and easiest way to demonstrate achievement was on standardized tests aligned to the state standards. The first fields that were required to demonstrate progress were reading and mathematics, which had to show improvement by 2004.[4] The federal expectation was that after ten years of assessing reading and mathematics, all students should be achieving AYP. Yes, 100 percent proficiency by 2014.

The intent of NCLB was obscured by the overemphasis on testing. The research community focused on NCLB's testing impact on teachers, on school environment, on the curriculum, and on student learning. The United States entered a culture of high-stakes testing in reading, mathematics, and science. Among the unintended consequences of NCLB was the demotion of those fields that were not tested. The devaluation of these subjects is measurable by examining the time allotment, their portion of the budget, and lack of curricular guidelines each subject receives.

For social studies, the NCLB era was awkward. Progress was required among "mathematics, reading or language arts, and [beginning in the 2005–2006 school year] science," but not limited to those subjects.[5] These three subjects had to demonstrate AYP or SEAs were required to make the district or school submit an improvement plan. As noted above, history and civics were specifically mentioned as part of NCLB, but what about social studies? None of the other fields are divided into their subdisciplines.[6] The lingering aftereffects of the National Standards for History (NSH) continued the national discrediting of social studies as a field. One theory frequently postulated concerning why social studies was not assessed was that each of the disciplines was "too contentious" to require testing.[7] Yet, no explanation of this "contentiousness" is ever provided.

States developed standards but the similarities between the social studies standards vary extensively, far more than with other subjects. The Fordham Institute, a conservative education think tank, evaluated state history standards in 1998, 2003, 2011, and 2021. The main criticism of their evaluation is the stated purpose of US history.[8] Nevertheless, the evaluators attempted to maintain some credibility by using consistent criteria. Additionally, their criteria align with the thinking of the Bradley Commission with a focus on chronological thinking, not "ahistoric themes organized into different social studies strands."[9] In other words, as long as it wasn't social studies. For the most part, Fordham's evaluation shows that once a state produces a good set of standards, the standards tend to maintain an above average level of performance. However, most state standards were "mediocre-to-awful."[10] Additionally, they identified many problems (at least as they view them) with most state standards.

Regarding accountability, some states included social studies in their state accountability system. Others maintained a low benchmark for social studies standards because they were not required to test, nor did they feel obliged to test. In the years after NCLB, about half of the states assessed social studies at some level in any given year.[11] Over a period of ten years (2004–2014), nineteen states tested social studies, and nine states either tested in 2004 and stopped or started after 2004 and were still testing in 2014.[12] The other twenty-two states and Washington, DC, did not assess any social studies (figure 10.1). Generally, those assessments are designed to demonstrate "rote memorization of names, dates, and loosely connected facts."[13]

NCLB could be considered a blessing and curse for social studies. Teachers discussed the perception about resources and time allocated to social studies prior to NCLB.[14] After NCLB, teachers bemoaned a marked drop in instructional allotment and resources. Yet, a study in Virginia found a slight increase in time allocation in first- to third-graders while a decrease in fourth- and fifth-grade classes.[15] Nevertheless, the majority of scholarship on this topic discussed the marginalization of the field.

The marginalization of social studies is an accepted construct because the focus has been on tested subjects.[16] For example, fifth-grade teachers in states that tested social studies estimated that they taught thirty minutes more than their non-tested peers.[17] Also, on the positive side, teachers note their curricular decisions are not as prescribed as those in tested subjects.[18] The impact on social studies is generally negative, but there were some definite positive side effects of NCLB.

On a related note, Sen. Robert Byrd (D-WV) amended NCLB to include the Teaching of American History (TAH) program. The amendment provided $100 million for local education agencies to join with other institutions (higher education, historical organizations, museums, etc.) to determine ways for teachers to improve history education.[19] TAH was similar to the "New" social studies projects of the 1960s, where a lot of work was done with little dissemination of the information gathered. The TAH did not develop a mechanism to evaluate the programs or practices, nor to define what constituted a necessary standard.[20] The federal government discontinued TAH in 2012 due to fiscal problems. In short, Congress eliminated programs that fostered social studies education when they deemed the programs nonessential and, thus, not deserving of federal funding.

THE COMMON CORE—WHERE DID SOCIAL STUDIES GO?

In 2006, SEAs and standard advocates began to meet regarding the need for a set of aligned state standards.[21] These meetings built the foundation for a new set of standards. Relying heavily upon Achieve, Inc., a nonprofit advocacy

The Realm of Accountability 133

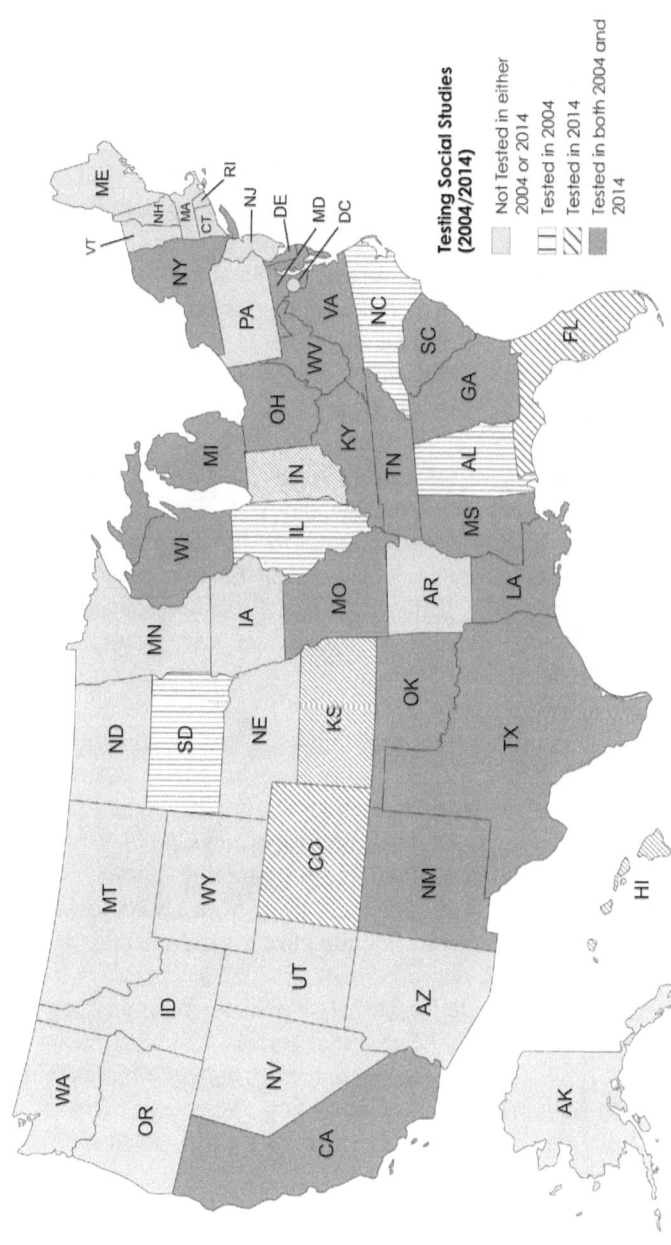

Figure 10.1 Testing of Social Studies between 2004–2014

and consulting firm created by the National Governors Association, SEAs set about formulating de facto national standards. These became known as the Common Core (CC).

The lessons from the NSH storm were considered when creating the Common Core standards; the standards were tasked to Achieve, Inc. to avoid the need for any federal funding. Consequently, this approach removed oversight at the federal level.[22] Following the German reform model, Achieve, Inc., also encouraged the federal government to promote standards but not require them. Because the CC were developed by a company, one major difference is that participants in the development process have not been identified. Achieve became the spokesperson. President Barack Obama's encouragement in 2012 was a carrot for SEAs that sought waivers for NCLB deadlines. States quickly adopted the CC standards.

Another lesson from national standards regarded the national assessment. Two consortia, Partnership for Assessment of Readiness for College and Careers (PARCC) and Smarter Balanced Assessment Consortium (SBAC), were tasked with creating assessments aligned to the CC. This assessment component became a problem again. Instead of periodic low-stakes sampling as with the NAEP, common assessments allow direct comparisons between educational reforms across states. There would be yearly data to compare groups of students and see whether reform efforts were successful.[23] This is a double-edged sword. While it is good to see what works, it is bad for politicians who will be blamed if education in their state is not improving as quickly as in other states.

As with NCLB, the CC focuses on language arts and mathematics. For social studies, there are two different strands within the CC. At the elementary level, social studies is linked to language arts. The *Common Core State Standards for English Language Arts in History/Social Studies, Science, and Technical Subjects* (CCSS-ELA) focuses on promoting literacy skills across the elementary grades. In a way, this shift away from fiction toward nonfiction was really a pedagogical shift intended to promote the understanding of upper-level texts with more dense content. Elementary teachers focused on decoding content of the nonfiction text, rather than simply helping students to read the words on the page.[24] For social studies, this shift meant a focus on document analysis, use of evidence, and discerning the biases of authors. This approach to social studies has been a key component of many recommendations throughout its history. Teachers also appreciated the integrated approach as articulated in the CCSS-ELA.[25]

Again, marginalization of social studies curricula became a concern as studies indicated that elementary teachers regularly spend less than three hours a week on social studies. The stated reason for this? Social studies was the least important subject.[26] The current hope, under the CCSS-ELA, is that increasing time allotted to social studies will reverse the marginalization.[27] Despite this, the debate over marginalization at the elementary level has not been as prevalent as in the first fifteen years of the twenty-first century.

In addition to the CCSS-ELA in the elementary grades, the CC consortium created the *College, Career, and Civic Life* (C3) Framework for Social Studies State Standards. The C3 standards were unveiled to the public in 2013. The C3 went through a process similar to the other CC standards: the committee would receive feedback and revise the standards. But Achieve did not set a date by which the C3 standards should be adopted. The C3 standards parallel the CCSS-ELA standards in the sense that they rely more upon skills over content.[28]

Some of the initial critiques of the C3 standards were that they blindly accepted democratic values as always good and that America is generally portrayed in only a positive light, without raising questions on social issues. The standards are ever more vocal, in the chaos that arises in arenas from the classroom to the library to student hairstyles to the school boards and administrations. In other words, it was a very traditional interpretation of citizenship education.[29] Others viewed the C3 as a progression in social studies pedagogy since teachers were required to focus on skills over content.[30] The hope was that rote memorization would be a pedagogical concept of the past, just like every other reform movement had sought.

Yet before the review process got underway, Achieve and the CC consortium were on the defensive. State governments backed out of the Common Core initiative. In June 2013, the Council of Chief State School Officers (CCSSO) announced that they were focusing on the implementation of CC standards for language arts and mathematics and thus did not have the resources to deal with revisions of the C3 standards. The NCSS took over responsibility for overseeing the revision and implementation of the C3 standards.[31]

At the same time, the College Board unveiled their updated Advanced Placement (AP) US History standards in 2014. The Republican National Committee (RNC) and other conservative organizations claimed that the new standards devalued America. Criticism ranged from an undue emphasis placed on ethnic groups to the negative image of American *heroes*. The College Board was accused of favoring criticism of America. The RNC informed them to strengthen content knowledge in the standards.

The new head of the College Board, David Coleman, acknowledged the concerns of the RNC. He announced that the College Board would release an early practice test that used the new standards.[32] Some speculated that the uproar might also have stemmed from Coleman's previous position as head of the Common Core. Nevertheless, the College Board, which oversees a purely privately funded test that universities have the choice whether or not to accept, has fallen into the same trap that ensnared previous attempts to develop social studies standards and for many of the same reasons: control over the national identity.

STATE AND LOCAL SOCIAL STUDIES CONTROVERSIES

Since the failure of the NSH, SEAs are tasked with writing and overseeing their state standards. In some states, the process has unfolded smoothly, but in others, conflicts have arisen over the standards—particularly social studies. For example, in 1995 Virginia summoned more than fifty educators, teachers, and state academics to replace the 1980 social studies standards. The committee's first draft received some criticism that it resembled the NSH standards. Yet, the most vocal complaints claimed "the social studies standards were politically-driven and ill-founded academically" based on a conservative mindset.[33]

Virginia responded by appointing a smaller group tasked with revising/creating a new nonpolitical set of social studies standards. This smaller group incorporated state politicians to guarantee accuracy and clarity with less inclusion of academics or teacher input. Upon the release of the second draft, state educators critiqued the standards for content and skills; yet few revisions were undertaken, and the standards were adopted. After a few years, these standards will be revised with less controversy and a few updates. With each revision, the controversy becomes less and less. This tends to be the typical pattern for social studies standards in many states.

Texas created its own unique path. Texas had adopted a set of standards under Governor Bush as part of the Texas miracle with plans to revise those standards every ten years. The standards came up for re-examination in 2009, when a team of teachers and state educators drafted revisions to the 1998 standards. Upon completion, a committee of six expert examiners appointed by the State Board of Education (SBOE) reviewed the revisions. These experts included two historians, a geography expert, a legal scholar, and two ministers.[34] When the SBOE opened discussion of these standards in a public debate overseen by fifteen state politicians, a firestorm erupted, surely an outcome that could have been anticipated.

There was an element of liberal versus conservative discussion over the standards, but the standards were really caught in a fight between Christian conservatives and more moderate conservatives.[35] Norma Gabler, the conservative education advocate from MACOS, testified at the hearings that Texas social studies standards must incorporate conservative ideals, otherwise students will continue to learn historical inaccuracies.[36] The committee listened to the influential Gabler and revised the standards. An SBOE member conflated history and religion as a united field within the new standards, demanding that America must be seen only as a Christian nation.[37]

Reactions to the hearings were intense, not only within the state but nationally and internationally as well. A university educator acknowledged that the standards did improve by being more inclusive of minorities: "the overwhelming voting power of SBOE conservatives imprinted these standards with too many fundamental errors."[38] The NAACP pointed out that the standards reverted to a 1940s version of history that indoctrinated students to a contrived history prior to the Civil Rights movement.[39] In other words, they infused history with a neo-confederate take on early American history and a return to the lost cause myth of the Civil War.[40]

The fate of the Texas standards is far more significant than "one more state culture war." Since Texas public schools are the biggest market for textbooks, this is also a cultural war for nearly all other states.[41] Most textbook companies use a master textbook based on their largest market and supplement their master textbook with each state's unique criteria. Consequently, Texas textbook standards greatly influence the textbooks for other states regardless of the standards those other states employ. In 2020, the *New York Times* evaluated two popular textbooks, one from Texas and another from California. Both textbooks were from the same publisher and credited the same authors, yet there were some significant differences.[42]

Aside from the large cultural debates, some textbook debates are more localized as happened with the Hindu controversy of 2005.[43] Two Hindu religious groups used the California revision process to *correct* facts about Hinduism and Indian history; however, the new information contradicted generally established literature in order to support the perspectives of the religious groups themselves.[44] These Hindu religious groups requested that their interpretation of history be imposed on the understanding of Indian history. Further, critics compared these Hindu religious attitudes and tactics with Christian-right attitudes and tactics towards social studies curriculum.[45] Ten years later, the same conflict reemerged over the same issues in California. Even when controversies die down, they tend to flare back up. Controversy is not limited to political leanings; religion and other social markers can also have significant influence on what content should or should not be included in social studies.

In another example, the McMinn County School Board in Tennessee had recently changed curriculum providers that used *Maus* curricula, a Pulitzer Prize–winning graphic novel, as part of their instruction on the Holocaust. They then made the decision to remove *Maus* from its eighth-grade curriculum. The school board further examined the curriculum beyond the Holocaust educational materials. This action aligned with a Tennessee law to prohibit materials that could make someone uncomfortable with content based on race or sex.[46]

Several teachers admitted that the banning of *Maus* caused them to worry about which topics they were allowed to discuss in the classroom. For social studies, the question of relevance to student learning is now in question. If this was an isolated incident, the fear would not capture national attention. But just like the Kanawa fight in the 1970s, this incident made national news. State legislatures lined up to either ban books or prevent the banning of books.[47] Teachers find themselves stuck in the middle. Comparisons could be made to the 1920s Butler Act and the subsequent Scopes trial over evolution in Tennessee schools.

Unsurprisingly, in this digital age, controversy is not limited to standards or textbooks. In a surprising announcement, H-Net's High School Social Studies blog announced that Boston Public School (BPS) had given "pink notices" to the district's history and social science administrators and curriculum coaches.[48] BPS planned to reorganize and eliminate history and social sciences departments, which were to be consumed by its English/language arts department. Thenceforth, social studies teachers would have to teach English, and language arts teachers would also teach social studies content. Social studies would cease to be a core academic discipline in Boston schools.

As the news filtered along the internet, the National Coalition for History (NCH) wrote to the interim superintendent, expressing its concern about using history "as easy targets for budget cuts."[49] NCH urged Boston to find other ways to cut their budget. The National Council for History Education picked up the story and published it in their *History Matters!* newsletter. On May 23, 2014, the interim superintendent addressed the issue by stating that Boston was not eliminating the social studies department.[50] History, language arts, and foreign languages were being merged under a new "humanities umbrella." The intent was for more cross-curricular planning of materials among the three departments. The story turned out to be false, yet educators rightly believed that the elimination of social studies could happen in any district with little warning. Kerry Dunne noted that the new head of the humanities umbrella did not have to hold a history licensure or have any history teaching experience.[51]

Over the last fifteen years, controversies over social studies have become more commonplace than just the few mentioned here. Some other examples include the second Hindu Controversy in California during 2016–2017; Pasco County (Tampa) arguments over new elementary social studies materials in 2012; the AP US history framework revisions sparked conflicts between students and a local Colorado school board; and Virginia's depiction of slavery in an elementary textbook. These do not include the ferocious debates that ensue whenever social studies standards come up for revision or update, including Minnesota (2003); Wisconsin (2013); Michigan (2015); Tennessee (2017); Hawaii (2017); and Texas (2022).

One of the most recent social studies controversies concerns PragerU, a conservative media company. PragerU started disseminating social studies education videos to SEAs, implying that they were an accredited institution of higher learning. Upon the discovery that they were not, the company simply responded by stating that their company promotes pro-American values. Several states backed away from use of these videos; however, in July 2023, the Florida Department of Education approved the use of their videos as supplemental K-12 materials. PragerU is an example of the recent polarization within American politics. This political polarization eventually evolved into the most recent culture war that launched in 2019.

1619 VERSUS 1776 CULTURE WAR

In 2019, the *New York Times Magazine* published a series of articles organized by Nikole Hannah-Jones that reexamined four hundred years of African American contributions in America. The *1619 Project* kicked off "a political firestorm" across America.[52] The most controversial aspect of the project is the assertation that America's origins should start with the introduction of slaves to Jamestown in 1619. According to another *New York Times* reporter, Hannah-Jones' assertions are significant because she stresses the "inextricable" nature of slavery to America's development.[53]

The *1619 Project* did not introduce any new theories regarding race; it simply brought older theories to the forefront. The political left saw this project as a major step forward in the conversation over race and inequality in America. Historians criticized Hannah-Jones's claim that colonists wanted to declare their independence to protect slavery.[54] Nevertheless, the popularity of the issue was extreme. Some teachers even sought resources that the Pulitzer Center provided for teacher's use at their discretion.

Despite wide interest in parts of society, national attention was on other issues than the publications of the *New York Times*. However, public attention shifted in the late spring of 2020. The world struggled amid the COVID-19 pandemic lockdown, which dramatically highlighted racial and economic disparities in America. Schools across the country shut down, and students were forced to finish the school year online. This shutdown highlighted the inequities among school districts. As suburban students quickly transitioned to online formats, rural, urban, and poorer districts struggled to transition due to issues of access.[55] Discussions about how to address these issues were shared, yet nothing could be done in the middle of the pandemic. Researchers are only now beginning to measure the impacts on student learning from the shutdown.

In any case, after two months in virtual lockdown, a police stop in Minneapolis, Minnesota, went terribly wrong. A police officer knelt on an African American, George Floyd, until he stopped breathing. The dissemination of a bystander's video sparked a national discussion about race and police abuse. The discussion spilled into demonstrations and protests across the United States.[56] These demonstrations utilized the language of the *1619 Project*, thus returning Hannah-Jones's articles to national attention.

Across the country, the surrogate for the *1619 Project* became the legal theoretical framework called Critical Race Theory (CRT). CRT is a framework that explains how laws and societal institutions are used to protect the advantages of a privileged class (white America) while ignoring the needs of minorities and other economically disadvantaged groups.[57] According to the Brookings Institute, concern for CRT arises because critics have portrayed CRT as all whites are oppressors while all minorities (particularly black America) are "hopelessly oppressed victims."[58]

President Donald Trump ordered the formation of the *1776 Commission* to counter the *1619 Project*, which he asserts "has vilified our Founders and our founding."[59] The Commission first addressed the founding principles of America. The founding principles begin with the adoption of the Declaration of Independence.[60] Throughout their report, the Commission stresses its desire to teach American children "accurate history" of the founding principles. The eighteen members of the Commission were picked not for their academic knowledge, but instead for their political leanings. Only one historian was on the Commission, with his specialty in ancient military history. The Commission was disbanded on President Joe Biden's first day in office.

Congress unexpectedly launched itself into the discussion during the summer of 2021. Sen. Tom Cotton (R-AR) introduced a bill, the *Saving American History Act*, that would prevent any federal funds from going to schools that utilized any part of the *1619 Project* or its theories (CRT). He and Rep. Ken Buck (R-CO) then addressed a letter to American parents about their concern that four thousand American classrooms were using the *1619 Project* as their curriculum.[61] The political right believed that this Project was pure propaganda designed to further polarize America.

Conservatives further claimed that CRT advocates were fomenting discord among society by creating ethnic instability.[62] In one interpretation, a reporter examining the data from a single survey conducted in Minneapolis-area schools in the aftermath of the George Floyd incident,[63] concluded that there must be at least 150,000 middle- and high-school teachers around the nation using CRT in their classroom. Fear that social studies teachers were teaching this highly inflammatory curriculum was rampant. The debate moved into the states and into SEAs. State legislatures passed laws to prevent the teaching of anything related to the *1619 Project*. More than twenty-two states initiated renewed evaluation of standards to guarantee that CRT was not in the state standards, especially in the fields of social studies. Yet, regardless of the state standards, state legislatures were still concerned that K-12 teachers were widely teaching CRT in their classrooms. In all, thirty-six states passed laws banning the teaching of CRT in schools.[64]

The debates over CRT did not simply end at the state level nor at the racial component. Pennridge School District outside Philadelphia adopted an ultra-conservative curriculum for the 2023–2024 school year based on the *1776 Commission* report.[65] In Beaufort County, North Carolina, parents urged the local school board to ban the textbook, not just because of the CRT curriculum, but also because it discussed LGBTQ issues. When the school board decided to adopt a new social studies curriculum, a special bill was introduced to the state legislature to authorize it.[66]

The connection between CRT and LGBTQ issues has become more commonplace because conservatives see both issues as an effort to force people to accept diversity. In California, Temecula Valley Unified school board rejected the new *Social Studies Alive* textbook because they believed it promoted LGBTQ issues. They favored a return to a seventeen-year-old textbook over a state-approved textbook that conforms with the latest state standards.[67] They could not necessarily prove that the new textbook was attempting LGBTQ issues, they just felt like it must.

Governor Rick DeSantis not only got the Florida legislature to ban CRT, he also convinced them to pass the "Don't Say Gay" law forbidding the discussion of LGBTQ in Florida schools. In January 2024, DeSantis eliminated sociology from the core curriculum of Florida universities due to the leftist leanings of sociologists. Students at Florida universities are required to take "a factual history course" instead.[68] The disciplines are starting to see some of the devaluing of their subjects. Over the last thirty years, educational reformers have used the mantra of data-driven reform. With each controversy, fear drives curricular decisions instead of data.

A common connection among all of these conservative furors has been Hillsdale College, a Christian Liberal Arts College located in Michigan. In recent years, the college has been active in various political circles, especially in the promotion of their version of civic education. Several states requested Hillsdale's assistance in reviewing textbooks and revising their state's curriculum to remove all traces of CRT.[69] The chairman of the *1776 Commission*, Larry Arn, was president of Hillsdale College. The conservative curriculum presented by the Commission was generated at Hillsdale College and distributed by its alumni. Concern over the influence of liberal institutions has been a common part of the culture wars, yet few people have shown the same concern about the influence of conservative institutions on the culture wars.

In terms of its impact on social studies standards, an examination of the recent South Dakota social studies process sheds some light upon this latest culture war. In 2021, South Dakota started the process of revising their social studies standards. The effort progressed like other revisions processes, beginning with a review of the six-year-old standards by about fifty educators in South Dakota. The committee then divided into smaller working groups to focus on more manageable standards.

The world history working group, composed of four members, was required to train on the C3 framework in order to incorporate it into the their draft standards.[70] This working group made three alterations to the world history standards: aligning the language with C3 framework, updating the language to the current literature, and developing new standards to represent underrepresented groups, specifically indigenous groups.[71] This last addition was designed to incorporate a 2018 state legislative recommendation on the inclusion of "indigenous culture in South Dakota" education.[72]

Then the SEA reviewed the various working group's drafts. They made no significant changes. Ten days after the final approval of the working group, the SEA published a "heavily altered document containing numerous changes that did not come from the world history work group members."[73] This was not the typical revision process. In the world history standards, the changes included the elimination of the C3 framework language, the addition of several new standards that focused on US history, and the removal of discussion on indigenous cultures.

The revisions soon became a political debate within the state. Multiple South Dakota organizations and groups condemned Gov. Kristi Noem and demanded a return to the working group's original standards. Stanley Kurtz, a national conservative commentator, decried Noem for mishandling the revision process by letting leftists co-opt the process.[74] She announced her intention to start fresh with new standards in 2022. In January, she announced a new fifteen-member standards commission to oversee the entire new social studies standards, not only world history. The members of the commission included three teachers (although one taught in Nebraska); Noem's chief of staff as chairman; the state historian; a tribal leader; the state director of Indian Education; two state legislators; the director of South Dakota's Catholic Conference; a director of a retirement home; a professor; a former military supervisor; and a former teacher who works in the banking industry.[75] This group did not draft new standards. They held four hearings on the new standards to gather public feedback.

Gov. Noem contracted professor emeritus William Morrisey to write her new social studies standards. The *Dakota Free Press*, a self-labelled liberal media, compared the contracts between the original committee and Morrisey. They concluded Morrisey's contract was vague on the deliverables and exhibited far less concern about the development.[76] Noem provided Morrisey more leeway to craft his standards based on his own personal and political interpretations. Morrisey himself was a professor at Hillsdale College. An appointee, liberal or conservative, is not uncommon. Yet the fact that Morrisey did not reside in South Dakota raised questions about the political motivation of the governor's office among educators.

Commentators noted the influence of Hillsdale College "Western Heritage" curriculum on the standards. Additionally, several mainstream media outlets started looking at the new commission. The media focused on the lack of educators. Dylan Kessler, the retirement center director, had graduated from Hillsdale College. Nearly all the commission's members were Republican party officials at some point, or, at the very least, notable Republican donors. The political impression was evident to various groups.

The South Dakota Superintendents Association as well as all nine tribal communities formally voted to oppose the social studies standards. The South Dakota Education Association pointed out that the commission and board "chose to ignore the educators, parents and community leaders of South Dakota who were almost unanimous in their opposition."[77] Several national organizations condemned the standards, including the AHA and several national Native organizations. The only national organization to commend the standards was the National Association of Scholars. Even Kurtz, who originally criticized Noem, admitted that the original standards were "actually very excellent," just not in line with conservative interpretations.[78]

The new standards sought to create a direct link between world history and the foundation of US history, including Native American history. The standards were designed to limit the influence of progressive educators and "left wing conspiracies everywhere."[79] Many educators were concerned about the overreliance on memorization and retelling of events, both of which are classified as low-level thinking skills.[80] Teachers began to worry about the access to resources, especially for AP classes, where standards from the College Board conflict with the South Dakota standards.[81] The culture wars continued and, as in other states, there appears to be no end in sight.

IMPLICATIONS

NCLB did not arise out of nothingness; it evolved out of federal involvement in public education. More to the point, NCLB did not make the federal government the final arbiter in the testing and standards debate. State governments decided the standards and criteria for AYP. SEAs used NCLB to wrestle control away from local districts with a carrot-and-stick approach (money and threats).[82] For twenty years, states used the NCLB/Every Student Succeeds Act (President Obama's reauthorization of NCLB) to control education policy. Yet, when federal accountability tried to hold states accountable, SEA insisted that the requirements were too strict. Looking at more recent conflicts, local school boards have used the same logic upon the SEAs to shake state control.

Regardless of who controls educational policy, standards are viewed as essential to the curriculum. SEAs assess those standards whether local districts adopt them or not. Now, a standardized testing culture exists within education. According to scholars, the standardized testing culture narrowly focuses the curriculum to measure "discrete pieces of information from an assumed uniform curriculum."[83] Further, the standardized testing culture changes teacher instruction methods, narrows the curriculum, and ignores the lowest and highest achieving students.[84]

For social studies, some scholars advocate the inclusion of social studies in the testing culture, while other scholars point out the very real advantages to remaining outside the testing culture. One way or the other, inclusion in the testing culture means that school districts cannot simply ignore social studies. About five years after NCLB, teachers and scholars started commenting on a perceived trend, especially in elementary education, where social studies was being marginalized.[85] Marginalization became an accepted aspect of social studies education for the subsequent ten years.

In educational research, the focus upon mathematics, reading, and science is evident when considering funding availabilities for those area's research ventures; social studies receives less concern among researchers because it has been marginalized in a test-heavy educational environment.[86] The initial conclusion of marginalization was that the only way to bring value back to social studies was to get social studies to be part of the testing culture.[87] A push for standards ensued, but not for social studies standards, for discipline standards instead. During a review of the Kentucky accountability system, evaluators noted that the major benefit and problem with content standards is the same: advocates are passionate about their content, and this seems especially true for history.[88]

States gather experts in their fields, often university professors from the field, yet should the states gather experts from among historians, from certain disciplines, or from all social studies disciplines? Individual disciplines within social studies promoted their own importance by devaluing social studies as an umbrella discipline, but by devaluing social studies, the disciplines also devalued any content associated with social studies. Without a generally unified field, discipline standards then competed against one another for resources and curricular time. This lesson should have been gleaned from the origins of social studies as a field a hundred years prior.

By the time Common Core became policy, the requirement that social studies have their own standards had been eliminated in favor of literacy standards. Even the discipline standards were subjugated into literacy standards. Literacy standards are acceptable for basic standards, but they do not address the purpose of social studies or the critical skills it teaches.[89] In fact, literacy standards are the opposite of most social studies standards that rely too much on content: CCSS-ELA standards rely solely on literacy skills.[90] The researchers who wanted social studies to be a part of testing culture might have had a point.

Other scholars viewed the exclusion of social studies from testing culture to be a good thing for the field. While they liked the creation of discipline standards, they believed that testing those standards would narrow the curriculum too much.[91] Teachers in non-tested states believed that they possessed more freedom to teach their discipline rather than holding to the standards.[92] If you do not test a subject, do states need to develop standards for that content? One way or another, standards are often developed in an ideal world with a dedication to content over skills.

Discipline standards soon lost the purpose of preparing citizens. Researchers sought to investigate student understanding of historical thinking rather than questions of citizenship.[93] Some teachers do focus on citizen education, yet they are often punished because high-stakes testing culture goes against their democratic pedagogy, especially in issue-centered curriculums.[94] Levinson believes that standards, assessments, and accountability help to foster the democratic character within education by establishing a system of checks on citizenship education.[95] Education is the core of *civic empowerment* that needs mechanisms to maintain oversight over the educational system. Yet, one aspect that Levinson did not predict in his vision was the polarization of American politics.

The polarization of politics in American society has had an immense influence on social studies education as multiculturalists argue for more inclusion of America's past sins while equally politically charged groups argue for an ideological agenda that imposes a WASP image on America.[96] Loveless implies that debates about content and pedagogy have been limited to schools of education and only occasionally appear in public forums.[97] The change happened when accountability allowed the public to track schools and measure if teachers are performing their duties of educating American youth. Educators bemoan the unintended consequences of large-scale assessments, especially of the narrowing of the curriculum, yet for their part, parents and politicians do not seem to criticize the narrowing of the curriculum.[98]

In the period between NCLB and Common Core, a first-year social studies teacher was called to the principal's office. The principal informed the teacher that she had gotten a call from a parent. The parent demanded to know why this teacher was imposing college-level material on her sixth-grade child. The teacher questioned which material was too advanced for his students. Handing a worksheet over, the principal demanded an explanation. Neither she nor the student's parents could explain the economic theory about levels of production. Certainly, a sixth-grader should not be exposed to such advanced material either. The teacher scrutinized the worksheet; he had definitely assigned it. He thought that it was advanced, but he found it in the textbook's instructional material. Further, he pulled up the state social studies standards for sixth grade and pointed to where it specifically required sixth-graders to learn this concept. The principal's response was, "Oh." By the end of the year, this teacher had moved on from the district.

This story highlights several problems for this age of accountability. Social studies standards contain a plethora of content and very little concern for skills. More troubling, the justification for the content does not always make sense to the stakeholders. Administrators themselves are rarely content experts, nor are they experts on the standards. The increasing involvement of parents as advocates has also become more significant. Whether for good or for ill, this increasing involvement can allow a small group to impose their personal ideology upon local curriculum. Finally, the goals of social studies are so scattered that any content can be deemed relevant, whether or not it achieves the learning outcomes for social studies. This is the problem that our unfortunate first-year teacher failed to understand.

Chapter 11

The Nation's Report Card

How do we as Americans guarantee student learning? It's simple: graduation. Students complete materials, teachers grade materials and, after thirteen years, students graduate. Accountability is not this simple, though. From the creation of the first school districts in America, districts wanted to guarantee that their students were learning the material and that their students were better than other school districts.[1] With the rise of *social efficiency* models, districts found ways to guarantee student learning. This guarantee of learning is associated with the business-minded goal of making America economically dominant.[2] Simply put, accountability is guaranteeing that money spent on education is achieving the goals of producing effective citizen workers for American business.

FEDERAL ACCOUNTABILITY BEGINS

The federal government began storing educational data as far back as 1867. Most of the information was general and not used for any discernable purpose. For nearly one hundred years, the federal government simply deposited the information into a warehouse. In 1963, John Gardner, cofounder of the Carnegie Corporation, was approached by US Commissioner of Education Francis Keppel to determine a way to measure education at a national level.[3] The Carnegie Corporation sponsored a committee headed by Ralph W. Tyler, director of Stanford's Center for Advanced Study of Behavioral Sciences, that would develop a national testing program.[4]

The Tyler Committee, including educators, curriculum specialists, and local administrators, set to work on a plan. They focused on skills in reading, writing, science, mathematics, social studies, citizenship, art, music, literature, and vocational education, drawing up objectives for each.[5] Tyler wanted to use the objectives and the measurement device to guide educational policy. The Committee was very aware that their small budget and size could not be replicated at a national level and that the federal government would need to take over at some point.

President Johnson's *War on Poverty*, which included education, provided the impetus for changing the Tyler Committee's theoretical work into a reality. The cornerstone of federal education policy for the last sixty years, the Elementary and Secondary Education Act (ESEA), included language to initiate a federal program to track education, specifically the achievement gaps. Today, the National Assessment of Educational Progress (NAEP), also known as the Nation's Report Card, dates its origin to ESEA.

The Department of Education saw the potential for the NAEP. For Tyler, he envisioned the national assessment as an educational census to inform policymakers. The national assessment would remain a low-stakes longitudinal assessment to track educational trends on skills over content.[6] Richard Jaeger, chief of Evaluation Design in Bureau of Elementary and Secondary Education, stated that the national assessment would "provide needed information for all of these decision makers."[7] Some of the original concern over the NAEP was whether it was a back door into establishing a national curriculum.[8] Yet, as long as schools, districts, and states demonstrated educational attainments over the cycles of the NAEP, federal dollars continued to flow.

In 1967, the Education Commission of the States (ECS), a nonprofit organization set up by Carnegie Corporation and former North Carolina governor Terry Sanford to advise educational policy, took over ownership of the Tyler Committee's work. Keeping with Tyler's vision, the assessment did not rely upon only multiple-choice questions but incorporated free response, short answer, and even group work.[9] Additionally, ECS prevented student, school, district, or state-level data sharing because NAEP would be a national snapshot of education. Finally, ECS encouraged teacher and education organizations to evaluate the NAEP to improve its focus as well as to provide assistance to local districts.[10]

In 1969, the first tests covered fourth-, eighth-, and twelfth-graders' knowledge of science, writing, and citizenship (see appendix C). About the first NAEP results, Jaeger stated that "State and Federal program managers must know the extent to which specifically needed services are being adequately provided and efficiently directed."[11] Then, every year, the NAEP would cycle through assessments of different subjects and skills. For example, in 1974, the Department of Education assessed student understanding of career development skills, and in another year, they measured basic learning skills. Some tests were repeated; some were done once and never repeated.

For the first ten years, ECS controlled the process and the assessment. The ECS was viewed as a trusted organization of state leaders who did not interfere with state education policy. Then, in the mid-1970s, congressional pushback sought the creation of an Assessment Policy Committee (APC) composed of state leaders and educators. The APC was given more authority over the NAEP in that they were to determine the objectives, select the questions, decide the methodology, and evaluate the data, which proved to be a significant amount of work for part-time committee members who had other responsibilities.[12] So the APC did not live up to the wishes of Congress.

For social studies, one of the first tests was citizenship. Citizenship covered "knowledges from the civics-political science areas and also includes a goodly portion of exercises covering citizenship behavior" that were "so crucial in our present society" that it needed to be evaluated separate from social studies.[13] The focus was not simply on political content knowledge. The assessors wanted to know whether students could address "ethical principles and interpersonal behaviors that . . . comprised democratic citizenship."[14] They were interested in the skills that made a *good* citizen.

As with any area associated with social studies, the Department of Education did "not create a precise definition of citizenship" that would align the tasks with the desired learning outcomes.[15] The Department of Education fell into the trap that social studies had fallen into in 1916—no clear definition for their stated purpose. Also, if it was separate from social studies, how would the testing for social studies differ? ECS encouraged the National Council for the Social Studies (NCSS) to conduct their own validity analysis of the citizenship objectives and assessment; they concluded that the major flaw in the NAEP objectives was that they wanted to measure how students were *good* citizens without defining what constituted *good*.[16]

In 1970, the Department of Education planned to measure social studies. Before they administered the test, the social studies objectives were deemed unacceptable. Of the ten tested areas, social studies was the only set of objectives that had to be redesigned.[17] Finally, in 1971, a social studies assessment was administered. The initial assessments for the ten areas were to serve as a baseline for future assessments.

As part of the evaluation process, NCSS generated a report on the citizenship and social studies assessments. While most of the criticism focused on citizenship, social studies had issues as well.[18] Professor Fair reconsidered the issue of whether social studies and citizenship should be linked.

> Much can be said in favor of two assessments rather than one focused on an area of critical yet controversial importance. Many will support the idea that citizenship is the responsibility of the school as a whole, not merely programs in social studies, or even that citizenship is as much the responsibility of out-of-school

institutions. But if social studies education can be thought of as emphasizing what is less likely to be learned informally in the culture at large, it can hardly be conceived as something without integral relation to individual lives and the requirements of society. Nor can citizenship be defensibly conceived as social participation without thought or knowledge. Neither is it sensible to think of citizenship as primarily political and social studies nonpolitical. Issues of distinction, overlap and emphasis are difficult to resolve.[19]

The issue of the relationship between history and the other social science disciplines arose in a fashion similar to the "New" social studies movement. Social scientists had attempted to divest themselves of citizen education as its only purpose while attempting to find a purpose in understanding man's relationship with society (see MACOS). Looking back, the removal of civic education from social studies left the field directionless.

Due to congressional interference and financial constraints on the Department of Education, the ten fields were condensed to five fields, with social studies and citizenship being merged into a single test. Why even include social studies since it duplicated the work of the citizenship assessment? The justification for social studies became the need to read charts. So, in 1976, the NAEP administered a citizenship/social studies assessment that was considerably smaller than the earlier ones.[20] However, the citizenship and social studies objectives remained separate, and they were measured independently.

Making comparisons between the first and second NAEP, the Department of Education pointed out that student understanding of national and international events remained strong. In terms of results, the general knowledge of students declined compared to the knowledge seen in the first assessments. Student understanding of governmental processes declined, but awareness of international affairs remained high. On a positive note, the results demonstrated a continual positive attitudinal shift towards other ethnic groups.[21] The results aligned with the results discovered in other assessments as well.

By the 1980s, the Department of Education was under siege from President Reagan. The National Center for Education Statistics (NCES), the official division within the Department of Education, conducted another citizenship/social studies assessment. This time the objectives were merged together.[22] The assessment was further reduced. For example, the testing of fourth-graders focused on social studies objectives with little examination of political rights and governmental process. The findings parallelled the NAEP findings in other areas that showed affluent students above the national average and lower socio-economic and minority students below the national average. Generally, the questions centered on attitudinal changes and student understanding of the political process. Even though the test changed over its three iterations, the types of exercises and focus keep the validity of its analysis intact.

Looking back at the NAEP and social studies over this period, the parallels became more evident. At first citizenship and social studies were separate, but by the end they were merged into a single vision. Like the "New" social studies movement, skills were a focus over content. The purpose was to see how students actually practiced citizenship, for if they practiced it then they were assumed to be *good* citizens. In terms of the federal role connected to social studies, the government allowed educators to determine direction, yet when questions arose, Congress tended to force change.

CHANGES INTRODUCED TO THE NAEP AND SOCIAL STUDIES

In the 1980s, the NAEP became a major focus of educational reflection. As noted above, President Reagan entered office with plans to eliminate the Department of Education (including NAEP), yet surveys conducted at the time showed a perceived lack of confidence in the local schools. Funds for NAEP had consistently fallen since the early 1970s from a high of $7 million in 1973 to $4 million in 1981.[23] As a consequence, NCES initiated its own evaluation of whether the NAEP had outlived its purpose and should be discontinued.[24] The following year, *A Nation at Risk* altered not only President Reagan's desire to end federal financial support for education but also the philosophical attitudes towards federal education policy.

The findings of its evaluation showed that the NAEP was underutilized. It demonstrated how "high quality assessment programs" could be linked to state and local standards.[25] Wirtz and Lapointe suggested that to better utilize the NAEP, Congress would need to change the organizational structure of process.[26] In 1984, state governors narrowly approved the release of state-level data where the general public could now compare state educational progress with other state educational policy.[27] While the state-level comparisons would lead to a change in overall leadership in the NAEP, the ECS and APC would not survive the shift in philosophy and were officially replaced in 1989 by the National Assessment Governing Board (NAGB). This shift in attitudes in the NAEP coincided with the rise of the national standards movement within educational organizations.

The most significant change came in the analysis of the NAEP. The original contract for the design and analysis of the NAEP shifted away from the ECS and went to a private organization, Educational Testing Service (ETS), which currently still holds the NAEP contract.[28] ETS was chosen due to their extensive experience with large-scale assessments, including the operation of the SAT (under the College Board) and total control over the GRE and National Teachers Examination. In many ways, ETS influenced two of the major national assessments with the SAT and the NAEP. Further, they had a vision for the NAEP; it should not be just another census report, but rather "a useful policy tool in the future" for the growing need for accountability.[29]

ETS introduced several new concepts: in statistical analysis, they revised the sampling and measurement theory; they introduced Item Response Theory (IRT), which permitted scaling due to exercise and sampling; and they suggested the increase of the frequency of the four key subjects: writing, mathematics, reading, and science.[30] Finally, ETS further expanded the additional information about the students, teachers, and schools.

Changes were made not only in the administration of the NAEP; social studies had its own philosophical shift as well. The Educational Excellence Network,[31] based at Vanderbilt University, proposed using the NAEP apparatus to measure student cultural literacy. Chester Finn and Diane Ravitch, co-directors of the Educational Excellence Network, received a grant from the National Endowment for the Humanities (NEH), then headed by William Bennett, to fund the Foundations of Literacy Project. The APC considered both sides of whether to accept this offer. The decision was informed by "a growing national concern that a number of young Americans lacked rudimentary knowledge of U.S. history and literature," and thus they permitted this one off-cycle series of assessments.[32]

Finn and Ravitch sought to demonstrate high school student knowledge in literature and US history with the stated purpose of gathering "information about basic knowledge in U.S. history and literature in a fair, accurate, and replicable process and to make it available in an accessible, intelligible form to prospective users."[33] The Foundations of Literacy Project did not claim to determine if those two areas were taught well, rather it claimed that they could determine how well students were prepared to be American citizens. They talked about the myth that social studies advocates want social science concepts, where they believe that history does not simply rely upon facts but can blend facts with concepts better than social studies.

The US history and literature assessments were a departure from established practices in several ways. First, the test focused only on seventeen-year-olds (eleventh-graders). The rationale was that the Foundations of Literacy Project wanted to see whether students had learned enough to possess "rudimentary knowledge" of the American citizenship canon.[34] Thus, the NAEP did not assess students at different levels for the first time. Second, Finn and Ravitch expanded the core background surveys to gain insight into the understanding of citizenship and cultural competence. They included survey questions about influences in the home, community, and the school. The APC decided to accept these core background questions and then utilize them in the four other NAEP assessments being administered that same year. Third, the objectives and questions for these two assessments were left for the Foundations of Literacy Project to determine. As requested by APC, five education/field experts were tasked with designing the objectives and questions for each test, then their draft was reviewed by a variety of experts.[35] The questions were limited only to knowledge content due to the nature of the grant given to the foundation. Unlike the other NAEP assessments, which consisted of diverse types of exercises including open response and short answers, the history and literature assessments were limited to multiple-choice questions.

Finally, upon the completion of the 1986 testing cycle, Finn and Ravitch analyzed and published their findings not as the typical NCES report, but as a book, *What Do Our 17-Year-Olds Know? A Report on the First National Assessment of History and Literature*. They declared that most eleventh-graders were culturally illiterate based on the NAEP results. Further, basic knowledge in both literature and history was far below the acceptable level even though that level was not defined. Similar to the *New York Times* survey in the 1940s, the Foundations of Literacy Project proved their hypothesis by providing the necessary instrument to validate their point. Additionally, the NAEP was not used as a census report to track the trend lines; it was used to make a statement about whether students possessed a common "American" knowledge.

Whereas the literature assessment did not have a life after 1986, the US history assessment was administered again in the 1988 cycle. During the planning of the 1988 US history assessment, one of the learning-area group members stated that they reviewed previous social studies assessments. The group member noted "two [sic] exams were entirely different from each other and were entirely different from" the assessment designed in 1988.[36] The group noted that the social studies assessments did not examine history, rather they measured whether students conducted themselves in accordance with the "right behavior as a citizen in America."[37] So, the focus on the new US history assessment was to measure student content knowledge deemed essential to be an American citizen, not whether students understood how to be a citizen. Ravitch and Finn repeatedly said that they wanted to evaluate students to see if they possessed a common knowledge of America's past. But they also inquired about student understanding of the Constitution, the Bill of Rights, and other mechanisms of government that are not historical objectives and instead belong to another social science discipline.

In addition to the US history assessment, the NCES administered their first civics assessment. Ironically, the civics assessment bridged back to the citizenship assessments of 1969, 1976, and 1981 and thus could be used to follow an educational trend line.[38] The Learning Area Committee that oversaw the objectives and questions for the US history and civics assessments were the same committee with "a parallel civics knowledge" that influenced the US history assessment; they even admitted that the focus tended to be on political history.[39] So, why did NCES use two assessments if they had the same committee creating similar assessments?

Following the example of the Foundation of Literacy Project, the National Geographic Society funded a NAEP assessment of twelfth-graders on geography.[40] Like US history, the geography assessment became part of the random rotation of assessments going forward. Due to the funding model, the assessment design for geography relied on only multiple-choice questions. Because NCES now fully supported the US history and civics assessments, these assessments conformed to a more traditional format of including open-ended items as well as multiple-choice questions.

Looking back at this period, the philosophical changes to the NAEP parallelled the shifts in attitudes about education. NCES needed to "adopt a more dynamic and more flexible approach both to its purpose and to its procedures."[41] There was a drastic shift not only in the NAEP but also in social studies. *What Do Our 17-Year-Olds Know?* was a significant shift in social studies similar to the impact of *A Nation at Risk* for education. Ravitch and Finn were able to eliminate social studies as a tested subject and replace it with history: their vision of history that projected a cultural indoctrination form of citizenship. As soon as history established itself as a distinct discipline, several other disciplines followed their example.

AGE OF ACCOUNTABILITY: SOCIAL STUDIES

One of the major problems with the ECS/APC model was that the committees were voluntary and offered little compensation. When the NAGB took over the reins of overseeing the NAEP in 1989, funding for NAEP and NAGB increased dramatically. NAGB had a dedicated staff, and their appointments came from the Secretary of Education. After the initial appointment, the NAGB nominated candidates from whom the Secretary would then choose appointees.[42] The major impetus for the creation of the NAGB was the desire for state-level comparisons on the NAEP.[43] Initially, the desire was to align the NAEP to developing national standards so that state-to-state comparison could be easily conducted. However, with the demise of national standards, the NAGB initiated a form of their own standards that they called the NAEP frameworks. One theory is that these frameworks would become de facto standards.

Like educational policy, which is influenced by local, state, and federal levels of government, the NAEP has more than one master. The NAGB, NCES, and ETS all influence the assessment in the framework, design, format, and dissemination of the information. Even though the NAGB is nominally in control, they neither design the test nor oversee its implementation. NCES does not determine the student learning outcomes (framework) but must create questions to measure them. ETS conducts the administrative and analysis portion, but they do not control the content or questions. Nevertheless, this is the system that currently runs the NAEP, with no one in total control and each influencing the process.

Since the shift to focusing upon specific disciplines rather than upon the broader umbrella of social studies in curriculum, the NAEP has followed a similar pattern. The NAGB felt the need to keep history as part of the NAEP assessment cycle because it believed history was the best way to measure the preparation of future citizens.[44] Former Assistant Secretary of Education over Assessment Chester Finn, the first chair of the NAGB, viewed US history as the avenue through which to understand citizenship. The importance of Finn is undeniable when it comes to the promotion of NAEP and standards, but he advocated disciplines over social studies.

Even though the NAGB advocated for state-to-state comparisons, they never conducted state-to-state comparisons with any of the social studies disciplines. In fact, the sampling of the states limits the size to about thirty-five to forty states during any given cycle. Hence, social studies did not warrant the state-to-state comparisons that NCES conducted for language arts, mathematics, or science.

During the middle of the 1990s cultural war, NAEP unveiled the framework for the 1994 US history assessment. The framework paralleled the NSH to a large degree, but no one criticized the NCES for its similarities.[45] In 1994, NCES conducted its first official NAEP-developed geography framework. Four years later, NCES measured civics using its new framework. The 1994/1998 assessments were considered the baseline for future assessments, so all the data gathered prior to 1994 was not included in the current trend lines.

As seen above, NCLB pressed Congress for a federal mandate to include history and civics standards, but these disciplines were not as critical as language arts, mathematics, or science. States began reporting that their students were learning more each year because test scores were going up, yet NAEP scores remained generally flat across the board.[46] At one point, President George W. Bush's Secretary of Education, Margaret Spellings, announced that NCLB was an education success story (2007), while in the same week the NCES released the recent trends from the US history and civics Nation's Report Card.[47] Both trend lines showed flatness or decreases in student learning for both disciplines. The impact of NCLB on social studies was not a trend upwards, but more like some disciplines being left behind. NCES does not speculate on why this is the trend; they simply state the facts as viewed from the data. One of the fallacies of testing is that *good* teachers raise test scores, and a *good* teacher is determined by improving test scores.[48] This is faulty logic.

The NAGB stated that they "sought breadth in the assessment schedule to the extent that assessments can be regularly administered and provide useful information to stakeholders"[49] In the run-up to the 2006 assessment cycle of US history and civics but not geography, the NAGB further determined to assess twelfth-grade students on their understanding of economics. Considering that economics courses are often limited to a single high school semester, the idea that NAEP needed to track them seemed a bit odd. No apparent justification from the NCES or the NAGB appears to explain why they made the decision in 2001 for an economics assessment. In the 2010 cycle, the NAGB brought back geography, along with US history and civics. Then, two years later, they assessed economics again. The results did not change significantly.

A pattern for social studies was emerging within the NAEP; the NCES assessed US history approximately every five years until the cycle became every four years. Civics went through long stretches in the 1990s and early 2000s but became part of the regular four-year cycle with US history. Geography was initially paired with US history, then replaced by civics, and finally brought back into the four-year cycle until discontinued in 2022 due to budgetary concerns. Economics has been administered only twice, with no current plans to administer it again (see appendix C).

In the early 2010s, the NAGB announced plans to introduce a world history assessment starting in the 2012 cycle along with the economics test, but that did not happen.[50] Then the world history assessment was tied to the US history, civics, and geography cycle in 2018, but again the NAGB changed its mind. Additionally, the NAGB determined that collecting data on fourth- and twelfth-graders in the social studies disciplines was not necessary. Starting in 2014, NCES collected data from only eighth-graders on US history, civics, and geography.

Lesley Muldoon, executive director of the NAGB, stated that "the value of a particular subject should not and does not depend on whether NAEP measures it."[51] The NAGB indicates that funding issues forced the cutting in 2018, but they had plans to assess the twelfth grade during the next cycle.[52] The NAGB did not include twelfth-graders in 2022. Director Muldoon did not understand the connection between elimination and value. As noted,

> Changes in the NAEP assessment schedule have significant educational implications because NAEP is used by many states, districts, and schools to establish policy (e.g., curriculum standards and graduation requirements) and to enact policy changes (e.g., course requirements, daily schedules, and time allocations

for subjects). Research trends suggest that testing practices are indicators of subject area priorities.⁵³

Social studies was even marginalized with regards to the NAEP. The NAGB marginalized social studies, and the national organizations did not even notice.

At the Fall 2023 meeting of the NAGB, their latest ten-year plan was unveiled. For social studies, they planned on assessing fourth- and twelfth-graders again but determined at the meeting to delete the fourth-grade assessment. Likewise, they are planning to introduce a full state-to-state comparison of US history and civics scores for the first time, but not until 2031 and then only for eighth-graders.⁵⁴ The first state-to-state comparisons were done in the 1990s in those valued subjects: reading, mathematics, science, and writing. Social studies is not important enough to test, but history has shown that many things can change in six years.

If budget concerns are a major obstacle for the NAEP, a return to social studies assessment could alleviate the problem. The science NAEP specifically divides content into three disciplines: physical, life, and earth/space sciences. The mathematics NAEP includes three disciplines: geometry, algebra, and statistics. So alternative solutions exist. The NAGB must have philosophical justification for assessing social studies in its specific disciplines instead of as a single field.

IMPLICATIONS

During the 1983 NAEP, students answered 60 percent of the questions correctly, implying a "certain common repertoire of knowledge" is generally apparent through the discipline.⁵⁵ This proves the broad appeal of consensus history within American schools in the late 1970s and early 1980s. Yet, since the redesign of the NAEP in the mid-1980s, student scores have remained flat with less than 50 percent considered proficient.

Since NCLB, both national political parties once again introduced legislation for some form of voluntary national standards in the form of the Standards to Provide Educational Achievement for All Kids (SPEAK) Act. This legislation was designed to encourage the NAGB to create voluntary national standards aligned with the NAEP.⁵⁶ Soon other groups (e.g., MacArthur and Gates Foundation) were advocating voluntary national standards in reading, mathematics, and science that were more rigorous than the ones created by individual states under NCLB.⁵⁷

In the most recent civics assessment, Johanek and Puckett discussed a noticeable achievement gap in the scores between whites and other minorities.[58] They noted that a part of the achievement gap might also be connected to the lack of relevance to those groups within the social studies curriculum. The desire of conservative groups to create patriotic citizens is challenging if all the examples are white males; the exclusion of other groups is problematic. The pedagogical argument for citizenship education has been to create patriotic citizens by teaching them but not engaging them.

How do stakeholders plan on measuring an effective civics program? One theory holds that the number of enlistments in the military by indoctrinated students should be tracked. Scholars theorized that educated citizens are more likely to participate in civic activities such as rallies and political activities. When *good* citizens simply vote their party line, is it a valid measure? Stakeholders do not know what a good civics program is supposed to achieve, and that does not bode well for the field of social studies. Consider this question: if teachers do not have a voice in creating policy, can they still effectively teach students to be citizen advocates?[59] The trends in social studies assessments are stagnant, yet stakeholders stress the importance of civic education because "they align to state legislative priorities or include important citizenship skills."[60] Social studies is important: stakeholders need to find common ground to define *good* citizenship, then determine how to produce a *good* citizen. That is when we can value social studies again.

Commenting on the declining 2022 US history and civics scores, Zachary Cote, executive director of Thinking Nation, suggests three factors that contribute to the decline: "decreased time spent on *social studies*, a lack of funding, and recent state legislation prohibiting the teaching of a full and honest history."[61] More importantly, he points out that history is not viewed as a discipline; rather the public sees history as content. For the NAEP, history has been viewed as content that assumes that students with the content knowledge must be active, knowledgeable, and *good* citizens. If citizenship is the purpose of history, someone needs to tell the AHA and OAH that their discipline is not fulfilling its role.

IMPLICATIONS: THE FUTURE OF SOCIAL STUDIES

Social studies is a field in conflict, suffering from an acute crisis of identity. The foundation of public education in the nineteenth century included it as a means for civic instruction, and that is its purpose. The labels may change over time, but the fundamental purpose of the field has not. So now that we have established that, how do we identify and define civic education?

In the 1890s, civic education was the focus of the upper and middle classes as they prepared to be active political participants. Not even thirty years later, civic education meant assimilation or acculturation: in other words, transforming diverse ethnic groups into a single American culture. Later, social studies was identified as a training place where students can become "informed and committed" citizens in "our free society."[62] Today, stakeholders acknowledge that civic education is important but permit it to be marginalized because they cannot agree on the path to *good* citizenship. Civic education is a constantly evolving identity, but consensus on what constitutes a *good* citizen is lost.

Social studies is crucial to sustaining our democracy. Stakeholders believe in the purpose of the field, but if any stakeholder feels like social studies is not being taught correctly, it makes headlines. Consider the *Problems of Democracy* course, the *New York Times* Survey, the MACOS controversy, the National Standards for History, and the *1619 Project*. At some point, those headlines turn into cultural wars in school board hearings, state legislatures, and even the halls of Congress. If stakeholders do not agree, how can teachers understand their roles? How can students understand the importance of the field? Soon America will have fourteen thousand different definitions for *good* citizenship: one for each school district in America. Or one for each social studies teacher.

The consequence of social studies' troubled history has increased doubt in the field's methodology as well as in its value in today's society.[63] A problem does exist. Whether or not stakeholders believe in social studies or its disciplines, the field is underrated. To promote the various disciplines over social studies, stakeholders must show the value of requiring those other disciplines. That action, in and of itself, devalues social studies, and by devaluing social studies, it unintentionally weakens any disciplines attached to social studies, including the one that a given stakeholder promotes. This decline is visible in the course of marginalization of the field over the last twenty-five years. Consider Florida and sociology.

By gaining an understanding of the development of the standards within the field of social studies, educators are better situated to determine their roles in the curriculum. Every state education agency (SEAs) had to develop individual standards for social studies as part of the No Child Left Behind (NCLB) Act.[64] At least ten states did not review their social studies standards between 2006 and 2014 when they were first implemented. Many states do not accumulate data on what social studies content or skills are being met, while other states adopted the Common Core literacy standards to replace their preexisting social studies standards.

Other states revise their standards on a semi-regular schedule. Unfortunately, when they revise them, controversy swirls around the new standards (e.g., Texas, South Dakota, California, Virginia). One set of standards is not going to make everyone happy, particularly if there is no consensus on what defines citizenship. Is citizenship simply doing your civic duty, like voting on election day, serving on a jury, and paying taxes? Is civic duty participating in the electoral process and making your voice heard? Is civic duty enlisting in the military and obeying orders? What is civic duty?

The various social studies disciplines are diverse, but so are the disciplines that comprise other fields. Conflicts between history and the other social sciences are at the heart of the problem. Historians do not use records to test a hypothesis, support an argument, or develop a theory; they raise questions from evidence and continually reframe questions as new evidence is discovered. Historians explore changes over time, especially the notion of chronology.[65] They focus on exploring the perspective of historical actors and relationships between causes and effects.

The social sciences tend to claim a more scientific approach in which evidence proves a theory.[66] Social scientists want to examine social constructs and explain how they relate to society, in other words, whether a political scientist interprets the writing in the Federalist Papers to understand their impact on the mechanisms of government or if a sociologist conducts surveys to explain how people's behaviors change over time. These approaches are different, but are they designed to achieve the same goals? The differences in epistemological approaches might be the biggest problem with social studies' attempts to blend different theories of knowledge to create a single authentic pedagogy for the field. At this point, the field probably will not establish a unified authentic pedagogy, yet it does need to address its identity crisis. How can the various disciplines work to create a *good* citizen when they cannot agree on a definition?

For social studies' life cycle, history can claim that it is the glue holding the field together. Thus, history's discipline advocates interpret history's role as essential over all other disciplines to the development of citizens. The political nature of citizenship thus promotes the idea that history is the essential discipline in the field. Yet, the three traditional functions for historical knowledge are: creating an imagined community (indoctrination), explaining how we got our rights and justifying them, and training to evaluate evidence (favored by historians).[67] At the dawn of the standards, historians did not isolate themselves from the other social sciences, nor did the social scientist seek to extricate history from the curriculum. While the other social sciences debate their importance to education, the bonds in the field of social studies are weakening. Sam Wineburg calls this notion *presentism*, as we attempt to put today's motives on past historical actors.[68]

For more than one hundred years, social studies educators have tried to prepare students to be citizens without a coherent definition to determine the path towards citizenship. In the 1880s, Union Army veterans within the Grand Army of the Republic sought to *correct* mistakes regarding the Civil War.[69] Southern states argued that the southern textbooks presented the *true* history of the war of southern independence. Arguments over the notion of *correct*, *true*, *right*, and *good* will continue, and social studies will have to adapt. America must be willing to admit that there is not one unified history that will not change over time. History is about gathering evidence and reframing the past as new evidence provides a more accurate picture. History is not stagnant.

As social studies became marginalized, the narrative shifted to focus more on skills and thinking than content. Social studies educators want students to think about issues; the main conflicts happen when including content in the framework. Historians want to begin with the past, whereas social studies practitioners argue for a more contemporary and relevant focus. Tosh suggests that historians suffer from the trap of thinking *about* history, thus students are taught to think *about* history.[70] He advocates that historians should think *with* history and teach students to also think *with* history. If social studies educators utilize history to make students think, we do not need to lecture them. Students become informed actors in the process.

Disconnecting history from the present to avoid political waters like multiculturalism or nationalism is problematic. Granted, a level of objectivity is obtained about historical decisions, but it comes at the cost of implications for the future.[71] By avoiding questions of relevance, the price of objectivity might be the consequential validity of all the disciplines in the social studies field. Paul Hanna lays out an interesting proposal with a very progressive view. He says that a child's world is not simply composed of history alone, but rather comprised of all the social sciences that help make them people. Thus, the field needs all the elements to generate a quality individual.[72] Social studies should blend the social sciences in the elementary grades, whereas the field should be divided up into the various disciplines in secondary grades as happens with science education. But to achieve that, the various stakeholders would have to forget their interpretations of the past and move the field forward.[73]

Social studies is often described as dry and boring. The curriculum tends to focus on assimilation of information. Teachers focus on students getting the *right* answers as determined by the state standards. The skills that students are trained to learn in traditional social studies classes include determining what is on the test, obtaining short-term recall for the test, and addressing specific individual points. A guiding principle of Jerome Bruner's that influenced the "New" social studies movement states that "the content of learning is the data of reflection we are saying, in a different context, that no content has meaning apart from the method by which it is verified and used, an assumption that is basic to many of the current projects in social studies."[74]

Content and context matter for social studies, and the teacher's role is to determine ways to blend them together. Tosh calls this blending the *organic relationship* between the past and present.[75] Kelly, Meuwissen, and VanSledright offer two alternatives for the future of social studies: continue the *humanist* model of memorizing facts or create a "rich history curriculum with powerful pedagogical practices and learning outcomes."[76] What does American society want in their social studies standards?

Standards are examined every ten years, but most of the focus of these reviews tends to be on content facts rather than skills. A gap exists between the expert-devised standards and what students actually learn. Grant states that social studies curriculum decision-making is accomplished by three diverse different groups: policymakers, professors, and teachers.[77] The level of influence on decisions tends to follow this order. People furthest away from the classroom seem to have the most important voice, and social studies teachers are left to interpret the standards and make them fit the reality of their classroom.

A major misconception within the field is that social studies educators are divided into two camps: social studies and the disciplines (primarily history). This division has been ongoing since the term social studies was first introduced in 1916. Barton claims current political ideology has fueled this debate in recent years; these political ideologies can be examined within questions about civic education.[78] *Traditionalists* (e.g., Ravitch, Finn, Nevins) feel that history content is the best way to teach citizenship. Further, they believe that the historical focus should create a shared narrative among Americans that is viewed as critical to citizenship. This group often claims that social studies usurped the traditional role of history in the curriculum.

Developmentalists (e.g., Counts, Saxe, VanSledright) tend to focus on determining the skills needed to be a *good* citizen and infusing them into the curriculum. This group is often concerned about the role of education in society and its impact upon elementary students in particular. This group wants to educate students to think critically about questions of citizenship to be *good* citizens. Early calls for a social studies curriculum never advocated for traditional history; they favored an interdisciplinary approach that focused on skills rather than content memorization as their idea of training citizens.[79] Still, these early calls for curriculum are the examples that *traditionalists* tend to idealize. Despite various disagreements about what constitutes *good* citizenship, these disparate groups tend to agree that standards for social studies should be developed around the purpose of educating *good* citizens.

The nature of curriculum as attributed to Herbert Spencer posed the question of what knowledge is most valuable.[80] When social studies makes the news, it is not necessarily about the skills students have but rather about the content they do not have. The *perceived* conflict between social studies and its disciplines has led to unintended consequences for the field as a whole. These struggles have led many disciplines to advocate for their own inclusion in the curriculum apart from social studies. Some have been more successful (i.e., history), but the field of social studies has never been a fully unified discipline.[81]

Disunity exists among the various social sciences, including history, sociology, government, anthropology, economics, geography, and the field of social studies education. Hertzberg argued that even in the standard definition of social studies, as articulated in the 1916 Final Report of Committee on Social Studies, there is no clear delineation of what comprises social studies.[82] The recommendations from the report advocate for a separate pedagogy among the various social sciences as well as a blending of the social sciences. The organization of the curriculum is different from state to state partly because there is not a single voice at the national level. The NCSS is the loudest advocate for social studies, but each discipline has their own agenda that does not always mesh with the NCSS agenda. For example, history has the National Council for History Education (NCHE), the American Historical Association (AHA), and the Organization of American Historians (OAH), who are all attempting to influence state curriculum decisions.

Educators cannot build consensus on the nature of the field of social studies. Some educators feel that history should be taught, but the design ideas are as fluid as the number of courses, the content, and the purpose.[83] Vinovskis wants history taught but she does not explain why or what the benefit it is for students other than giving them historical training.[84] Cultural wars often happen when there is a movement away from content knowledge in favor of a focus on developing skills. Content is what *humanistic* interest groups want to measure, but *social meliorism* and *developmentalism* are more concerned with skills. When objective skills become the focus, the differences between the social sciences become the most acute. Each social science interest group wants to stress their own *humanistic* interests over an interdisciplinary approach to social science.

In the 1950s, Arthur Bestor argued that social studies stressed present times and issues of relevance, while history as a discipline trained the mind.[85] He claimed that if students studied social studies, they would become interested only in the present; thus, social studies should become history education. Consider the four beliefs by historians that led to this conclusion: (1) historians believed that they controlled all aspects of the curriculum (including textbooks and content) prior to the Committee on Social Studies' Final Report; (2) many current historians believe the Final Report usurped historians and replaced them with educationalists who wanted to eliminate history from the curriculum; (3) historians believed that social studies represented a true blending of the social sciences and that they should not, therefore, foster the subject;[86] and (4) the educationalists in the 1920s and 1930s were determined to replace history with social studies courses.[87] Fallacies are connected to these interpretations, but these fallacies were believed to be fact by many of the individuals working on the NSH. Moreover, historians have often claimed that social studies has been corrupted for political motives, but they neglect to mention the fact that history has also been corrupted for political reasons.

Examining the debates over the NSH, Nash, Crabtree, and Dunn gave the impression that the failure of the NSH was not understandable.[88] They decided that the standards failure was due to bad political timing. Yet time allows historians to gain some perspective, and the failure is not an inexplicable mystery. The NSH failure is part of a larger narrative in the dispute over the pedagogy of social studies. In many ways, the very origins of social studies have plagued the field, and the constant debate over pedagogy has often hindered the development of value for the field.

Savit identifies legal cases going through the courts concerning adequate funding for social studies programs within states.[89] The "courts could require states to provide students with the level of education outlined in state standards" but adds that this still would not address the issue of good standards.[90] Kidwell examined state policy and civic education in K-12 and concluded that, due to the general lack of quality found in state standards for civics, much of the understanding of civics came from individual teachers.[91] As seen in the NSH, when skills are the focus in social studies, conflict often arises due to the disunity among the field on its purpose, which is to prepare citizens. The content tends to be too broad, and teachers are not able to cover all the material adequately. And since textbooks are a critical part of any classroom, they provide a way to control the curriculum to maintain the dominant culture over minorities.[92]

Under Reagan, "progressives in social studies were swimming against a rising tide"; *social efficiency* controlled by *humanistic* interest groups influenced the curriculum, and teachers simply went along for the ride.[93] At first, the left-leaning academy suggested that education be placed back into the hands of the teachers and principals, favoring more teacher-centered activities; this was not the trend in education.[94] Going forward, social studies suffered from the actions taken by individuals who believed that they were doing what was necessary to develop better citizens. Social studies educators are threatened with being marginalized, yet most educators do not understand why it has happened or how to fix it. Former Supreme Court Justice Sandra Day O'Connor called for more civics education, but social studies is being left behind. The fact that social studies is not tested is part of the explanation. Pederson noted that the trend of states testing social studies was decreasing following NCLB, whereas states were increasing their assessment in science and writing even though they were not part of the initial accountability mandate.[95] However, ignoring Justice O'Connor highlights a serious disconnect in the continually fracturing field. Social studies educators must examine those disconnects and cohesively unite in a single voice to restore the field to a place in the curriculum.

Without any action, social studies will remain a field in crisis. Even the highly regarded New York Regents exam contemplated the discontinuation of its social studies exam because students were struggling with passing the global history test.[96] The New York Board of Education ended up altering the exam to include a geographic component that was phased in by 2020. New York had to merge the disciplines because relying on pure history is simply relying on rote memorization, which will doom the field. Without change, social studies, along with its various disciplines, will find itself in the dustbin of history.

Appendix A

Chart of Major Social Studies Committees

Table A.1 Committee Memberships Based on Profession

		University Instructors		Government, Administrators, & Other	
	Historians	Social Scientists	Education	Positions	Teachers
Madison Conference (1892–1894) Published 1893	Charles Kendall Adams (Wisconsin)*; James Harvey Robinson (UPenn); Albert Bushnell Hart (Harvard); William Scott (Wisconsin)	Woodrow Wilson (Princeton); Edward Bourne (Adelbert College, Cleveland); Jesse Macy (Grinnell College, IA)		Abram Brown (Principal, Central HS, Columbus OH); Ray Green Huling (Principal, New Bedford, MA); Henry Warren (Headmaster, Albany Academy, NY)	
Committee of Seven (1897–1898) Published 1899	Herbert Baxter Adams (John Hopkins); Albert Bushnell Hart (Harvard); Andrew C. McLaughlin (Michigan)*; Charles H. Haskins (Wisconsin); Lucy M. Salmon (Vassar Univ); H. Morse Stephens (Cornell)			George L. Fox (Hopkins Grammar School, New Haven)	
Committee of Eight (1905–1909) Published 1909	James Alton James*; Henry E. Bourne; Eugene C. Brooks; Wilbur F. Gordy; Mabel Hill; Julius Sachs; Henry W. Thurston; J. H. Van Sickle			James Sullivan (Boys' High School, Brooklyn)	
Committee of Five (1907–1909) Published 1911	Andrew C. McLaughlin (Chicago)*; Charles Haskins (Harvard); James H. Robinson (Columbia); Charles W. Mann (Lewis Institute, Chicago; died in 1909).				

Chart of Major Social Studies Committees

AHA's Committee on the Preparation of Teachers of History in Schools (1911–1913)	Dana C. Munro (Wisconsin)*	Edgar Dawson (Hunter College)	Charles E. Chadsey (Superintendent of Denver 1909–1912 & Detroit 1912–1920); Kendric C. Babcock (Arizona & Bureau of Education 1910–1913)	Robert A. Maurer (Central High School, Washington, DC)
MVHA's Committee on the Certification of High School Teachers of History (1911)	Guernsey Jones (Nebraska); Frank M. Anderson (Minnesota); Eugene C. Barker (Texas); Henry E. Bourne (Western Reserve University); James Field Willard (Colorado); James A. Woodburn (Indiana); Frederic L Paxson (Wisconsin)*; Jonas Viles (Missouri); William C. Wilcox (Iowa); St. George L. Sioussat (Vanderbilt); Earl W. Dow (Michigan); Evarts B. Greene (Illinois); Lawrence M. Larson (Illinois); Orrin G. Libby (North Dakota); John H. Reynolds (Arkansas); Franklin L. Riley (Mississippi)	John W. Townsend		

(Continued)

Table A.1 (Continued)

	University Instructors			Government, Administrators, & Other	
	Historians	Social Scientists	Education	Positions	Teachers
MVHA's Second Committee on the Certification of High School Teachers of History (1913)	Wayland J. Chase* (Wisconsin); A. C. Krey; St. George L. Sioussat (Vanderbilt); Henry W. Elson; Guernsey Jones (Nebraska); Samuel B. Harding; Carl C. Eckhardt; Frederic Duncan; William E. Dodd; Paul C. Phillips; Harlow Lindley; Frank H. Hodder; Norman M. Trenholme; James E. Winston; David Y. Thomas	Henry E. Bourne (Western Reserve University)			
Committee of Nine (1911)			Charles H. Judd (Chicago)	William M. Butler (Principal, Yeatman HS, St. Louis); Frank B. Dyer (Superintendent, Cincinnati); Charles W. Evans (Principal, East Orange HS, NJ); Alexis F. Lange (Dean, Berkley); W. D. Lewis (Principal, William Penn HS, Philadelphia); William Orr (Deputy State Commissioner of Massachusetts); W. H. Smiley (Principal, East Eide HS, Denver)	Clarence D. Kingsley (Manual Training HS, Brooklyn)

Chart of Major Social Studies Committees 171

Committee					
Committee on Social Studies (1911–1918) Final Report 1916	James Harvey Robinson (Columbia); William H. Mace (Syracuse)	W. A. Arey (Hampton Institute, VA); E. C. Branson (UNC); Blanche Evans Hazard (Cornell	J. Lynn Barnard (School of Pedagogy, Philadelphia)	Clarence D. Kingsley (Massachusetts Education Department); Thomas Jesse Jones (ED)*; Arthur William Dunn (ED); George G. Bechtel (Principal, Northwestern HS, Detroit); F. L. Boyden (Principal, Deerfield, MA); W. J. Hamilton (Superintendent, Two Rivers, WI); William A. Wheatley (Superintendent, Middletown, CT);	Henry R. Burch (West Philadelphia HS); F. W. Carrier (Somerville HS, MA); Jessie C. Evans (William Penn HS for Girls, Philadelphia); Frank P. Goodwin (Woodward HS, Cincinnati); S. B. Howe (Newark HS, NJ); J. Herbert Low (Manual Training HS, Brooklyn); William T. Morrey (Bushwick HS, Brooklyn); John Pettibone (New Milford HS, CT)
Committee on History and Education for Citizenship in the Schools (Replaced by Committee on History in the Schools	Joseph Schafer*; William C Bagley; Frank S. Bogardus; Julian A. C. Chandler; Guy S. Ford; Samuel B. Harding* (Original Chair); Daniel C. Knowlton; Andrew C. McLaughlin				
AHA's Committee on History Teaching in the Schools	Guy Stanton Ford (Minnesota); Albert E. McKinley (University of Pennsylvania, Philadelphia); Eugene M. Violette (Kirksville, MO)		Henry E. Bourne (Western Reserve University, Cleveland, O-I);	Henry Johnson* (Teachers College, Columbia, NY)	Philip P. Chase (Milton, MA); Daniel C. Knowlton (Lincoln School, New York, NY)

(Continued)

Table A.1 (Continued)

	University Instructors			Government, Administrators, & Other Positions	Teachers
	Historians	Social Scientists	Education		
Commission on the Social Studies (1929–1940) Published 1934 (Several Books)	Avery O. Craven (Chicago); Guy Stanton Ford (Minnesota); Carlton J. H. Hayes (Columbia); Henry Johnson (Columbia); A. C. Krey (Minnesota)*	Charles A Beard (Formerly Columbia); Leon C. Marshall (John Hopkins); Charles E. Merriam (Chicago); Jesse F. Steiner (Washington)	George Counts (Columbia); Ernest Horn (Iowa); Jesse H. Newlon (Columbia)	Isaiah Bowman (Director of American Geographical Society); Frank Ballou (Superintendent, Washington, DC); Ada Comstock (President of Radcliffe College); Edmund E. Day (Director of Social Sciences, Rockefeller Foundation)	
Commission on Social Studies (1957–1959) Social Studies and the Social Sciences (1962)			Dorothy McClure Fraser (City College of New York); Howard R. Anderson (Washington); Samuel P. McCutchen (NYU); William H. Cartwright (Duke); Jack Allen (Vanderbilt); John H. Haefner (Iowa);	Lewis Paul Todd (*Social Education* Editor, NCSS)	

Council on Education Excellence (1981) Nation at Risk (1983)	Gerald Holton (Harvard)	David P Gardner* (Utah, President); Yvonne W. Larson (San Diego School Board); William O. Baker (Bell Telephone Lab); Anne Campbell (Former Commissioner of Education, NE); Emeral A. Crosby (Principal, Northern HS, Detroit); Charles A. Foster (Foundation for Teaching Economics); Norman C. Francis (Xavier University of LA, President); A. Bartlett Giamatti (President, Yale); Shirley Gordon (Highline CC, WA, President); Robert V Haderlein (National School Boards Association); Annette Kirk (Kirk Associates); Margaret S. Marston (VA State Board of Education); Albert H. Quie (Former Governor, MN); Francisco D. Sanchez (Superintendent, Albuquerque Public Schools); Glenn T. Seaborg (Berkley, Chemistry); Richard Wallace (Principal, Lutheran HS East, Cleveland Heights, OH)	Jay Sommer (New Rochelle HS, NY; National Teacher of the Year)

(Continued)

Table A.1 (Continued)

	Historians	University Instructors / Social Scientists	Education	Government, Administrators, & Other Positions	Teachers
National Commission on Social Studies in the Schools NCSSS (1987)	William H. McNeill (Chicago)*; David M. Katzman (Kansas); Thomas C. Holt (Chicago)	Paul Bohannan (UCLA); Christopher L. Salter (Missouri)	Thomas E. Cronin (Colorado College); Matthew T. Downey (Berkley); Hazel W. Hertzberg (Columbia); Howard Mehlinger (Dean, Indiana)	Jean Craven (Albuquerque Public Schools)*; Ronalda Cadiente (Indian Studies Program, Juneau, AK); Carol Hamilton Cobb (Nashville); Gary K. Hart (CA State Senator); Judith Rényi (Humanities and Arts Teaching, Philadelphia); Fay D. Metcalf (Executive Director)	Zenda F. Gutierrez (Zachry Middle School, San Antonio, TX); Kevin O'Reilly (Hamilton-Wenham Reg HS, Beverly, MA)
Bradley Commission (1988)	Kenneth T. Jackson (Columbia)*; Gordon Craig (Stanford); Nathan I. Huggins (Harvard); Michael Kammen (Cornell); William E. Leuchtenburg (UNC); Leon F. Litwack (UC, Berkeley); William H. McNeill (Chicago); C. Vann Woodward (Yale)		Charlotte Crabtree (UCLA); Hazel Whitman Hertzberg (Columbia); Diane Ravitch (Columbia)		Charles Shotland (Blind Brook High School, NY); John M. Arévalo (Harlandale High School, San Antonio); Louise Cox Byron (Booker T. Washington HS, Atlanta); Claudia J. Hoone (Public School #58, Indianapolis); Marjorie Wall Bingham (St. Louis Park Senior High School, MN)

Chart of Major Social Studies Committees

National Standards for History; National Standards for US History; National Standards for World History; National Standards for Grades K-4 (1994)	Gary B. Nash* (UCLA); Joyce Appleby (UCLA & President OAH); Pedro Castillo (Oakes & UC, Santa Cruz); Ainslie T. Embree (Columbia); Elizabeth Fox-Genovese (Emory); Carol Gluck (Columbia); Darlene Clark Hine (Mich State); Akira Iriye (Harvard); Kenneth Jackson (Columbia); Morton Keller (Brandeis); William Leuchtenburg (UNC & AHA); Bernard Lewis (Princeton); William McNeill (Chicago); John J Patrick (Indiana & SS Development Center); Theodore K. Rabb (Princeton & NCHE); C. Frederick Risinger (Indiana & SS Development Center)	Charlotte Crabtree* (UCLA); Earl Bell (Chicago, Organization of History Teachers)	Charlotte Anderson (President, NCSS); Samuel Banks (Executive Director, Baltimore Public Schools); Diane Brooks (CA Department of Education & President CSSSS); Michael R. Winston (Vice President Howard & President Alfred Harcourt Foundation); Warren Solomon (Consultant, MO Department of Elementary and Secondary Education); Gilbert T. Sewall (Director, American Textbook Council); Alan Morgan (State Superintendent, NM & President CCSSO); Barbara Talbert Jackson (President, ASCD); Bill Honig (Superintendent, CA Department of Education & President, CCSSO)	David Battini (Durham HS, Cairo, NY); David Baubach (Woolslair Elementary Gifted Center, Pittsburgh, PA); Mary Bicouvaris (Hampton Roads Academy, Newport News, VA)
Common Core (3C)	Undisclosed			

Appendix B

Timeline of Social Studies Standards

Table B.1 Events Related to the Development of Social Studies Standards

Date	Event
1867	National Center of Education Statistics begins collecting data on schools
	American Social Sciences Association begins
1884	American Historical Association begins holding meetings
	American Economic Association
1892	Committee of Ten initiated by NEA
1894	Madison Conference is called to examine history education in public schools
	American Psychological Association
1897	Committee of Seven (AHA)
1898	Recommendations from Committee of Seven
	American Political Science Association
1900s	Hampton Institute begins teaching social studies
1905	American Sociology Association
1909	Committee on History in Elementary Education publishes report
1911	Committee of Eight (AHA)
	Committee on History in Secondary Education (Committee of Five—AHA)
1912	Committee on Social Studies begins deliberations
1914	National Council of Geography Teachers formed
1916	Recommendations from the Committee on Social Studies published
1921	National Council of Social Studies (NCSS) inaugurated
	Committee of Eight (AHA)
1929	Rugg publishes his first textbook series
1932	AHA Commission on the Social Studies begins meeting
	Publication of AHA Commission on the Social Studies (total of 17 volumes)
1935	NCSS and AHA sever official ties
1939	Forbes and NAM launch attacks on social studies textbooks
1942	Nevins publishes article about lack of US history in public schools
1943	New York Times conducts survey of knowledge on American history

(Continued)

Table B.1 (Continued)

Date	Event
1953	Bestor publishes Educational Wastelands
1957	Launch of Sputnik
	National Defense Education Act
1959	Wood Hole Conference
1960	Bruner publishes Process of Education
1961	Charles R. Keller article; beginning of "New" social studies movement
	"New" social studies project begins
1962	Publication of ACLS/NCSS joint volume
	Endicott House Meetings
1963	Tyler Committee set up
1965	Elementary and Secondary Education Act (ESEA)
1967	Teaching of Social Studies in High Schools is published (introduction of "New" social studies into social studies teacher preparation)
	"Newer" social studies starts
1969	First NAEP tests are administered
	First NAEP test of citizenship is administered
1972	First NAEP test of social studies is administered
1974	Kanawha Book controversy
1975	Congressional hearings over MACOS and other education projects
	OAH survey on state of history education
1977	NCSS survey of the state of social studies in schools
1983	A Nation at Risk is published, sparking a national crisis in education
1984	First NAEP test is given in US History
1987	Publication of What Do Our 17-Year-Olds Know?
1988	Civics assessment administrated for NAEP
	Field test of geography assessment for NAEP
1989	Bradley Commission publishes its findings on history education
	Charlottesville Education Summit
	America 2000 proposed
1990	National Council of History Education is formed
1992	NEH funds National Standards for History
	NEH funds national standards for Geography, Economics, Civics
	NCSS requests funds for developing social studies standards but it is denied
1994	Goals 2000 signed into law
	NCSS privately develops Standards for Social Studies
	ESEA reauthorized as Improving America's Schools Act
	Cheney publishes an editorial in Wall Street Journal
	National Standards for History are officially published
1995	Senate votes no confidence in National Standards for History, resulting in the discontinuation of all education standards
1996	Revised National Standards for History are published (excluding teaching examples)
	Voluntary National Standards for all subjects are adopted by the federal government
2002	ESEA reauthorized (renamed No Child Left Behind) mandating states to develop standards for Reading, Mathematics, Science, and Social Studies

(Continued)

Table B.1 (Continued)

Date	Event
2005	Religion and Hindu controversy in California
2006	NCSS revises its standards for Social Studies
2009	Texas issues an updated set of social studies standards
	Common Core publishes Literacy in Social Studies and other places
2013	C3 disseminate to the public with no timetable for implementation
2014	NAGB announce that the NAEP tests for US History, Geography, and Civics will now assess only eighth-graders
	Revised AP Framework for US History released
	Boston public schools reorganization mishap
	Republican National Committee criticize the new AP US History standards
2016	Second Hindu Controversy
2019	Publication of 1619 Project
2020	1776 Commission established by President Trump
2021	South Dakota Standards revision
2024	AP administer the first African American studies exam

Appendix C

NAEP Schedule

Table C.1 History of the NAEP Assessments (1969–2032)

Year*	Content	Grades	Framework Changes or Other Assessment Changes
1969/70	Citizenship	4, 8, 12	Not listed on NAGB website
	Science	4, 8, 12	
	Writing	4, 8, 12	Not listed on NAGB website
1970/1971	Literature	4, 8, 12	
	Reading	4, 8, 12	
1971/1972	Music	4, 8, 12	
	Social Studies	4, 8, 12	
1972/1973	Mathematics	4, 8, 12	
	Science	4, 8, 12	
1973/1974	Career/Occupational Development	4, 8, 12	
	Writing	4, 8, 12	
1974/1975	Art	4, 8, 12	
	Index of Basic Skills	4, 8, 12	
	Reading	4, 8, 12	
1975/1976	Mathematics	8, 12	
	Citizenship/Social Studies	4, 8, 12	
1976/1977	Basic Life Skills	12	
	Science	4, 8, 12	
	Energy	12	High school dropouts
	Health	12	High school dropouts
	Reading	12	High school dropouts
1977/1978	Mathematics	4, 8, 12	
	Consumer Skills	12	
1978/1979	Writing	4, 8, 12	
	Art	4, 8, 12	
	Music	4, 8, 12	

(Continued)

Table C.1 (Continued)

Year*	Content	Grades	Framework Changes or Other Assessment Changes
1979/1980	Reading	4, 8, 12	Listed also as combined
	Literature	4, 8, 12	Listed also as combined
1980/1981			
1981/1982	Science	4, 8, 12	
	Mathematics	4, 8, 12	
	Citizenship/Social Studies	4, 8, 12	
1982/1983			
1984	Reading	4, 8, 12	
	Writing	4, 8, 12	
1985	Adult Literacy	Adult	
1986	Reading	3, 4, 7, 8, 11, 12	
	Mathematics	3, 4, 7, 8, 11, 12	
	Science	3, 4, 7, 8, 11, 12	
	Computer Competence	3, 4, 7, 8, 11, 12	
	US History	11	
	Literature	11	
1987			
1988	Reading	4, 8, 12	
	Writing	4, 8, 12	
	Civics	4, 8, 12	
	Document Literacy	8, 12	
	US History	4, 8, 12	
	Geography	12	
1989			
1990	Mathematics	4, 8, 12	New Framework; State (8)
	Reading	4, 8, 12	
	Science	4, 8, 12	
1991			
1992	Mathematics	4, 8, 12	State (4, 8)
	Writing	4, 8, 12	
	Reading	4, 8, 12	New Framework; State (4)
1993			
1994	Reading	4, 8, 12	State (3)
	US History	4, 8, 12	New Framework
	Geography	4, 8, 12	New Framework
1995			
1996	Mathematics	4, 8, 12	State (4, 8)
	Science	4, 8, 12	New Framework; State (8)
1997	Music	8	Also Arts Probe
	Theatre	8	Also Arts Probe
	Visual Arts	8	Also Arts Probe
1998	Reading	4, 8, 12	State (4, 8)
	Writing	4, 8, 12	New Framework; State (8)
	Civics	4, 8, 12	New Framework

(*Continued*)

Table C.1 (Continued)

Year*	Content	Grades	Framework Changes or Other Assessment Changes
1999			
2000	Mathematics	4, 8, 12	State (4, 8)
	Science	4, 8, 12	State (4, 8)
	Reading	4	
2001	Geography	4, 8, 12	
	US History	4, 8, 12	
2002	Reading	4, 8, 12	State (4, 8)
	Writing	4, 8, 12	State (4, 8)
2003	Reading	4, 8	State (4, 8)
	Mathematics	4, 8	State (4, 8)
2004			
2005	Reading	4, 8, 12	State (4, 8)
	Science	4, 8, 12	State (4, 8)
	Mathematics	4, 8, 12	New Framework; State (4, 8)
2006	US History	4, 8, 12	
	Civics	4, 8, 12	
	Economics	12	New Framework
2007	Reading	4, 8	State (4, 8)
	Mathematics	4, 8	State (4, 8)
	Writing	8, 12	State (8, 12)
2008	Art	8	
2009	Reading	4, 8, 12	New Framework; State (4, 8, 12)
	Science	8	New Framework; State (8)
	Mathematics	4, 8, 12	New Framework; State (4, 8, 12)
2010	US History	4, 8, 12	
	Civics	4, 8, 12	
	Geography	4, 8, 12	
2011	Reading	4, 8	State (4, 8)
	Writing	8, 12	New Framework
	Mathematics	4, 8	State (4, 8)
	Science		State (8)
2012	Economics	12	
2013	Reading	4, 8, 12	State (4, 8, 12)
	Mathematics	4, 8, 12	State (4, 8, 12)
2014	US History	8	
	Civics	8	
	Geography	8	
	Technology and Engineering Literacy	8	New Framework
2015	Mathematics	4, 8, 12	State (4, 8)
	Reading	4, 8, 12	State (4, 8)
	Science	4, 8, 12	State (4, 8)
2016	Arts	8	
2017	Writing	4, 8	State (4, 8)
	Mathematics	4, 8	State (4, 8)
	Reading	4, 8	State (4, 8)

(*Continued*)

Table C.1 (Continued)

Year*	Content	Grades	Framework Changes or Other Assessment Changes
2018	Civics	8	
	Geography	8	
	US History	8	
	Technology & Engineering Literacy	8	
2019	Mathematics	4, 8, 12	State (4, 8)
	Reading	4, 8, 12	State (4, 8)
	Science	4, 8, 12	
2020			
2021			Postponed due to COVID-19
2022	Civics	8	
	US History	8	
	Mathematics	4, 8, 12	State (4, 8)
	Reading	4, 8, 12	State (4, 8)
2023			
2024	Reading	4, 8, 12	State (4, 8)
	Mathematics	4, 8, 12	State (4, 8)
	Science	8	
2025			
2026	Reading	4, 8	New Framework; State (4, 8)
	Mathematics	4, 8	New Framework; State (4, 8)
	Civics	8	
	US History	8	
2027			
2028	Reading	4, 8, 12	State (4, 8, 12)
	Mathematics	4, 8, 12	State (4, 8, 12)
	Science	4, 8	New Framework; State (8)
2029			
2030	Reading	4, 8	State (4, 8)
	Mathematics	4, 8	State (4, 8)
	Civics	8, 12	New Framework; State (8)
	US History	8, 12	New Framework; State (8)
2031			
2032	Reading	4, 8, 12	State (4, 8, 12)
	Mathematics	4, 8, 12	
	Science	4, 8, 12	
	Writing	4, 8, 12	New Framework

There are some questions about the accuracy of the schedule of assessment; I could not find a complete schedule (additionally, what is proposed is not always the final schedule). As noted, the NAGB does not list the Citizenship nor the Writing NAEP from 1969–1970; yet all the technical reports through to the 1980s list these two assessments, as does the NCES literature. I used grades instead of ages; some literature lists both grades and ages, some only grades, some only ages. Without access to the actual assessments, I tried to make my best judgment when it comes to dates, subjects, and grades of students. For the purposes of this assessment, I stuck with grades to simplify the process but a nine-year-old could have been in third, fourth, or fifth grade technically.

* Until 1983, tests were given in the Fall and Spring, thus the years are both given.

Notes

CHAPTER 1

1. The term social studies did not come into general usage until 1910. So to keep accurate, social sciences will be substituted until the term is used.

2. David B. Tyack, Thomas James, & Aaron Benavot, *Law and the Shaping of Public Education, 1785–1954* (Madison, WI: University of Wisconsin Press, 1987), 24.

3. Robert B. Townsend, *History's Babel: Scholarship, Professionalization, and the Historical Enterprise in the United States, 1880–1940* (Chicago: University of Chicago Press, 2013).

4. Mason Locke (Parson) Weems wrote *The Life of Washington*, George Washington's first biography, in 1800. This is the first literary mention of George Washington chopping a cherry tree. Washington Irving's *A History of the Life and Voyages of Christopher Columbus* is often depicted as a fictional account of the life of Christopher Columbus. Several scholars believe that Irving developed the myth of the flat world to sensationalize Columbus.

5. David Warren Saxe, *Social Studies in Schools: A History of the Early Years* (Albany, NY: State University of New York Press, 1991).

6. Hazel Whitman Hertzberg, *Social Studies Reform, 1880–1980* (Boulder, CO: Social Science Education Consortium, Inc., 1981).

7. David Warren Saxe, Framing a Theory for Social Studies Foundations, *Review of Educational Research 62*, No. 3 (1992), 268.

8. Hertzberg, 1981.

9. Saxe, 1991; Townsend, 2013.

10. American Sociological Society was renamed to the American Sociological Association in 1959.

11. Lawrence Goldman, "Exceptionalism and Internationalism: The Origins of American Social Science Reconsidered," *Journal of Historical Sociology 11*, No. 1 (1998).

12. Herbert M. Kliebard, *The Struggle for the American Curriculum, 1893–1958*, third ed. (New York, NY: Routledge, 2004).

13. Saxe, 1991, 30.

14. Saxe, 1991.

15. Barry Joyce, *The First US History Textbooks: Constructing and Disseminating the American Tale in the Nineteenth Century* (Lanham, MD: Lexington Books, 2015).

16. Frances Fitzgerald, *America Revised: History Schoolbooks in the Twentieth Century* (New York, NY: Vintage Books, 1979), 19.

17. Michael Whelan, "Albert Bushnell Hart and the Origins of Social Studies Education," *Theory & Research in Social Education 22*, No. 4 (1994).

18. Townsend, 2013.

19. Whelan, 1994.

20. Whelan, 1994, 430.

21. National Education Association of the United States, *Committee on Secondary School Studies. Report of the Committee of Ten on Secondary School Studies [appointed at the Meeting of the National Educational Association July 9, 1892: With the Reports of the Conferences Arranged by this Committee and Held December 28–30, 1892]*, No. 205 (Washington, DC: US Government Printing Office, 1893), 189.

22. Townsend, 2013.

23. Townsend, 2013.

24. The National Education Association started in 1857. It is currently the largest national teachers' union in the United States.

25. Kliebard, 2004.

26. Thomas D. Snyder, *120 Years of American Education: A Statistical Portrait* (Washington, DC: US Department of Education, Office of Educational Research and Improvement, National Center for Education Statistics, 1993).

27. Ronald W. Evans, *The Social Studies Wars: What Should We Teach the Children?* (New York, NY: Teachers College Press, 2004), 7.

28. Evans, 2004, 7. Geography was also part of the subjects examined in 1892 but it was grouped with the natural sciences and thus was not considered part of the Madison Conference.

29. Townsend, 2013.

30. National Education Association of the United States, 1893, 28.

31. Evans, 2004, 7.

32. Chara Haeussler Bohan, Frans Doppen, Joseph Feinberg, & Carolyn O'Mahony, "Citizens of Today and Tomorrow: An Exploration of Preservice Social Studies Teachers' Knowledge and Their Professors' Experiences with Citizenship," *Curriculum & Teaching Dialogue 10*, No. 1 & 2 (2008).

33. National Education Association of the United States, 1893, 162.

34. Townsend, 2013.

35. N. Ray Hiner, "Professions in Process: Changing Relations between Historians and Educators, 1896–1911," *History of Education Quarterly 12*, No. 1 (1972).

36. Hertzberg, 1981.

37. Townsend, 2013, 62.

38. Hertzberg, 1981.
39. Townsend, 2013.
40. Bohan, Doppen, Feinberg, & O'Mahony, 2008.
41. Andrew Cunningham McLaughlin, Herbert B. Adams, George Levi Fox, Albert Bushnell Hart, Charles Homer Haskins, Lucy Maynard Salmon, & Henry Morse Stephens, *The Study of History in Schools: Report to the American Historical Association* (New York, NY: Macmillan Company, 1898), 87, fn 1.
42. Saxe, 1991, 58.
43. Hertzberg, 1981.
44. Howard Rai Boozer, *The American Historical Association and the Schools, 1884–1956* [Unpublished doctoral dissertation], Washington University, St. Louis, MO (1960), 101.
45. Boozer, 1960, 102.
46. The idea that a golden age existed in education is a fallacy. See Anne-Lise Halvorsen, "'Don't Know Much about History': The *New York Times* 1943 Survey of US History and the Controversy It Generated," *Teachers College Record 114*, No. 1 (2012); David C. Berliner & Bruce J. Biddle, *The Manufactured Crisis: Myths, Fraud, and the Attack on America's Public Schools* (Reading, MA: Addison-Wesley Publishing Company, 1995).
47. McLaughlin, Adams, Fox, Hart, Haskins, Salmon, & Stephens, 1898.
48. Bohan, Doppen, Feinberg, & O'Mahony, 2008.
49. Townsend, 2013.
50. Saxe, 1991.
51. Gary B. Nash, Charlotte Antoinette Crabtree, & Ross E. Dunn, *History on Trial: Culture Wars and the Teaching of the Past* (New York, NY: Knopf, 1997), 34.
52. Saxe, 1991.
53. Townsend, 2013.
54. Townsend, 2013.
55. Saxe, 1991.
56. Townsend, 2013.
57. Townsend, 2013.
58. Townsend, 2013.
59. Townsend, 2013.
60. McLaughlin, Adams, Fox, Hart, Haskins, Salmon, & Stephens, 1898.
61. Bohan, Doppen, Feinberg, & O'Mahony, 2008.
62. Hertzberg, 1981.
63. Whelan, 1994.
64. Diane Ravitch, "The Plight of History in American Schools." In P. Gagnon & The Bradley Commission on History in Schools (Eds.), *Historical Literacy: The Case for History in American Education* (New York, NY: Macmillan Publishing Company, 1989); Hertzberg, 1981.
65. Hertzberg, 1981, 16.
66. Saxe, 1991.
67. Oliver M. Keels, "In the Beginning—Albert McKinley and the Founding of *The Social Studies*," *The Social Studies 100*, No. 1 (2009). Original was printed in 1994.

68. Saxe, 1991.
69. Townsend, 2013.
70. Townsend, 2013.
71. Townsend, 2013.
72. Kliebard, 2004.
73. H. A. Hollister, "The Programme of Studies for High Schools," *The School Review 16*, No. 4 (1908), 252.

CHAPTER 2

1. Thomas S. Vontz, "Perspectives on Civic Education, 1898–1916," Report (1997).
2. Tyack, James, & Benavot, 1987.
3. Mona Siegel, "'History Is the Opposite of Forgetting': The Limits of Memory and the Lessons of History in Interwar France," *The Journal of Modern History 74*, No. 4 (2002).
4. In 1877, *Le tour de France par deux enfants* was published with G. Bruno as the author. Subsequent information revealed that G. Bruno was female writer Augustine Fouillée.
5. Some French schools were using this textbook into the 1970s.
6. Kory E. Olson, "Creating Map Readers: Republican Geographic and Cartographic Discourse in G. Bruno's (Augustine Fouillée) 1905 *Le Tour de la France par Deux Enfants*," *Modern & Contemporary France 19*, No. 1 (2011), 40.
7. Olson, 2011.
8. For Civic Republicanism see: Andrew Peterson, *Civic Republicanism and Civic Education: The Education of Citizens* (New York, NY: Springer, 2011); Italy Snir and Yuval Eylon, "Civic Republicanism and Education: Democracy and Social Justice in School," *Studies in Philosophy and Education* 36 (2017); Geoffrey Hinchliffe, "Civic Republicanism, Citizenship and Education." In A. Peterson, G. Stahl, & H. Soong (Eds.), *The Palgrave Handbook of Citizenship and Education* (London, UK: Palgrave Macmillan, 2020). For political liberalism see: Nomi Maya Stolzenberg, "'He Drew a Circle That Shut Me Out': Assimilation, Indoctrination, and the Paradox of a Liberal Education," *Harvard Law Review 106*, No. 3 (1993); Wayne Journell, "Standardizing Citizenship: The Potential Influence of State Curriculum Standards on the Civic Development of Adolescents," *PS: Political Science & Politics 43*, No. 2 (2010); Renato Rosaldo, "Cultural Citizenship and Educational Democracy," *Cultural Anthropology 9*, No. 3 (1994); Gerard Delanty, "Citizenship as a Learning Process: Disciplinary Citizenship versus Cultural Citizenship," *Int. of Lifelong Education 22*, No. 6 (2003); Tim Fowler, "The Limits of Civic Education: The Divergent Implications of Political and Comprehensive Liberalism," *Theory and Research in Education 9*, No. 1 (2011).
9. Fowler, 2011.
10. Susan Gibson, "'Why Do We Learn This Stuff?' Students' Views on the Purpose of Social Studies," *Canadian Social Studies 45*, No. 1 (2012); Bruce Haynes,

"Introduction: Special Issue: Patriotism and Citizenship Education," *Educational Philosophy and Theory 41*, No. 4 (2009); J. L. Nelson, "Defining Social Studies." In W. B. Stanley (Ed.), *Critical Issues in Social Studies Research for the 21st Century* (pp. 15–38) (Greenwich, CT: Information Age Publishing, 2001).

11. Hiner, 1972, 41. Italics are mine.

12. Similar attitudes can be seen in Irish and German immigrants during the 1840s; yet they were able to become part of American society more readily. Neither Native Americans nor African Americans could be seen as completely joining American culture.

13. Jill Lepore, *The Name of War: King Philip's War and the Origins of American Identity* (New York, NY: Vintage Books, 2009).

14. Robert Carlson, *The Quest for Conformity: Americanization through Education* (New York, NY: John Wiley and Sons, Inc. 1975).

15. In addition to Robert Carlson's book *The Quest for Conformity*, also see Jon Reyhner & Jeanne Eder, *American Indian Education: A History* (Norman, OK: University of Oklahoma Press, 2004). Carlson also has a new book on Americanization that came out in 2022.

16. Jon Reyhner, "American Indian Boarding Schools: What Went Wrong? What Is Going Right?" *Journal of American Indian Education 57*, No. 1 (Spring 2018).

17. David Wallace Adams, "Fundamental Considerations: The Deep Meaning of Native American Schooling, 1880–1900," *Harvard Educational Review 58*, No. 1 (1988).

18. Angelique EagleWoman and G. William Rice, "American Indian Children and US Indian Policy," *Tribal Law Journal 2015, 16* (2016).

19. Brenda J. Child, "Indian Boarding Schools," *Journal of Curriculum and Pedagogy 13*, No. 1 (2016).

20. Hampton Agricultural and Normal University would become Hampton University, a historically Black University. However, it did not hand out its first bachelor's degree until 1926 and was not accredited until the 1930s.

21. Nancy Elizabeth Jones-Oltjenbruns, A Historical Case Study of the Arikara, Hidatsa, and Mandan Indians at Hampton Normal and Agricultural Institute, Virginia, 1878–1911 [Unpublished doctoral dissertation]. (Virginia Commonwealth University, Richmond, VA, 2012), 89–90.

22. Native Americans would attend the institute until 1923. After 1923, the Hampton Institute would focus more on higher education of African Americans.

23. Thomas Jesse Jones, *Social Studies in the Hampton Curriculum* (Hampton, VA: Hampton Institute Press, 1906).

24. Jones-Oltjenbruns, 2012, 209.

25. Jones-Oltjenbruns, 2012.

26. Francis Kennedy, *First Person Accounts as Written by American Indian Students at Hampton Institute, 1878–1923*, edited by J. L. Brudvig (1994), http://www.twofrog.com/hamptonstories4.html.

27. Jones, 1906.

28. Michael Lybarger, "Origins of the Modern Social Studies: 1900–1916," *History of Education Quarterly 23*, No. 4 (1983), 461.

29. Jones, 1906; Evans, 2004; Saxe, 1992.

30. Jones, 1906.

31. The blending of ethnic superiority and Social Darwinism contributed to the notion that there exists an American exceptionalism over other groups. Social Darwinism was an important aspect of these groups because they viewed their WASP identity as being superior.

32. Jeffery Mirel, *Patriotic Pluralism: Americanization Education and European Immigrants* (Cambridge, MA: Harvard University Press, 2010).

33. Barbara Beatty, "'The Letter Killeth:' Americanization and Multicultural Education in Kindergartens in the United States, 1856–1920, Vol. 42." In R. L Wollons (Ed.), *Kindergartens and Cultures* (New Haven, CT: Yale University Press, 2000).

34. Mirel, 2010.

35. Mirel, 2010.

36. Anne Brophy, "'The Committee . . . Has Stood Out against Coercion': The Reinvention of Detroit Americanization, 1915–1931," *Michigan Historical Review* 29, No. 2 (2003).

37. Mirel, 2010.

38. Brophy, 2003, 5.

39. Mirel, 2010.

40. Saxe, 1991.

41. Matthew J. Brown & Sabrina Starnaman, "Unless We Americanize Them They Will Foreignize Us," Pragmatism, Progressivism, and Americanization [Working paper].

42. Saxe, 1991.

43. Saxe, 1991.

44. Kliebard, 2004.

45. Hiner, 1972, 41.

46. Mirel, 2010.

47. Mirel, 2010.

48. Kliebard, 2004.

49. Mirel, 2010.

50. Mirel, 2010.

51. Townsend, 2013, 65.

52. Saxe, 1991.

53. Saxe, 1991.

54. Saxe, 1991.

55. As quoted in Saxe, 1991, 100.

56. Saxe, 1991.

57. Saxe, 1991.

58. Andrew C. McLaughlin, Charles H. Haskins, James Harvey Robinson, & James Sullivan, "The Study of History in Secondary Schools: Report of the Committee of Five," *Annual Report of the American Historical Association* (1911), 241.

59. This committee was originally called the Committee on the Certification of High School Teachers of History but this would be confused with a similar committee founded by the MVHA in 1913.

60. Normal Schools were learning centers designed to educate teachers, many were funded by the state. Eventually they would form School/College of Education at various universities.

61. Was the former president of University of Arizona. While at the Bureau of Education, he created the first ranking system of universities. Many critics deemed it a disaster, and he got no support. One story goes that President Taft was angered by the ranking of the University of Cincinnati in the second tier and thus he opposed the ranking, highly apocryphal.

62. Townsend, 2013.

63. C. Gregg Jorgensen, *John Dewey and the Dawn of Social Studies: Unraveling Conflicting Interpretations of the 1916 Report* (Charlotte, NC: Information Age Publishing, 2012), 29.

64. Hiner, 1972, 41.

65. Bohan, Doppen, Feinberg, & O'Mahony, 2008.

66. Hiner, 1972, 48–49.

67. Mirel, 2010, 3.

68. Theodore Roosevelt, "Address to the Knights of Columbus" delivered at Carnegie Hall in New York City on October 12, 1915, in Phillip Davis (Ed.), *Immigration and Americanization: Selected Readings* (Boston, MA: Ginn, 1920), 645.

69. Tyack, James, & Benavot, 1987.

70. Christine A. Woyshner, Joseph Watras, & Margaret Crocco (Eds.), *Social Education in the Twentieth Century: Curriculum and Context for Citizenship, Vol. 32* (New York, NY: Peter Lang, 2004), xiii.

71. As cited in Tyack, James, & Benavot, 1987, 169.

72. Bohan, Doppen, Feinberg, & O'Mahony, 2008, 14.

73. Hertzberg, 1981.

74. N. Ray Hiner, "Professions in Process: Changing Relations among Social Scientists, Historians, and Educators, 1880–1920," *The History Teacher 6*, No. 2 (1973).

75. Mirel, 2010.

76. Mirel, 2010.

77. Mirel, 2010, 28.

78. Maria Lauret, "Americanization Now and Then: The 'Nation of Immigrants' in the Early Twentieth and Twenty-First Centuries," *Journal of American Studies 50*, No. 2 (2016).

79. Bohan, Doppen, Feinberg, & O'Mahony, 2008.

80. McLaughlin, Haskins, Robinson, & Sullivan, 1911, 231.

81. Saxe, 1991.

82. Wallace Foster, *A Patriotic Primer for the Little Citizen* (Indianapolis, IN: Levey Bros. & Company, 1898), 11.

83. Foster, 1898, 11–12.

CHAPTER 3

1. Tyack, James, & Benavot, 1987, 112.

2. Georg G. Iggers, "Historicism: The History and Meaning of the Term," *Journal of the History of Ideas 56*, No. 1 (1995), 147.

3. Townsend, 2013.

4. Townsend, 2013.

5. Townsend, 2013, 72.

6. J. Madison Gathany, "Practical Aims and Methods in the Teaching of Civics," *The History Teacher's Magazine 4*, No. 1 (1913), 22.

7. Mississippi Valley Historical Association, founded in 1907, changed its name to the Organization of American Historians in 1965.

8. Townsend, 2013.

9. Townsend, 2013.

10. Frederic L. Paxson, "Certification of High-School Teachers of History: Report of the Chairman of the Committee," *The History Teacher's Magazine 4*, No. 6 (1913).

11. Townsend, 2013.

12. Wayland Chase was an active editor on McKinley's board (*The History Teacher's Magazine*) contributing many recommendations on history and civics sources for teachers.

13. Wayland Chase, "Report of the Certification of High School Teachers of History," *Proceedings of the Mississippi Valley Historical Association* (1914–15), 8. (Cedar Rapids, IA: Publisher Torch Press, 1916). Edited by Milo M Quaife.

14. Calvin O. Davis, "The Report of the Committee of Nine, 1911," *Junior-Senior High School Clearing House 6,* No. 9 (May 1932), 550–55.

15. Davis, 1932, 550.

16. As quoted by Davis, 1932, 551.

17. William A. Galston, "The Politics of Polarization: Education Debates in the United States." In Susan Fuhrman & Marvin Lazerson (Eds.), *The Institutions of American Democracy: The Public Schools* (New York, NY: Oxford University Press, 2005).

18. Saxe, 1991.

19. Several scholars have noted the influence of Dewey and Snedden. Traditionally, Snedden's influence is often believed to have had lasting impact. See W. H. Drost, "Social Efficiency Reexamined: The Dewey-Snedden Controversy," *Curriculum Inquiry 7,* No. 1 (1977); David F. Labaree, "How Dewey Lost: The Victory of David Snedden and Social Efficiency in the Reform of American Education." In D. Tröhler, T. Schlag, & F. Osterwalder (Eds.), *Pragmatism and Modernities* (New York, NY: Brill Publishers, 2010); Thomas Fallace, "John Dewey's Influence on the Origins of the Social Studies: An Analysis of the Historiography and New Interpretation," *Review of Educational Research 79*, No. 2 (2009); C. G. Jorgensen, *John Dewey and the Dawn of Social Studies: Unraveling Conflicting Interpretations of the 1916 Report* (Chalotte, NC: Information Age Publishing, 2012).

20. Murry R. Nelson, *The Social Studies in Secondary Education: A Reprint of the Seminal 1916 Report with Annotations and Commentaries* (Bloomington, IN: ERIC Clearinghouse for Social Studies/Social Science Education, 1994).

21. Saxe, 1991.

22. Saxe, 1991.

23. Saxe, 1991.

24. Saxe, 1991.

25. Saxe, 1991, 146–47.

26. "NCSS Social Studies Standards." *Social Studies*, www.socialstudies.org/standards.
27. Saxe, 1991.
28. Thomas Jesse Jones as quoted by Saxe, 1991, 146.
29. Lybarger, 1983.
30. Saxe, 1991.
31. Saxe, 1991.
32. Nelson, 1994, 14.
33. Anne-Lise Halvorsen & Jeffery Mirel, "Educating Citizens: Social Problems meet Progressive Education in Detroit, 1930–1952." In Kenneth W. Wong & Robert Rothman (Eds.), *Clio at the Table: Using History to Inform and Improve Education Policy* (New York, NY: Peter Lang, 2009).
34. Lybarger, 1983, 466.
35. Nelson, 1994, 17.
36. Nelson, 1994, 38.
37. Saxe, 1992.
38. Nelson, 1994, 7.
39. Jorgenson, 2012.
40. National Education Association of the United States, Commission on the Reorganization of Secondary Education, *Cardinal Principles of Secondary Education*, 35 (Washington, DC: US Government Printing Office, 1928), 32. Further reference will be *Cardinal Principles*, 1928.
41. See Boozer, 1960. He goes through all the AHA committees and their purposes.
42. Keels, 2009.
43. Keels, 2009, 10.
44. The National Board for Historical Service was a government organization set up by the AHA at the behest of the US government.
45. Townsend, 2013.
46. Townsend, 2013.
47. Townsend, 2013.
48. *Annual Report of the American Historical Association*, 1918 (Washington, DC: US Government Printing Office, 1921), 42. Italics added for emphasis.
49. Henry Johnson, "Report of Committee on History and Education for Citizenship: Part 2, History in the Grades," *The Historical Outlook 12*, No. 6 (1921), 93.
50. Boozer, 1960, 148.
51. Arthur Dunn, "Civics in Schools, with Special Reference to Grades Nine and Twelve," *Social Studies 12*, No. 6 (1921), 223.
52. Joseph Schafer, "Report of Committee on History and Education for Citizenship," *The Historical Outlook 12*, No. 3 (1921), 90.
53. Townsend, 2013.
54. Anna Stewart, "The Social Sciences in Secondary Schools," *The Historical Outlook 12*, No. 2 (1921), 53.
55. Edmund Noyes, "Comment upon Committee's Report," *The Historical Outlook 12*, No. 4 (1921), 142.

56. Harold Rugg, "How Shall We Reconstruct the Social Studies Curriculum? An Open Letter to Professor Henry Johnson," *The Historical Outlook 12*, No. 5 (1921).

57. Dunn, 1921.

58. Howard C. Hill, "History for History's Sake," *The Historical Outlook 12*, No. 9 (1921), 313.

59. Jorgenson, 2012; Saxe, 1991.

60. Galston, 2005, 58.

61. Tyack, James, & Benavot, 1987.

62. Joan K. Smith, "Progressive School Administration Ella Flagg Young and the Chicago Schools, 1905–1915," *Journal of the Illinois State Historical Society (1908–1984) 73*, No. 1 (1980), 33.

63. Hiner, 1973.

64. Richard Hofstadter, *Anti-Intellectualism in American Life* (New York, NY: Vintage, 1966), 333–34.

65. Hofstadter, 1966.

66. Erling M. Hunt, "Changing Perspectives in the Social Studies." In Erling M. Hunt (Ed.), *High School Social Studies: Perspectives* (Boston, MA: Houghton Mifflin Company, 1962).

67. Hazel W. Hertzberg, "History and Progressivism: A Century of Reform Proposals." In Paul Gagnon & The Bradley Commission on History in Schools (Eds.), *Historical Literacy: The Case for History in American Education* (New York, NY: Macmillan Publishing Company, 1989).

68. George E. DeBoer, *A History of Ideas in Science Education: Implications for Practice* (New York, NY: Teachers College Press, 1991).

69. Saxe, 1991.

70. Saxe, 1991.

71. *Cardinal Principles*, 1928, 14.

72. Saxe, 1991.

73. Saxe, 1992.

74. Saxe, 1991.

75. Jorgensen, 2012.

76. Hertzberg, 1989.

77. Saxe, 1991.

78. Jorgensen, 2012. When discussing Krug's interpretations, Jorgensen notes that social efficiency had a more controlling aspect towards society. While other scholars (e.g., Ravitch, Saxe, and Evans) focus less on the controlling aspect of social studies, they point to other aspects to highlight their perspectives. The significance is that Krug published his interpretations during the 1960s at a time of general social upheavals looking for explanations for why rights were denied to certain groups.

79. Jorgensen, 2012.

80. Kenneth T. Jackson & Barbara B. Jackson, "Why the Time Is Right to Reform the History Curriculum." In Paul Gagnon (Ed.), *Historical Literacy: The Case for History in American Education* (New York, NY: Macmillan Publishing Company, 1989).

81. Hertzberg, 1989.

82. Paleoconservatism is a branch of US conservatism that developed in the 1980s in reaction to a neoconservative movement. Paleoconservatives favored a society based on "traditional" Christian values and a focus on family. For the purpose of this study, I will use conservative with the understanding that not all conservatives are the same. Nor are they motivated by the same reasons.

83. Robert Lerner, Althea K. Nagai, & Stanley Rothman, *Molding the Good Citizen: The Politics of High School History Texts* (Westport, CT: Praeger, 1995).

84. Ravitch, 1989.

85. Saxe, 1991.

86. Saxe, 1991.

87. Saxe, 1991.

88. Bohan, Doppen, Feinberg, & O'Mahony, 2008.

89. Keels, 2009, 10.

90. Lerner, Nagai, & Rothman, 1995; Julie A. Reuben, "Patriotic Purposes: Public Schools and the Education of Citizens." In Susan Fuhrman & Marvin Lazerson (Eds.), *The Institutions of American Democracy: The Public Schools* (New York, NY: Oxford University Press, 2005).

91. Reuben, 2005.

92. *Cardinal Principles*, 1928, 14.

93. Hertzberg, 1981.

94. Saxe, 1991.

95. Edwin R. Carr, *The Social Studies* (New York, NY: The Center for Applied Research in Education, 1965), 25.

96. Mirel, 2010.

97. The law required it to be in place by 1931; Mirel, 2010.

98. As cited in Saxe, 1992, 270.

99. Saxe, 1991.

CHAPTER 4

1. Townsend, 2013.

2. Evans, 2004.

3. Saxe, 1991.

4. National Council for the Social Studies, "A National Council for the Social Studies" [Announcement] in *The Historical Outlook 12*, No. 4 (April 1921), 144.

5. Townsend, 2013.

6. Boozer, 1960.

7. Keels, 2009.

8. Evans, 2004, 35.

9. Townsend, 2013.

10. Townsend, 2013.

11. Evans, 2004, 35.

12. Thomas Fallace, "Did the Social Studies Really Replace History in American Secondary Schools," *Teachers College Record 110,* No. 10 (2008); Fitzgerald, 1979.

13. Townsend, 2013, 129.
14. Townsend, 2013.
15. Townsend, 2013.
16. Mark M. Krug, John B. Poster, & William B. Gillies III (Eds.), *The New Social Studies: Analysis of Theory and Materials* (Itasca, IL: F. E. Peacock Publishers, Inc., 1970).
17. The *Cardinal Principles* called for a course that dealt with problems in America's democracy. Various names were used for this course, including *Problems of America*, *Problems of American Democracy*, *Problems of Contemporary Life*, and *Problems of Democracy*. To simplify, I choose to stick to *Problems of Democracy*, which appears to be the most common name for the course.
18. Evans, 2004.
19. Kliebard, 2004.
20. Evans, 2004.
21. Hertzberg, 1981.
22. Hiner, 1973.
23. Dunn, 1921, 219.
24. Reuben, 2005.
25. Reuben, 2005.
26. Mirel, 2010, 63.
27. Mirel, 2010.
28. Mirel, 2010. Also see Fitzgerald, 1979.
29. Mirel, 2010.
30. Mirel, 2010.
31. Evans, 2004, 5.
32. Fitzgerald, 1979.
33. Kliebard, 2004.
34. Evans, 2004, 40.
35. Alice B. McGuirk, *A Study of the Achievement of Pupils Who Studied the Harold Rugg's Fused Course in Social Studies as Compared with Those Who Studied Separate History and Geography Courses* [Unpublished master's thesis], Indiana State Teachers College, Terre Haute, IN (1933), 37.
36. Larry Lloyd Kraus, *Curriculum, Public Policy, and Criticism: An Analysis of the Controversies Surrounding "Man: A Course of Study"* [Unpublished doctoral dissertation], The University of Texas at Austin (1977), 14–16.
37. Townsend, 2013.
38. Townsend, 2013.
39. Townsend, 2013.
40. Townsend, 2013.
41. Hunt, 1962.
42. Hertzberg, 1981.
43. Townsend, 2013.
44. Townsend, 2013.
45. Hertzberg, 1981.

46. Hunt, 1962.
47. Hertzberg, 1981.
48. Hertzberg, 1981.
49. Townsend, 2013.
50. Townsend, 2013.
51. Townsend, 2013, 175.
52. Gerald Lee Gutek, *George S. Counts and American Civilization: The Educator as Social Theorist* (Chicago, IL: Mercer University Press, 1984), 154.
53. Hertzberg, 1981.
54. Gutek, 1984.
55. Gutek, 1984, 85.
56. Gutek, 1984.
57. Arnold K. King, From History to Social Studies in the Secondary School, *The High School Journal 29*, No. 1 (1946), 18.
58. Lerner, Nagai, & Rothman, 1995.
59. Hertzberg, 1981.
60. Townsend, 2013.
61. Townsend, 2013; Hertzberg, 1981.
62. Hertzberg, 1981.
63. Hunt, 1962.
64. Freedom Kline Capps, The Discipline of History as Portrayed in the Journal "Social Education," 1937–1982 [Unpublished doctoral dissertation], University of Missouri, Columbia, MO (1984).
65. Gerald Lee Gutek, *The Educational Theory of George S. Counts* (Columbus, OH: Ohio State University Press, 1970), 29.
66. Gutek, 1970; Gutek, 1984.
67. Gutek, 1984.
68. Woyshner, Watras, & Crocco, 2004.
69. Hertzberg, 1981.
70. Hertzberg, 1981, 61.
71. See Krug, Ravitch, Hertzberg, & Finn.
72. Fallace, 2008, 2265.
73. Hertzberg, 1981.
74. Hertzberg, 1981.
75. Charles H. Judd, "The Teaching of Civics," *The School Review 26*, No. 7 (1918), 528.
76. Nash, Crabtree, & Dunn, 1997.
77. Hertzberg, 1981.
78. King, 1946.
79. Townsend, 2013.
80. Mirel, 2010.
81. Mirel, 2010.
82. Mirel, 2010.
83. Mirel, 2010.

CHAPTER 5

1. Hertzberg, 1981.
2. Saxe, 1991.
3. Saxe, 1991.
4. Gutek, 1970, 92.
5. Caroline J. Conner and Chara H. Bohan, "The Second World War's Impact on the Progressive Educational Movement: Assessing Its Role," *The Journal of Social Studies Research 38*, No. 2 (2014).
6. Kevin Boland Johnson, *Guardians of Historical Knowledge: Textbook Politics, Conservative Activism, and School Reform in Mississippi, 1928–1982* [Unpublished doctoral dissertation], Mississippi State University, Starkville, MS (2014).
7. Gutek, 1970, 75–76.
8. Mirel, 2010.
9. Mirel, 2010.
10. Karen L. Riley & Barbara Slater Stern, "'A Bootlegged Curriculum': The American Legion versus Harold Rugg," *International Journal of Social Education 18*, No. 2 (2002).
11. Hertzberg, 1981.
12. Fitzgerald, 1979, 37.
13. Fitzgerald, 1979, 37.
14. Halvorsen, 2012.
15. Townsend, 2013.
16. Conner & Bohan, 2014.
17. Halvorsen, 2012.
18. Halvorsen, 2012.
19. Townsend, 2013.
20. Hertzberg, 1981.
21. Conner & Bohan, 2014.
22. Halvorsen, 2012.
23. Hertzberg, 1981.
24. Conner & Bohan, 2014.
25. Hertzberg, 1981.
26. Halvorsen, 2012.
27. Halvorsen, 2012.
28. Halvorsen, 2012.
29. Kliebard, 2004.
30. Hertzberg, 1981.
31. Tyack, James, & Benavot, 1987, 191.
32. Hertzberg, 1981.
33. Hertzberg, 1981.
34. Hertzberg, 1981.
35. Hertzberg, 1981.
36. Kraus, 1977, 16.

37. Halvorsen & Mirel, 2009.
38. Hertzberg, 1981.
39. Halvorsen & Mirel, 2009.
40. Halvorsen & Mirel, 2009.
41. Halvorsen & Mirel, 2009.
42. Halvorsen & Mirel, 2009.
43. Kliebard, 2004, 183.
44. Kliebard, 2004, 183.
45. Hertzberg, 1981, 78.
46. Hertzberg, 1981.
47. Hertzberg, 1981.
48. Evans, 2004.
49. Nash, Crabtree, & Dunn, 1997.
50. Hunt, 1962.
51. Evans, 2004.
52. Hertzberg, 1981.
53. Hertzberg, 1981.
54. Hertzberg, 1981.
55. Kliebard, 2004, 266.
56. Nash, Crabtree, & Dunn, 1997.
57. Kliebard, 2004, 270.
58. As quoted in Byron G. Massialas & Andreas M. Kazamias (Eds.), *Crucial Issues in the Teaching of Social Studies: A Book of Readings* (Englewood Cliffs, NJ: Prentice-Hall, Inc., 1964), 20.
59. A. E. Bestor, *Educational Wastelands: The Retreat from Learning in Our Public Schools* (Eastford, CT: Martino Fine Books, 2016), 46. (Original work published 1953.)
60. Hunt, 1962.
61. Riley & Stern, 2002, 26.
62. Halvorsen, 2012.
63. Halvorsen, 2012.
64. Halvorsen, 2012.
65. Jackson & Jackson, 1989.
66. Nelson, 2001.
67. Hertzberg, 1981.
68. Tyack, James, & Benavot, 1987.
69. Y. Zhao & J. D. Hoge, "What Elementary Students and Teachers Say about Social Studies," *The Social Studies 96*, No. 5 (2005), 216–21.
70. Nash, Crabtree, & Dunn, 1997.
71. Hunt, 1962.
72. J. A. Michener, "Who Is Virgil T. Fry? The Remarkable Facts about a Man Who Is Either a Master Teacher or a Big Fraud," *The Clearing House: A Journal of Educational Strategies, Issues and Ideas 19*, No. 2 (1944), 73.
73. Michener, 1944, 73.
74. Michener, 1944, editor note, 69.

CHAPTER 6

1. Charles R. Keller, "Needed: Revolution in the Social Studies." In B. G. Massialas & A. M. Kazamias (Eds.), *Crucial Issues in the Teaching of Social Studies: A Book of Readings* (Englewood Cliffs, NJ: Prentice-Hall, Inc., 1964).
2. Keller, 1964.
3. Andrew Norman Cruikshanks, *The Social Studies Curriculum in the Secondary School: 1893–1955* [Unpublished doctoral dissertation], Stanford University, Stanford, CA (1957), 192.
4. Cruikshanks 1957, 192.
5. See Douglas Edwin Wilson, *Curriculum Reform in History and the Social Studies, 1960–1965: A Survey of the Literature* [Unpublished master's thesis], Kansas State University, Manhattan, KS (1965).
6. Cruikshanks, 1957, 220.
7. Cruikshanks, 1957, 199.
8. Cruikshanks, 1957, 203.
9. Jamie Cohen-Cole, *The Open Mind: Cold War Politics and the Sciences of Human Nature* (Chicago, IL: University of Chicago Press, 2014), 195.
10. See Leo P. Ribuffo, What Is Still Living in "Consensus" History and Pluralist Social Theory, *American Studies International 38,* No. 1 (2000). Ribuffo claims that consensus history is not an appropriate label because historians did not always agree (consensus). He suggests another term coined in 1973 as counterprogressivists. Consensus history is a more familiar term.
11. John Higham, "The Cult of the American Consensus," *Commentary, 28* (1959).
12. Hertzberg, 1981.
13. Linda Symcox, *Whose History? The Struggle for National Standards in American Classrooms* (New York, NY: Teachers College Press, 2002).
14. Nash, Crabtree, & Dunn, 1997, 77.
15. Ronald W. Evans, "National Security Trumps Social Progress: The Era of the New Social Studies in Retrospect." In B. S. Stern (Ed.), *The New Social Studies: People, Projects, & Perspectives* (pp. 1–37) (Charlotte, NC: Information Age Publishing. 2010).
16. Evans, 2010.
17. Lynda Carl Falkenstein, *Man: A Course of Study—A Case Study of Diffusion in Oregon* [Unpublished doctoral dissertation], Stanford University, Stanford, CA (1977), 4.
18. Evans, 2010.
19. Evans, 2010.
20. Cohen-Cole, 2014.
21. Cohen-Cole, 2014.
22. Evans, 2004.
23. Evans, 2004.
24. Shirley H. Engle, "Decision Making: The Heart of Social Studies Instruction," In B. G. Massialas & A. M. Kazamias (Eds.), *Crucial Issues in the Teaching of Social Studies: A Book of Readings* (Englewood Cliffs, NJ: Prentice-Hall, Inc., 1964).

25. Engle, 1964.
26. Hertzberg, 1981.
27. Hertzberg, 1981.
28. Carr, 1965.
29. "Progress in Social Studies," *New York Times*, June 16, 1961, 32.
30. Evans, 2010.
31. Cohen-Cole, 2014.
32. Carr, 1965.
33. Maurice P. Hunt & Lawrence E. Metcalf, *Teaching High School Social Studies: Problems in Reflective Thinking and Social Understanding* (New York, NY: Harper & Row, 1968).
34. Massialas & Kazamias, 1964.
35. Cohen-Cole, 2014.
36. Lynn R. Nelson & Frederick D. Drake, "Secondary Teachers' Reactions to the New Social Studies," *Theory & Research in Social Education 22*, No. 1 (1994).
37. Hertzberg, 1981.
38. Evans, 2010.
39. Hunt & Metcalf, 1968.
40. Evans, 2010.
41. Cohen-Cole, 2014.
42. Nash, Crabtree, & Dunn, 1997, 81.
43. Fenton says that Carnegie Mellon collected material from 130 centers in 1970. Nelson & Drake (1994) claim it was only 100. See Edwin Fenton, "The New Social Studies Reconsidered." In M. M. Krug, J. B. Poster, & W. B. Gillies III (Eds.), *The New Social Studies: Analysis of Theory and Materials* (Itasca, IL: F. E. Peacock, 1970).
44. Evans, 2004, 127.
45. Evans, 2010.
46. Hertzberg, 1981, 132.
47. William Weber, "The Amherst Project and Reform of History Education, 1959–1972," *The History Teacher 51*, No. 1 (2017), 38
48. Charles Samec, *A History of the Amherst Project: Revising the Teaching of American History 1959 to 1972* [Unpublished doctoral dissertation], Loyola University, Chicago, IL (1976), 22.
49. Weber, 2017, 57.
50. Semac, 1976, 77.
51. Weber, 2017, 48.
52. Samec, 1976, 38.
53. Jeffery Byford & William Russell, "The New Social Studies: A Historical Examination of Curriculum Reform," *Social Studies Research and Practice 2*, No. 1 (2007), 42.
54. Joseph M. Cirrincione, *The Role of Values in the Teaching of Geography* [Unpublished doctoral dissertation], Ohio State University, Columbus, OH (1970), 20.
55. Cirrincione, 1970, 26.
56. Cirrincione, 1970, 27.

57. Donald J. Patton, *From Geographic Discipline to Inquiring Student. The High School Geography Project. Final Report* (Washington, DC: Association of American Geographers, 1970), 5.

58. Ronald J. B. Carswell, "Teacher Education and Dissemination of Information." In D. J. Patton (Ed.), *From Geographic Discipline to Inquiring Student. The High School Geography Project. Final Report* (Washington, DC: Association of American Geographers, 1970), 47.

59. Robert B. Pratt, *Evolution of a Curriculum Project: The High School Geography Project* (Boulder, CO: Social Science Education Consortium, Inc., 1976), 22.

60. Pratt, 1976, 29.

61. Marion J. Rice, "The Case for the Disciplines in the Organization of Social Studies Curricula for Elementary and Secondary Schooling" (Paper Presented at College and University Faculty Association, National Council for the Social Studies, Boston, MA, November 21, 1972), 1.

62. Carole L. Hahn, "Attributes and Adoption of New Social Studies Materials," *Theory & Research in Social Education 5*, No. 1 (1977), 22.

63. Marion J. Rice, *Evaluation in the Anthropology Curriculum Project* (Report), Anthropology Curriculum Project, University of Georgia, Athens, GA (1969), 4.

64. Rice, 1969, 2.

65. Rice 1972, 4–5.

66. Hertzberg, 1981, 108–109.

67. Barbara Slater Stern, *The New Social Studies: People, Projects, & Perspectives* (Charlotte, NC: Information Age Publishing, 2010), ix.

68. Ian Tyrrell, American Exceptionalism in an Age of International History, *The American Historical Review* (1991).

69. Carr, 1965.

70. Hertzberg, 1981.

71. Hertzberg, 1981, 93.

72. Cohen-Cole, 2014.

73. Krug, Poster, & Gillies, 1970.

74. Krug, Poster, & Gillies, 1970.

75. Krug, Poster, & Gillies, 1970.

76. Keller, 1964.

77. Keller, 1964, 41.

78. Krug, Poster, & Gillies, 1970.

79. Carr, 1965.

80. Hertzberg, 1989.

81. Leonard S. Kenworthy, "Some Persistent Problems of the Social Studies, 1903–1978–2003" (Talk presented at Middle States Council for the Social Studies in Wilmington, DE, April 14, 1978), 13.

82. Hertzberg, 1989.

83. Krug, Poster, & Gillies, 1970.

84. H. Stuart Hughes, "The Historian and the Social Scientist." In B. G. Massialas & A. M. Kazamias (Eds.), *Crucial Issues in the Teaching of Social Studies: A Book of Readings* (Englewood Cliffs, NJ: Prentice-Hall, Inc., 1964).

85. Carolyn Jo Johnson McIntosh, *A Study of Teachers' Attitudes toward the "New" Social Studies* [Unpublished doctoral dissertation], University of North Texas, Denton, TX (1973), 66.
86. Krug, Poster, & Gillies, 1970.
87. Hunt & Metcalf, 1968.
88. Hunt & Metcalf, 1968.
89. Jackson & Jackson, 1989.
90. Jackson & Jackson, 1989.
91. Susan Moore Johnson, "Working in Schools." In S. Fuhrman & M. Lazerson (Eds.), *The Institutions of American Democracy: The Public Schools* (New York, NY: Oxford University Press, 2005).
92. Wilson, 1965, 54.
93. Wilson, 1965, 54.
94. Hunt & Metcalf, 1968.
95. Hunt & Metcalf, 1968.
96. Edwin Fenton, "Inquiry Techniques in the New Social Studies," *The High School Journal 55*, No. 1 (1971), 28.
97. Nicholas Helburn, "The High School Geography Project: A Retrospective View," *The Social Studies 89*, No. 5 (1998), 217.
98. Marion J. Rice & Wilfrid C. Bailey, *The Development of a Sequential Curriculum in Anthropology, Grades 1–7. Final Report* (Washington, DC: Department of Education, 1971), 51.
99. Rice, 1969, 7.
100. Byford and Russell, 2007, 46.
101. Pratt, 1976, 78.
102. Samec, 1976, 58.
103. Gross, 1976.
104. Weber, 2017, 58.
105. Suzanne Wiggins Helburn, "ECON12 and the New Social Studies: Love's Labor Lost?" *The Social Studies 88*, No. 6 (1997), 275.
106. Weber, 2017, 58.
107. Johnson, 2005.
108. Orry Walz, "Anthropology: Adrenalin for a Tired High School Curriculum," *The Clearing House: A Journal of Educational Strategies, Issues and Ideas 48*, No. 4 (1973), 208.
109. Gerald W. Marker, "Why Schools Abandon 'New Social Studies' Materials," *Theory & Research in Social Education 7*, No. 4 (1980), 35–36.
110. Marker, 1980, 55.
111. Marker, 1980, 55.
112. Fred M. Newmann, "The Analysis of Public Controversy: New Focus for Social Studies." In M. M. Krug, J. B. Poster, & W. B. Gillies III (Eds.), *The New Social Studies: Analysis of Theory and Materials* (Itasca, IL: F. E. Peacock, 1970).
113. Hertzberg (1981) attributes these to critiques to Standard Education Professor Richard Gross and Duke History Professor William Cartwright, respectively.
114. Nelson & Drake, 1994.

115. John D. Haas, *The Era of the New Social Studies* (Boulder, CO: Social Science Education Consortium, 1977).

116. Tim Joe Wells, *Oklahoma Secondary Social Supplies Teachers and the Usage of New National Social Studies Projects* [Unpublished doctoral dissertation], Oklahoma State University, Stillwater, OK (1973), 34.

CHAPTER 7

1. Hunt & Metcalf, 1968, 288.
2. Originally this group formed a company called the Educational Services Inc., but they merged with the Institute for Educational Innovation in January 1967 to form the Educational Development Center (EDC). Most of the literature refers to the EDC as the backing of MACOS even before 1967. For less confusion, I will utilize the EDC rather than the various early names.
3. Falkenstein, 1977.
4. Cohen-Cole, 2014.
5. Donald Oliver would eventually set up the Harvard Social Studies Project with Fred Newmann and James Shaver.
6. Harry F. Wolcott, "The Middlemen of MACOS," *Anthropology & Education Quarterly 38*, No. 2 (2007), 203.
7. Cohen-Cole, 2014.
8. Nancy C. Lutkehaus, "Putting 'Culture' into Cultural Psychology: Anthropology's Role in the Development of Bruner's Cultural Psychology," *Ethos 36*, No. 1 (2008).
9. Lutkehaus, 2008, 49.
10. Jerome Bruner, *Toward a Theory of Instruction* (Cambridge, MA: Harvard University Press, 1966), 90.
11. Bruner, 1966, 92.
12. Suan Hegeman, "Arctic Pedagogy: Indigenous People and the MACOS Culture War," *Lateral 10*, No. 2 (2021).
13. Hegeman, 2021.
14. Wolcott, 2007, 200.
15. Luktehaus, 2008, 53.
16. By Bruner as recounted in Lutkehaus, 2008, 54.
17. Erika Lorraine Milam, "Salmon, Gulls, and Baboons? Oh My," *The Journal of the History of Childhood and Youth 4*, No. 3 (2011).
18. Milam, 2011, 362.
19. Peter B. Dow, "MACOS: The Study of Human Behavior as One Road to Survival," *The Phi Delta Kappan 57*, No. 2 (1975), 80.
20. Symcox, 2002.
21. Krug, Poster, & Gillies, 1970.
22. Falkenstein, 1977, 24.
23. Wolcott, 2007, 200.
24. As quoted in Falkenstein, 1977, 14.

25. Floyd Fenocchio as quoted in Kraus, 1977, 2.
26. Hegeman, 2021.
27. Cohen-Cole, 2014.
28. Falkenstein, 1977, 107.
29. Cohen-Cole, 2014.
30. Falkenstein, 1977, 30.
31. Joe Allen Weedman, *A Case for Anthropology as the Integrating Force in Pre-Collegiate Social Studies* [Unpublished doctoral dissertation], Texas Tech University, Lubbock, TX (1976), 28.
32. Evans, 2010.
33. Hegeman, 2021.
34. Hegeman, 2021, 6.
35. Cohen-Cole, 2014, 218.
36. Cohen-Cole, 2014.
37. Cohen-Cole, 2014.
38. Peter Woolfson, "The Fight over MACOS: An Ideological Conflict in Vermont," *Council on Anthropology and Education Quarterly 5*, No. 3 (1974), 27.
39. Woolfson, 1974, 28.
40. Falkenstein, 1977, 165.
41. Ken Hechler, *Toward the Endless Frontier: History of the Committee on Science and Technology, 1959–79* (Washington, DC: US House of Representatives, 1980), 517.
42. Hechler, 1980, 517–18.
43. Evans, 2004, 144.
44. Evans, 2010.
45. Hegeman, 2021.
46. James J. Kilpatrick as quoted in Kraus, 1977, 82.
47. Hegeman, 2021.
48. Kraus, 1977, 87.
49. Karen B. Wiley, *The NSF Science Education Controversy: Issues, Events, Decisions* (Boulder, CO: Social Science Education Consortium, Inc., 1976).
50. Lee Dembert, "The Proper Study of Mankind," *New York Times*, April 25, 1976.
51. Hechler, 1980, 516.
52. Hechler, 1980, 520.
53. As quoted by Wolcott, 2007, 202.
54. Wolcott, 2007, 201.
55. Dow, 1975, 80.
56. Wolcott, 2007, 201.
57. Falkenstein, 1977, 180.
58. Dembert, 1976.
59. Lloyd Tredwell & David Zodikoff, "A Study of the Effects of Jerome Bruner's 'Man: A Course of Study' on Social Studies Achievement in Fifth Grade" (Paper presented to the Asian American Conference at the University of Massachusetts, December 6, 1974), 8.

60. Percy D. Peckham & Arthur E. Ware, "An Evaluation of 'Man: A Course of Study'" (Evaluation for Bellevue Public Schools, Bellevue, WA, 1973).

61. Kraus, 1977, 80.

62. Falkenstein, 1977, 171.

63. Falkenstein, 1977.

64. Hegeman, 2021.

65. Hegeman, 2021.

66. Hegeman, 2021.

67. Hechler, 1980, 649.

68. Tyack, James, & Benovat, 1987.

69. Julian Vasquez Heilig, Keffrelyn Brown, & Anthony Brown, "The Illusion of Inclusion: A Critical Race Theory Textual Analysis of Race and Standards," *Harvard Educational Review 82*, No. 3 (2012); Lerner, Nagai, & Rothman, 1995.

70. Lerner, Nagai, & Rothman, 1995.

71. Hertzberg, 1981.

72. Evans, 2004.

73. Kraus, 1977, 18.

74. Evans, 2010, 21.

75. Evans, 2010.

76. Evans, 2010.

77. John Guenther, "More Humanistic Social Studies Programs through Minicourses" (Paper presented at the Annual Meeting of the National Council for the Social Studies, Atlanta, GA, November 27–29, 1975).

78. Hertzberg, 1981.

79. Guenther, 1975.

80. Paul Ringel, "Schoolhouse Rock! for a New Generation: What Should It Look Like?" *The Public Historian 43*, No. 1 (2021), 84.

81. Talia Brenner, "America Rock's Education: Presenting National Narratives on American Televisions," *The Virginia Tech Undergraduate Historical Review 7* (2018), 29.

82. Brenner, 2018, 34–35.

83. Ringel, 2021, 84.

84. Hertzberg, 1981.

85. Hertzberg, 1981.

86. William E. Gardner, "The Social Studies—Its Role in General Education." In W. E. Gardner & F. A. Johnson (Eds.), *Social Studies in the Secondary Schools: A Book of Readings* (Boston, MA: Allyn and Bacon, Inc., 1970).

87. Cohen-Cole, 2014.

88. Mary Campbell Gallagher, "Lessons from the Sputnik-era Curriculum Reform Movement: The Institutions We Need for Educational Reform." In S. Stotsky (Ed.), *What's at Stake in the K-12 Standards Wars: A Primer for Educational Policy Makers* (New York, NY: Peter Lang Publishing, Inc., 2000).

89. Wolcott, 2007, 198.

90. Daniel Selakovich, "Has the New Social Studies Failed?" *The High School Journal 59*, No. 3 (1975), 135.

91. Carr, 1965.
92. Selakovich, 1975, 134.
93. Wolcott, 2007, 199.
94. Kraus, 1977, 27–28.
95. Kraus, 1977, 60.
96. Kraus, 1977, 76–77.
97. Kraus, 1977, 78.
98. Woyshner, Watras, & Crocco, 2004, xv.
99. Dembert, 1976.
100. Milam, 2011, 366.
101. Woolfson, 1974, 30.
102. Hegeman, 2021.
103. Hegeman, 2021.
104. Selakovich, 1975, 135.
105. Hegeman, 2021.
106. Hegeman, 2021.
107. Cohen-Cole, 2014.
108. Cohen-Cole, 2014.
109. Jack Hassard, Defunding the Common Core: Back to the Future [Blog]. Available from http://nepc.colorado.edu (National Education Policy Center, May 2, 2013).
110. Jerome S. Bruner, *The Process of Education* (Revised edition) (Cambridge, MA: Harvard University Press, 2009), 19–20. Originally published in 1960.
111. Edwin Reynolds, interview by Mary Ellen Zuverink, December 5, 1984, interview, transcript, and recording, Oral History of Teaneck (2), History of Teaneck Township, Archive collection of the Teaneck Public Library. Retrieved from https://archive.teanecklibrary.org/OralHistory2/reynolds.html.
112. Reynolds, 1984.

CHAPTER 8

1. The Department of Education was separated in 1979 by President Carter from the Department of Health, Education, and Welfare, which was created in 1953 under President Eisenhower. The federal oversight of education dates back to 1867 under President Andrew Johnson as the Office of Education.
2. Evans, 2004.
3. Evans, 2004, 150.
4. Ronald W. Evans, *Schooling Corporate Citizens: How Accountability Reform Has Damaged Civic Education and Undermined Democracy* (New York, NY: Routledge, 2014).
5. National Commission on Educational Excellence, "A Nation at Risk: The Imperative for Educational Reform" (Report to the Nation and the Secretary of Education). In D. T. Gordon (Ed.), *A Nation Reformed? American Education 20 Years after* A Nation at Risk (Cambridge, MA: Harvard Education Press, 2003).

6. Evans, 2004.
7. Maris A. Vinovskis, "Missed Opportunities: Why the Federal Response to A Nation at Risk Was Inadequate." In D. T. Gordon (Ed.), *A Nation Reformed? American Education 20 Years after* A Nation at Risk (Cambridge, MA: Harvard Education Press, 2003), 129.
8. David T. Gordon, "The Limits of Ideology: Curriculum and the Culture Wars." In D. T. Gordon (Ed.), *A Nation Reformed? American Education 20 Years after* A Nation at Risk (Cambridge, MA: Harvard Education Press, 2003).
9. David T. Gordon, "Introduction." In D. T. Gordon (Ed.), *A Nation Reformed? American Education 20 Years after* A Nation at Risk (Cambridge, MA: Harvard Education Press, 2003).
10. Symcox, 2002.
11. Vinovskis, 2003.
12. Symcox, 2002.
13. Richard F. Elmore, "Change and Improvement in Educational Reform." In D. T. Gordon (Ed.), *A Nation Reformed? American Education 20 Years after* A Nation at Risk (Cambridge, MA: Harvard Education Press, 2003).
14. Scott Geoffrey Grant, "Research on History Tests." In S. G. Grant (Ed.), *Measuring History: Cases of State-Level Testing across the United States* (Charlotte, NC: Information Age Publishing, 2006).
15. Susan Fuhrman & Marvin Lazerson (Eds.), *The Institutions of American Democracy: The Public Schools* (New York, NY: Oxford University Press, 2005).
16. Maris A. Vinovskis, *Overseeing the Nation's Report Card: The Creation and Evolution of the National Assessment Governing Board (NAGB)* (Washington, DC: National Assessment Governing Board, 2001).
17. Vinovskis, 2001.
18. Evans, 2004, 153.
19. Maris A. Vinovskis, "No Child Left Behind and Highly Qualified U.S. History Teachers: Some Historical and Policy Perspectives." In K. W. Wong & R. Rothman (Eds.), *Clio at the Table: Using History to Inform and Improve Education Policy* (New York, NY: Peter Lang, 2009).
20. Newmann, 1970, 7.
21. Newmann, 1970, 11.
22. Michael Henry, "A Fifty-Year Perspective on History Teaching's 'Crisis,'" *OAH Magazine of History 7,* No. 3 (1993).
23. Fallace, 2008.
24. Evans, 2004; Henry, 1993.
25. Nash, Crabtree, & Dunn, 1997.
26. Diane Ravitch & Chester E. Finn, *What Do Our 17-Year-Olds Know? A Report on the First National Assessment of History and Literature* (New York, NY: Harper & Row, Publishers, 1987), 251.
27. Ravitch & Finn, 1987.
28. Edward B. Fiske, "Schools Criticized on the Humanities," *New York Times,* September 8, 1987.
29. Symcox, 2002.

30. Symcox, 2002.
31. Hertzberg, 1989.
32. Bradley Commission on History in Schools, "Building a History Curriculum: Guidelines for Teaching History in Schools." In P. Gagnon & The Bradley Commission on History in Schools (Eds.), *Historical Literacy: The Case for History in American Education* (New York, NY: Macmillan Publishing Company, 1989).
33. Bradley Commission, 1989.
34. Bradley Commission, 1989.
35. Bradley Commission, 1989, 17.
36. Ravitch, 1989.
37. William H. McNeill, Michael Kammen, & Gordon A. Craig, "Why Study History? Three Historians Respond." In P. Gagnon & The Bradley Commission on History in Schools (Eds.), *Historical Literacy: The Case for History in American Education* (New York, NY: Macmillan Publishing Company, 1989), 104.
38. John Arévalo, Marjorie Bingham, Louise Cox Byron, Claudia J. Hoone, & Charles Shotland, "Obstacles Teachers Confront: What Needs to Change." In P. Gagnon & The Bradley Commission on History in Schools (Eds.), *Historical Literacy: The Case for History in American Education* (New York, NY: Macmillan Publishing Company, 1989).
39. Suzanne M. Wilson & Gary Sykes, "Toward Better Teacher Preparation and Certification." In P. Gagnon & The Bradley Commission on History in Schools (Eds.), *Historical Literacy: The Case for History in American Education* (New York, NY: Macmillan Publishing Company, 1989).
40. Wilson & Sykes, 1989.
41. Wilson & Sykes, 1989, 277.
42. Evans, 2004.
43. Wilson & Sykes, 1989.
44. Hanna Schissler, "Containing and Regulating Knowledge: Some Thoughts on Standards and Canonization as a Response to the Complex Demands of a Globalizing World." In L. Symcox & A. Wilschut (Eds.), *National History Standards: The Problem of the Canon and the Future of Teaching History* (Charlotte, NC: Information Age Publishing, Inc., 2009), 98.
45. Joseph Crespino, "Civil Rights and the Religious Right." In B. J. Schulman & J. E. Zelizer (Eds.), *Rightward Bound: Making America Conservative in the 1970s* (Cambridge, MA: Harvard University Press, 2009).
46. Fuhrman & Lazerson, 2005, xxvii.
47. Newmann, 1970, 8.
48. Fuhrman & Lazerson, 2005.
49. Symcox, 2002.
50. Symcox, 2002, 76.
51. Symcox, 2002, 77.
52. McNeill, Kammen, & Craig, 1989.
53. McNeill, Kammen, & Craig, 1989.
54. Matthew T. Downey, History in the Schools, *National Council for the Social Studies Bulletin 74* (1985); R. E. Gross, *The Status of the Social Studies in the Public*

Schools of the United States: Facts and Impressions of a National Survey [Paper presented at annual meeting of the National Council for Social Studies, Washington, DC, 1976].

55. Hertzberg, 1989.

56. Hertzberg, 1989; Nelson, 1994; National Education Association of the United States, 1893.

57. Hertzberg, 1989.

58. Ravitch, 1989, 68.

59. Keith C. Barton, "Wars and Rumors of War: The Rhetoric and Reality of History Education in the United States." In T. Taylor & R. Guyver (Eds.), *History Wars and the Classroom: Global Perspectives* (Charlotte, NC: Information Age Publishing, Inc., 2012).

60. Stephen J. Thornton & Keith C. Barton, "Can History Stand Alone? Drawbacks and Blind Spots of a "Disciplinary" Curriculum," *Teachers College Record 112*, No. 9 (2010).

61. Robert L. Dahlgren, "The Attack on Social Studies Teachers and Teaching in 1970s and 1980s Hollywood Movies," *The Councilor: A Journal of the Social Studies 74*, No. 2 (2013), 7.

CHAPTER 9

1. Lawrence C. Stedman, "The Sandia Report and U.S. Achievement: An Assessment," *Journal of Educational Research 87*, No. 3 (1994); Symcox, 2002.

2. Nash, Crabtree, & Dunn, 1997.

3. Kathryn A. McDermott, "Growing State Intervention in Low-Performing Schools: Laws and Regulation in Three Waves of Reform." In K. W. Wong & R. Rothman (Eds.), *Clio at the Table: Using History to Inform and Improve Education Policy* (New York, NY: Peter Lang, 2009), 92.

4. Susan Fuhrman, "Riding Waves, Trading Horses: The Twenty-Year Effort to Reform Education." In D. T. Gordon (Ed.), *A Nation Reformed? American Education 20 Years After* A Nation at Risk (Cambridge, MA: Harvard Education Press, 2003).

5. McDermott, 2009.

6. Nash, Crabtree, & Dunn, 1997, 150.

7. Nash, Crabtree, & Dunn, 1997,

8. *Goals 2000: Educate America Act and the Improving America's Schools Act*, Pub. L. 103-227 § Stat. H.R. 1804 (1994); McDermott, 2009.

9. Walter C. Parker, *Renewing the Social Studies Curriculum* (Alexandria, VA: Association for Supervision and Curriculum Development, 1991).

10. Nash, Crabtree, & Dunn, 1997.

11. Symcox, 2002.

12. Evans, 2004.

13. Cleo H. Cherryholmes, "Social Studies for Which Century?" *Social Education 54*, No. 7 (1990).

14. Evans, 2004.

15. Evans, 2004.
16. Symcox, 2002.
17. Symcox, 2002, 74.
18. Nash, Crabtree, & Dunn, 1997.
19. Symcox, 2002.
20. Symcox, 2002.
21. Symcox, 2002.
22. Nelson, 2001, 18.
23. Nelson, 2001, 16.
24. Jere Brophy & Janet Alleman, "Meaningful Social Studies for Elementary Students," *Teachers and Teaching: Theory and Practice 15*, No. 3 (2009).
25. Saxe, 1992.
26. Vinovskis, 2009.
27. Nash, Crabtree, & Dunn, 1997.
28. Nash, Crabtree, & Dunn, 1997.
29. Donald Schneider, "Teaching Social Studies: The Standards Movement," *The Clearing House 67*, No. 1 (1993).
30. Nash, Crabtree, & Dunn, 1997.
31. See Bicouvaris for a full list of participants and focus groups. Mary Vassilikou Bicouvaris, *Building a Consensus for the Development of National Standards in History* [Unpublished doctoral dissertation], Old Dominion University, Norfolk, VA (1994).
32. National Center for History in the Schools, *National Standards for History, Basic Edition* (Los Angeles, CA: UCLA Press, 1996).
33. Nash, Crabtree, & Dunn, 1997.
34. Nash, Crabtree, & Dunn, 1997, 175.
35. Nash, Crabtree, & Dunn, 1997.
36. Western Civilization courses are generally believed to have started at Columbia University in 1919. James Harvey Robinson is often connected. The course became widely popular in K-12 and universities until the 1980s. See Gilbert Allardyce, "The Rise and Fall of the Western Civilization Course," *The American Historical Review 87*, No. 3 (1982), where he discusses the origins and its evolution through the 1960s. Stanley Kurtz, *The Lost History of Western Civilization* (New York: NY: National Association of Scholars, 2020) tells a slightly different end to Western Civilization courses focusing on discrediting Allardyce's thesis.
37. Symcox, 2002.
38. Symcox, 2002.
39. National Geographic Society Committee on Research and Exploration, *Geography for Life: The National Geography Standards* (1994).
40. Center for Civic Education, *National Standards for Civics and Government* (Calabasas, CA: Center for Civic Education, 1994).
41. Council for Economic Education, *Voluntary National Content Standards in Economics* (second ed.) (2010).
42. Stephen Buckles & Michael Watts, "National Standards in Economics, History, Social Studies, Civics, and Geography: Complementarities, Competition, or Peaceful Coexistence?" *The Journal of Economic Education 29*, No. 2 (1998).

43. Evans, 2004.
44. As quoted by Evans, 2004, 165.
45. Parker, 1991.
46. Evans, 2004.
47. Evans, 2004, 169.
48. Richard H. Kohn, "History and the Culture Wars: The Case of the Smithsonian Institution's *Enola Gay* Exhibition," *The Journal of American History 82*, No. 3 (1995).
49. Joseph M. Skelly, as read into the Congressional Record 140, Number 127 (September 13, 1994), by Rep. Duncan Hunter. Ironically, members of Congress wanted to create their own version of pseudo-history that places all the blame on the Japanese. The history of the atomic bomb is more complex and widely debated by historians even today.
50. Nash, Crabtree, & Dunn, 1997.
51. Nash, Crabtree, & Dunn, 1997.
52. Evans, 2004.
53. Michael C. Johanek & John Puckett, "The State of Civic Education: Preparing Citizens in an Era of Accountability." In S. Fuhrman & M. M. Lazerson (Eds.), *The Institutions of American Democracy: The Public Schools* (New York, NY: Oxford University Press, 2005).
54. Sheldon M. Stern, "Why the Battle over History Standards?" In S. Stotsky (Ed.), *What's at Stake in the K-12 Standards Wars: A Primer for Educational Policy Makers* (New York, NY: Peter Lang Publishing, Inc., 2000).
55. Nash, Crabtree, & Dunn, 1997, 7.
56. Stern, 2000.
57. C. Frederick Risinger, "The National History Standards: A View from the Inside," *The History Teacher 28*, No. 3 (1995), 389.
58. Nash, Crabtree, & Dunn, 1997.
59. Stern, 2000, 153.
60. Stern, 2000.
61. Nash, Crabtree, & Dunn, 1997.
62. Catherine Cornbleth & Dexter Waugh, "Research News and Comment: The Great Speckled Bird: Education Policy-in-the-Making," *Educational Researcher 22*, No. 7 (1993).
63. Linda Darling-Hammond, "National Standards and Assessments: Will They Improve Education?" *American Journal of Education 102*, No. 4 (1994).
64. Darling-Hammond, 1994, 481.
65. Nash, Crabtree, & Dunn, 1997.
66. Evans, 2004.
67. Johanek & Puckett, 2005.
68. Williamson M. Evers, "Implementing Standards and Testing." In C. E. Finn Jr. & R. Sousa (Eds.), *What Lies Ahead: For America's Children and Their Schools* (Stanford, CA: Hoover Institution Press, 2014).
69. John Tosh, *Why History Matters* (New York, NY: Palgrave Macmillan, 2008).

70. Katherine G. Simon, "Classroom Deliberations." In S. Fuhrman & M. Lazerson (Eds.), *The Institutions of American Democracy: The Public Schools* (New York, NY: Oxford University Press, 2005).

71. Symcox, 2002, 101; Symcox was assistant to Charlotte Crabtree during the NSH.

72. Symcox, 2002, 4.

73. Nash, Crabtree, & Dunn, 1997, 77.

74. Peter Seixas, "Historical Understanding among Adolescents in a Multicultural Setting," *Curriculum Inquiry 23*, No. 3 (1993).

75. Stern, 2000.

76. Symcox, 2002.

77. Symcox, 2002.

78. Symcox, 2002.

79. Kurtz, 2020.

80. Nash, Crabtree, & Dunn, 1997.

81. Symcox, 2002.

82. Tony Taylor & Robert Guyver, "Introduction." In T. Taylor & R. Guyver (Eds.), *History Wars and the Classroom: Global Perspectives* (Charlotte, NC: Information Age Publishing, Inc., 2012), xiii.

83. Risinger, 1995.

84. Symcox, 2002, 151.

85. Robert M. Costrell, "Discipline-based Economics Standards: Opportunity and Obstacles." In S. Stotsky (Ed.), *What's at Stake in the K-12 Standards Wars: A Primer for Educational Policy Makers* (New York, NY: Peter Lang Publishing, Inc., 2000).

86. Buckles & Watts, 1998.

87. Costrell, 2000.

88. Costrell, 2000.

89. Evans, 2004.

90. Symcox, 2002.

91. Nash, Crabtree, & Dunn, 1997.

92. Costrell, 2000.

93. Costrell, 2000, 170.

94. Costrell, 2000.

95. Arie Wilschut, "Canonical Standards or Orientational Frames Reference? The Cultural and Educational Approach to the Debate about Standards in History Teaching," In L. Symcox & A. Wilschut (Eds.), *National History Standards: The Problem of the Canon and the Future of Teaching History* (Charlotte, NC: Information Age Publishing, Inc., 2009), 128–29.

96. Keith C. Barton & Linda S. Levstik, "'Back When God Was Around and Everything': Elementary Children's Understanding of Historical Time," *American Educational Research Journal 33*, No. 2 (1996).

97. Sam Wineburg, *Historical Thinking and Other Unnatural Acts: Charting the Future of Teaching the Past* (Philadelphia, PA: Temple University Press, 2001).

98. Bruce A. VanSledright & Christine Kelly, "Reading American History: The Influence of Multiple Sources on Six Fifth Graders," *The Elementary School Journal 98*, No. 3 (1998).

99. Keith C. Barton & Alan W. McCully, "History, Identity, and the School Curriculum in Northern Ireland: An Empirical Study of Secondary Students' Ideas and Perspectives," *Journal of Curriculum Studies 37*, No. 1 (2005).

100. Keith C. Barton, "The Denial of Desire: How to Make History Education Meaningless." In L. Symcox & A. Wilschut (Eds.), *National History Standards: The Problem of the Canon and the Future of Teaching History* (Charlotte, NC: Information Age Publishing, 2009).

101. Ross E. Dunn, "The Two World Histories." In L. Symcox & A. Wilschut (Eds.), *National History Standards: The Problem of the Canon and the Future of Teaching History* (Charlotte, NC: Information Age Publishing, Inc., 2009).

102. Symcox, 2002, 2–3.

103. Stern, 2000.

104. Robert J. Marzano & John S. Kendall, *Awash in a Sea of Standards* (Report) (Aurora, CO: Mid-Continent Research for Education and Learning, 1998).

CHAPTER 10

1. Walt Haney, "The Myth of the Texas Miracle in Education," *Education Policy Analysis Archives 8* (2000), 41.

2. Haney, 2000.

3. Martin Carnoy & Susanna Loeb, "Does External Accountability Affect Student Outcomes? A Cross-State Analysis," *Educational Evaluation and Policy Analysis 24*, No. 4 (2002).

4. Meira Levinson, *No Citizen Left Behind* (Cambridge, MA: Harvard University Press, 2012).

5. No Child Left Behind Act of 2001 (NCLB), Pub. L. No. 107-110, § 115 Stat. 1425 (2002), 115.

6. NCLB, 2002. The only social studies disciplines mentioned are history (28), Civics & Government (15), economics (18), and geography (5).

7. Levinson, 2012, 254.

8. David Randall, Critique of the Fordham Institute's "The State of State Standards for Civics and U.S. History in 2021," *National Association of Scholars* (July 29, 2021). Fordham Foundation was directed by Chester Finn and was an outgrowth of the Education Excellence Network.

9. Sheldon M. Stern & Jeremy A. Stern, *The State of State U.S. History Standards, 2011* (Washington, DC: The Thomas B. Fordham Institute, 2011), 7.

10. Stern & Stern, 2011, 2.

11. Grant, 2006.

12. Michael Learn, *Consequential Validity and Social Studies Education: An Examination of Standards, Assessment Policies, and Teacher Preparation* [Unpublished doctoral dissertation], North Dakota State University, Fargo, ND (2019).

13. Joshua L. Kenna & William B. Russell III, "The Culture and History of Standards-Based Educational Reform and Social Studies in America," *Journal of Culture and Values in Education 1*, No. 1 (2018), 42.

14. Neil O. Houser, "Social Studies on the Back Burner: Views from the Field," *Theory & Research in Social Education 23*, No. 2 (1995); Zhao & Hoge, 2005.

15. Gail McEachron, "Study of Allocated Social Studies Time in Elementary Classrooms in Virginia: 1987–2009," *The Journal of Social Studies Research 34*, No. 2 (2010).

16. Patricia Velde Pederson, "What Is Measured Is Treasured: The Impact of the No Child Left Behind Act on Nonassessed Subjects," *The Clearing House: A Journal of Educational Strategies, Issues and Ideas 80*, No. 6 (2007).

17. Paul G. Fitchett, Tina L. Heafner, & Richard G. Lambert, "Examining Elementary Social Studies Marginalization: A Multilevel Model," *Educational Policy 20*, No. 10 (2012).

18. Kenneth E. Vogler, "Comparing the Impact of Accountability Examinations on Mississippi and Tennessee Social Studies Teachers' Instructional Practices," *Educational Assessment 13*, No. 1 (2008).

19. Vinovskis, 2009.

20. Vinovskis, 2009.

21. Evers, 2014.

22. Evers, 2014.

23. Evers, 2014.

24. John K. Lee, "The Status of Social Studies and the Common Core State Standards: An Opportunity for Reform." In J. Passe & P. G. Fitchett (Eds.), *The Status of Social Studies: Views from the Field* (Charlotte, NC: Information Age Publishing, Inc., 2013).

25. Lee, 2013.

26. Fitchett, Heafner, & Lambert, 2012.

27. Lee, 2013.

28. Wayne Au, "Coring Social Studies within Corporate Education Reform: The Common Core State Standards, Social Justice, and the Politics of Knowledge in U.S. Schools," *Critical Education 4*, No. 5 (2013).

29. Au, 2013.

30. Joshua L. Kenna & William B. Russell III, "Implications of Common Core State Standards on the Social Studies," *The Clearing House: A Journal of Educational Strategies, Issues and Ideas 87*, No. 2 (2014).

31. Catherine Gewertz, "Chiefs Group Terminates Role in Social Studies Framework" [Blog]. Retrieved from *Curriculum Matters* (June 7, 2013).

32. Catherine Gewertz, "Incoming College Board Head Wants SAT to Reflect Common Core," *Education Week* (May 16, 2012).

33. Stephanie van Hover, David Hicks, & Jeremy Stoddard, "The Development of Virginia's History and Social Studies Standards of Learning (SOLs), 1995–2010," *The Virginia Newsletter 86*, No. 2 (2010), 2.

34. Keith Erekson, "Culture War Circus: How Politics and the Media Left History Education Behind." In K. A. Erekson (Ed.), *Politics and the History Curriculum: The Struggle over Standards in Texas and the Nation* (New York, NY: Palgrave Macmillan, 2012).

35. Erekson, 2012.

36. Abbie Strunc, "Rewriting the Standards, Not History: A Critical Discourse Analysis of the Texas State Board of Education Social Studies Standards Revisions," *National Journal of Urban and Public Education 11*, No. 2 (2017); see also, Gene B Preuss, "'As Texas Goes, So Goes the Nation' Conservatism and Culture Wars in the Lone Star State." In K. A. Erekson (Ed.), *Politics and the History Curriculum: The Struggle over Standards in Texas and the Nation* (New York, NY: Palgrave Macmillan, 2012).

37. Jill Lepore, *The Whites of Their Eyes: The Tea Party's Revolution and the Battle over American History* (Princeton, NJ: Princeton University Press, 2010).

38. Julio Noboa, "Names, Numbers, and Narratives: A Multicultural Critique of the US History Standards." In K. A. Erekson (Ed.), *Politics and the History Curriculum: The Struggle over Standards in Texas and the Nation* (New York, NY: Palgrave Macmillan, 2012).

39. Lepore, 2010.

40. Edward H. Sebesta, "Neo-Confederate Ideology in the Texas History Standards." In K. A. Erekson (Ed.), *Politics and the History Curriculum: The Struggle over Standards in Texas and the Nation* (New York, NY: Palgrave Macmillan, 2012).

41. Erekson, 2012. California would be the biggest, but they permit local control in high school. For these textbooks, high school is generally where the most contentious aspects of debate happen.

42. See Dana Goldstein, "Two States. Eight Textbooks. Two American Stories," *New York Times,* January 7, 2020, 12.

43. Duane Campbell, "California Must Change Its History Books before Adopting Common Core" [Blog post]. Retrieved from http://choosingdemocracy.blogspot.com /2013/09/california-must-change (September 11, 2013).

44. Purnima Bose, "Hindutva Abroad: The California Textbook Controversy," *The Global South 2*, No. 1 (2008).

45. Bose, 2008.

46. Sophie Kasakove, "The Fight over 'Maus' Is Part of a Bigger Cultural Battle in Tennessee," *New York Times*, March 4, 2022. Retrieved on October 6, 2023.

47. See Kasakove, 2022. Arkansas passed a law criminalizing some books; Illinois passed a law preventing the banning of any pools in public schools and libraries; students and authors are suing Florida and a school district that removed a book about penguins with two fathers.

48. Joseph J. Ferreira Jr., "Boston Public Schools to Eliminate History & Social Science Departments" (2014, May 21), *H-Net*, https://networks.h-net.org/node /14773/discussions/27470/boston-public-schools-eliminate-history-social-science -departments.

49. Lee White, "Letter to John McDonough, Boston Public Schools from the National Coalition for History" (May 28, 2014), https://historycoalition .org/wp-content/uploads/2014/05/NCH-Superintendent-McDonough-BPS-History -final.pdf.

50. Boston Public Schools, "Q: IS BPS REALLY ELIMINATING ITS HISTORY AND SOCIAL STUDIES DEPARTMENT? A: NO" [Press release] (May 23 2014),

https://www.bostonpublicschools.org/site/default.aspx?PageType=3&DomainID=4&ModuleInstanceID=14&ViewID=047E6BE3-6D87-4130-8424-D8E4E9ED6C2A&RenderLoc=0&FlexDataID=4091&PageID=1.

51. Kerry Dunne, (2014, May 24), As a follow-up to the post from Friday, here is a link to a response from the Interim Superintendent of Schools for the Boston Public Schools [Comment on the blog post "Boston Public Schools to Eliminate History & Social Science Departments"], *H-Net*, https://networks.h-net.org/node/14773/discussions/27470/boston-public-schools-eliminate-history-social-science-departments.

52. A. J. Angulo & Jack Schneider, "Between Recent Political Controversies and Long-Standing Education Histories," *History of Education Quarterly,* 62 (2022), 133.

53. Jake Silverstein, "The 1619 Project and the Long Battle over U.S. History," *New York Times Magazine*, November 9, 2021, https://www.nytimes.com/2021/11/09/magazine/1619-project-us-history.html#:~:text=That%20project%20made%20a%20bold,be%20considered%20the%20country's%20origin.

54. Silverstein, 2021.

55. Paul M. Ong, *COVID-19 and the Digital Divide in Virtual Learning, Fall 2020* (Los Angeles, CA: UCLA Center for Neighborhood Knowledge, 2020).

56. Derrick Bryson Taylor, "George Floyd Protests: A Timeline," *New York Times,* June 8, 2020.

57. Christopher L. Busey, Kristen E. Duncan, & Tianna Dowie-Chin, "Critical What What? A Theoretical Systematic Review of 15 Years of Critical Race Theory Research in Social Studies Education, 2004–2019," *Review of Educational Research,* 93, No. 3 (2023).

58. Rashawn Ray & Alexandra Gibbons, *Why Are States Banning Critical Race Theory?* (Washington, DC: Brookings Institute, November 2021), https://www.brookings.edu/articles/why-are-states-banning-critical-race-theory/.

59. Exec. Order # 13,958, 85 Fed. Reg. 215 (2 November 2020).

60. Larry P. Arnn, Carol Swain, and Matthew Spalding (Eds.), *The 1776 Report* (Monroe, IL: Encounter Books, 2021).

61. Tom Cotton & Ken Buck, "When *New York Times* Fake News Replaces American History," *National Review,* June 30, 2021.

62. Jarrett Stepman, "Critical Race Theory Infiltrates Government, Classrooms," *The Daily Signal*, January 12, 2021.

63. John Murawski, "No Critical Race Theory in Schools? Here's the Abundant Evidence Saying Otherwise," *Real Clear Investigations*, December 22, 2021. Murawski does not address the fact that George Floyd was killed the year prior; nor that the trial of the police officer involved was current events in the city. Minnesota also has implemented an ethnic studies requirement for graduation in 2022.

64. Angulo & Schneider, 2022.

65. Judd Legum & Rebecca Crosby, "Pennsylvania School District Requires Social Studies Classes to Incorporate Right-Wing Propaganda," *Popular Information*, September 7, 2023.

66. Greg Childress, "Bill to Allow Controversial Social Studies Curriculum in Beaufort County Schools Surprised Its Leaders," *NC Newsline*, April 20, 2023.

67. Diana Lambert, Mallika Seshadri, & John Fensterwald, "Temecula Board Again Votes to Reject Textbooks, Despite Warnings from Newsom," *Ed Source*, July 19, 2023.

68. Anemona Hartocollis, "Florida Eliminates Sociology as a Core Course at Its Universities," *New York Times*, January 24, 2024.

69. Tyler Kingkade, "Conservatives Are Changing K-12 Education and One Christian College Is at the Center," *NBC News.com*, July 20, 2023.

70. Stephen Jackson, "The Place of World History in South Dakota's Failed 2021 Social Studies Standards Revision Process," *World History Connected 20*, No. 1 (2023).

71. Jackson, 2023, 4–5.

72. Jackson, 2023, 5.

73. Jackson, 2023, 5.

74. Jackson, 2023, 7.

75. Jacob Newton, "Noem Helped Select Social Studies Commission Members," *KELOLAND.com*, April 27, 2022. Mark Miller (chair), Joe Circle Bear (tribal leader), Janet Finzen (NE teacher), Stephanie Hiatt (former teacher, currently in banking), Benjamin Jones (state historian), Dylan Kessler (retirement director), Aaron Levisay (FM supervisor at US military), Christopher Motz (SD Catholic conference), Shaun Nielsen (teacher), Fred Osborn (director of Indian Education), Jon Schaff (government professor at Northern State University), Mary Shuey (former teacher), State Rep. Tamara St. John, Samantha Walder (award-winning elementary teacher with focus on LA), State Senator John Wiik.

76. Cory Allen Heidelberger, "Hillsdale's Morrisey Wrote Social Studies Standards—Contract Says So," *Dakota Free Press*, September 18, 2023.

77. South Dakota Education Association, "SDEA Responds to the Adoption of Social Studies Standards by the South Dakota Board of Education Standards," *SDEA.org*, April 17, 2023.

78. David Wegner, "Letter to the Editor: What Was Behind the South Dakota Standards Review?" *Mitchell republic.com*, September 24, 2022.

79. Jackson, 2023, 11; See also Tyler O'Neil, "'Model for Rest of the Country': South Dakota History Standards Scrap Critical Race Theory, Build on Hillsdale Foundation," *The Daily Signal*, May 9, 2023.

80. Jazzmine Jackson, "Superintendents Join Opposition to Proposed Social Studies Standards," *KELOLAND.COM*, April 11, 2023.

81. C. J. Keene, "Some Educators Apprehensive over Implementation of Social Studies Standards," *SDPB Radio*, June 25, 2023.

82. Jesse H. Rhodes, *An Education in Politics: The Origin and Evolution of No Child Left Behind* (Ithaca, NY: Cornell University Press, 2012).

83. Simon, 2005, 115.

84. Margaret E. Goertz, "Standards-Based Reform: Lessons from the Past, Directions for the Future." In K. W. Wong & R. Rothman (Eds.), *Clio at the Table: Using History to Inform and Improve Education Policy* (New York, NY: Peter Lang. 2009).

85. See Kathleen Kennedy Manzo, "Social Studies Losing out to Reading, Math," *Education Week 24*, No. 27 (2005).

86. Vinovskis, 2009.
87. Pederson, 2007.
88. George K. Cunningham, "Learning from Kentucky's Failed Accountability System." In W. M. Evers & H. J. Walberg (Eds.), *Testing Student Learning, Evaluating Teaching Effectiveness* (Stanford, CA: Hoover Institution Press, 2004).
89. Au, 2013.
90. Au, 2013.
91. Kenneth E. Vogler & David Virtue, "'Just the Facts, Ma'am': Teaching Social Studies in the Era of Standards and High-Stakes Testing," *The Social Studies 98*, No. 2 (2007).
92. Tina L. Heafner, George B. Lipscomb, & Tracy C. Rock, "To Test or Not to Test? The Role of Testing in Elementary Social Studies, a Collaborative Study Conducted by NCPSSE and SCPSSE," *Social Studies Research and Practice 1*, No. 2 (2006).
93. Vinovskis, 2009.
94. Simon, 2005.
95. Levinson, 2012.
96. Tom Loveless, "Strengthening the Curriculum." In C. E. Finn Jr. & R. Sousa (Eds.), *What Lies Ahead: For America's Children and Their Schools* (Stanford, CA: Hoover Institution Press, 2014).
97. Loveless, 2014.
98. Loveless, 2014.

CHAPTER 11

1. William J. Reese, *Testing Wars in the Public Schools: A Forgotten History* (Cambridge, MA: Harvard University Press, 2013).
2. Evans, 2004.
3. Rebecca Jacobsen & Richard Rothstein, "What NAEP Once Was, and What NAEP Could Once Again Be," *Economic Policy Institute* (2014).
4. Luther J. Carter, "Educational Testing: National Program Enters Critical Phase," *Science 156*, No. 3775 (1967).
5. Carter, 1967.
6. Thomas P. Southwick, "Education Assessment: Results a Step toward Accountability," *Science 169*, No. 3943 (1970).
7. Richard M. Jaeger, Evaluation of National Educational Programs: The Goals and the Instruments (Paper presented at American Educational Research Association, March 1970), 1.
8. Frank B. Womer & Wayne H. Martin, "The National Assessment of Educational Progress," *Studies in Educational Evaluation 5*, No. 1 (1979).
9. Frank B. Womer, *What Is National Assessment?* (Ann Arbor, MI: National Assessment of Educational Progress, 1970), 8.
10. Ina V. S. Mullis, "White Paper on 50 years of NAEP Use: Where NAEP Has Been and Where It Should Go Next" (Paper commissioned by the NAEP Validity Studies Panel, American Institutes for Research, 2019).

11. Jaeger, 1970, 5.
12. Robert F. Boruch, *The Governance of the National Assessment of Educational Progress: A Brief Review and Some Options*, Report No. A-158-5 (Washington, DC: National Institute of Education, 1982).
13. Womer, 1970, 3–4.
14. Jacobsen & Rothstein, 2014, 2.
15. Francis P. Hunkins, *Validity of Social Studies and Citizenship Exercising—Task 2. Final Report* (Washington, DC: NCSS, 1973), 7.
16. A. Guy Larkins, *Critique of NAEP Objectives: Citizenship and Social Studies [and] Critique of NAEP Procedures—Task 1. Final Report Parts 1 and 2* (Washington, DC: NCSS, 1973), 3.
17. Womer, 1970, 3–4.
18. Larkins, 1973.
19. Jean Fair, "National Assessment and Social Studies Education: The Setting." In J. Fair (Ed.), *National Assessment and Social Studies Education: A Review of Assessments in Citizenship and Social Studies by the National Council for the Social Studies* (Washington, DC: US Government Printing Office, 1975), 2.
20. J. Stanley Ahrnann, "A Response from National Assessment." In J. Fair (Ed.), *National Assessment and Social Studies Education: A Review of Assessments in Citizenship and Social Studies by the National Council for the Social Studies* (Washington, DC: US Government Printing Office, 1975).
21. Robert W. Sweet Jr., *Director's Report to the Congress on the National Assessment of Educational Progress* (Washington, DC: National Institute of Education, 1982).
22. National Assessment of Educational Progress, *Citizenship and Social Studies Achievement of Young Americans: 1981–1982 Performance and Changes between 1976 and 1982* (Denver, CO: Education Commission of the States, 1983), ED236247.
23. Willard Wirtz & Archie Lapointe, *Measuring the Quality of Education: A Report on Assessing Educational Progress* (Washington, DC, 1982).
24. Wirtz & Lapointe, 1982.
25. Samuel Messick, Albert Beaton, & Frederic Lord, *National Assessment of Educational Progress Reconsidered: A New Design for a New Era* (Princeton, NJ: Educational Testing Service, 1983), 10.
26. Wirtz & Lapointe, 1982.
27. Vinovskis, 2001.
28. Vinovskis, 2001.
29. Messick, Beaton, & Lord, 1983, 5.
30. Vinovskis, 2001.
31. In 1998, the Educational Excellence Network was resurrected and came under the auspices of the Thomas B. Fordham Foundation.
32. Albert E. Beaton, *Implementing the New Design: The NAEP 1983–84. Technical Report* (Washington, DC: NAEP, 1987), 41.
33. National Assessment of Educational Progress, *Foundations of Literacy: A Description of the Assessment of a Basic Knowledge of United States History and Literature* (Princeton, NJ: Educational Testing Service, 1986), 7.

34. Ina V. Mullis, Walter MacDonald, & Nancy A. Mead, "Developing the 1986 National Assessment Objectives, Items, and Background Questions." In A. Beaton (Ed.), *Expanding the New Design: The NAEP 1985–86 Technical Report* (Princeton, NJ: Educational Testing Service, 1988), 41.

35. Historical experts were Diane Brooks, California State Department of Education, Sacramento, CA; Henry N. Drewry, Princeton University, Princeton, NJ; Dana Kurfman, Prince Georges County Public Schools, Landover, MD; Donald V. Rogan, New Trier High School, Evanston, IL; and Stephan Thernstrom, Harvard University, Cambridge, MA. Literature experts were E. D. Hirsch, University of Virginia, Charlottesville, VA; Anna K. Johnston, Colchester High School, Colchester, VT; Helen Lojek, Boise State University, Boise, ID; Richard Rodriguez, Author, San Francisco, CA; and Patrick Welch, T. C. Williams High School, Arlington, VA.

36. Ernest R. House & Nancy Lawrence, "Report on Content Definition Process in Social Studies Testing" (Paper presented at Annual Meeting of American Educational Research Association, San Francisco, CA, 1989), 4.

37. House & Lawrence, 1989, 5.

38. Eugene G. Johnson, *Focusing the New Design: The NAEP 1988 Technical Report* (Princeton, NJ: National Assessment of Educational Progress (NAEP), Educational Testing Service, 1990).

39. House & Lawrence, 1989, 7.

40. Johnson, 1990.

41. Wirtz & Lapointe, 1982, 74.

42. Vinovskis, 2001.

43. Vinovskis, 2001.

44. Vinovskis, 2009.

45. Symcox, 2002.

46. Diane Ravitch, *The Death and Life of the Great American School System: How Testing and Choice Are Undermining Education* (New York, NY: Basic Books, 2010).

47. Vinovskis, 2009.

48. Ravitch, 2010.

49. National Assessment Governing Board, *Governing Board Updates NAEP Assessment Schedule: Reading and Mathematics Prioritized, with Additional State and District Data in Science, Technology and Engineering, U.S. History and Civics Governing Board Approves Updated NAEP Assessment Schedule* [Press Release] (July 24, 2019). Retrieved from https://www.nagb.gov/news-and-events/news-releases/2019/release-20190724-assessment-schedule.html.

50. NAGB, 2019.

51. NAGB, 2019.

52. National Assessment Governing Board, *Governing Board Approves Updated NAEP Assessment Schedule* [Press Release] (November 25, 2015). Retrieved from https://www.nagb.gov/news-and-events/news-releases/2015/new-assessment-schedule-112515.html.

53. Tina L. Heafner, "Advocacy for Social Studies: The Need to Respond to the Updated NAEP Schedule," *Social Education 83*, No. 5 (2019), 299.

54. National Assessment Governing Board, *Governing Board Sets 10-Year Vision with the Nation's Report Card Assessment Schedule* [Press Release] (November 17, 2023). Retrieved from https://www.nagb.gov/news-and-events/news-releases/2023/10-year-vision-assessment-schedule.html.

55. Newmann, 1970, 11.

56. Elizabeth Debray-Pelot, "Education Interest Groups and Policy Agendas in the 109th and 110th Congresses: Applying an Advocacy Coalition Framework." In K. W. Wong & R. Rothman (Eds.), *Clio at the Table: Using History to Inform and Improve Education Policy* (New York, NY: Peter Lang, 2009).

57. Debray-Pelot, 2009.

58. Johanek & Puckett, 2005.

59. Johnson, 2005.

60. NAGB, 2023.

61. Zachary Cote, "OpEd: Our Response to the NAEP Scores," *Thinking Nation*, May 22, 2023, https://www.thinkingnation.org/oped-our-response-to-the-naep-scores/.

62. National Commission on Educational Excellence, 2003, 185.

63. Perry M. Marker, "The Future Is Now: Social Studies in the World of 2056." In E. W. Ross (Ed.), *The Social Studies Curriculum: Purposes, Problems, and Possibilities* (3rd ed.) (Albany, NY: State University of New York Press, 2006).

64. No Child Left Behind Act, 2002.

65. Tracy L. Steffes, *School, Society, and State: A New Education to Govern Modern America, 1890–1940* (Chicago, IL: University of Chicago Press. 2012).

66. Steffes, 2012.

67. Tosh, 2008.

68. Wineburg, 2001.

69. Tyack, James, & Benovat, 1987.

70. Tosh, 2008.

71. Tosh, 2008.

72. Paul R. Hanna, *Assuring Quality for the Social Studies in Our Schools* (Stanford, CA: Hoover Institution Press, 1987).

73. Hanna, 1987.

74. Hunt & Metcalf, 1968, 283.

75. Tosh, 2008.

76. Timothy Kelly, Kevin Meuwissen, & Bruce A. VanSledright, "What of History? Historical Knowledge within a System of Standards and Accountability," *International Journal of Social Education 22*, No. 1 (2007), 138.

77. Scott Geoffrey Grant, "Understanding What Children Know about History: Exploring the Representation and Testing Dilemmas," *Social Studies Research and Practice 2*, No. 2 (2007).

78. Barton, 2012.

79. McLaughlin, Adams, Fox, Hart, Haskins, Salmon, & Stephens, 1899.

80. Loveless, 2014.

81. Thornton & Barton, 2010.

82. Hertzberg, 1981.

83. Vinovskis, 2009.
84. Vinovskis, 2009.
85. Symcox, 2002.
86. Nelson, 1994.
87. Fallace, 2008.
88. Nash, Crabtree, & Dunn, 1997.
89. Eli Savit, "Can Courts Repair the Crumbling Foundation of Good Citizenship? An Examination of Potential Legal Challenges to Social Studies Cutbacks in Public Schools," *Michigan Law Review 107* (2009).
90. Savit, 2009, 1303.
91. Frances L. Kidwell, *The Relationship between Civic Education and State Policy: An Evaluative Study* [Unpublished doctoral dissertation]. University of Southern California, Los Angeles, CA (2005).
92. Sandra Foster, "A Qualitative Understanding of Preservice Teachers' Critical Examination of Textbook Curriculum Units as Political Text." In H. Hickman & B. J. Porfilio (Eds.), *The New Politics of the Textbook: Problematizing the Portrayal of Marginalized Groups in Textbooks* (Rotterdam, Netherlands: Sense Publishers, 2012).
93. Evans, 2004, 154.
94. Symcox, 2002.
95. Pederson, 2007.
96. Catherine Gewertz, "New York May Ease Test Requirements for Graduation," *Education Week*, September 16, 2014.

Bibliography

Adams, D. W. (1988). "Fundamental Considerations: The Deep Meaning of Native American Schooling, 1880–1900." *Harvard Educational Review*, 58(1), 1–29.

Ahrnann, J. S. (1975). "A Response from National Assessment." In J. Fair (Ed.), *National Assessment and Social Studies Education: A Review of Assessments in Citizenship and Social Studies by the National Council for the Social Studies* (pp. 95–97). Washington, DC: US Government Printing Office.

Allardyce, G. (1982). "The Rise and Fall of the Western Civilization Course." *The American Historical Review*, 87(3), 695–725.

Anderson, L.W. (2009). "Upper Elementary Grades Bear the Brunt of Accountability." *Phi Delta Kappan*, 90(6), 413 18.

Angulo, A. J., & Schneider, J. (2022). "Between Recent Political Controversies and Long-Standing Education Histories." *History of Education Quarterly*, 62, 133–35.

Annual Report of the American Historical Association, 1918. (1921). Washington, DC: US Government Printing Office.

Arévalo, J., Bingham, M., Byron, L. C., Hoone, C. J., & Shotland, C. (1989). "Obstacles Teachers Confront: What Needs to Change." In P. Gagnon & The Bradley Commission on History in Schools (Eds.), *Historical Literacy: The Case for History in American Education* (pp. 251–67). New York, NY: Macmillan Publishing Company.

Arnn, L. P., Swain, C., & Spalding, M. (Eds.). (2021). *The 1776 Report*. Monroe, IL: Encounter Books.

Au, W. (2010). "The Idiocy of Policy: The Anti-Democratic Curriculum of High-Stakes Testing." *Critical Education*, 1(1), 1–16.

Au, W. (2013). Coring Social Studies within Corporate Education Reform: The Common Core State Standards, Social Justice, and the Politics of Knowledge in U.S. Schools. *Critical Education*, 4(5), 1–15.

Bain, R. B. (2004). *NAEP 12th Grade World History Assessment: Issues and Options* [Commissioned Paper]. Washington, DC: National Assessment Governing Board.

Bain, R. B., & Shreiner, T. L. (2005). "Issues and Options in Creating a National Assessment in World History." *The History Teacher, 38*(2), 241–71.

Barbour, M., Evans, M., & Ritter, J. (2007). "Situating the Georgia Performance Standards in the Social Studies Debate: An Improvement for Social Studies Classrooms or Continuing the Whitewash." *Journal of Social Studies Research, 31*(1), 27–33.

Barr, H. (1997). "Defining Social Studies." *Teachers and Curriculum, 1*(1), 6–12.

Barr, R. D., Barth, J. L., & Shermis, S. S. (1978). *The Nature of Social Studies*. Palm Springs, CA: ETC Publications.

Barth, J. L. (1991). *Elementary and Junior High/Middle School Social Studies Curriculum, Activities, and Materials* (Vol. 1). Lanham, MD: University Press of America.

Barton, K. C. (2009). "The Denial of Desire: How to Make History Education Meaningless." In L. Symcox & A. Wilschut (Eds.), *National History Standards: The Problem of the Canon and the Future of History Teaching* (pp. 265–82). Charlotte, NC: Information Age Publishing.

Barton, K. C. (2012). "Wars and Rumors of War: The Rhetoric and Reality of History Education in the United States." In T. Taylor & R. Guyver (Eds.), *History Wars and the Classroom: Global Perspectives* (pp. 187–202). Charlotte, NC: Information Age Publishing, Inc.

Barton, K. C., & Levstik, L. S. (1996). "'Back When God Was Around and Everything': Elementary Children's Understanding of Historical Time." *American Educational Research Journal, 33*(2), 419–54.

Barton, K. C., & McCully, A. W. (2005). History, Identity, and the School Curriculum in Northern Ireland: An Empirical Study of Secondary Students' Ideas and Perspectives. *Journal of Curriculum Studies, 37*(1), 85–116. doi: 10.1080/0022027032000266070.

Beard, C. A. (1932). *A Charter for the Social Sciences in the Schools* [Report of the Commission on the Social Studies, part 1]. New York, NY: Charles Scribner & Sons.

Beard, C. A. (1934). *The Nature of the Social Sciences: In Relation to Objectives of Instruction* [Report of the Commission on the Social Studies, part vii]. New York, NY: Charles Scribner & Sons.

Beaton, A. E. (1987). *Implementing the New Design: The NAEP 1983–84. Technical Report*. Washington, DC: National Assessment of Educational Progress.

Beatty, B. (2000). "'The Letter Killeth': Americanization and Multicultural Education in Kindergartens in the United States, 1856–1920." In R. L Wollons (Ed.), *Kindergartens and Cultures* (pp. 42–55). New Haven, CT: Yale University Press.

Berliner, D. C., & Biddle, B. J. (1995). *The Manufactured Crisis: Myths, Fraud, and the Attack on America's Public Schools*. Reading, MA: Addison-Wesley Publishing Company.

Berliner, D. C., & Glass, G. V. (Eds.). (2014). *50 Myths and Lies That Threaten America's Public Schools: The Real Crisis in Education*. New York, NY: Teachers College Press.

Bernicker, B. (2016, September 19). The Decline of Civic Education and the Effect on Our Democracy [Blog]. Retrieved from https://www.everyday-democracy.org/news/decline-civic-education-and-effect-our-democracy.

Bestor, A. E. (2016). *Educational Wastelands: The Retreat from Learning in Our Public Schools.* Eastford, CT: Martino Fine Books. (Original work published 1953.)

Bicouvaris, M. V. (1994). *Building a Consensus for the Development of National Standards in History* [Unpublished doctoral dissertation]. Old Dominion University, Norfolk, VA.

Bleazby, J. (2015). "Why Some School Subjects Have a Higher Status Than Others: The Epistemology of the Traditional Curriculum Hierarchy." *Oxford Review of Education, 41*(5), 671–89.

Bluey, R. B. (2008, July 7). Federal Education Law Blamed for Decline in Civics Teaching. CNS.com. Retrieved from http://www.cnsnews.com/news.article/federal-education-law-blamed-decline-civics-teaching.

Bohan, C. H., Doppen, F., Feinberg, J., & O'Mahony, C. (2008). "Citizens of Today and Tomorrow: An Exploration of Preservice Social Studies Teachers' Knowledge and Their Professors' Experiences with Citizenship." *Curriculum & Teaching Dialogue, 10*(1 & 2), 117–34.

Bolick, C. M., Adams, R., & Willox, L. (2010). "The Marginalization of Elementary Social Studies in Teacher Education." *Social Studies Research and Practice, 5*(2), 1–22.

Booher-Jennings, J. (2006). "Rationing Education in an Era of Accountability." *Phi Delta Kappan, 87*(10), 756–61.

Boozer, H. R. (1960). *The American Historical Association and the Schools, 1884–1956* [Unpublished doctoral dissertation]. Washington University, St. Louis, MO.

Boruch, R. F. (1982). *The Governance of the National Assessment of Educational Progress: A Brief Review and Some Options* [Report No. A-158-5]. Washington, DC: National Institute of Education.

Bose, P. (2008). "Hindutva Abroad: The California Textbook Controversy." *The Global South, 2*(1), 11–34. doi: 10.1353/gbs.0.0002.

Boston Public Schools. (2014, May 23). Q: IS BPS REALLY ELIMINATING ITS HISTORY AND SOCIAL STUDIES DEPARTMENT? A: NO [Press release]. https://www.bostonpublicschools.org/site/default.aspx?PageType=3&DomainID=4&ModuleInstanceID=14&ViewID=047E6BE3-6D87-4130-8424-D8E4E9ED6C2A&RenderLoc=0&FlexDataID=4091&PageID=1.

Boyer, T. L. (2009). *Teacher Perceptions of the Ohio Graduation Test for Social Studies* [Unpublished doctoral dissertation]. Ohio University, Athens, OH.

Bradley Commission on History in Schools. (1989). Building a History Curriculum: Guidelines for Teaching History in Schools. In P. Gagnon & The Bradley Commission on History in Schools (Eds.), *Historical Literacy: The Case for History in American Education* (pp. 3–15). New York, NY: Macmillan Publishing Company.

Brasof, M. (2012, November 15). What Future Can Social Studies Education Have under the Common Core? [Commentary Blog]. Retrieved from Philadelphia Public School Notebook, http://legacy.thenotebook.org/blog/125326/what-future-can-social-studies-education-have-under-common-core.

Brenner, T. (2018). "America Rock's Education: Presenting National Narratives on American Televisions." *The Virginia Tech Undergraduate Historical Review, 7.*

Brophy, A. (2003). "'The Committee... Has Stood Out against Coercion': The Reinvention of Detroit Americanization, 1915–1931." *Michigan Historical Review*, 29(2), 1–39. doi:10.2307/20174032.

Brophy, J., & Alleman, J. (2009). "Meaningful Social Studies for Elementary Students." *Teachers and Teaching: Theory and Practice*, 15(3), 357–76.

Brophy, J., Alleman, J., & Knighton, B. (2009). *Inside the Social Studies Classroom*. New York, NY: Routledge.

Brown, M. J., & Starnaman, S. (N.D.). "Unless We Americanize Them They Will Foreignize Us." Pragmatism, Progressivism, and Americanization [Working paper].

Bruner, J. S. (1966). *Toward a Theory of Instruction*. Cambridge, MA: Harvard University Press.

Bruner, J. S. (2009). *The Process of Education* (Revised edition). Cambridge, MA: Harvard University Press (originally published in 1960).

Buckles, S., & Watts, M. (1998). "National Standards in Economics, History, Social Studies, Civics, and Geography: Complementarities, Competition, or Peaceful Coexistence?" *The Journal of Economic Education*, 29(2), 157–66.

Burroughs, S., Groce, E., & Webeck, M. (2005). "Social Studies Education in the Age of Testing and Accountability." *Educational Measurement: Issues and Practice*, 24(3), 13–20.

Busey, C. L., Duncan, K. E., & Dowie-Chin, T. (2023). "Critical What What? A Theoretical Systematic Review of 15 Years of Critical Race Theory Research in Social Studies Education, 2004–2019." *Review of Educational Research*, 93(3), 412–53.

Bush, G. (1991). *America 2000: An Education Strategy: Sourcebook*. Washington, DC: US Government Printing Office.

Busteed, B. (2013, January 7). The School Cliff: Student Engagement Drops with Each School Year. *Gallup Blog*. Retrieved from http://www.gallup.com/opinion/gallup/170525/school-cliff-student241engagement-drops-school-year.aspx.

Byford, J., & Russell, W. (2007). "The New Social Studies: A Historical Examination of Curriculum Reform." *Social Studies Research and Practice*, 2(1), 38–48.

Campbell, D. (2013, September 11). California Must Change Its History Books before Adopting Common Core [Blog post]. Retrieved from http://choosingdemocracy.blogspot.com/2013/09/california-must-change.

Campbell, D. E. (2014). *Putting Civics to the Test: The Impact of State-Level Civics Assessments on Civic Knowledge* [AEI Program on American Citizenship Report]. Retrieved from American Enterprise Institute for Public Policy Research.

Capps, F. K. (1984). *The Discipline of History as Portrayed in the Journal "Social Education," 1937–1982* [Unpublished doctoral dissertation]. University of Missouri, Columbia, MO.

Carlson, R. (1975). *The Quest for Conformity: Americanization through Education*. New York, NY: John Wiley and Sons, Inc.

Carnoy, M., & Loeb, S. (2002). "Does External Accountability Affect Student Outcomes? A Cross-State Analysis." *Educational Evaluation and Policy Analysis*, 24(4), 305–31.

Carpenter, J. J. (2006). "'The Development of a More Intelligent Citizenship': John Dewey and the Social Studies." *Education and Culture*, 22(2), 31–42.

Carr, E. R. (1965). *The Social Studies*. New York, NY: The Center for Applied Research in Education, Inc.

Carr, P. G. (2015). *The Nation's Report Card: 2014 U.S. History, Geography, and Civics at Grade 8*. Washington, DC: National Center for Education Statistics, US Department of Education. Available from http://nces.ed.gov/whatsnew/commissioner/remarks2015/04_29_2015.asp.

Carswell, R. J. B. (1970). "Teacher Education and Dissemination of Information." In D. J. Patton (Ed.), *From Geographic Discipline to Inquiring Student. The High School Geography Project. Final Report* (pp. 45–56). Washington, DC: Association of American Geographers.

Carter, L. J. (1967). "Educational Testing: National Program Enters Critical Phase." *Science*, 156(3775), 622–26.

Center for Civic Education. (1994). *National Standards for Civics and Government*. Calabasas, CA: Center for Civic Education.

Chase, W. (1916). "Report of the Certification of High School Teachers of History." In M. M. Quaife (Ed.), *Proceedings of the Mississippi Valley Historical Association (1914–15)*, 8. Cedar Rapids, IA: Publisher Torch Press.

Cherryholmes, C. H. (1990). "Social Studies for Which Century?" *Social Education*, 54(7), 438–42.

Child, B. J. (2016). "Indian Boarding Schools." *Journal of Curriculum and Pedagogy*, 13(1), 25–27.

Childress, G. (2023). Bill to Allow Controversial Social Studies Curriculum in Beaufort County Schools Surprised Its Leaders. *NC Newsline*.

Cirrincione, J. M. (1970). *The Role of Values in the Teaching of Geography* [Unpublished doctoral dissertation]. The Ohio State University, Columbus, OH.

Cohen, A. (2013). *Conceptions of Citizenship and Civic Education: Lessons from Three Israeli Civics Classrooms* [Unpublished doctoral dissertation]. Columbia University, New York, NY.

Cohen-Cole, J. (2014). *The Open Mind: Cold War Politics and the Sciences of Human Nature*. Chicago, IL: University of Chicago Press.

Coley, R. J., & Sum, A. (2012). *Fault Lines in Our Democracy: Civic Knowledge, Voting Behavior, and Civic Engagement in the United States*. Princeton, NJ: Education Testing Service.

Conner, C. J., & Bohan, C. H. (2014). "The Second World War's Impact on the Progressive Educational Movement: Assessing Its Role." *The Journal of Social Studies Research*, 38(2), 91–102.

Cornbleth, C., & Waugh, D. (1993). "Research News and Comment: The Great Speckled Bird: Education Policy-in-the-Making." *Educational Researcher*, 22(7), 31–37.

Costrell, R. M. (2000). "Discipline-Based Economics Standards: Opportunity and Obstacles." In S. Stotsky (Ed.), *What's at Stake in the K-12 Standards Wars: A Primer for Educational Policy Makers* (pp. 169–210). New York, NY: Peter Lang Publishing, Inc.

Cote, Z. (2023, May 22). "OpEd: Our Response to the NAEP Scores." *Thinking Nation*, https://www.thinkingnation.org/oped-our-response-to-the-naep-scores/.

Cotton, T., & Buck, K. (2021, June 30). When *New York Times* Fake News Replaces American History. *National Review*.

Council for Economic Education. (2010). *Voluntary National Content Standards in Economics* (second ed.). Available from http://www.councilforeconed.org/ea/standards/standards.pdf.

Counts, G. (1934). *The Social Foundations of Education: Report of the Commission on the Social Studies*. New York, NY: Scribner's.

Crespino, J. (2008). Civil Rights and the Religious Right. In B. J. Schulman & J. E. Zelizer (Eds.), *Rightward Bound: Making America Conservative in the 1970s* (pp. 90–105). Cambridge, MA: Harvard University Press.

Crocco, M. S. (2004). "Dealing with Difference in the Social Studies: A Historical Perspective." *International Journal of Social Education*, *18*(2), 106–20.

Cruikshanks, A. N. (1957). *The Social Studies Curriculum in the Secondary School: 1893–1955* [Unpublished doctoral dissertation]. Stanford University, Stanford, CA.

Cunningham, G. K. (2004). "Learning from Kentucky's Failed Accountability System." In W. M. Evers & H. J. Walberg (Eds.), *Testing Student Learning, Evaluating Teaching Effectiveness* (pp. 245–301). Stanford, CA: Hoover Institution Press.

Dahlgren, R. L. (2013). "The Attack on Social Studies Teachers and Teaching in 1970s and 1980s Hollywood Movies." *The Councilor: A Journal of the Social Studies*, *74*(2), Article 7.

Darling-Hammond, L. (1994). "National Standards and Assessments: Will They Improve Education?" *American Journal of Education*, *102*(4), 478–510.

Davis, C. O. (1932). "The Report of the Committee of Nine, 1911." *Junior-Senior High School Clearing House*, *6*(9), 550–55.

DeBoer, G. E. (1991). *A History of Ideas in Science Education: Implications for Practice*. New York, NY: Teachers College Press.

DeBoer, G. E. (2000). "Scientific Literacy: Another Look at Its Historical and Contemporary Meanings and Its Relationship to Science Education Reform." *Journal of Research in Science Teaching*, *37*(6), 582–601.

Debray-Pelot, E. D. (2009). Education Interest Groups and Policy Agendas in the 109th and 110th Congresses: Applying an Advocacy Coalition Framework. In K. W. Wong & R. Rothman (Eds.), *Clio at the Table: Using History to Inform and Improve Education Policy* (pp. 131–56). New York, NY: Peter Lang.

Dee, T. S., & Jacob, B. (2011). "The Impact of No Child Left Behind on Student Achievement." *Journal of Policy Analysis and Management*, *30*(3), 418–46.

Dee, T. S., Jacob, B., & Schwartz, N. L. (2013). "The Effects of NCLB on School Resources and Practices." *Educational Evaluation and Policy Analysis*, *35*(2), 252–79.

Delanty, G. (2003). "Citizenship as a Learning Process: Disciplinary Citizenship versus Cultural Citizenship." *International Journal of Lifelong Education*, *22*(6), 597–605.

Dembert, L. (1976, April 25). "The Proper Study of Mankind." *New York Times*.

Denton, D. W., & Sink, C. (2015). "Preserving Social Studies as Core Curricula in an Era of Common Core Reform." *Journal of Social Studies Education Research*, 6(2), 1–17.

Dewey, J. (1937). *Education and Democracy: An Introduction to the Philosophy of Education*. New York, NY: Macmillan Company.

Doppen, F., Misco, T., & Patterson, N. (2008). "The State of K-12 Social Studies Instruction in Ohio." *Social Studies Research and Practice*, 3(3), 1–25.

Dorn, S. (2014). "Testing like William the Conqueror: Cultural and Instrumental Uses of Examinations." *Education Policy Analysis Archives*, 22(119), 1–16.

Dorn, S., & Ydesen, C. (2015). "Towards a Comparative and International History of School Testing and Accountability." *Education Policy Analysis*, 22(115), 1–11.

Dougherty, J. (2009). "Conflicting Questions: Why Historians and Policymakers Miscommunicate on Urban Education." In K. W. Wong & R. Rothman (Eds.), *Clio at the Table: Using History to Inform and Improve Education Policy* (pp. 251–62). New York, NY: Peter Lang.

Dow, P. B. (1975). "MACOS: The Study of Human Behavior as One Road to Survival." *The Phi Delta Kappan*, 57(2), 79–81.

Downey, M. T. (1985). *History in the Schools*. National Council for the Social Studies Bulletin 74. Washington, DC: National Council for the Social Studies.

Driscoll, D. (2013, June 12). *Tough Budget Decisions for National Assessment of Education Progress: Statement of National Assessment Governing Board*. Washington, DC: National Assessment Governing Board. Available from http://www.nagb.org.

Drost, W. H. (1977). "Social Efficiency Reexamined: The Dewey-Snedden Controversy." *Curriculum Inquiry*, 7(1), 19–32.

Dunn, A. W. (1921). "Civics in Schools, with Special Reference to Grades Nine and Twelve." *Social Studies*, 12(6), 219–23.

Dunn, R. E. (2009). "The Two World Histories." In L. Symcox & A. Wilschut (Eds.), *National History Standards: The Problem of the Canon and the Future of Teaching History* (pp. 55–69). Charlotte, NC: Information Age Publishing, Inc.

Dunne, K. (2014, May 24). As a follow-up to the post from Friday, here is a link to a response from the Interim Superintendent of Schools for the Boston Public Schools [Comment on the blog post "Boston Public Schools to Eliminate History & Social Science Departments" *H-Net*]. https://networks.h-net.org/node/14773/discussions/27470/boston-public-schools-eliminate-history-social-science-departments.

EagleWoman, A., & Rice, G. W. (2016). "American Indian Children and US Indian Policy." *Tribal Law Journal, 2015*, 16.

Eckers, S. M. (2018). The Effect of Elimination of State Social Studies Assessment on Content Knowledge of Elementary Students [Unpublished doctoral dissertation]. Hofstra University, Hempstead, NY.

Elmore, R. F. (2003). "Change and Improvement in Educational Reform." In D. T. Gordon (Ed.), *A Nation Reformed? American Education 20 Years after* A Nation at Risk (pp. 23–38). Cambridge, MA: Harvard Education Press.

Engle, S. H. (1964). "Decision Making: The Heart of Social Studies Instruction." In B. G. Massialas & A. M. Kazamias (Eds.), *Crucial Issues in the Teaching of Social*

Studies: A Book of Readings (pp. 28–35). Englewood Cliffs, NJ: Prentice-Hall, Inc. (Excerpted from *Social Education*, 1960, November 24, pp. 301–6).

Epstein, D. (1993). "Defining Accountability in Education." *British Educational Research Journal, 19*(3), 243–57.

Ercikan, K. (1997). "Linking Statewide Tests to the National Assessment of Educational Progress: Accuracy of Combining Test Results across States." *Applied Measurement in Education, 10*(2), 145–59. doi: 10.1207/s15324818ame1002_3.

Erekson, K. A. (2012). "Culture War Circus: How Politics and the Media Left History Education Behind." In K. A. Erekson (Ed.), *Politics and the History Curriculum: The Struggle over Standards in Texas and the Nation* (pp. 2–17). New York, NY: Palgrave Macmillan US.

Evans, R. W. (2004). *The Social Studies Wars: What Should We Teach the Children?* New York, NY: Teachers College Press.

Evans, R. W. (2010). "National Security Trumps Social Progress: The Era of the New Social Studies in Retrospect." In B. S. Stern (Ed.), *The New Social Studies: People, Projects, & Perspectives* (pp. 1–37). Charlotte, NC: Information Age Publishing.

Evans, R. W. (2014). *Schooling Corporate Citizens: How Accountability Reform Has Damaged Civic Education and Undermined Democracy*. New York, NY: Routledge.

Evers, W. M. (2014). "Implementing Standards and Testing." In C. E. Finn Jr. & R. Sousa (Eds.), *What Lies Ahead: For America's Children and Their Schools* (pp. 87–118). Stanford, CA: Hoover Institution Press.

Evers, W. M., & Walberg, H. J. (2004). *Testing Student Learning, Evaluating Teaching Effectiveness*. Sanford, CA: Hoover Institution Press.

Executive Order 13958, FR Doc. 2020-24793, https://www.federalregister.gov/documents/2020/11/05/2020-24793/establishing-thepresidents-advisory-1776-commission.

Fair, J. (1975). "National Assessment and Social Studies Education: The Setting." In J. Fair (Ed.), *National Assessment and Social Studies Education: A Review of Assessments in Citizenship and Social Studies by the National Council for the Social Studies* (pp. 1–4). Washington, DC: US Government Printing Office.

Falkenstein, L. C. (1977). *Man: A Course of Study—A Case Study of Diffusion in Oregon* [Unpublished doctoral dissertation]. Stanford University, Stanford, CA.

Fallace, T. (2008). "Did the Social Studies Really Replace History in American Secondary Schools." *Teachers College Record, 110*(10), 2245–70.

Fallace, T. (2009). "John Dewey's Influence on the Origins of the Social Studies: An Analysis of the Historiography and New Interpretation." *Review of Educational Research, 79*(2), 601–24.

Fallace, T., & Fantozzi, V. (2013). "Was There Really a Social Efficiency Doctrine? The Uses and Abuses of an Idea in Educational History." *Educational Researcher, 42*(3), 142–50.

Fenton, E. (1967). "The New Social Studies: Implications for School Administration." *National Association of Secondary School Principals Bulletin, 51*(317), 62–80.

Fenton, E. (1970). "The New Social Studies Reconsidered." In M. M. Krug, J. B. Poster, & W. B. Gillies III (Eds.), *The New Social Studies: Analysis of Theory and Materials* (pp. 176–82). Itasca, IL: F. E. Peacock. (Excerpted from speech to NY Council for the Social Studies April 9, 1968.)

Fenton, E. (1971). "Inquiry Techniques in the New Social Studies." *The High School Journal, 55*(1), 28–40.

Ferreira, J. J. Jr. (2014, May 21). Boston Public Schools to Eliminate History & Social Science Departments. *H-Net*, https://networks.h-net.org/node/14773/discussions/27470/boston-public-schools-eliminate-history-social-science-departments.

Finn, C. (2003). "Forward." In J. Leming, L. E. Ellington, & K. Porter-Magee (Eds.), *Where Did Social Studies Go Wrong?* (pp. i–vii). Washington, DC: Thomas B. Fordham Foundation.

Fiske, E. B. (1987, September 8). "Schools Criticized on the Humanities." *New York Times*.

Fitchett, P. G., & Heafner, T. L. (2013). "Making Critical Connections between Social Studies Teaching and Student Achievement using NAEP Data Explore." *The Teacher Educator, 48*(4), 296–310.

Fitchett, P. G., Heafner, T. L., & Lambert, R. G. (2012). "Examining Elementary Social Studies Marginalization: A Multilevel Model." *Educational Policy, 20*(10), 1–29. doi: 10.1177/0895904812453998.

Fitzgerald, F. (1979). *America Revised: History Schoolbooks in Twentieth Century.* New York, NY: Vintage Books.

Fleming, D. B. (1977). "Social Studies Standardized Achievement Tests: Are They Worth It?" *Peabody Journal of Education, 54*(4), 292–95.

Forte, E. (2010). "Examining the Assumptions Underlying the NCLB Federal Accountability Policy on School Improvement." *Educational Psychologist, 45*(?), 76–88.

Foster, S. (2012). "A Qualitative Understanding of Preservice Teachers' Critical Examination of Textbook Curriculum Units as Political Text." In H. Hickman & B. J. Porfilio (Eds.), *The New Politics of the Textbook: Problematizing the Portrayal of Marginalized Groups in Textbooks* (pp. 3–16). Rotterdam, Netherlands: Sense Publishers.

Foster, W. (1898). *A Patriotic Primer for the Little Citizen.* Indianapolis, IN: Levey Bros. & Company.

Fowler, T. (2011). "The Limits of Civic Education: The Divergent Implications of Political and Comprehensive Liberalism." *Theory and Research in Education, 9*(1), 87–100.

Fragnoli, K. (2005). "Historical Inquiry in a Methods Classroom: Examining Our Beliefs and Shedding Our Old Ways." *The Social Studies, 96*(6), 247–51.

Francis, A. T. (2014). "Value of Content: An Invisible Problem for Beginning Social Studies Teachers." *The Ohio Social Studies Review, 51*(2), 45–55.

Fraser, J. W. (2007). *Preparing America's Teachers: A History.* New York, NY: Teachers College Press.

Frohman, L. (2006). "NCSS Standards and the History Major: Are They Really Irreconcilable?" *AHA Perspectives, 44*(6), 43–47.

Fuhrman, S. (2003). "Riding Waves, Trading Horses: The Twenty-Year Effort to Reform Education." In D. T. Gordon (Ed.), *A Nation Reformed? American Education 20 Years After A Nation at Risk* (pp. 7–22). Cambridge, MA: Harvard Education Press.

Fuhrman, S., & Lazerson, M. (Eds.). (2005). *The Institutions of American Democracy: The Public Schools*. New York, NY: Oxford University Press.

Fusarelli, L. D. (2005). "Gubernatorial Reactions to No Child Left Behind: Politics, Pressure, and Education Reform." *Peabody Journal of Education, 80*(2), 120–36.

Gagnon, P., & The Bradley Commission on History in Schools (Eds.). (1989). *Historical Literacy: The Case for History in American Education*. New York, NY: Macmillan Publishing Company.

Gallagher, M. C. (2000). "Lessons from the Sputnik-era Curriculum Reform Movement: The Institutions We Need for Educational Reform." In S. Stotsky (Ed.), *What's at Stake in the K-12 Standards Wars: A Primer for Educational Policy Makers* (pp. 281–312). New York, NY: Peter Lang Publishing, Inc.

Galston, W. A. (2005). "The Politics of Polarization: Education Debates in the United States." In S. Fuhrman & M. M. Lazerson (Eds.), *The Institutions of American Democracy: The Public Schools* (pp. 57–80). New York, NY: Oxford University Press.

Gardner, W. E. (1970). "The Social Studies—Its Role in General Education." In W. E. Gardner & F. A. Johnson (Eds.), *Social Studies in the Secondary Schools: A Book of Readings* (pp. 11–15). Boston, MA: Allyn and Bacon, Inc.

Gathany, J. M. (1913). "Practical Aims and Methods in the Teaching of Civics." *The History Teacher's Magazine, 4*(1), 20.

Gaudelli, W. (2002). "U.S. Kids Don't Know U.S. History: The NAEP Study, Perspectives, and Presuppositions." *The Social Studies, 93*(5), 197–201.

Gerwin, D., & Visone, F. (2006). "The Freedom to Teach: Contrasting History Teaching in Elective and State-Tested Courses." *Theory and Research in Social Education, 34*(2), 259–82.

Gewertz, C. (2012, May 16). "Incoming College Board Head Wants SAT to Reflect Common Core." *Education Week*.

Gewertz, C. (2013, June 7). Chiefs Group Terminates Role in Social Studies Framework [Blog]. Retrieved from *Curriculum Matters* at http://blogs.edweek.org/edweek/curriculum/2013/06/chiefs_group_terminates_role_i.html.

Gewertz, C. (2014, September 16). "New York May Ease Test Requirements for Graduation." *Education Week*.

Gibson, S. (2012). "'Why Do We Learn This Stuff?' Students' Views on the Purpose of Social Studies." *Canadian Social Studies, 45*(1), 43–58.

Goals 2000: Educate America Act and the Improving America's Schools Act, Pub. L. 103-227 § Stat. H.R. 1804 (1994).

Goertz, M. E. (2009). "Standards-Based Reform: Lessons from the Past, Directions for the Future." In K. W. Wong & R. Rothman (Eds.), *Clio at the Table: Using History to Inform and Improve Education Policy* (pp. 201–19). New York, NY: Peter Lang.

Goldman, L. (1998). "Exceptionalism and Internationalism: The Origins of American Social Science Reconsidered." *Journal of Historical Sociology, 11*(1), 1–36.

Goldstein, D. (2015). *The Teacher Wars: A History of America's Most Embattled Profession*. New York, NY: Anchor.

Goldstein, D. (2020, January 20). "Two States. Eight Textbooks. Two American Stories." *New York Times*.

Good, A. J., Heafner, T. L., Rock, T. C., O'Connor, K. A., Passe, J., Waring, S. M., & Byrd, S. (2010). "The De-Emphasis on Social Studies in Elementary Schools: Teacher Candidate Perspective." *Current Issues in Education*, *13*(4), 1–19.

Good, T. L., McCaslin, M., Tsang, H. Y., Zhang, J., Wiley, C. R., Bozack, A. R., & Hester, W. (2006). "How Well Do 1st-Year Teachers Teach: Does Type of Preparation Make a Difference?" *Journal of Teacher Education*, *57*(4), 410–30.

Goodman, J., & Adler, S. (1985). "Becoming an Elementary Social Studies Teacher: A Study of Perspectives." *Theory & Research in Social Education*, *13*(2), 1–20.

Gordon, D. T. (2003). "Introduction." In D. T. Gordon (Ed.), *A Nation Reformed? American Education 20 Years after* A Nation at Risk (pp. 1–6). Cambridge, MA: Harvard Education Press.

Gordon, D. T. (2003). "The Limits of Ideology: Curriculum and the Culture Wars." In D. T. Gordon (Ed.), *A Nation Reformed? American Education 20 Years after* A Nation at Risk (pp. 99–114). Cambridge, MA: Harvard Education Press.

Gradwell, J. M. (2006). "Teaching in Spite of, Rather than Because of, the Test: A Case of Ambitious History Teaching in New York State." In S. G. Grant (Ed.), *Measuring History: Cases of State-Level Testing across the United States* (pp. 157–76). Greenwich, CT: Information Age Publishing.

Grant, S. G. (2006). "Research on History Tests." In S. G. Grant (Ed.), *Measuring History: Cases of State-Level Testing across the United States* (pp. 29–56). Charlotte, NC: Information Age Publishing.

Grant, S. G. (2007). "Understanding What Children Know about History: Exploring the Representation and Testing Dilemmas." *Social Studies Research and Practice*, *2*(2), 196–208.

Grant, S. G., & Horn, C. (2006). "The State of State-Level History Tests." In S. G. Grant (Ed.), *Measuring History: Cases of State-Level Testing across the United States* (pp. 9–28). Greenwich, CT: Information Age Publishing.

Grant, S. G., & Salinas, C. (2008). "Assessment and Accountability in the Social Studies." In L. S. Levstik & C. A. Tyson (Eds.), *Handbook of Research in Social Studies Education* (pp. 219–36). New York, NY: Routledge.

Gross, R. E. (1976, November). The Status of the Social Studies in the Public Schools of the United States: Facts and Impressions of a National Survey [Paper presented at annual meeting of the National Council for Social Studies, Washington, DC].

Gross, R. E., & Dynneson, T. L. (1983). "What Should We Be Teaching the Social Studies?" Fastback 199, *Phi Delta Kappa*.

Gudmundsdottir, S., & Shulman, L. (1987). "Pedagogical Content Knowledge in Social Studies." *Scandinavian Journal of Educational Research*, *31*(2), 59–70.

Guenther, J. (1975, November 27–29). *More Humanistic Social Studies Programs through Mini-courses* [Paper presented at the Annual Meeting of the National Council for the Social Studies, Atlanta, GA].

Gutek, G. L. (1970) *The Educational Theory of George S. Counts*. Columbus, OH: Ohio State University Press.

Gutek, G. L. (1984). *George S. Counts and American Civilization: The Educator as Social Theorist*. Chicago, IL: Mercer University Press.

Gutherie, J. W., & Springer, M. G. (2004). "*A Nation at Risk* Revisited: Did 'Wrong' Reasoning Result in 'Right' Results? At What Costs." In K. K. Wong, J. W. Guthrie, & D. N. Harris (Eds.), *A Nation at Risk: A 20-year Reappraisal* (pp. 7–35). New York, NY: Psychology Press (Routledge).

Ha, J. M. (2006). *The Use of NAEP Data in a State Context* [Unpublished doctoral dissertation]. Oregon State University, Corvallis, OR.

Haas, J. D. (1977). *The Era of the New Social Studies*. Boulder, CO: Social Science Education Consortium.

Hahn, C. L. (1977). "Attributes and Adoption of New Social Studies Materials." *Theory & Research in Social Education*, 5(1), 19–40.

Halvorsen, A. (2012). "'Don't Know Much about History': The *New York Times* 1943 Survey of U.S. History and the Controversy It Generated." *Teachers College Record*, 114(1), 1–32.

Halvorsen. A., & Mirel, J. E. (2009). "Educating Citizens: Social Problems Meet Progressive Education in Detroit, 1930–1952." In K. W. Wong & R. Rothman (Eds.), *Clio at the Table: Using History to Inform and Improve Education Policy* (pp. 9–36). New York, NY: Peter Lang.

Hamilton, L. S., Stecher, B. M., & Yuan, K. (2008). *Standards-Based Reform in the United States: History, Research, and Future Directions* [No. RP-1384]. Santa Monica, CA: RAND Corporation.

Haney, W. (2000). "The Myth of the Texas Miracle in Education." *Education Policy Analysis Archives*, 8, 41.

Hanna, P. R. (1987). *Assuring Quality for the Social Studies in Our Schools*. Stanford, CA: Hoover Institution Press.

Hannah-Jones, N., & Watson, R. (2021). *The 1619 Project: Born on the Water*. New York, NY: Penguin.

Hanushek, E. A., & Raymond, M. E. (2005). Does School Accountability Lead to Improved Student Performance? *Journal of Policy Analysis and Management*, 24(2), 297–327.

Harrington, J. M. (2009). The Perceptions of High School Educators about the Impact of the Massachusetts Comprehensive Assessment System (MCAS) on Instructional Practices [Unpublished doctoral dissertation]. University of Pennsylvania, Philadelphia, PA.

Hartocollis, A. (2024, January 24). "Florida Eliminates Sociology as a Core Course at Its Universities." *New York Times*.

Haskins, C. H., Robinson, J. H., Wesley, C. W., Sullivan, J., & McLaughlin, A. C. [Committee of Five]. (1912). *The Study of History in Secondary Schools: Report to the American Historical Association*. New York, NY: The Macmillan Company.

Hassard, J. (2013, May 2). Defunding the Common Core: Back to the Future [Blog]. Available from http://nepc.colorado.edu (National Education Policy Center).

Hawley, T. S. (2010). "Purpose into Practice: The Problems and Possibilities of Rationale-Based Practice in Social Studies." *Theory & Research in Social Education*, *38*(1), 131–62.

Haynes, B. (2009). "Introduction to Special Issue: Patriotism and Citizenship Education." *Educational Philosophy and Theory*, *41*(4), 365–77.

Heafner, T. L. (2019). "Advocacy for Social Studies: The Need to Respond to the Updated NAEP Schedule." *Social Education*, *83*(5), 299–300.

Heafner, T. L., & Fitchett, P. G. (2012). "Tipping the Scales: National Trends of Declining Social Studies Instructional Time in Elementary Schools." *Journal of Social Studies Research*, *36*(2), 190–215.

Heafner, T. L., & Fitchett, P. G. (2015). "An Opportunity to learn US History: What NAEP Data Suggest Regarding the Opportunity Gap." *The High School Journal*, *98*(3), 226–49.

Heafner, T. L., Good, A. J., O'Connor, K. A., Passe, J., Rock, T., Byrd, S., Oldendorf, S. B., & Groce, E. (2007). "Is Social Studies 'History' in North Carolina's Elementary Schools?" *Social Studies Research and Practice*, *2*(3), 502–9.

Heafner, T. L., Lipscomb, G. B., & Rock, T. C. (2006). "To Test or Not to Test? The Role of Testing Elementary Social Studies, a Collaborative Study Conducted by NCPSSE and SCPSSE." *Social Studies Research and Practice*, *1*(2), 145–64.

Hechler, K. (1980). *Toward the Endless Frontier: History of the Committee on Science and Technology, 1959–79*. Washington, DC: US House of Representatives.

Heffner, A. (2012, April 12). "Former Supreme Court Justice Sandra Day O'Connor on the Importance of Civics Education." *Washington Post*. Available from https://www.washingtonpost.com/lifestyle/magazine/former-supreme-court-justice-sandra-day-oconnor-on-the-importance-of-civics-education/2012/04/10/gIQA-8aUnCT_story.html?utm_term=.369c5cf9f554.

Hegeman, S. (2021). "Arctic Pedagogy: Indigenous People and the MACOS Culture War." *Lateral*, *10*(2).

Heidelberger, C. A. (2023, September 18). Hillsdale's Morrisey Wrote Social Studies Standards—Contract Says So. *Dakota Free Press*, https://dakotafreepress.com/2022/08/17/hillsdales-morrisey-wrote-social-studies-standards-contract-says-so/.

Heilig, J. V., Brown, K., & Brown, A. (2012). "The Illusion of Inclusion: A Critical Race Theory Textual Analysis of Race and Standards." *Harvard Educational Review*, *82*(3), 403–24.

Helburn, N. (1998). "The High School Geography Project: A Retrospective View." *The Social Studies*, *89*(5), 212–18.

Helburn, S. W. (1997). "ECON12 and the New Social Studies: Love's Labor Lost?" *The Social Studies*, *88*(6), 268–76.

Henry, M. (1993). "A Fifty-Year Perspective on History Teaching's 'Crisis.'" *OAH Magazine of History*, *7*(3), 5–8.

Hertzberg, H. W. (1981). *Social Studies Reform, 1880–1980*. Boulder, CO: Social Science Education Consortium, Inc.

Hertzberg, H. W. (1989). "History and Progressivism: A Century of Reform Proposals." In P. Gagnon & The Bradley Commission on History in Schools (Eds.),

Historical Literacy: The Case for History in American Education (pp. 69–99). New York, NY: Macmillan Publishing Company.

Higham, J. (1959). "The Cult of the American Consensus." *Commentary, 28*, 93.

Hill, H. C. (1921). "History for History's Sake." *The Historical Outlook, 12*(9), 310–15.

Hinchliffe, G. (2020). "Civic Republicanism, Citizenship and Education." In A. Peterson, G. Stahl, & H. Soong (Eds.), *The Palgrave Handbook of Citizenship and Education*. London, UK: Palgrave Macmillan, Cham. https://doi.org/10.1007/978-3-319-67828-3_9.

Hiner, N. (1972). "Professions in Process: Changing Relations between Historians and Educators, 1896–1911." *History of Education Quarterly, 12*(1), 34–56. doi:10.2307/367147.

Hiner, N. R. (1973). "Professions in Process: Changing Relations among Social Scientists, Historians, and Educators, 1880–1920." *The History Teacher, 6*(2), 201–18.

Hofstadter, R. (1966). *Anti-Intellectualism in American Life* (Vol. 713). New York, NY: Vintage.

Hollister, H. A. (1908). The Programme of Studies for High Schools. *The School Review, 16*(4), 252–57.

Holloway, J. E., & Chiodo, J. J. (2009). "Social Studies IS Being Taught in the Elementary School: A Contrarian View." *Journal of Social Studies Research, 33*(2), 235–61.

Holt, E. W. (2006). *Qualifications of Public Secondary School History Teachers, 1999–2000* [Issue Brief No. NCES 2006-004]. Washington, DC: US Department of Education.

House, E. R., & Lawrence, N. (1989). "Report on Content Definition Process in Social Studies Testing." Paper presented at Annual Meeting of American Educational Research Association, San Francisco, CA.

House, E. R., & Lawrence, N. (1990). *Report on Content Definition Process in Social Studies Testing* (CSE Technical Report 310). Los Angeles, CA: UCLA Center for Research on Evaluation, Standards, and Student Testing.

Houser, N. O. (1995). "Social Studies on the Back Burner: Views from the Field." *Theory & Research in Social Education, 23*(2), 147–68.

Hughes, H. S. (1964). "The Historian and the Social Scientist." In B. G. Massialas & A. M. Kazamias (Eds.), *Crucial Issues in the Teaching of Social Studies: A Book of Readings* (pp. 84–95). Englewood Cliffs, NJ: Prentice-Hall, Inc. (Reprinted from *American Historical Review*, 1960, October, 66:1, pp. 20–46).

Hunkins, F. P. (1973). *Validity of Social Studies and Citizenship Exercising—Task 2. Final Report*. Washington, DC: National Council for the Social Studies.

Hunt, E. M. (1962). "Changing Perspectives in the Social Studies." In E. M. Hunt (Ed.), *High School Social Studies: Perspectives* (pp. 3–28). Boston, MA: Houghton Mifflin Company.

Hunt, M. P., & Metcalf, L. E. (1968). *Teaching High School Social Studies: Problems in Reflective Thinking and Social Understanding*. New York, NY: Harper & Row.

Hunter, D. (1994, September 13). 140 Cong. Rec., 127 (Statement by Rep. Hunter).

Hutton, L. A., & Burstein, J. H. (2008). "The Teaching of History-Social Studies: Left Behind or Behind Closed Doors?" *Social Studies Research and Practice*, *3*(1), 96–108.

Iggers, G. G. (1995). "Historicism: The History and Meaning of the Term." *Journal of the History of Ideas*, *56*(1), 129–52.

Jackson, J. (2023, Apr 11). Superintendents Join Opposition to Proposed Social Studies Standards. *KELOLAND.COM*, https://www.keloland.com/keloland-com-original/superintendents-join-opposition-to-proposed-social-studies-standards/.

Jackson, K. T., & Jackson, B. B. (1989). "Why the Time Is Right to Reform the History Curriculum." In P. Gagnon & The Bradley Commission on History in Schools (Eds.), *Historical Literacy: The Case for History in American Education* (pp. 3–15). New York, NY: Macmillan Publishing Company.

Jackson, S. (2023). "The Place of World History in South Dakota's Failed 2021 Social Studies Standards Revision Process." *World History Connected*, *20*(1).

Jacobsen, R., & Rothstein, R. (2014). "What NAEP Once Was, and What NAEP Could Once Again Be." *Economic Policy Institute*.

Jaeger, R. M. (1970, March). Evaluation of National Educational Programs: The Goals and the Instruments. Paper presented at American Educational Research Association, Minneapolis, MN.

Jamison, E. A., Jamison, D. T., & Hanushek, E. A. (2007). "The Effects of Education on Income Growth and Mortality Decline." *Economics of Education Review*, *26*(6), 771–88.

Jamnah, D., & Zimmerman, J. (2022). "Policy Dialogue: The War over How History Is Taught." *History of Education Quarterly*, *62*(2), 231–39.

Johanek, M. C., & Puckett, J. (2005). "The State of Civic Education: Preparing Citizens in an Era of Accountability." In S. Fuhrman & M. M. Lazerson (Eds.), *The Institutions of American Democracy: The Public Schools* (pp. 130–59). New York, NY: Oxford University Press.

Johnson, E. G. (1990). *Focusing the New Design: The NAEP 1988 Technical Report*. Princeton, NJ: National Assessment of Educational Progress (NAEP), Educational Testing Service.

Johnson, E. G. (1992). "The Design of the National Assessment of Educational Progress." *Journal of Educational Measurement*, *29*(2), 95–110.

Johnson, H. (1921). "Report of Committee on History and Education for Citizenship: Part II, History in the Grades." *Historical Outlook*, *12*(6), 93–95.

Johnson, K. B. (2014). Guardians of Historical Knowledge: Textbook Politics, Conservative Activism, and School Reform in Mississippi, 1928–1982 [Unpublished doctoral dissertation]. Mississippi State University, Starkville, MS.

Johnson, S. M. (2005). "Working in Schools." In S. Fuhrman & M. Lazerson (Eds.), *The Institutions of American Democracy: The Public Schools* (pp. 160–87). New York, NY: Oxford University Press.

Jones, M. G., Jones, B. D., & Hargrove, T. Y. (2003). *The Unintended Consequences of High-Stakes Testing*. Lanham, MD: Rowman & Littlefield Publishers, Inc.

Jones, T. J. (1906). *Social Studies in the Hampton Curriculum*. Hampton, VA: Hampton Institute Press.

Jones-Oltjenbruns, N. E. (2012). *A Historical Case Study of the Arikara, Hidatsa, and Mandan Indians Attending Hampton Normal and Agricultural Institute, Virginia, 1878–1911* [Unpublished doctoral dissertation]. Virginia Commonwealth University, Richmond, VA.

Jordan, C. A. (2007). "Social Studies Has Often Been Expendable: The Erosion of Curricular Time and the NCLB Act." *Michigan Social Studies Journal, 17,* 20–38.

Jordan, P. D. (1942). "The *New York Times* Survey of United States History." *The Mississippi Valley Historical Review, 29*(2), 238–42.

Jorgensen, C. G. (2012). *John Dewey and the Dawn of Social Studies: Unraveling Conflicting Interpretations of the 1916 Report.* Charlotte, NC: Information Age Publishing, Inc.

Journell, W. (2010). "Standardizing Citizenship: The Potential Influence of State Curriculum Standards on the Civic Development of Adolescents." *PS: Political Science & Politics, 43*(2), 351–58.

Joyce, B. (2015). *The First US History Textbooks: Constructing and Disseminating the American Tale in the Nineteenth Century.* Lanham, MD: Lexington Books.

Judd, C. H. (1918). "The Teaching of Civics." *The School Review, 26*(7), 511–32.

Kaestle, C. F. (2001). "Federal Aid to Education since World War II: Purposes and Politics." In J. Jennings (Ed.), *The Future of the Federal Role in Elementary and Secondary Education. A Collection of Papers* (pp. 13–36). Washington, DC: Center on Education Policy.

Kaestle, C. F. (2013). *Testing Policy in the United States: A Historical Perspective.* Retrieved from Gordon Commission website: http://www.gordoncommission.org/rsc/pdf/kaestle_testing_policy_us_historical_perspective.

Kaladis, J. (2013, September 23). Bring Back Social Studies. *The Atlantic.* Available from https://www.theatlantic.com/education/archive/2013/09/bring-back-social-studies/279891/.

Kallen, H. M. (1915). "Democracy versus the Melting Pot: A Study of American Nationality." *The Nation, 100*(2590), 190–94.

Kasakove, S. (2022, March 4). The Fight over "Maus" Is Part of a Bigger Cultural Battle in Tennessee. *New York Times.* https://www.nytimes.com/2022/03/04/us/maus-banned-books-tennessee.html.

Kazin, M. (2021, February 1). "The 1776 Follies." *New York Times.*

Keels, O. M. (1994). "In the Beginning—Albert McKinley and the Founding of *The Social Studies.*" *The Social Studies, 100*(1), 6–13.

Keene, C. J. (2023, June 25). Some Educators Apprehensive over Implementation of Social Studies Standards. *SDPB Radio,* https://listen.sdpb.org/education/2023-06-25/some-educators-apprehensive-over-implementation-of-social-studies-standards.

Keller, C. R. (1964). "Needed: Revolution in the Social Studies." In B. G. Massialas & A. M. Kazamias (Eds.), *Crucial Issues in the Teaching of Social Studies: A Book of Readings* (pp. 38–45). Englewood Cliffs, NJ: Prentice-Hall, Inc. (Reprinted from *Saturday Review,* pp. 60–62, 1961, September 16).

Kelly, T., Meuwissen, K., & VanSledright, B. (2007). "What of History? Historical Knowledge within a System of Standards and Accountability." *International Journal of Social Education, 22*(1), 115–45.

Kenna, J., & Russell, W. (2018). "The Culture and History of Standards-Based Educational Reform and Social Studies in America." *Journal of Culture and Values in Education*, *1*(1), 26–49.

Kenna, J. L., & Russell, W. (2014). "Implications of Common Core State Standards on the Social Studies." *The Clearing House: A Journal of Educational Strategies, Issues and Ideas*, *87*(2), 75–82.

Kennedy, F. (1994). *First Person Accounts as Written by American Indian Students at Hampton Institute, 1878–1923*. J. L. Brudvig (Ed.). Retrieved from http://www.twofrog.com/hamptonstories4.html.

Kenworthy, L. S. (1978, April 14). *Some Persistent Problems of the Social Studies, 1903–1978–2003*. Talk presented at Middle States Council for the Social Studies in Wilmington, DE.

Kidwell, F. L. (2005). *The Relationship between Civic Education and State Policy: An Evaluative Study* [Unpublished doctoral dissertation]. University of Southern California, Los Angeles, CA.

King, A. K. (1946). "From History to Social Studies in the Secondary School." *The High School Journal*, *29*(1), 9–19.

Kingkade, T. (2023, July 20). Conservatives Are Changing K-12 Education and One Christian College Is at the Center. NBCNews.com, https://www.nbcnews.com/news/us-news/hillsdale-college-1776-curriculum-k12-education-conservative-rcna93397.

Kliebard, H. M. (2004). *The Struggles for the American Curriculum, 1893–1958* (third ed.). New York, NY: Routledge.

Kohn, R. H. (1995). "History and the Culture Wars: The Case of the Smithsonian Institution's *Enola Gay* Exhibition." *The Journal of American History*, *82*(3), 1036–63.

Kraus, L. L. (1977). *Curriculum, Public Policy, and Criticism: An Analysis of the Controversies Surrounding "Man: A Course of Study"* [Unpublished doctoral dissertation]. The University of Texas, Austin, TX.

Krug, M. M., Poster, J. B., & Gillies III, W. B. (Eds.). (1970). *The New Social Studies: Analysis of Theory and Materials*. Itasca, IL: F. E. Peacock Publishers, Inc.

Kuhn, T. S. (2012). *The Structure of Scientific Revolutions* (fourth ed.). Chicago, IL: University of Chicago Press.

Kurtz, S. (2020). *The Lost History of Western Civilization*. New York, NY: National Association of Scholars.

Labaree, D. F. (2010). "How Dewey Lost: The Victory of David Snedden and Social Efficiency in the Reform of American Education." In D. Tröhler, T. Schlag, & F. Osterwalder (Eds.), *Pragmatism and Modernities* (pp. 163–88). New York, NY: Brill Publishers.

Lambert, D., Seshadri, M., & Fensterwald, J. (2023). "Temecula Board Again Votes to Reject Textbooks, Despite Warnings from Newsom." *Ed Source*.

Larkins, A. G. (1973). *Critique of NAEP Objectives: Citizenship and Social Studies [and] Critique of NAEP Procedures—Task 1. Final Report Parts 1 and 2*. Washington, DC: National Council for the Social Studies.

Lauret, M. (2016). "Americanization Now and Then: The 'Nation of Immigrants' in the Early Twentieth and Twenty-first Centuries." *Journal of American Studies*, *50*(2), 419–47.

Learn, M. (2019). *Consequential Validity and Social Studies Education: An Examination of Standards, Assessment Policies, and Teacher Preparation* [Unpublished doctoral dissertation]. North Dakota State University, Fargo, ND.

Lee, J. K. (2013). "The Status of Social Studies and the Common Core State Standards: An Opportunity for Reform." In J. Passe & P. G. Fitchett (Eds.), *The Status of Social Studies: Views from the Field* (pp. 315–27). Charlotte, NC: Information Age Publishing, Inc.

Lee, P., & Howson, J. (2009). "Two Out of Five Did Not Know That Henry VIII Had Six Wives: History Education, Historical Literacy, and Historical Consciousness." In L. Symcox & A. Wilschut (Eds.), *National History Standards: The Problem of the Canon and the Future of Teaching History* (pp. 211–61). Charlotte, NC: Information Age Publishing, Inc.

Legum, J., & Crosby, R. (2023). "Pennsylvania School District Requires Social Studies Classes to Incorporate Right-Wing Propaganda." *Popular Information*.

Leming, J., Ellington, L., & Porter-Magee, K. (Eds.). (2003). *Where Did Social Studies Go Wrong?* Washington, DC: Thomas B. Fordham Foundation.

Leming, J. S., Ellington, L., & Schug, M. (2006). "The State of Social Studies: A National Random Survey of Elementary and Middle School Social Studies Teachers." *Social Education*, 70(5), 322–27.

Lepore, J. (2009). *The Name of War: King Philip's War and the Origins of American Identity*. New York, NY: Vintage Books.

Lepore, J. (2010). *The Whites of Their Eyes: The Tea Party's Revolution and the Battle over American History*. Princeton, NJ: Princeton University Press.

Lerner, R., Nagai, A. K., & Rothman, S. (1995). *Molding the Good Citizen: The Politics of High School History Texts*. Westport, CT: Praeger.

Lévesque, S. (2008). *Thinking Historically: Educating Students for the Twenty-First Century*. Toronto, ON: University of Toronto Press.

Levinson, M. (2012). *No Citizen Left Behind*. Cambridge, MA: Harvard University Press.

Libresco, A. S. (2006). "Elementary Social Studies in 2005: Danger or Opportunity? A Response to Jeff Passe." *The Social Studies*, 97(5), 193–95.

Linethal, E. T., & Engelhardt, T. (Eds.). (1996). *History Wars: The Enola Gay and Other Battles for the American Past*. New York, NY: Macmillan.

Linn, R. L., & Baker, E. L. (1996). *Assessing the Validity of the National Assessment of Educational Progress: NAEP Technical Review* [NCES Report CSE-TR-416]. Washington, DC: National Center of Educational Statistics.

Lobes, L. S. (1998). "Surveying State Standards: National History Education Network's 1997 Report on State Social Studies Standards." *The History Teacher*, 31(2), 221–34.

Loewen, J. W. (2013). *Teaching What Really Happened: How to Avoid the Tyranny of Textbooks and Get Students Excited about Doing History*. New York, NY: Teachers College Press.

Longstreet, W. S. (1985). "Citizenship: The Phantom Core of Social Studies Curriculum." *Theory and Research in Social Education*, 13(2), 21–29.

Loveless, T. (2005). "Test-based Accountability: The Promise and the Perils." *Brookings Papers on Education Policy*, (1), 7–45.

Loveless, T. (2007). "The Peculiar Politics of No Child Left Behind. Standards-based Reform and the Poverty Gap: Lessons for No Child Left Behind." In A. Gamoran (Ed.), *Standards-based Reforms and the Poverty Gap: Lessons for No Child Left Behind* (pp. 253–85). Washington, DC: Brookings Institution Press.

Loveless, T. (2014). "Strengthening the Curriculum." In C. E. Finn Jr. & R. Sousa (Eds.), *What Lies Ahead: For America's Children and Their Schools* (pp. 137–48). Stanford, CA: Hoover Institution Press.

Lutkehaus, N. C. (2008). "Putting 'Culture' into Cultural Psychology: Anthropology's Role in the Development of Bruner's Cultural Psychology." *Ethos*, *36*(1), 46–59.

Lybarger, M. (1983). "Origins of the Modern Social Studies: 1900–1916." *History of Education Quarterly*, *23*(4), 455–68.

MacIver, M. A. (2007). "What Reform Left Behind: A Decade of Change at One Urban High School." *Education and Urban Society*, *40*(1), 3–35.

Madaus, G. F. (1988). "The Distortion of Teaching and Testing: High-Stakes Testing and Instruction." *Peabody Journal of Education*, *65*(3), 29–46.

Manna, P. (2006). "Control, Persuasion, and Educational Accountability: Implementing the No Child Left Behind Act." *Educational Policy*, *20*(3), 471–94.

Manzo, K. K. (2005). "Social Studies Losing out to Reading, Math." *Education Week*, *24*(27).

Marchant, G. J. (2015). "How Plausible Is Using Averaged NAEP Values to Examine Student Achievement?" *Comprehensive Psychology*, *4*(1), 1–4.

Marker, G. W. (1980). "Why Schools Abandon 'New Social Studies' Materials." *Theory & Research in Social Education*, *7*(4), 35–57.

Marker, P. M. (2006). "The Future Is Now: Social Studies in the World of 2056." In E. W. Ross (Ed.), *The Social Studies Curriculum: Purposes, Problems, and Possibilities* (3rd ed.) (pp. 77–96). Albany, NY: State University of New York Press.

Martin, D., Maldonado, S. I., Schneider, J., & Smith, M. (2011). *A Report on the State of History Education: State Policies and National Programs* (second ed.). Fairfax, VA: Teachinghistory.org, National History Education Clearinghouse.

Martinez, M. (2012, May 3). Justice Sandra Day O'Connor Seeks to Reverse America's Decline in Civics. CNN.com. Available from http://www.cnn.com/2012/05/02/us/california-sandra-day-oconnor-civics/.

Marzano, R. J., & Kendall, J. S. (1997). "National and State Standards: The Problems and the Promise." *National Association of Secondary School Principals Bulletin*, *81*(26), 26–41. doi: 10.1177/019263659708159006.

Marzano, R. J., & Kendall, J. S. (1998). *Awash in a Sea of Standards* (Report). Aurora, CO: Mid-Continent Research for Education and Learning. Available from http://mcrel.org/PDF/Standards/5982IR_AwashInASea.pdf.

Massialas, B. G., & Cox, C. B. (1964). "History and Reflective Thinking." In B. G. Massialas & A. M. Kazamias (Eds.), *Crucial Issues in the Teaching of Social Studies: A Book of Readings* (pp. 149–55). Englewood Cliffs, NJ: Prentice-Hall, Inc. (Reprinted from *Indiana Teacher*, 1960, December.)

Massialas, B. G., & Kazamias, A. M. (Eds.). (1964). *Crucial Issues in the Teaching of Social Studies: A Book of Readings*. Englewood Cliffs, NJ: Prentice-Hall, Inc.

McDermott, C. (2015, October 27). Souter, Gregg Call for Renewed Focus on Civics Education. *New Hampshire Public Radio.* Available from http://nhpr.org/post/souter-gregg-call-renewed-focus-civics-education#stream/0.

McDermott, K. A. (2007). "'Expanding the Moral Community' or 'Blaming the Victim'? The Politics of State Education Accountability Policy." *American Educational Research Journal, 44*(1), 77–111.

McDermott, K. A. (2009). "Growing State Intervention in Low-Performing Schools: Laws and Regulation in Three Waves of Reform." In K. W. Wong & R. Rothman (Eds.), *Clio at the Table: Using History to Inform and Improve Education Policy* (pp. 91–108). New York, NY: Peter Lang.

McDonnell, L. M. (2013). "Educational Accountability and Policy Feedback." *Educational Policy, 27*(2), 170–89.

McDonough, J. (2014, May 23). Q: Is BPS Really Eliminating Its History and Social Studies Department? A: No [Discussion board]. Posted to Boston Public Schools, available from http://bostonpublicschools.org/site/default.aspx?PageType=3&DomainID=4&ModuleInstanceID=14&ViewID=047E6BE3-6D87-4130-8424-D8E4E9ED6C2A&RenderLoc=0&FlexDataID=4091&PageID=1.

McEachron, G. (2010). "Study of Allocated Social Studies Time in Elementary Classrooms in Virginia: 1987–2009." *The Journal of Social Studies Research, 34*(2), 208–20.

McGuire, M. E. (2007). "What Happened to Social Studies? The Disappearing Curriculum." *Phi Delta Kappan, 88*(8), 620–24.

McGuirk, A. B. (1933). A Study of the Achievement of Pupils Who Studied the Harold Rugg's Fused Course in Social Studies as Compared with Those Who Studied Separate History and Geography Courses [Unpublished master's thesis]. Indiana State Teachers College, Terre Haute, IN.

McIntosh, C. J. J. (1973). *A Study of Teachers' Attitudes toward the "New" Social Studies* [Unpublished doctoral dissertation]. University of North Texas, Denton, TX.

McLaughlin, A. C., Adams, H. B., Fox, G. L., Hart, A. B., Haskins, C. H., Salmon, L. M., & Stephens, H. M. [Committee of Seven]. (1898). *The Study of History in Schools: Report to the American Historical Association.* New York, NY: The Macmillan Company.

McLaughlin, A. C., Haskins, C. H., Robinson, J. H., & Sullivan, J. (1911). "The Study of History in Secondary Schools: Report of the Committee of Five." *Annual Report of the American Historical Association,* 209–42.

McNeill, W. H., Kammen, M., & Craig, G. A. (1989). "Why Study History? Three Historians Respond." In P. Gagnon & The Bradley Commission on History in Schools (Eds.), *Historical Literacy: The Case for History in American Education* (pp. 103–18). New York, NY: Macmillan Publishing Company.

Means, B., Padilla, C., & Gallagher, L. (2010). *Use of Education Data at the Local Level: From Accountability to Instructional Improvement.* Washington, DC: US Department of Education, Office of Planning, Evaluation, and Policy Development. Available from http://www.ed.gov/about/offices/list/opepd/ppss/reports.html#edtech.

Messick, S. (1985). "Response to Changing Assessment Needs: Redesign of the National Assessment of Educational Progress." *American Journal of Education*, *94*(1), 90–105.

Messick, S. (1989). "Meaning and Values in Test Validation: The Science and Ethics of Assessment." *Educational Researcher*, *18*(2), 5–11.

Messick, S., Beaton, A., & Lord, F. (1983). *National Assessment of Educational Progress Reconsidered: A New Design for a New Era.* Princeton, NJ: Educational Testing Service.

Michener, J. A. (1944). "Who Is Virgil T. Fry? The Remarkable Facts about a Man Who Is Either a Master Teacher or a Big Fraud." *The Clearing House: A Journal of Educational Strategies, Issues and Ideas*, *19*(2), 69–73.

Milam, E. L. (2011). "Salmon, Gulls, and Baboons? Oh My." *The Journal of the History of Childhood and Youth*, *4*(3), 361–67.

Mirel, J. (2002). "The Decline of Civic Education." *Daedalus*, *131*(3), 49–55.

Mirel, J. E. (2010). *Patriotic Pluralism: Americanization Education and European Immigrants*. Cambridge, MA: Harvard University Press.

Misco, T., Patterson, N., & Doppen, F. (2011). "Policy in the Way of Practice: How Assessment Legislation Is Affecting Social Studies Curriculum and Instruction in Ohio." *International Journal of Education Policy & Leadership*, *6*(7), 1–13.

Mitsakos, C. L. (1981). "The Nature and Purposes of Social Studies." In J. Allen (Ed.), *Education in the 80's: Social Studies* (pp. 13–21). Washington, DC: National Education Association.

Mondale, S., & Patton, S. B. (Eds.). (2001). *School: The Story of American Public Education*. Boston, MA: Beacon Press.

Moses, M. S., & Nanna, M. J. (2007). "The Testing Culture and the Persistence of High Stakes Testing Reforms." *Education and Culture*, *23*(1), 55–72.

Mueller, R. G. W., & Colley, L. M. (2015). "An Evaluation of the Impact of End-of-Course Exams and ACT-QualityCore on U.S. History Instruction in a Kentucky High School." *The Journal of Social Studies Research*, *39*(2), 95–106.

Mullis, I. V. (2019). White Paper on 50 Years of NAEP Use: Where NAEP Has Been and Where It Should Go Next. Commissioned by NAEP Validity Studies (NVS) Panel, American Institutes for Research.

Mullis, I. V., MacDonald, W., & Mead, N. A. (1988). "Developing the 1986 National Assessment Objectives, Items, and Background Questions." In A. Beaton (Ed.), *Expanding the New Design: The NAEP 1985–86 Technical Report*. Princeton, NJ: Educational Testing Service.

Murawski, J. (2021). No Critical Race Theory in Schools? Here's the Abundant Evidence Saying Otherwise. *Real Clear Investigations*, https://www.realclearinvestigations.com/articles/2021/12/22/no_critical_race_theory_in_schools_heres_the_abundant_evidence_saying_otherwise_808528.html.

Myers, C. B., Dougan, A. M., Baber, C. R., Dumas, W., Helmkamp, C. J., Lane, J. W., Morganett, L., Solomon, W., & Theisen, R. (2006). *National Standards for Social Studies Teachers*. Silver Spring, MD: National Council for the Social Studies.

Nagy, P. (2000). "The Three Roles of Assessment: Gatekeeping, Accountability, and Instructional Diagnosis." *Canadian Journal of Education*, *25*(4), 262–79.

Nash, G. B., Crabtree, C., & Dunn, R. E. (1997). *History on Trial: Culture Wars and the Teaching of the Past*. New York, NY: Knopf.
National Assessment Governing Board. (2009). *Civics Framework for the 2010 National Assessment of Educational Progress: NAEP Civics Project*. Washington, DC: National Assessment Governing Board.
National Assessment Governing Board. (2009). *U.S. History Framework for the 2010 National Assessment of Educational Progress*. Washington, DC: National Assessment Governing Board.
National Assessment Governing Board. (2015, November 25). *Governing Board Approves Updated NAEP Assessment Schedule*. Retrieved from https://www.nagb.gov/news-and-events/news-releases/2015/new-assessment-schedule-112515.html.
National Assessment Governing Board. (2019, July 24). Governing Board Updates NAEP Assessment Schedule: Reading and Mathematics Prioritized, with Additional State and District Data in Science, Technology and Engineering, U.S. History and Civics Governing Board Approves Updated NAEP Assessment Schedule [Press Release]. Retrieved from https://www.nagb.gov/news-and-events/news-releases/2019/release-20190724-assessment-schedule.html.
National Assessment Governing Board. (2023, November 17). *Governing Board Sets 10-Year Vision with the Nation's Report Card Assessment Schedule* [Press Release]. Retrieved from https://www.nagb.gov/news-and-events/news-releases/2023/10-year-vision-assessment-schedule.html.
National Assessment of Educational Progress. (1983). *Citizenship and Social Studies Achievement of Young Americans: 1981–1982 Performance and Changes between 1976 and 1982*. Denver, CO: Education Commission of the States. ED236247.
National Assessment of Educational Progress. (1986). *Foundations of Literacy: A Description of the Assessment of a Basic Knowledge of United States History and Literature*. Princeton, NJ: Educational Testing Service.
National Center for History in the Schools. (1996). *National Standards for History, Basic Edition*. Los Angeles, CA: UCLA Press, 1996. Available from http://nchs.ucla.edu/standards/.
National Commission on Educational Excellence. (2003). "A Nation at Risk: The Imperative for Educational Reform" [Report to the Nation and the Secretary of Education]. In D. T. Gordon (Ed.), *A Nation Reformed? American Education 20 Years After* A Nation at Risk (pp. 165–94). Cambridge, MA: Harvard Education Press. (Reprint of 1983 Report.)
National Council for the Social Studies. (1921). "A National Council for the Social Studies [Announcement]." *The Historical Outlook*, *12*(4), 144.
National Council for the Social Studies. (1964). "A Guide to Content in the Social Studies." In B. G. Massialas & A. M. Kazamias (Eds.), *Crucial Issues in the Teaching of Social Studies: A Book of Readings* (pp. 20–27). Englewood Cliffs, NJ: Prentice-Hall, Inc. (Reprinted 1958, Washington, DC: National Council for the Social Studies.)
National Education Association of the United States. (1893). *Committee on Secondary School Studies. Report of the Committee of Ten on Secondary School Studies* [As appointed at the Meeting of the National Educational Association July 9,

1892: With the Reports of the Conferences Arranged by this Committee and Held December 28–30, 1892], No. 205. Washington, DC: US Government Printing Office.

National Education Association of the United States. (1928). Commission on the Reorganization of Secondary Education. *Cardinal Principles of Secondary Education, 35.* Washington, DC: US Government Printing Office.

National Geographic Society Committee on Research and Exploration. (1994). *Geography for Life: The National Geography Standards.* Available from http://www.ncge.org/i4a/pages/index.cfm?pageid=3314.

National Research Council. (2008). *Common Standards for K-12 Education? Considering the Evidence.* Summary of a Workshop Series. Alexandra Beatty, Rapporteur. Committee on State Standards in Education. Washington, DC: National Academies Press.

Nelson, J. L. (2001). "Defining Social Studies." In W. B. Stanley (Ed.), *Critical Issues in Social Studies Research for the 21st Century* (pp. 15–38). Greenwich, CT: Information Age Publishing.

Nelson, L. R., & Drake, F. D. (1994). Secondary Teachers' Reactions to the New Social Studies. *Theory & Research in Social Education*, 22(1), 44–73.

Nelson, M. R. (1994). *The Social Studies in Secondary Education: A Reprint of the Seminal 1916 Report with Annotations and Commentaries.* Bloomington, IN: ERIC Clearinghouse for Social Studies/Social Science Education.

Newmann, F. M. (1970). "The Analysis of Public Controversy: New Focus for Social Studies." In M. M. Krug, J. B. Poster, & W. B. Gillies III (Eds.), *The New Social Studies: Analysis of Theory and Materials* (pp. 211–28). Itasca, IL: F. E. Peacock. (Reprinted from *School Review*, 1965, 73(4)).

Newton, J. (2022, April 27). Noem Helped Select Social Studies Commission Members. *KELOLAND*.com, https://www.keloland.com/keloland-com-original/noem-helped-select-social-studies-commission-members/.

No Child Left Behind Act of 2001, Pub. L. No. 107-110, § 115 Stat. 1425 (2002).

Noboa, J. (2012). "Names, Numbers, and Narratives: A Multicultural Critique of the U.S. History Standards." In K. A. Erekson (Ed.), *Politics and the History Curriculum: The Struggle over Standards in Texas and the Nation* (pp. 102–25). New York, NY: Palgrave Macmillan US.

Noyes, E. (1921). "Comment upon Committee's Report." *The Historical Outlook*, 12(4), 142.

O'Connor, K. A., Heafner, T., & Groce, E. (2007). "Advocating for Social Studies: Documenting the Decline and Doing Something about It." *Social Education*, 71(5), 255–60.

O'Neil, T. (2023, May 9). "Model for Rest of the Country": South Dakota History Standards Scrap Critical Race Theory, Build on Hillsdale Foundation. *The Daily Signal*, https://www.dailysignal.com/2023/05/09/model-rest-country-south-dakota-history-standards-scrap-critical-race-theory-build-hillsdale-foundation/.

Olneck, M. R. (1989). "Americanization and the Education of Immigrants, 1900–1925: An Analysis of Symbolic Action." *American Journal of Education*, 97(4), 398–423.

Olson, K. E. (2011). "Creating Map Readers: Republican Geographic and Cartographic Discourse in G. Bruno's (Augustine Fouillée) 1905 *Le Tour De La France par Deux Enfants.*" *Modern & Contemporary France, 19*(1), 37–51.

Ong, P. M. (2020). COVID-19 and the Digital Divide in Virtual Learning, Fall 2020. *UCLA Center for Neighborhood Knowledge.*

Pace, J. L. (2008). "Inequalities in History–Social Science Teaching under High-Stakes Accountability: Interviews with Fifth-Grade Teachers in California." *Social Studies Research and Practice, 3*(1), 24–40.

Pace, J. L. (2011). "The Complex and Unequal Impact of High Stakes Accountability on Untested Social Studies." *Theory & Research in Social Education, 39*(1), 32–60.

Parker, W. C. (1991). *Renewing the Social Studies Curriculum.* Alexandria, VA: Association for Supervision and Curriculum Development.

Passe, J. (2006). "New Challenges in Elementary Social Studies." *The Social Studies, 97*(5), 189–92. doi: 10.3200/TSSS.97.5.189-192.

Passe, J., & Fitchett, P. G. (Eds.). (2013). *The Status of Social Studies: Views from the Field.* Charlotte, NC: Information Age Publishing.

Patton, D. J. (1970). From Geographic Discipline to Inquiring Student. The High School Geography Project. Final Report. Washington, DC: Association of American Geographers.

Paxson, F. L. (1913). "Certification of High-School Teachers of History: Report of the Chairman of the Committee." *The History Teacher's Magazine, 4*(6), 169–72.

Paxton, R. J. (2003). "Don't Know Much about History—Never Did." *Phi Delta Kappan, 85*(4), 264–73.

Peckham, P. D., & Ware, A. E. (1973). *"An Evaluation of 'Man: A Course of Study.'"* Evaluation for Bellevue Public Schools, Bellevue, WA.

Pederson, P. V. (2007). "What Is Measured Is Treasured: The Impact of the No Child Left Behind Act on Nonassessed Subjects." *The Clearing House: A Journal of Educational Strategies, Issues and Ideas, 80*(6), 287–91.

Pellegrino, J. W. (2014). "Assessment as a Positive Influence on 21st Century Teaching and Learning: A Systems Approach to Progress." *Psicología Educativa, 20*(2), 65–77.

Peterson, A. (2011). *Civic Republicanism and Civic Education: The Education of Citizens.* New York, NY: Springer.

Phipps, S., & Adler, S. (2003). "Where's the History?" *Social Education, 67*(4), 296–98.

Podgursky, M. (2002). NAEP Background Questions: What Can We Learn from NAEP about the Effect of Schools and Teachers on Student Achievement? [Discussion paper]. Washington, DC: National Assessment Governing Board.

Popham, W. J. (2001). "Uses and Misuses of Standardized Tests." *National Association of Secondary School Principals Bulletin, 85*(24), 24–31.

Powers, C., & Wood, R. (1984). "National Assessment: A Review of Programs in Australia, the United Kingdom, and the United States." *Comparative Education Review, 28*(3), 355–77.

Pratt, R. B. (1976). *Evolution of a Curriculum Project: The High School Geography Project.* Boulder, CO: Social Science Education Consortium, Inc.

Preuss, G. B. (2012). "'As Texas Goes, So Goes the Nation:' Conservatism and Culture Wars in the Lone Star State." In K. A. Erekson (Ed.), *Politics and the History Curriculum: The Struggle over Standards in Texas and the Nation* (pp. 18–38). New York, NY: Palgrave Macmillan US.

Progress in Social Studies. (1961, June 16). *New York Times*, 32.

Randall, D. (2021, July 29). Critique of the Fordham Institute's "The State of State Standards for Civics and U.S. History in 2021." *National Association of Scholars*.

Ravitch, D. (1989). "The Plight of History in American Schools." In P. Gagnon & The Bradley Commission on History in Schools (Eds.), *Historical Literacy: The Case for History in American Education* (pp. 51–68). New York, NY: Macmillan Publishing Company.

Ravitch, D. (1996). "50 States, 50 Standards? The Continuing Need for National Voluntary Standards in Education." *The Brookings Review*, *14*(3), 6–10.

Ravitch, D. (2000). *The Great School Wars: A History of the New York City Public Schools*. Baltimore, MD: John Hopkins University Press.

Ravitch, D. (2002). "Education after the Culture Wars." *Daedalus*, *131*(3), 5–21.

Ravitch, D. (2010). *The Death and Life of the Great American School System: How Testing and Choice Are Undermining Education*. New York, NY: Basic Books.

Ravitch, D., & Finn, C. E. (1987). *What Do Our 17-Year-Olds Know? A Report on the First National Assessment of History and Literature*. New York, NY: Harper & Row, Publishers.

Ray, R., & Gibbons, A. (2021). Why Are States Banning Critical Race Theory? Brookings Institute, https://www.brookings.edu/articles/why-are-states-banning-critical-race-theory/.

Reese, W. J. (2013). *Testing Wars in Public Schools: A Forgotten History*. Cambridge, MA: Harvard University Press.

Reich, G. A. (2009). "Testing Historical Knowledge: Standards, Multiple-Choice Questions and Student Reasoning." *Theory & Research in Social Education*, *37*(3), 325–60.

Reuben, J. A. (2005). "Patriotic Purposes: Public Schools and the Education of Citizens." In S. Fuhrman & M. Lazerson (Eds.), *The Institutions of American Democracy: The Public Schools* (pp. 9–24). New York, NY: Oxford University Press.

Reyhner, J. (2018). "American Indian Boarding Schools: What Went Wrong? What Is Going Right?" *Journal of American Indian Education*, *57*(1), 58–78.

Reyhner, J., & Eder, J. (2004). *American Indian Education: A History*. Norman, OK: University of Oklahoma Press.

Reynolds, E. (1984, December 5). Interview by M. E. Zuverink. Interview, transcript, and recording. Oral History of Teaneck (2), History of Teaneck Township, Archive collection of the Teaneck Public Library. Retrieved from https://archive.teanecklibrary.org/OralHistory2/reynolds.html.

Rhodes, J. (2012). *An Education in Politics: The Origins and Evolution of No Child Left Behind*. Ithaca, NY: Cornell University Press.

Ribuffo, L. P. (2000). "What Is Still Living in 'Consensus' History and Pluralist Social Theory." *American Studies International*, *38*(1), 42–60.

Rice, M. J. (1969). *Evaluation in the Anthropology Curriculum Project* [Report]. Anthropology Curriculum Project, University of Georgia, Athens, GA.

Rice, M. J. (1972, November 21). *The Case for the Disciplines in the Organization of Social Studies Curricula for Elementary and Secondary Schooling* [Paper Presentation]. College and University Faculty Association, National Council for the Social Studies, Boston, MA.

Rice, M. J., & Bailey, W. C. (1971). The Development of a Sequential Curriculum in Anthropology, Grades 1–7. Final Report. Washington, DC: Department of Education.

Riley, K. L., & Stern, B. S. (2002). "'A Bootlegged Curriculum:' The American Legion versus Harold Rugg." *International Journal of Social Education, 18*(2), 62–72.

Ringel, P. (2021). "Schoolhouse Rock! for a New Generation: What Should It Look Like?" *The Public Historian, 43*(1), 82–101.

Risinger, C. F. (1995). "The National History Standards: A View from the Inside." *The History Teacher, 28*(3), 387–93.

Robelen, E. W. (2010). "Rewriting of States' Standards on Social Studies Stirs Debate." *Education Week, 29*(27), 1–18.

Rochester, J. M. (2003). "The Training of Idiots: Civics Education in America's Schools." In J. Leming, L. E. Ellington, & K. Porter-Magee (Eds.), *Where Did Social Studies Go Wrong?* (pp. 6–39). Washington, DC: Thomas B Fordham Foundation.

Rock, T. C., Heafner, T., O'Connor, K., Passe, J., Olendorf, S., Good, A., & Byrd, S. (2006). "One State Closer to a National Crisis: A Report on Elementary Social Studies Education in North Carolina Schools." *Theory & Research in Social Education, 34*(4), 455–83.

Roosevelt, T. (1915). "'Address to the Knights of Columbus' delivered at Carnegie Hall in New York City on October 12, 1915," in P. Davis (Ed.), *Immigration and Americanization: Selected Readings* (pp. 645–60). Boston, MA: Ginn.

Rosaldo, R. (1994). "Cultural Citizenship and Educational Democracy." *Cultural Anthropology, 9*(3), 402–11.

Ruff, C. S. (2013). *Perspectives on the Hidden Curriculum within the Social Studies* [Unpublished master's thesis]. Ohio University, Athens, OH.

Rugg, H. (1921). "How Shall We Reconstruct the Social Studies Curriculum? An Open Letter to Professor Henry Johnson." *The Historical Outlook, 12*(5), 184–89.

Ruswick, B. (2015). "What Does It Mean to Be an American? Training History Students and Prospective Teachers to See the Assumptions in Their Textbooks." *The History Teacher, 48*(4), 667–92.

Rutherford, D. J., & Boehm, R. G. (2004). "Round Two: Standards Writing and Implementation in the Social Studies." *The Social Studies, 95*(6), 231–38.

Samec, C. (1976). *A History of the Amherst Project: Revising the Teaching of American History 1959 to 1972* [Unpublished doctoral dissertation]. Loyola University, Chicago, IL.

Savage, T. (2003). "Assessment and Quality Social Studies." *The Social Studies, 94*(5), 201–6.

Savit, E. (2009). "Can Courts Repair the Crumbling Foundation of Good Citizenship? An Examination of Potential Legal Challenges to Social Studies Cutbacks in Public Schools." *Michigan Law Review, 107*, 1269–1303.

Sawchuk, S. (2013, July 24). When Bad Things Happen to Good NAEP Data. *Education Week.* Available from http://www.edweek.org/ew/articles/2013/07/24/37naep.h32.html?tkn.

Saxe, D. W. (1991). *Social Studies in Schools: A History of the Early Years.* Albany, NY: State University of New York Press.

Saxe, D. W. (1992). "Framing a Theory for Social Studies Foundations." *Review of Educational Research, 62*(3), 259–77.

Saxe, D. W. (1997). "The Unique Mission of the Social Studies." In E. W. Ross (Ed.), *The Social Studies Curriculum: Purposes, Problems, and Possibilities* (pp. 39–55). Albany, NY: State University of New York Press.

Saye, J., & Social Studies Inquiry Research Collaborative (SSIRC). (2013). "Authentic Pedagogy: Its Presence in Social Studies Classrooms and Relationship to Student Performance on State-Mandated Tests." *Theory & Research in Social Education, 41*(1), 89–132.

Schafer, J. (1921). "Report of Committee on History and Education for Citizenship." *Historical Outlook, 12*(3), 87–93.

Schissler, H. (2009). "Containing and Regulating Knowledge: Some Thoughts on Standards and Canonization as a Response to the Complex Demands of a Globalizing World." In L. Symcox & A. Wilschut (Eds.), *National History Standards: The Problem of the Canon and the Future of Teaching History* (pp. 95–113). Charlotte, NC: Information Age Publishing, Inc.

Schmoker, M., & Marzano, R. J. (1999). "Realizing the Promise of Standards-Based Education." *Educational Leadership, 56*(6), 17–21.

Schneider, D. (1993). "Teaching Social Studies: The Standards Movement." *The Clearing House, 67*(1), 5–7.

Schroeder, K. (2007). "NCLB and Civics." *Education Digest, 72*(8), 76–77.

Schwartz, R. B., & Robinson, M. A. (2000). "Goals 2000 and the Standards Movement." *Brookings Papers on Education Policy,* (1), 173–206.

Sebesta, E. H. (2012). "Neo-Confederate Ideology in the Texas History Standards." In K. A. Erekson (Ed.), *Politics and the History Curriculum: The Struggle over Standards in Texas and the Nation* (pp. 148–68). New York, NY: Palgrave Macmillan US.

Seixas, P. (1993). "Historical Understanding among Adolescents in a Multicultural Setting." *Curriculum Inquiry, 23*(3), 301–27.

Seixas, P. (1993). "Parallel Crises: History and the Social Studies Curriculum in the USA." *Journal of Curriculum Studies, 25*(3), 235–50.

Selakovich, D. (1975). "Has the New Social Studies Failed?" *The High School Journal, 59*(3), 130–36.

Serwer, A. (2019). "The Fight over the 1619 Project Is Not about the Facts." *The Atlantic, 23.*

Shedd, J. (2000). "Why and How Should History Departments Train Secondary Social Studies Teachers?" *The History Teacher, 34*(1), 29–33.

Siegel, M. (2002). "'History Is the Opposite of Forgetting': The Limits of Memory and the Lessons of History in Interwar France." *The Journal of Modern History*, *74*(4), 770–800.

Silverstein, J. (2021, November 9). The *1619 Project* and the long battle over U.S. history. *New York Times Magazine*, https://www.nytimes.com/2021/11/09/magazine/1619-project-us-history.html#:~:text=That%20project%20made%20a%20bold,be%20considered%20the%20country's%20origin.

Simon, K. G. (2005). "Classroom Deliberations." In S. Fuhrman & M. Lazerson (Eds.), *The Institutions of American Democracy: The Public Schools* (pp. 107–29). New York, NY: Oxford University Press.

Singer, A. (2014, October 27). Common Core and the End of History [Blog]. Available from http://www.huffingtonpost.com/alan-singer/common-core-history-exams_b_6050456.html.

Smith, J. (1980). "Progressive School Administration Ella Flagg Young and the Chicago Schools, 1905–1915." *Journal of the Illinois State Historical Society (1908–1984)*, *73*(1), 27–44.

Smith, O. B. (1943). "Social Studies in General Education." *The Journal of Higher Education*, *14*(8), 404–8.

Snir, I., & Eylon, Y. (2017). "Civic Republicanism and Education: Democracy and Social Justice in School." *Studies in Philosophy and Education*, *36*, 585–600.

Snyder, T. D. (1993). *120 Years of American Education: A Statistical Portrait* [Report]. Washington, DC: National Center for Education Statistics.

Sorensen, K. (2006). *Is Social Studies Being Taught in Elementary Schools? A Study of One District* [Unpublished master's thesis]. Brigham Young University, Provo, UT.

South Dakota Education Association. (2023, April 17). SDEA Responds to the Adoption of Social Studies Standards by the South Dakota Board of Education Standards [Press release]. https://www.sdea.org/blog/5477/sdea-responds-to-the-adoption-of-social-studies-standards-by-the-south-dakota-board-of-education-standards#:~:text=%E2%80%9CToday's%20decision%20by%20the%20Board,almost%20unanimous%20in%20their%20opposition.

Southwick, T. P. (1970). "Education Assessment: Results a Step toward Accountability." *Science*, *169*(3943), 358–59.

Stanley, W. B. (2005). "Social Studies and the Social Order: Transmission or Transformation?" *Social Education*, *69*(5), 282–86.

Stearns, P. N., Seixas, P. C., & Wineburg, S. (Eds.). (2000). *Knowing, Teaching, and Learning History: National and International Perspectives*. New York, NY: New York University Press.

Stedman, L. C. (1994). "The Sandia Report and U.S. Achievement: An Assessment." *Journal of Educational Research*, *87*(3), 133–46.

Steffes, T. L. (2012). *School, Society, and State: A New Education to Govern Modern America, 1890–1940*. Chicago, IL: University of Chicago Press.

Stepman, J. (2021). Critical Race Theory Infiltrates Government, Classrooms. *The Daily Signal*, https://www.dailysignal.com/2021/01/12/critical-race-theory-infiltrates-government-classrooms/?_gl=1*1znnua*_ga*NjQ4NzE0MTkyLjE2OTYx

MDg5MjI.*_ga_W14BT6YQ87*MTY5NzcONTA0MS4zLjAuMTY5NzcONTA0 MS42MC4wLjA.

Stern, B. S. (Ed.) (2010). *The New Social Studies: People, Projects, & Perspectives*. Charlotte, NC: Information Age Publishing.

Stern, J. A., Brody, A. E., Gregory, J. A., Griffith, S., & Pulvers, J. (2021). *The State of State Standards for Civics and US History in 2021*. Washington, DC: Thomas B. Fordham Institute.

Stern, S. M. (2000). "Why the Battle over History Standards?" In S. Stotsky (Ed.), What's at Stake in the K-12 Standards Wars: A Primer for Educational Policy Makers (pp. 149–68). New York, NY: Peter Lang Publishing, Inc.

Stern, S. M., & Stern, J. A. (2011). *The State of State U.S. History Standards, 2011*. Washington, DC: The Thomas B. Fordham Institute.

Stevens, R., Wineburg, S., Herrenkohl, L. R., & Bell, P. (2005). "Comparative Understanding of School Subjects: Past, Present, and Future." *Review of Educational Research*, 75(2), 125–57.

Stewart, A. (1921). "The Social Sciences in Secondary Schools." *The Historical Outlook*, 12(2), 50–56.

Stolzenberg, N. M. (1993). "'He Drew a Circle That Shut Me Out': Assimilation, Indoctrination, and the Paradox of a Liberal Education." *Harvard Law Review*, 106(3), 581–667. https://doi.org/10.2307/1341657.

Strunc, A. (2017). "Rewriting the Standards, Not History: A Critical Discourse Analysis of the Texas State Board of Education Social Studies Standards Revisions." *National Journal of Urban and Public Education*, 11(2), 39–51.

Swanson, C. B., & Stevenson, D. L. (2002). "Standards-Based Reform in Practice: Evidence on State Policy and Classroom Instruction from the NAEP State Assessments." *Educational Evaluation and Policy Analysis*, 24(1), 1–27.

Sweet Jr., R. W. (1982). *Director's Report to the Congress on the National Assessment of Educational Progress*. Washington, DC: National Institute of Education.

Symcox, L. (2002). *Whose History? The Struggle for National Standards in American Classrooms*. New York, NY: Teachers College Press.

Symcox, L. (2009). "Introduction." In L. Symcox & A. Wilschut (Eds.), *National History Standards: The Problem of the Canon and the Future of Teaching History* (pp. 1–11). Charlotte, NC: Information Age Publishing, Inc.

Taylor, D. B. (2020, June 8). "George Floyd Protests: A Timeline." *New York Times*.

Taylor, T., & Guyver, R. (2012). "Introduction." In T. Taylor & R. Guyver (Eds.), *History Wars and the Classroom: Global Perspectives* (pp. xi–xix). Charlotte, NC: Information Age Publishing, Inc.

Thornton, S. J. (2005). *Teaching Social Studies That Matters: Curriculum for Active Learning*. New York, NY: Teachers College Press.

Thornton, S. J., & Barton, K. C. (2010). "Can History Stand Alone? Drawbacks and Blind Spots of a 'Disciplinary' Curriculum." *Teachers College Record*, 112(9), 2471–95.

Tosh, J. (2008). *Why History Matters*. New York, NY: Palgrave Macmillan.

Townsend, R. B. (2013). *History's Babel: Scholarship, Professionalization, and the Historical Enterprise in the United States, 1880–1940*. Chicago, IL: University of Chicago Press.

Tredwell, L., & Zodikoff, D. (1974). "A Study of the Effects of Jerome Bruner's 'Man: A Course of Study' on Social Studies Achievement in Fifth Grade." Paper presented to the Asian American Conference at the University of Massachusetts, Amherst, MA.

Tyack, D., James, T., & Benavot, A. (1987). *Law and the Shaping of Public Education, 1785–1954*. Madison, WI: University of Wisconsin Press.

Tyrrell, I. (1991). "American Exceptionalism in an Age of International History." *The American Historical Review*, 1031–55.

US Department of Education, Institute of Education Sciences. (2016). *NAEP 2010 Sample Design*. Retrieved from NAEP website on April 27, 2019, https://nces.ed.gov/nationsreportcard/tdw/sample_design/2010/2010_sampdsgn_new.aspx.

US Department of Education, Institute of Education Services. (2010a). *Civics, Geography, & U.S. History Teacher Background Questionnaire: 2010, Grade 4* (Survey G1TQCGHW-D). Washington, DC: US Department of Education.

US Department of Education, Institute of Education Services. (2010b). *Civics, Geography, & U.S. History Teacher Background Questionnaire: 2010, Grade 8* (Survey G2TQCGH-D). Washington, DC: US Department of Education.

US Department of Education, National Center for Education Statistics. (2011). National Assessment of Educational Progress: The Nation's Report Card: Civics 2010. (NCES 2011-466).

US Department of Education, National Center for Education Statistics. (2011). *National Assessment of Educational Progress: The Nation's Report Card: U.S. History 2010*. (NCES 2011-468).

US Department of Education, National Center for Education Statistics. (2011). *National Assessment of Educational Progress: The Nation's Report Card: Geography 2010*. (NCES 2011-467).

US Department of Education, National Center for Education Statistics. (2017). *Timeline for National Assessment of Educational Progress (NAEP) Assessments from 1969 to 2024*. Accessed on June 25, 2018, https://nces.ed.gov/nationsreportcard/about/assessmentsched.aspx.

US Department of Education, National Center for Education Statistics. (2018). *Technical Documentation on the Web*. Retrieved from https://nces.ed.gov/nationsreportcard/tdw/.

US Department of Education, National Center for Education Statistics. (n.d.). *Assessment Schedule*. Retrieved from https://nces.ed.gov/nationsreportcard/about/calendar.aspx.

US Department of Education. (2002, June). *Meeting the Highly Qualified Teachers Challenge: The Secretary's Annual Report on Teacher Quality*. Washington, DC: US Department of Education, Office of Postsecondary Education.

Useem, E. L. (2007). "Learning from Philadelphia's School Reform: The Impact of NCLB and Related State Legislation." *No Child Left Behind and the Reduction of the Achievement Gap: Sociological Perspectives on Federal Educational Policy*, 297–321.

van der Leeuw-Roord, J. (2009). "Yearning for Yesterday: Efforts of History Professionals in Europe at Designing Meaningful and Effective School History Curricula." In L. Symcox & A. Wilschut (Eds.), *National History Standards: The*

Problem of the Canon and the Future of Teaching History (pp. 73–94). Charlotte, NC: Information Age Publishing, Inc.

VanFossen, P. J. (2005). "'Reading and Math Take So Much of the Time . . .': An Overview of Social Studies Instruction in Elementary Classrooms in Indiana." *Theory & Research in Social Education, 33*(3), 376–403.

VanFossen, P. J., & McGrew, C. (2008). "Is the Sky Really Falling? An Update on the Status of Social Studies in the K-5 Curriculum in Indiana." *International Journal of Social Education, 23*(1), 139–79.

van Hover, S., & Yeager, E. (2007). "'I Want to Use My Subject Matter to . . .': The Role of Purpose in One U.S. Secondary History Teacher's Instructional Decision Making." *Canadian Journal of Education, 30*(3), 670–90.

van Hover, S., Hicks, D., & Stoddard, J. (2010). "The Development of Virginia's History and Social Studies Standards of Learning (SOLs), 1995–2010." *The Virginia Newsletter, 86*(2), 1–6.

van Hover, S., Hicks, D., Stoddard, J., & Lisanti, M. (2010). "From Roar to a Murmur: Virginia's History & Social Science Standards, 1995–2009." *Theory & Research in Social Education, 38*(1), 80–113.

VanSledright, B. (2002). "Confronting History's Interpretive Paradox While Teaching Fifth Graders to Investigate the Past." *American Educational Research Journal, 39*(4), 1089–1115.

VanSledright, B. (2011). *The Challenge of Rethinking History Education: On Practices, Theories, and Policy.* New York, NY: Routledge.

VanSledright, B., & Kelly, C. (1998). "Reading American History: The Influence of Multiple Sources on Six Fifth Graders." *The Elementary School Journal, 98*(3), 239–65.

Vinovskis, M. A. (1999). *The Road to Charlottesville: The 1989 Education Summit* (Report). Alexandria, VA: National Education Goals Panel.

Vinovskis, M. A. (2001). Overseeing the Nation's Report Card: The Creation and Evolution of the National Assessment Governing Board (NAGB). Washington, DC: National Assessment Governing Board.

Vinovskis, M. A. (2003). "Missed Opportunities: Why the Federal Response to *A Nation at Risk* Was Inadequate." In D. T. Gordon (Ed.), *A Nation Reformed? American Education 20 Years after* A Nation at Risk (pp. 115–30). Cambridge, MA: Harvard Education Press.

Vinovskis, M. A. (2009). "No Child Left Behind and Highly Qualified U.S. History Teachers: Some Historical and Policy Perspectives." In K. W. Wong & R. Rothman (Eds.), *Clio at the Table: Using History to Inform and Improve Education Policy* (pp. 221–47). New York, NY: Peter Lang.

Vinovskis, M. A. (2015). *From* A Nation at Risk *to* No Child Left Behind*: National Education Goals and the Creation of Federal Education Policy.* New York, NY: Teachers College Press.

Vogler, K. E. (2003). "Where Does Social Studies Fit in a High-Stakes Testing Environment?" *The Social Studies, 94*(5), 207–11.

Vogler, K. E. (2008). "Comparing the Impact of Accountability Examinations on Mississippi and Tennessee Social Studies Teachers' Instructional Practices." *Educational Assessment, 13*(1), 1–32.

Vogler, K. E., & Virtue, D. (2007). "'Just the Facts, Ma'am': Teaching Social Studies in the Era of Standards and High-Stakes Testing." *The Social Studies*, 98(2), 54–58.

Vontz, Thomas S. (1997). "Perspectives on Civic Education, 1898–1916." Ed 420 597. https://files.eric.ed.gov/fulltext/ED420597.pdf.

Wagner, R. B. (1989). *Accountability in Education: A Philosophical Inquiry*. New York, NY: Routledge.

Walberg, H. J. (2004). "Examinations for Educational Productivity." In W. M. Evers & H. J. Walberg (Eds.), *Testing Student Learning, Evaluating Teaching Effectiveness* (pp. 3–26). Stanford, CA: Hoover Institution Press.

Walz, O. (1973). "Anthropology: Adrenalin for a Tired High School Curriculum." *The Clearing House: A Journal of Educational Strategies, Issues and Ideas*, 48(4), 206–9.

Watts, H. (2021). "Charting the Present of Teaching the Past: Propaganda and 1776 in the History Classroom." *Teaching History: A Journal of Methods*, 46(2), 45–48.

Weber, W. (2017). "The Amherst Project and Reform of History Education, 1959–1972." *The History Teacher*, 51(1), 37–64.

Weedman, J. A. (1976). *A Case for Anthropology as the Integrating Force in Pre-Collegiate Social Studies* [Unpublished doctoral dissertation]. Texas Tech University, Lubbock, TX.

Wegner, D. (2022, September 24). Letter to the Editor: What Was Behind the South Dakota Standards Review? Mitchell Republic.com, https://www.mitchellrepublic.com/opinion/letters/letter-what-was-behind-the-south-dakota-standards-review.

Wells, T. J. (1973). *Oklahoma Secondary Social Supplies Teachers and the Usage of New National Social Studies Projects* [Unpublished doctoral dissertation]. Oklahoma State University, Stillwater, OK.

Weltman, B. (2000). "Reconsidering Arthur Bestor and the Cold War in Social Education." *Theory & Research in Social Education*, 28(1), 11–39.

Westheimer, J., & Kahne, J. (2003). "Educating the 'Good' Citizen: Political Choices and Pedagogical Goals." *PS: Political Science & Politics*, 37(2), 241–47. doi: 10.1017/S1049096504004160.

Whelan, M. (1994). "Albert Bushnell Hart and the Origins of Social Studies Education." *Theory & Research in Social Education*, 22(4), 423–40.

White, L. (2014, May 28). Letter to John McDonough, Boston Public Schools from the National Coalition for History. https://historycoalition.org/wp-content/uploads/2014/05/NCH-Superintendent-McDonough-BPS-History-final.pdf.

White, S. (1994). *The 1994 NAEP Teacher Background Questionnaire* (Report NCES 94-666). Washington, DC: US Department of Education, National Center for Education Statistics.

Whittington, D. (1991). "What Have 17-Year-Olds Known in the Past?" *American Educational Research Journal*, 28(4), 759–80.

Wiley, K. B. (1976). *The NSF Science Education Controversy: Issues, Events, Decisions*. Boulder, CO: Social Science Education Consortium, Inc.

Wills, J. S. (2007). "Putting the Squeeze on Social Studies: Managing Teaching Dilemmas in Subject Areas Excluded from State Testing." *Teacher College Record*, 109(8), 1980–2046.

Wilschut, A. (2009). "Canonical Standards or Orientational Frames Reference? The Cultural and Educational Approach to the Debate about Standards in History Teaching." In L. Symcox & A. Wilschut (Eds.), *National History Standards: The Problem of the Canon and the Future of Teaching History* (pp. 117–39). Charlotte, NC: Information Age Publishing, Inc.

Wilson, D. E. (1965). Curriculum Reform in History and the Social Studies, 1960–1965: A Survey of the Literature [Unpublished master's thesis]. Kansas State University, Manhattan, KS.

Wilson, S. M., & Sykes, G. (1989). "Toward Better Teacher Preparation and Certification." In P. Gagnon & The Bradley Commission on History in Schools (Eds.), *Historical Literacy: The Case for History in American Education* (pp. 268–86). New York, NY: Macmillan Publishing Company.

Wineburg, S. (2001). *Historical Thinking and Other Unnatural Acts: Charting the Future of Teaching the Past*. Philadelphia, PA: Temple University Press.

Wirtz, W., & Lapointe, A. (1982). *Measuring the Quality of Education: A Report on Assessing Educational Progress*. Washington, DC.

Wiseman, A. W. (2010). "The Uses of Evidence for Educational Policymaking: Global Contexts and International Trends." *Review of Research in Education*, *34*(1), 1–24.

Wolcott, H. F. (2007). "The Middlemen of MACOS." *Anthropology & Education Quarterly*, *38*(2), 195–206.

Womer F. B. (1970). *What Is National Assessment?* Ann Arbor, MI: National Assessment of Educational Progress, 1970.

Womer, F. B., & Martin, W. H. (1979). "The National Assessment of Educational Progress." *Studies in Educational Evaluation*, *5*(1), 27–37.

Woolfson, P. (1974). "The Fight over MACOS: An Ideological Conflict in Vermont." *Council on Anthropology and Education Quarterly*, *5*(3), 27–30.

Woyshner, C., Watras, J., & Crocco, M. S. (Eds). (2004). *Social Education in the Twentieth Century: Curriculum and Context for Citizenship*. New York, NY: Peter Lang Publishing, Inc.

Yeager, E. A., & van Hover, S. (2006). "Virginia vs. Florida: Two Beginning History Teachers' Perceptions of the Influence of High-Stakes Tests on Their Instructional Decision-Making." *Social Studies Research and Practice*, *1*(3), 340–58.

Zhao, Y., & Hoge, J. D. (2005). "What Elementary Students and Teachers Say about Social Studies." *The Social Studies*, *96*(5), 216–21.

Zimmerman, J. (2005). *Whose America? Culture Wars in the Public Schools*. Cambridge, MA: Harvard University Press.

Index

Page numbers in italics refer to figures and tables.

accountability, 129, 130, 131, 144, 145, 146; federal, 147–51; social studies, 154–57
Achieve, Inc. (National Governors Association), 132, 134, 135
achievement, student, 20, 69, 71, 103, 130–31, 157–58
ACL. *See* American Council of Learned Societies
ACP. *See* Anthropology Curriculum Project
ACT. *See* American College Testing Program
active learners, 118
Adamic, Louis, 55
Adams, Charles Francis, 8
Adams, Herbert Baxter, "HB," 3–4, 7
Addams, Jane, 19, 55
adequate yearly progress (AYP), 130, 131, 143
adult-centered classroom, in traditional factions, 38
Advanced Placement (AP) US history, 135, 138
AEA. *See* American Economic Association
African Americans, 16, 139–43

AHA. *See* American Historical Association
amalgamationist movement, 19
America 2000 (Bush, H. W.), 113–14, 115, 116, 117, 123, 126, 130
American College Testing Program (ACT), 103
American Council of Learned Societies (ACL), 73
American Economic Association (AEA), 2–3, 6
American exceptionalism, 70, 80, 118
American Historical Association (AHA), 3, 4, 7, 8–11, 20, 21; *Commission on the Social Studies*, 49–52; Committee of Five, 34; Committee of Seven, 32, 53, 54; Committee on Teacher Certification, 28–29; convention of, 18; Final Report of, 37, 40–41, 46; history courses altered by, 24; Krey and, 49; study sequence of, *21*; teachers and, 44, 67
American history, 1, 6, 7, 9, 11, 14; courses in, 24, 45–46; generations in, 57; neo-confederate take on, 137; pluralist vision of, 55; textbooks on, 47–49

American identity, 15–17, 27, 94, 120–22, 127, 159
Americanization, 16, 17–18, 23, 24, 36, 58; curriculum *versus*, 19–22; immigrant, 27
American Legion, 23, 58, 66
American Political Science Association (APSA), 44, 61
American Revolution, 1, 73
American Rock (ABC), 95, 97
American Social Science Association (ASSA), 2, 3, 43–44
American society, 51
American Textbook Council, 106
Amherst College, 77
Amherst High School, 77
Amherst Project, 77–78, 83–84
Anderson, Benedict, 109
Anglo-Saxon culture, 15, 16, 18, 20
anthropology centered, curriculum, 79, 88
Anthropology Curriculum Project (ACP), 79
AP. *See* Advanced Placement
APC. *See* Assessment Policy Committee
APSA. *See* American Political Science Association
Archibald, George, 91, 92, 98, 100
area studies courses, 95
Arizona, 90–91
Armstrong, Samuel C., 16
Arn, Larry, 141
ASSA. *See* American Social Science Association
assessment, social studies, 60, 148–49, 150, 153–54, 156–58
Assessment Policy Committee (APC), 149, 151, 152–53, 154
assimilation, of Native Americans, 16, 93
assimilationist approach, 18, 19, 24, 108
Association of American Geographers, 78

Association of History Teachers of the Middle States and Maryland, 29
attitudes, traditional faction, 53, 67
AYP. *See* adequate yearly progress

banning books, 138
Barton, Keith, 109, 127, 162
basic skills, 99
Beard, Charles A., 51
beliefs, education, 11, 31, 47, 80, 81, 82; historians and, 163–64; multiculturalism, 15; traditional, 98
Bell, Terrel H., 102, 103
Bennett, William, 152
Bestor, Arthur, 65, 66, 163
Biden, Joe, 140
Bill of Rights, US, 153
"binding heritage," of history education, 107
boarding schools, for African and Native Americans, 15–16
book banning, 138
Boston Public School (BPS), 88–89, 138
BPS. *See* Boston Public School
Bradley Commission (Bradley Foundation), 106–8, 110–11, 113, 116–17, 124, 131
British bias, in US education, 48
Brookings Institute, 140
Brown, Howard Elmer, 70
Brown v. Topeka, 67
Bruner, Jerome, 72, 74, 78, 80, 87, 88–89; ideology of, 90; MACOS and, 93, 94, 97–100; NSS and, 161; Skinner and, 91–92
Buck, Ken, 140
Building America (Hanna and Mendenhall), 49
Bureau of Education, US, 22, 31
Bush, George H. W., 113–14, 115, 116, 117, 123, 126, 130
Bush, George W., 129, 130, 136, 155
Bushman, Bruner on, 88
Butler Act (1920), 138
Byrd, Robert, 132

Index

C3. *See College, Career, and Civic Life*
California Board of Education, 62, 89
California History-Social Science, framework, 124
California History-Social Studies, framework, 115
California reform, models of, 115, 116
Cardinal Principles, on education by CRSE, 30–31, 33, 38, 54
Cardinal Principles of Secondary Education (Kingsley), 33, 36, 37, 40, 41
Carlisle Indian Industrial School, 15, 17
Carnegie Corporation, 50, 147, 148
Carnegie Mellon University, 74, 83
CC. *See* Common Core
CCSSO. *See* Council of Chief State School Officers
Charlottesville, Virginia, 114
CHEC. *See* Committee on History and Education for Citizenship
Cheney, Lynne, 115, 117, 121, 122
Cherokee tribe, 15
child-centered, education methods, 3, 22, 25, 30, 36, 72, 125
child labor laws, 27
Christian Broadcasting Network, 99
Christian Coalition (Robertson), 123
Christian Family Renewal, 93
Christian values, 99, 137
citizenship, social studies and, xii–xiii, 13–15, 23–24, 99, 104–5, 111; assessment of, 150; civic duty and, 31, 37, 158–60; interpretations of, 121; models for, 64–65; tests for, 149; vision of, 55, 107–9
civic competence, 120
civic duty, 159–60
civic empowerment, 145
civic identity, 27
civic nationalists, 18, 19, 121
civics, education, 6, 13–14, 18, 19, 22, 39; agenda, 23–24; assessment, 153–54, 156; citizenship and, 31, 37, 158–60; disciplines in, 17, 111,

155; ideology, 9, 30, 40, 74, 87, 146; NCLB and, 131, 155; relevance of, 21, 41, 76, 83, 138; removal of, 150; stakeholders for, 43, 119, 123, 130, 146
civilization, western, 61, 66, 67, 118, 125
Civil Rights, 69, 137
Civil War, 137, 160–61
Clinton, Bill, 114, 123, 130
Cohen-Cole, Jamie, 80
Cold War, 64, 68, 69, 70, 80, 102, 123
Coleman, David, 135
College, Career, and Civic Life (C3), 135, 142
College Board, 6, 37, 135–36
college-ready, curriculum, 5
colonial period, ethnic groups, 15–17
Columbia University, 48, 52, 58
Columbus, Christopher, 2
commission, on social studies, AHA, 49–52, 54
Commissioner of Education, New York, 116
Commissioner of Education, US, 147
Commission on the Reorganization of Secondary Education (CRSE), 30–31, 33, 37, 38, 54
Commission on the Social Studies (AHA), 49–52
committee, discipline-specific, 5, 43
committee memberships, by profession, *168*
Committee of Articulation. *See* Committee of Nine
Committee of Five, AHA, 20, 21, 34
Committee of Nine, NEA, 29
Committee of Preparation of Teachers of History in Schools, 22
Committee of Seven, AHA, 7–11, 20, 21, 32, 53, 54
Committee of Ten, NEA, 1, 5, 20, 27, 29, 102–3
Committee on American History in Schools and Colleges, 59, 60

Committee on History and Education for Citizenship (CHEC), 34, 35, 50
Committee on Social Science, 31
Committee on Social Studies, 31–32, 35, 37, 39, 40, 73; accessibility for teachers in, 75; Final Report of, 163; historians on, 75, 81
Committee on Social Studies, NEA, 50
Committee on Teacher Certification, AHA, 28–29
Committee on Teaching, AHA, 50
Common Core (CC), 100, 129, 132, 134–35, 145; social studies standards and, 159
Common Core State Standards for English Language Arts in History/Social Studies, Science, and Technical Subjects (CCSS-ELA), 134–35, 145
communist plot, of progressive education, 64
community, social studies, 43–45
"complex thinking skills," 105
concepts, historical, 127
conceptualization, of social studies, *xii*
Conclusions and Recommendations (AHA), 51
conflict, textbooks, 93–95
Congress, US, MACOS and, 92
Conlan, John B., 91–92, 93
consensus history movement (NCHS), 70, 73, 80, 81, 105, 108
conservative radio pundits, 121
conservatives, on education, 37, 38, 80, 90, 99, 101–2; battles of, 94, 124, 158; ideals of, 136; social meliorism and, 125; standards and, 110, 116, 121, 122. *See also* paleoconservatives
Constitution, US, 13, 41, 153
content, patriotic, 47
content knowledge, 60, 65, 67, 105–6, 118, 119; context and, 161; history, 162; political, 149; skills over, 89, 151, 163

core disciplines, social studies, 32, 73–74
corruption, of MACOS, 91
Costrell, Robert M., 126
Cote, Zachary, 158
Cotton, Tom, 140
Council of Chief State School Officers (CCSSO), 103–4, 135
Council of Economic Education, 119–20
Counts, George, 51, 52, 53, 55, 57–58, 62
COVID-19, 139–40
Cox, Dealous, 93
Crabtree, Charlotte, 117
crises, education, xiii, xiv, 101, 102–5, 108, 165
Critical Race Theory (CRT), 140–41
critical thinking, xii–xiii, 24, 78, 84, 92
critics, of MACOS, 98–99
critiques, of education reform, 93–94
CRSE. *See* Commission on the Reorganization of Secondary Education
CRT. *See* Critical Race Theory
"cultural imperialism," 23
cultural pluralism, 15, 19, 24, 30, 47–48, 55; acceptance of, 122; favoring, 83, 118
culture wars, xiii, 108, 120–21, 129, 137, 155; *1619 Project versus 1776 Commission*, 139–43; battles in, 57–61; skills over content in, 163
curriculum, xiv, 3, 11, 29–30, 31–32, 43–55; of African and Native American boarding schools, 15–16; Americanization *versus*, 19–22; anthropology, 79; centers for, 76, 84; debates on, 57, 66; high school, 104; history, 1, 5, 106; interest groups influence on, 164; MACOS, 89–90; national, 113–15; NSS and, *81*; postsecondary, 94; project models for, 71–72; secondary education, 128; social studies, 59, 76, 88, 100, 103; teacher-proof, 66, 97–98

Dakota Free Press (media), 142–43
Darling-Hammond, Linda, 122–23
data-driven, education reform, 141
Dawson, Edgar, 45
DBQs. *See* document-based questions
DCEP. *See* Detroit Citizenship Education Project
debates, on curriculum, 57, 66
Declaration of Independence, US, 41, 140
decline, of social studies, 109
"Decline and Fall of History Teaching" (Ravitch), 105
Denver, Colorado, 63
Department of Education, US, 101, 102, 148, 149, 150
DeSantis, Rick, 141
Detroit, Michigan, 18, 62
Detroit Citizenship Education Project (DCEP), 62
developmental faction, of education methods. *See* child-centered education methods
Dewey, John, 22, 30, 38, 53, 63, 90; *developmentalism* of, 119, 162
Diamond, Stanley, 62
discipline movement, 116
disciplines, of social studies, xi–xii, 32, 73–75, 83, 104, 128; civic education as, 17, 111, 155; geography as, 78, 119, 165; history as, 1, 46, 47–48, 54, 60–61, 80–82, 105, 107, 109–10, 124, 160–62; language arts as, 63, 134, 135, 138; NAEP and, 155, 157; social sciences as, 16, 47, 72, 79, 99, 115; standards of, 113–17, 120–21, 126, 131, 136, 142–44, 145–46; value of, 84, 159, 161
discovery-based, teaching methods, 90
discussion-based, lecture model, 77
document-based questions (DBQs), 84
doldrums, in social studies, 69, 74
"Don't Say Gay," 141
Dow, Peter, 88
Drake, F. D., 84

Dunn, Arthur William, 31, 32, 33
Dunne, Kerry, 138

economics, civic education and, 101, 102, 119, 125, 126, 156
ECS. *See* Education Commission of the States
EDC. *See* Educational Development Course
education, civic, 6, 13–14, 19, 22–24, 123; battles in, 94, 124, 158; citizenship, 31, 37, 158–60; conservatives on, 37, 38, 80, 99, 102; crises in, xiii, xiv, 101, 102–5, 108, 165; disciplines, xi–xii, 1–2, 17, 111, 155; economics, 119, 125, 126, 156; federal government, xiv, 66, 69, 71, 98, 108; history, 7–8, 10, 20, 27, 105; Holocaust materials for, 137; MACOS, 87–100; pedagogy for, 43, 62; policies for, 144, 148, 149, 151, 154; public school, 5, 34, 73; secondary, 20, 29, 30, 50, 52, 66; social studies, xi–xiv, 32–33, 40; world history, 106, 142, 156. *See also* models, of education; reformers, education
Educational Development Course (EDC), 87–88, 89, 92
Educational Excellence Network, 152
educationalists, 89, 163
Educational Testing Service (ETS), 151–52, 155
Educational Wastelands (Bestor), 66
Education Commission of the States (ECS), 148, 149, 151, 154
educators, xiv, 37, 39, 46, 47, 60; curriculum of, 29–30, 52; historians and, 22, 27, 81, 82, 105, 160; social studies, 64, 65, 68, 69, 97, 164–65
Elementary and Secondary Education Act (ESEA), 69, 71, 102, 129, 130, 148. *See also;* No Child Left Behind
elementary education, 10, 20, 48, 67, 89, 127; social sciences and, 161; teachers of, 134

Eliot, Charles W., 4–5
Endicott House Conference, 74, 87
Enola Gay (exhibit), 120–21
enrollment, high school, social studies course, *74*, 104
Eskimo, Bruner focus on, 88
ethnic groups, education of, 15–17, 19, 140
ETS. *See* Educational Testing Service
Eurocentric models, of education, 61
Evaluation Design, in Bureau of Elementary and Secondary Education, 148
Every Student Succeeds Act (Obama), 144
Evolution of Man and Society (Oliver), 88

factual knowledge, 49, 60, 125, 141, 150, 162
Fair, Jean, 149–50
Farrand, Max, 49
federal government, education and, xiv, 66, 69, 71, 98, 108; accountability for, 147–51; ESEA and, 130; funding, 76, 78, 79, 117, 123, 128; humanism and, 99; interference of, 101; money, 87; oversight of, 90–94, 103; public education and, 143; reform mandates of, 102; TAH discontinued by, 132
Feldmesser, Robert, 74
Fenton, Edwin, 74, 75, 83
Ferris Beuhler's Day Off (film), 111
field-testing, by Getises, 78
the fifties, education in, 69–71
Final Report, AHA, 37, 40–41, 46
Finn, Chester, 105, 118, 152, 153, 154, 155
FitzGerald, Frances, 94
Florida, 90, 141
Floyd, George, 140
Forbes (magazine), 58
Ford, Guy Stanton, 59
Ford, Henry, 18, 93
Fordham Institute, 131

Ford Motor Company, 18
Foster, Wallace, 25
Fouillée, Augustine, 14
Foundations of Literacy Project (NEH), 152, 153, 154
frameworks, for state social studies standards, x, 1, 30, 52, 62, 74; AP US history, 135, 138; C3, 135, 142; California History-Social Science, 124; California History-Social Studies, 115; CRT as, 140; NAEP, 154; student learning outcomes and, 155; teachers and, 125–26
France, education in, 13–14
frequency, of "New" Social Studies Projects, *76*
Frontier Group, 22
Fry, Virgil T. (fictional character), 78
funding, education, 28, 63, 71, 78, 91, 164; assessment, 154; federal government, 76, 79, 117, 123, 128
fusion model, of education, 63
future, of social studies, 158–65

Gabler, Norma, 91, 93, 136–37
Gallagher, Mary Campbell, 97
Gardner, John, 147
generations, of Americans, 57
geography, discipline of, xi, 78, 119, 154, 156, 165
Geography in an Urban Age (Amherst Project), 78
German immigrants, 18
Getis, Arthur, 78
Getis, Judy, 78
G.I. Bill, 63–64, 66
Glenn, Don, 90
Goals 2000 (Clinton), 114, 130
Gobitis v. Minerville, 61
golden age, history education, 10, 40, 124
good citizens, 17, 24, 25, 27, 28, 40; civic activities and, 158; identity of, 159; skills for, 162; Soviet Union in relation to, 68; students as, 80, 109, 149, 151

good teacher, 44, 156
Gorton, Slade, 122
graduation, students and, 35, 147
Grand Army of the Republic, 160
grants, education, 50, 52, 71, 91, 152
Great Depression, 51, 52, 53, 57, 101, 111, 125
Gross, Richard, 97

Haas, J. D., 84–85
Halvorsen, Anne-Lise, 67
Hampton Normal and Agricultural Institute, "Hampton Institute," 16–17, 18, 31, 33
Hanna, Paul R., 49, 161
Hannah-Jones, Nikole, 139–43
hardships, economic, 101
Harris, William, 92, 98
Hart, Albert Bushnell, 4, 7, 8, 10
Harvard University, 4, 6, 72
Hearst, William Randolph, 48, 58
Hegeman, Suan, 99
Helburn, Nicholas, 83
Heritage Foundation, 90
Hertzberg, Hazel Whitman, 10, 38, 39, 52–53, 80, 109–10, 163
hidden agenda, in standards, 121
high school, social studies in, xi, 43, *74, 96*, 104
High School Geography Project (HSGP), 78, 79, 83
Hillsdale College, Michigan, 141, 143
Hindu controversy, 137
historians, educators and, 22, 27, 80–81, 82, 105, 160; four beliefs by, 163–64; social scientists and, 75; standards of, 115; Tosh on, 161; traditional factions and, 39; university, 110, 125
historical identity, for national standards, 120–22, 127
Historical Literacy (Bradley Foundation), 106
historical narrative, multicultural approach to, 71

The Historical Outlook (NCSS), 35, 44–45, 52. *See also Social Education; The Social Studies*
History and Social Science, Massachusetts model of, 126
history education, 1–2, 6–10, 27, 57–68, 73, 107; assessment in, 153–54, 155; British Bias in US, 48; disciplines of, 1, 46, 47–48, 54, 80–82, 105, 109, 124, 160–62; France, 13–14; *golden age*, 124; NCLB and, 131; "New" movement for, 11, 28, 37–39, 45; *Problems of Democracy* course, 32–33, 35, 39–40, 44, 46–47, 51; skills for, 119; social meliorism faction of, 14, 31, 40; social studies curriculum in, 43, 45–49, 88, 100; social studies education *versus*, 34–37; survey on, 59–60, 66–67, 97; textbooks on, 21, 69–70; in US, 94, 95, 123, 135, 152; value of, 110–11, 151, 161
History Matters! (newsletter) (NCHE), 138
The History Teacher Magazine (McKinley), 22, 28, 97
H-Net's High School Social Studies (blog), 138
Hofstadter, Richard, 37, 81
Holocaust, educational materials, 137
Holocaust Center, 100
House Labor and Education Committee, 94
Howe, Harold, 94
HSGP. *See* High School Geography Project
Hughes, H. Stuart, 82
Hughes, John, 111
humanistic factors, in education, 3–4, 6, 37, 66, 99, 107, 163
Hunt, Erling, 59, 68, 82, 83, 87
Hunter, Duncan, 120

IASA. *See Improving America's Schools Act*
identity, civic, 27

ideology, civic education, 9, 30, 40, 74, 87, 146; of Bruner, 90; conservative, 101–2, 136; political, 3, 20, 38, 54, 107, 162
Illinois, 41
Imagined Communities (Anderson), 109
immigrants, Americanization of, 17–19, 20, 27, 55
immorality hearing, in Oregon schools, 93
Improving America's Schools Act (IASA), 114
indigenous culture, South Dakota, 142
inquiry model, of teaching approach, 21, 43, 58, 79, 84
institutions, democratic, 47
instructional materials, NSS scholars, 84
interdisciplinary approach, to social studies, 74
interest groups influence, on curriculum, 164
interference, of federal government, 101
interpretations, of citizenship, 121
interwar period, 93–94
IRT. *See* Item Response Theory
Item Response Theory (IRT), 152

Jackson, Andrew, 15
Jaeger, Richard, 148
James, James Alton, 35
Jamestown, 139
Japan, *Enola Gay* exhibit and, 120–21
Jehovah's Witness, students of, 61
Johanek, Michael C., 157–58
John Birch Society, 90
Johnson, Henry, 34–35
Johnson, Lyndon B., 69, 71, 101, 148
Jones, Thomas Jesse, 17, 31, 32
Jorgensen, on social efficiency, 38

Kanawha County, West Virginia, 61, 94–95
Kansas, 95, *96*
Keller, Charles R., 75, 81, 84

Kelley, Dr. (fictional character), 68
Kellor, Francis A., 23
Kendall, John S., 128
Kennedy, Francis, 16–17
Kennedy, John F., 75
Kentucky, 144
Kenworthy, Leonard, 82
Keppel, Francis, 147
Kidwell, Frances L., 164
King, A. K., 54
Kingsley, Clarence D., 29–31, 33, 36, 37, 39, 40, 41
Kirkendall, Richard, 97
Kliebard, Herbert M., 3, 18
Krey, August C., 49, 50, 51
Kurtz, Stanley, 142

Lake City, Florida, 90
language arts, social studies disciplines and, 63, 134, 135, 138
Lapointe, Archie, 151
leadership, NCSS, 116
learners, passive and active, 118
Learning Area Committee, NCES, 153–54
Leland, Waldo Gifford, 28
Le Tour de France (primary school reader), 13–14
Levinson, Meira, 145
Levstik, L. S., 127
LGBTQ issues, 141
listening, passive and active, 118
literacy skills, 134, 145
"little citizens" (patriotic primer), 25
Longview, Texas, 91
Lorraine, France, 13–14
Loveless, Tom, 145
loyalty oaths, state-mandated, 64
Lybarger, Michael, 109–10
Lynde and Harry Bradley Foundation, 106–8, 110–11, 113, 116–17, 124, 131

Madison Conference, 4, 5–11, *6*, 20, 54, 75

Man (MACOS) (Bruner), 21, 43, 58, 87–94, 97–100
Man and his Changing Society (Rugg, H.), 48, 64
The Many Lives of Kiviok (Dow), 88
marginalization, of social studies, 132, 134, 144, 157, 164
Marker, Gerald W., 84
Martz, C. E., 45
Marzano, Robert J., 128
Maus (graphic novel), 137, 138
McCarthyism, 64
McCully, A. W., 127
McKinley, Albert, 28, 44–45
McMaster, John Bach, 18
McMinn County School Board, Tennessee, 137
memorization, 2, 6, 9, 20, 53, 67; history and, 107, 165; pedagogical practice as, 21, 46; problems of, 35, 74, 80; survey participants and, 59–60
Mendenhall, James, 49
Metcalf, Lawrence E., 82, 83, 87
Michener, James A., 68
Michigan, 41
middle school, xi–xii
Middle States Association (MSA), 9
Milam, Erika Lorraine, 99
mini courses, education models as, 95, 100
minimums, for graduation, 35
Minneapolis, Minnesota, 140
Mississippi State Textbook Purchasing Board, 58
Mississippi Valley Historical Association (MVHA), 28–29, 59
Mississippi Valley Historical Review (MVHA), 59
models, of education, 33, 39, 53, 59, 63, 65; California reform, 115, 116; child-centered, 22, 30, 72; citizenship, 64–65; curriculum project, 71–72; discussion-based, 77; Eurocentric, 61; inquiry, 21, 43, 58, 79, 84;

Massachusetts, 126; mini courses, 95, 100; national assessment, 113; national standards, 129; NCHS, 124; "New" history, 11, 21, 24, 28, 37–38, 45; "New" social studies, 82–83, 85, 87; one-size-fits-all, 108, 109; patriotic education renewed, 23–24; preparatory-school, 27; progressive, 33, 36, 55, 62, 64, 110; social efficiency, 147; standards, 114, 125, 126, 130; teacher-centered, 3, 119; Texas, 129
Morrisey, William, 142–43
Morrissett, Irving, 83
MSA. *See* Middle States Association
Muldoon, Leslie, 156
multicultural approach, to historical narrative, 71, 106
multiculturalism, 15, 122
multicultural pluralism, 113
MVHA. *See* Mississippi Valley Historical Association

NAACP, 137
NAEP. *See* National Assessment for Educational Progress
NAGB. *See* National Assessment Governing Board
NAM. *See* National Association of Manufacturers
NAS. *See* National Association of Scholars
NASSP. *See* National Association of Secondary School Principals
National American Committee, 23
national assessment, 113, 114, 123, 134, 148, 152
National Assessment for Educational Progress (NAEP), xiv, 103, 105, 114, 148, 150, 151–57
National Assessment Governing Board (NAGB), 151, 154–55, 156–57
National Association of Manufacturers (NAM), 58
National Association of Scholars (NAS), 143

National Association of Secondary School Principals (NASSP), 46
national average assessments, NAEP findings on, 150–51
National Center for Education Statistics (NCES), 102, 103, 150, 151, 153–56
National Center for History in the Schools (NCHS), 117, 118, 119, 122, 124, 125
National Coalition for History (NCH), 138
National Commission on Excellence in Education (NCEE), 101–3, 104, 108
National Commission on Social Studies in the Schools (NCSSS), 115
National Council for Geographic Education, 78
National Council for History Education (NCHE), 107, 138, 163
National Council for the Social Studies (NCSS), 44, 45, 46, 49, 52, 53; agenda of, 163; C3 and, 135; Commission on Social Studies for, 73; ECS and, 149; education of, 62; Ford, G., and, 59; *The Historical Outlook*, 35 (*See also Social Education*; *The Social Studies*); recommendations of, *116*; *Social Education*, 72; standards project, 120; *The Teaching the Social Studies*, 67
national curriculum, 113–15
National Defense Education Act (NDEA), xiv
National Education Association (NEA), 1, 4–5, 19, 20, 27, 30; Committee of Nine, 29; Committee of Ten, 102–3; *Committee on Social Studies* and, 50; NCSS department in, 45
National Endowment for the Humanities (NEH), 115, 117, 121, 126, 152, 154
National Endowment of the Arts (NEA), 126
National Geographic Society, 154
National Governors Association, 134
nationalists, civic, 18, 19, 121

National Science Foundation (NSF), 71, 78, 91, 92, 98
National Standards for History (NSH), 117–27, 131, 136, 164
national standards movement, 113, 120–22, 124, 126, 127, 129
National Teachers Examination, 152
A Nation at Risk (NCEE), 102, 103, 108, 113, 151, 154
Native Americans, 15–17, 18, 93, 143
"nature study," 2
NCEE. *See* National Commission on Excellence in Education
NCES. *See* National Center for Education Statistics
NCH. *See* National Coalition for History
NCHE. *See* National Council for History Education
NCHS. *See* National Center for History in the Schools
NCLB. *See* No Child Left Behind
NCSSS. *See* National Commission on Social Studies in the Schools
NDEA. *See* National Defense Education Act
NEA. *See* National Education Association; National Endowment of the Arts
NEH. *See* National Endowment for the Humanities
NEHTA. *See* New England History Teachers' Association
Nelson, L. R., 84
Netsilik tribe, 88–89, 90, 92, 93
Nevins, Allen, 58–59
New England History Teachers' Association (NEHTA), 9
New Hampshire, 13
Newmann, Fred M., 84
news, on social studies, 61–62
"New" social studies (NSS), 72, 74, 75–77, *76*, 79, 99; Bruner and, 161; historian in, 80; movement for, 82–83, 85, 87, 151; problems

with, 97–98; scholars of, 84; Social Studies Curriculum, *81*
New Viewpoints in the Social Sciences (NCSS), 73, 80
New York Board of Education, 165
New York City, NY, 48, 116, 165
New York Regents, exam, 165
New York Times, 59, 60, 66, 67, 92, 99; *1619 Project* of, 139–43; textbook evaluation by, 137
No Child Left Behind (NCLB) (2002), 129, 130–32, 134, 143–44, 155, 157, 159
Noem, Kristi, 142, 143
non-college-bound students, 1, 8, 11, 21–22, 40
North Carolina, 141, 148
North Central History Teachers' Association Convention, 19
Northern Ireland, 127
notions, of citizenship, 13–15
Noyes, Edmund S., 36
NSF. *See* National Science Foundation
NSH. *See* National Standards for History
NSS. *See* "New" social studies

OAH. *See* Organization of American Historians
Obama, Barack, 134, 144
O'Connor, Sandra Day, 164–65
Office of Science and Technology Policy, US, 93
Oklahoma, 85
Oliver, Donald, 88
Olver, Rose, 77
one-size-fits-all models, of education, 108, 109
Oregon, 92, 93, 98
organic relationship, between past and present, 161–62
Organization of American Historians (OAH, formerly MVHA), 96, 97, 107, 158
Organization of the National Council of Geography Teachers, 44

oversight, federal government, 90–94, 103

paleoconservatives, 39, 93, 95
pandemic. *See* COVID-19
PARCC. *See* Partnership for Assessment of Readiness for College and Careers
parents, 141, 146
Parker, W. C., 120
Partnership for Assessment of Readiness for College and Careers (PARCC), 134
passive learners, 118
past, present relationship with, 161–62
patriotic education, movement for, 23–24, 47
Paxson Report, 28–29
PEA. *See* Progressive Education Association
pedagogical methods, for teachers, 5, 8, 21, 43, 46, 58; problem-centered, 75; rote memorization, 2, 6, 9, 20, 53, 59–60, 67, 107; social studies education, 62, 124, 160, 164
Pederson, Patricia Velde, 164
Pennridge School District, Philadelphia, 141
Pennsylvania Education Association, 41
philosophy, social studies, 43
Piaget, Jean, 89, 127
Piagetian notion, 127
pinnacle project, MACO, 87–90
placement assimilation, of ethnic groups, 16
placement indoctrination, of ethnic groups, 16
pluralistic vision, of America, 55
polarization, American politics, 145
policies, education, 144, 148, 149, 151, 154; politics and, xiii, 14, 87, 99, 101
policymakers, 65, 75–76, 81, 127, 148, 162
political corruption, of NSH, 164
politicization, of social studies, 48

270 *Index*

postsecondary academics, 9, 22, 30, 52, 61, 70; diversity in curriculum of, 94; history problems with, 97
Powell, Adam Clayton, 94
PragerU (media company), 139
preparatory-school model, 27
present, past relationship to, 161–62
presentism (Wineburg), 160
problems, NSS, 97–98
Problems of Democracy course, 32–33, 35, 40, 44, 46–47, 51; downfall of, 64, 68; model of, 65
The Process of Education (Bruner), 72
professions, of committee memberships, *168*
programs, civics education, 158
Progressive Education Association (PEA), 52–53, 55
progressive education model, 33, 36, 55, 62, 64, 110
Progressive Era, 2
progressivism, political ideology of, 3, 20, 38, 54, 107, 162
projects, NSS, 81, 82, 84, 85, 98, 99; pinnacle, 87–90; standards, 120
Project Social Studies, 75–76
public debates, televised, 122
public hearings, by NCEE, 102
public school education, 5, 13, 27, 29, 34, 73, 143
Puckett, John, 157–58
Pulitzer Center, 139
purpose, social studies, xi–xii

racism, 88, 121, 139
Ravitch, Diane, 105, 107, 109, 116, 117, 124; Finn and, 152, 153, 154
Reagan, Ronald, 99, 101–2, 150, 164
recommendations, of NCSS, *116*
reformers, education, 3–4, 23–24, 27, 37–40, 123–24; beliefs of, 80, 81, 82; California models of, 115, 116; critiques of, 93–94; data-driven, 141; federal mandates and, 102; politicians and, 101; standards-based, 114

relevance, civic education, 21, 37, 41, 76, 83, 138; issues of, 158, 161, 163
removal, of civics education, 150
republicanism, 14
Republican National Committee (RNC), 135
Reynolds, Edwin, 100
Risinger, Frederick, 122
RNC. *See* Republican National Committee
Robertson, Pat, 99, 123
Robinson, Harvey, 11
role, in society of African and Native Americans, 16
Rugg, Earle, 44, 46, 48
Rugg, Harold O., 36, 44, 48, 49, 57, 58, 64
Russell, William R., 63

Salmon, Lucy M., 8
Sandia National Labs, reports of, 113
Sanford, Terry, 148
SAT. *See* Scholastic Aptitude Test
Savit, Eli, 164
Saxe, David Warren, 38, 39, 41
SBAC. *See* Smarter Balanced Assessment Consortium
SBOE. *See* State Board of Education
scapegoating, of social studies, 105–6, 110
Schafer, James, 34–35, 36
Schissler, Hanna, 108
scholars, on testing culture, 144, 145
Scholastic Aptitude Test (SAT), 113–14, 152
school board, Oakland, 115–16
school districts, American, 147
Schoolhouse Rock (TV series), 95
scope, of NCSS, *104*, *116*
seamless web, of Beard, 51
SEAs. *See* State Education Agencies
secondary education, 20, 29, 30, 50, 52, 66, 128
Secretary of Education, 154
segregation, of ethnic groups, 16

Seixas, Peter, 124
Selakovich, Daniel, 99
Senate, US, history standards rejected by, 122–23
Senesh, Lawrence, 75
sequence, of NCSS, *104*, *116*
1776 Commission (Trump), 139–43
Sewell, Gilbert, 106
sex education, MACOS taught, 93
single field, social studies as, xi
1619 Project (Hannah-Jones), 139–43
sixth-grader, worksheet, 146
skills, 16, 46, 60, 61, 72, 80; basic, 99; cognitive, 83; content over, 89, 151, 163; for *good* citizens, 162; history, 119; literacy, 134, 145; social sciences, 79; social studies, 1–2, 120, 127; thinking, 105, 118, 126
Skinner, B. F., 91–92
slant, political, xiii
Slovenian immigrant, 55
Smarter Balanced Assessment Consortium (SBAC), 134
Smedstad, Alton O., 91
Smithsonian Institute, 120
Snedden, David, 30–31
Sobol, Thomas, 116
Social Education (NCSS), 52, 72–73
social efficiency, 3, 18, 20, 30, 31, 36; Denver schools and, 63; Jorgenson on, 38; model of, 53, 147; social studies and, 37
socialization, political, 87
social meliorism, history faction of, 11, 14, 31, 40, 47, 53; conservatives and, 125; Counts, G. aligned with, 62; "Great Society" in, 95; Rugg, H. favoring, 48
social problems, in society, 2, 29, 32, 33, 41, 65; NSS model integration of, 77, 97–98
Social Science Education Consortium (Morrissett), 83
social sciences, 1–11, 24, 30–34, 44, 47, 50–51; Cold War and, 69; disciplines of, 16, 72, 79, 99, 115; elementary grades and, 161; history conflicts in, 160; Newmann perceived value of, 84
social studies, xi–xiv, *xii*, 30–34, 40, 111, 126; assessment of, 150, 153, 158; C3 state standards framework for, 135, 142; CC and, 132, 134; citizenship and, xii–xiii, 13–15, 23–24, 99, 104–5; Cold War in relation to, 80; commission on, 49–52, 54; controversies of, 87–100, 136–39; core discipline within, 73–74; courses on, *46*; curricular materials for, 76; curriculum of, 43–47, 48, 59; Department of Education and, 149; disciplines of, xii, 16, 60, 72, 80; educators and, 64, 65, 68, 69, 84–85, 97, 145–46; future of, 158–65; Hertzberg and, 163; history-dominated field of, 39; history education *versus*, 35–37; interdisciplinary approach to, 74; marginalization of, 132, 134, 144, 157, 164; NAEP and, 151–57; pedagogy for, 124, 160, 164; *Problems of Democracy* and, 35, 40; scapegoating, 105–6, 110; skills related to, 1–2, 127; standards of, 113–17, 120–21, 128, 131, 136, 142–43, 146, 159; testing, *133*, 151; testing culture and, 144, 145; textbook series on, 54, 58, 59, 60
Social Studies Alive (textbook), 141
The Social Studies and the Social Sciences (ACLS/NCSS), 73–74
society, American, 16, 51
South Dakota, 142, 143
Soviet Union, 64, 66, 68, 69
SPAN, scope and sequence, *104*
SPEAK. *See* Standards to Provide Educational Achievement for All Kids
Spellings, Margaret, 155
Spencer, Herbert, 162

Sputnik, 65, 66, 69, 71
stages of development, for students (Piaget), 89
stakeholders, civic education, 43, 119, 123, 130, 146, 158, 159
standardized tests, 129, 130–31, 132, 135, 141, 144, 145
standards, education, 4–5, 7–11, 114, 119–22; history, 162; literacy, 145; movement for, 125, 126, 130; social studies, 113–17, 120–21, 128, 131, 136, 142–44, 146, 159
Standards to Provide Educational Achievement for All Kids (SPEAK) Act, 157
Stanford's Center for Advanced Study of Behavioral Sciences, 147
State Board of Education (SBOE), 136, 137
state controversies, social studies and, 136–39
State Education Agencies (SEAs), 98, 103, 108, 130, 142, 144; NCLB and, 159; state standards and, 132
state-level, testing, 141, 148, 151, 154
state-mandated, loyalty oaths, 64
state standards, education, 114, 131, 132, 136, 151, 161; C3 and, 135; CRT and, 141
Stein, Ben, 111
Steinbacher, John, 91
Stever, H. Guyford, 92, 93
Stewart, Anna, 35
student learning, guarantee of, 147
students, 1, 8, 11, 21–22, 61, 71; achievements of, 20, 69, 103, 130–31, 157–58; assessments of, 148; Boston, 88–89; *good* citizens as, 80, 109, 149, 151; knowledge of, 150; learning outcomes framework for, 155; social studies material of, 75; test scores of, 113–14
study, for Social Studies Curriculum (NSS), *81*
study, Madison Conference, *6*
study, sequence of, AHA, *21*

subject, of history, 1–2
suburban schools, 108
success, civic education, 15, 18, 61, 82, 85, 90; History-Social Studies framework, of California, 115; identity study of Barton as, 127; NCLB, 131, 155; social studies, 77
Supreme Court, US, 61, 67
survey, for Social Studies Courses (OAH), *96*
survey, on history knowledge, 59–60, 66–67, 97
Symcox, Linda, 109, 124, 125, 126
systemic, education reform, 123

TAH. *See* Teaching of American History
teacher-centered model, 3, 119
teacher-proof, curriculum, 66, 82, 87, 97–98
teachers, xi, xiii, 5, 8, 9, 28–29; AHA and, 44, 67; Committee on Social Studies and, 75; on curriculum, 106; elementary education, 134; frameworks for, 125–26; *good*, 156; inquiry model for, 21, 79, 84; lesson plans by, 97, 104; MACOS training for, 58, 90; NCLB impact on, 131; pedagogical methods for, 21, 43, 46; quality content for, 164; social studies, 84–85, 110, 111, 138, 145; standards of, 162; Teachers College for, 65
Teachers College, Columbia University, 48, 58, 65
teaching methods, 21, 32, 39, 46, 50, 74; child-centered, 22, 30, 72, 125; discovery-based, 90; issues-centered courses, 65; traditional, 57
Teaching of American History (TAH) program, 132
The Teaching of Community Civics (Dunn), 33
The Teaching the Social Studies (NCSS), 67
Teaneck, New Jersey, 100
Terre Haute, Indiana, 49

testing, standardized, 129, 130–31, 132, 135, 141, 144, 145; social studies, *133*, 150–51; state-level, 148, 154
tests, for citizenship, 149
test scores, student, 113–14
Texas, 91, 129, 130, 136
textbooks, education, 21, 47–49, 90, 93–95, 105–6, 107; history, 69–70; master, 137; *Social Studies Alive*, 141; social studies series, 54, 58, 59, 60; un-American, 64
thinking skills, 105, 118, 126; critical, xii–xiii, 24, 78, 84, 92
Third Republic, France, 13
thirteen colonies, US, 59–60
time allotted, for standardized tests, 132, 135
Tosh, Josh, 161–62
traditional factions, in education, 3–4, 6, 7, 14, 20–21, 98; adult-centered classroom in, 38; attitudes of, 53, 67; conservatives and, 94; historians establishing, 39; history content and, 162; progressive models and, 36; supporting Committee on Social Studies, 35; teaching methods of, 57
Trump, Donald, 139–43
Turner, Frederick Jackson, 70, 100
Tuskegee Institute, 16
Twenty-Four Cities, course of study, 70
Tyler, Ralph W., 147–48
Tyler Committee, 147–48

un-American, textbooks, 64
Union Army veterans, 160
United States (US), xi, 17, 57, 80, 94, 101; AP frameworks for history of, 138, 153–54; Congress of, 61, 67, 92; Constitution, 13, 41, 153; Declaration of Independence, 41, 140; Department of Education, 22, 31, 102, 116, 147, 148, 149, 150; history education in, 94, 95, 123, 135, 152, 155; Office of Science and Technology Policy, 93; Supreme Court, 61, 67; thirteen colonies of, 59–60

University of Georgia, 79
University of Oregon, 92, 98
US. *See* United States

value, of education, 84, 99, 110–11, 137, 151, 159, 161
Vanderbilt University, 152
VanSledright, B., 127
Vinovskis, M. A., 163
Virginia, 61, 94–95, 114, 136
vision, of citizenship, 55, 107–9

War on Poverty, 71
War on Poverty (Johnson), 148
Warren, Saxe, 10
Washington, Booker T., 16
Washington, George, 2
WASP. *See* White Anglo-Saxon Protestant
Watts Riots, 77
Wesley, Edgar, 59, 67
western civilization, 61, 66, 67, 118, 125
West Virgina v. Barnette, 61
What Do Our 17-Year-Olds Know? (Ravitch and Finn), 105, 153, 154
What Happened on Lexington Green? (Amherst Project), 77
White, Andrew D., 3–4
White Anglo-Saxon Protestant (WASP), 15–20, 23, 48, 58, 82–83, 94
"Who is Virgil T. Fry?" (Michener), 68
Wilschut, Arie, 127
Wineburg, Sam, 127, 160
Wirtz, Willard, 151
Wolcott, H. F., 98
Woods Hole Conference, 72
worksheet, of sixth-grader, 146
world history, 106, 142, 156
World War I, 14, 23, 34, 36
World War II, 57, 59, 60, 63, 73, 106

YMCA, 18
Young, Ella Flagg, 36–37
Your Life in a Democracy (Brown), 70

Zacharias, Jerrold R., 71

About the Author

Michael Learn is currently assistant professor at North Dakota State College of Science, where he teaches various introductory-level history, philosophy, and political science courses. He has taught social studies courses from sixth grade through to college over the past twenty years. During those twenty years of educating, he reflected upon the teaching and purpose of social studies, culminating in his obtaining of a doctorate in institutional effectiveness focusing on standards and social studies testing. At home, Michael and his wife, Tracy, are sending off their only children, Gus and Eli, to college and are left to care for two dogs, a cat, and a grand-gecko.

www.ingramcontent.com/pod-product-compliance
Lightning Source LLC
Chambersburg PA
CBHW021821300426
44114CB00009BA/261